黒人奴隷の着装の研究

アメリカ独立革命期ヴァージニアにおける奴隷の被服の社会的研究

濱田雅子 ◆ 著

東京堂出版

口絵

◎本文であげた図版のうち、カラー図版を一括して掲げた。
◎図版番号は本文の様式にあわせてある。適宜参照されたい。

口絵1-2-1　ジェームズタウン（復元）、植民者とタバコの花
　　　　　筆者撮影　1999年7月17日

口絵1-3-1　カーターズ・グローブ・プランテーション（復元）
　　　　　奴隷小屋とタバコ畑　筆者撮影　1999年7月18日

口絵1-3-2　同左　タバコの葉を詰める樽と乾燥させたタバコの葉っぱ
　　　　　筆者撮影　1999年7月18日

口絵1-4-1　フル・ドレスまたは宮廷用コート（フランス製）1775～1810年　Mr. Mark A. Clark 寄贈、Dewitt Wallace Gallery of Decorative Arts, Colonial Willamsburg Foundation, Virginia所蔵（access number 1971－433）．

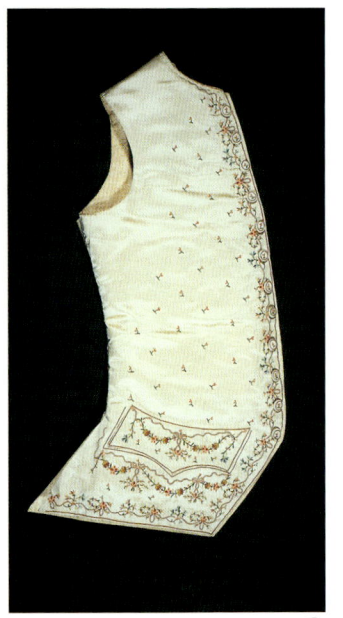 

①　　　　　　　　　　　　　　　　　②
口絵1-4-3 ①②　ウェストコート右半面/正面
Smithsonian Institution所蔵（access number 85－17618/17617）

①　　　　　　　　　　　　　　　　　②
口絵1-4-4 ①②　ブリーチズ　前面/背面
Smithsonian Institution所蔵（access number 85－17635/17636）

口絵1-4-2　左＝刺繍が施さ
右＝縞柄のグリ
出典：Carl Köh
York, 1928, p.3

① ②　口絵1-4-6 ①②　ポロネーズ型ドレス　前面/側面　Smithsonian Institution所蔵（access number 85－17568/17564）

ドレス・コート　1780年
のタフタ製のドレス・コート（中産階級用）
History of Costume, Dover Pub., New

①②　口絵1-4-7 ①②　コルセット　前面/側面
Smithsonian Institution所蔵（access number 85－17605/17606）

口絵2-3-1　ブロード・クロスとカルゼ
出典：Florence Montgomery, *Textiles in America, 1650〜1870: A Dictionary Based on Original Documents, Prints and Paintings, Commercial Records, American Merchant' Papers, Shopkeepers' Advertisements and Pattern Books with Original Swatches of Cloth*, W. W. Norton & Company, New York, A Winterthur/ Barra Book, 1984.掲載の図版　PL.D-102 A, B.

口絵2-3-2　キャリマンコ
出典：Montgomery, D-64.

口絵2-3-3　カシミア
出典：Montgomery, PL.D-88.

口絵2-3-4　コーティング
出典：Montgomery, PL.D-2.

口絵2-3-6　デュロイ
出典：Montgomery, PL.D－55 P

口絵2-3-5　ダッフィル
出典：Montgomery, PL.D－21.

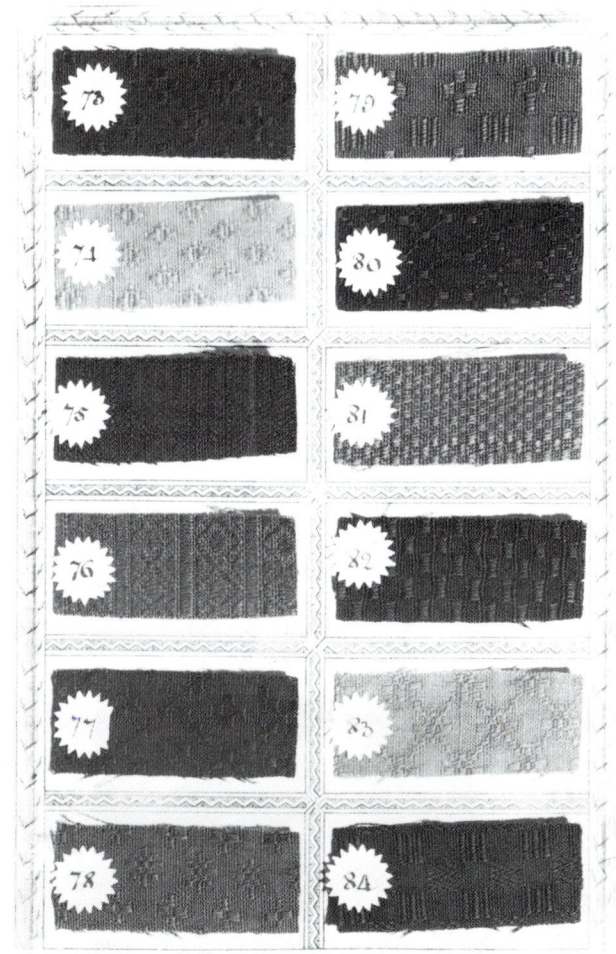

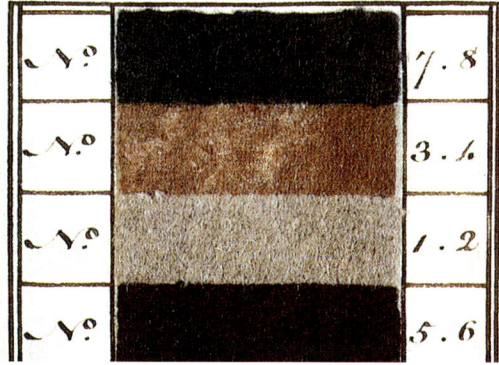

口絵2-3-8　フランネル
出典：Montgomery, PL.D－60 T.

口絵2-3-9　フリーズ
出典：Montgomery, PL.D－100 A.

口絵2-3-7　エヴァーラスティング
出典：Montgomery, D－48.

口絵2-3-10　プレインズ
出典：Montgomery, PL.D－60 L.

口絵2-3-11　プラッシュ
出典：Montgomery, PL.D－87.

口絵2-3-12　サガスィー
出典：Montgomery, PL.D－59 H.

口絵2-3-13　サージ
出典：Montgomery, PL.D－60 Q.

口絵2-3-14　シャグ
出典：Montgomery, PL.D－103 A.

口絵2-3-15　シャルーン
出典：Montgomery, PL.D－103 A.

口絵2-3-17 ベルベット
出典：Montgomery, PL.D-62 Y.

口絵2-3-16 プレード
出典：Montgomery, PL.D-32.

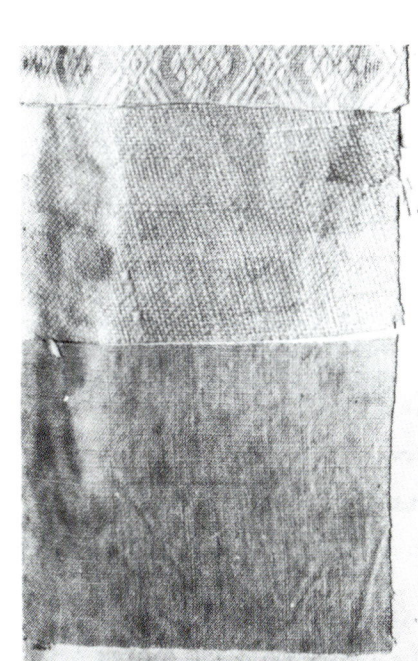

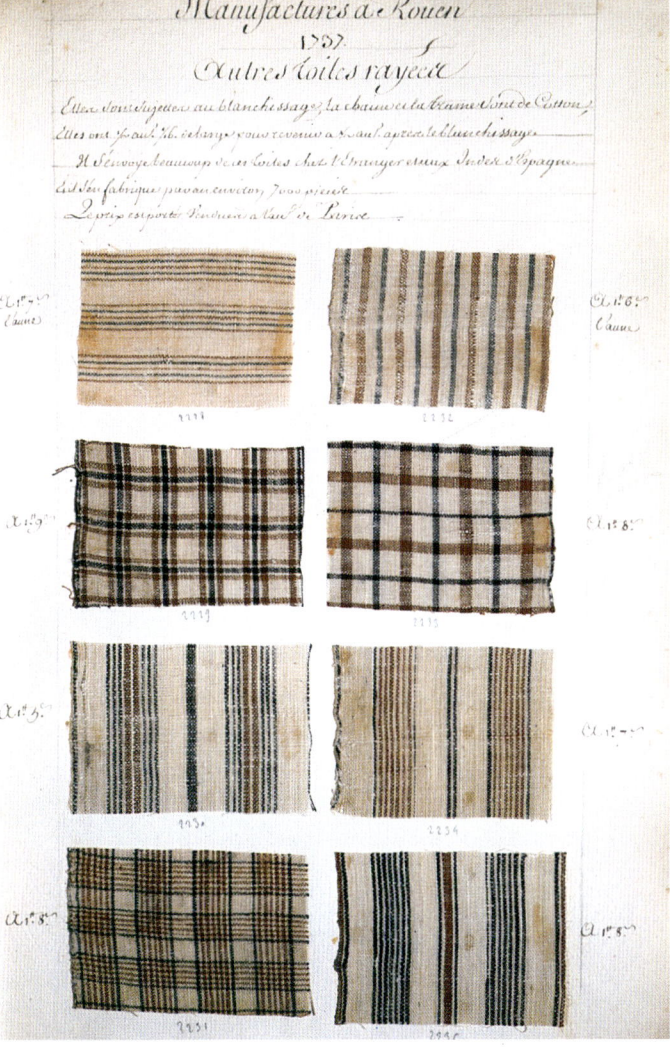

口絵2-3-18 キャリコ
出典：Montgomery, Fig. D-40. P.220.

口絵2-3-19 コットン
出典：Montgomery, PL.D-94.

口絵2-3-20　ディミティー
出典：Montgomery, Fig. D−41.

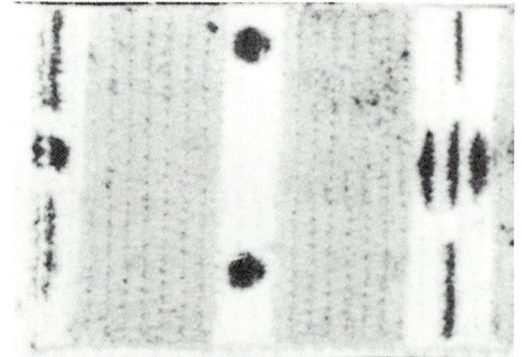

口絵2-3-21　スィックセット　または　コットン
出典：Montgomery, Fig.D−97, p.362.

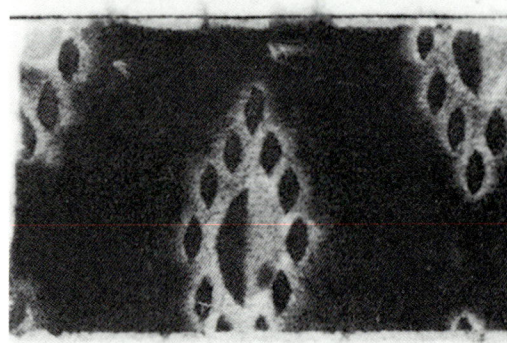

口絵2-3-22　ベルブレット　または　コットン
出典：Montgomery, Fig.D−97, p.362

口絵2-3-23　チェック
出典：Montgomery, PL.D−62 V.

口絵2-3-24　リネン
出典：Montgomery, PL.D−62 T.

口絵3-1-1① お仕着せのコート（イギリス製）1790〜1800
DeWitt Wallace Gallery of Decorative Arts, Colonial Williamsburg Foundation, Williamsburg, Virginia所蔵（access number 1954-1032）．筆者撮影　1999年8月6日．

口絵3-1-2　マウント・ヴァーノンの奴隷の従僕（1765年）彼のコートはオフ・ホワイトで、赤いカフスと衿が付いている。ブリーチズは白で、ウェストコートは赤である。コートには赤い裏が付いている。ウェストコートとカフスと衿は赤と白で縁取られている。靴下は格子縞模様で、靴とブリーチズの膝の部分には、粗末なバックルが付いている。円い帽子は巻き上げられ、白いテープで縁取られている。コートには内ポケットは付いているかもしれないが、外ポケットは付いていない。Peter F. Copeland著、濱田雅子訳『アメリカ史にみる職業着―植民地時代〜独立革命期―』（せせらぎ出版、1998年10月）、p.174
本書の原題は" Working Dress in Colonial and Revolutionary America, Greenwood Press, Westport, Connecticut, 1977

口絵3-1-1② 同　ポケットの部分

口絵3-1-1③ 同　袖の部分

口絵4-2-1①　ヴァージニア・クロス製の男子または少年用コート
DeWitt Wallace Gallery of Decorative Arts, Colonial Williamsburg Foundation, Williamsburg, Virginia所蔵(access number 1964-174 a-b).
筆者撮影　1999年8月6日.

口絵4-2-1②　同　コートの上部

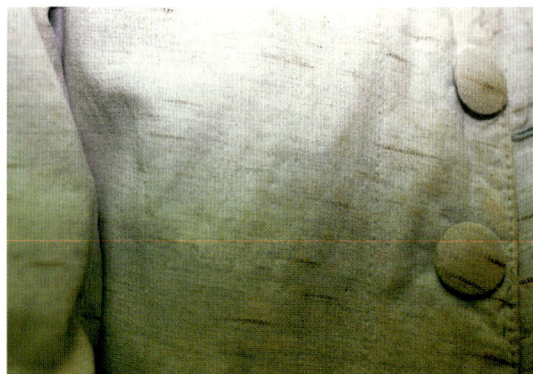

口絵4-2-1③　同　前身頃のヴァージニア・クロスの拡大写真

口絵4-2-1④　同　衿

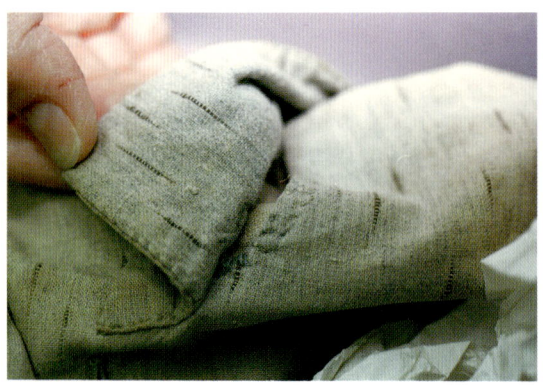

口絵4-2-1⑤　同　ポケットの部分

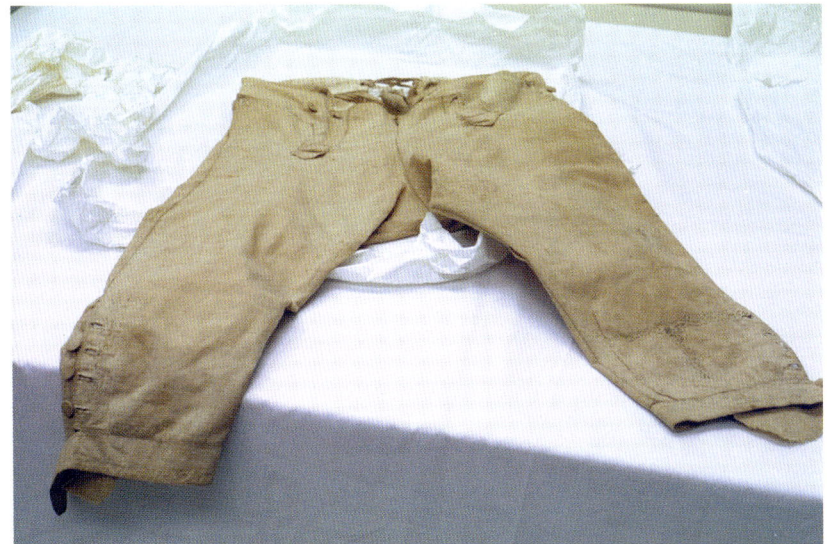

口絵4-2-2① ヴァージニア・クロス製男子または少年用ブリーチズ
DeWitt Wallace Gallery所蔵.（access number 1954-174 a-b）
筆者撮影 1999年8月6日．

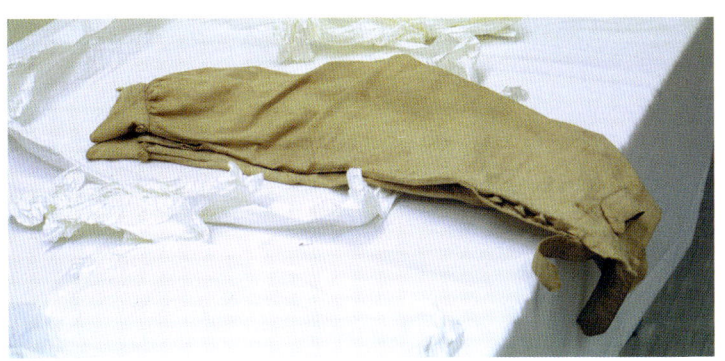

口絵4-2-2② 同 中心から折りたたんだ写真

口絵4-2-2③ 同 ウェスト部分の内側

口絵4-2-2④ 同 裾口

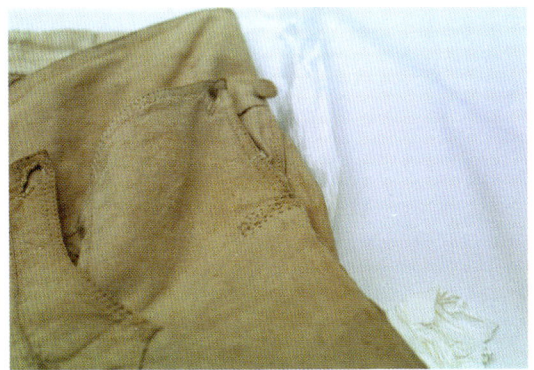

口絵4-2-2⑤ 同 脇ポケット

口絵4-2-2⑥ 同 裾口の内側

口絵4-2-3① パッチワーク・キルト 奴隷により製作 1800年頃
The Valentine Museum, Richmond, Virginia 所蔵 (access number 50.127.1). 寄贈者 Dr. & Mrs. Emett H. Terrell
当美術館提供のスライドからプリント

口絵4-2-3② 同 筆者撮影 1999年8月3日

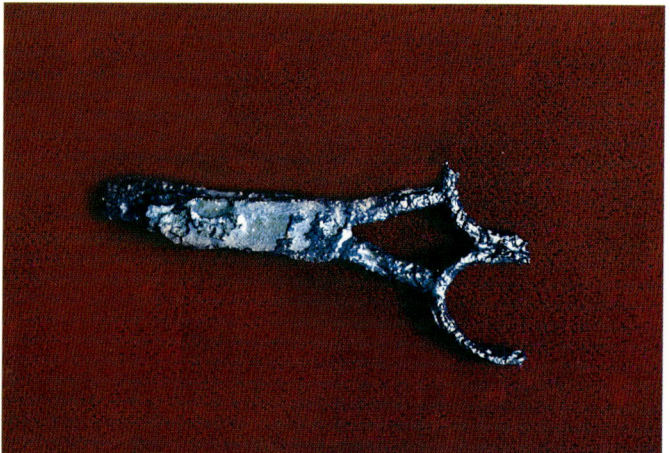

口絵4-2-6① 鋏の発掘品、全長 8.7センチ パレス・プランテーション出土
Department of Archaeological Research, Colonial Williamsburg Foundation, Williamsburg, Virginia 所蔵 (access number 067-40AA-279).
筆者撮影 1999年8月17日

口絵4-2-3③ 同 筆者撮影
1999年8月3日
左手のプリントはアメリカ製の
ブロック・プリント

口絵4-2-3④ 同 筆者撮影
1999年8月3日

口絵4-2-6② 指貫の発掘品　奴隷が使用　同左所蔵　パレス・プランテーション出土
　　右　大人用　直径　1.4センチ（access number　0024-33AS-050CD）
　　左　子ども用　直径1.1センチ（access number　098-33AS-054BJ）
　　筆者撮影　1999年8月17日

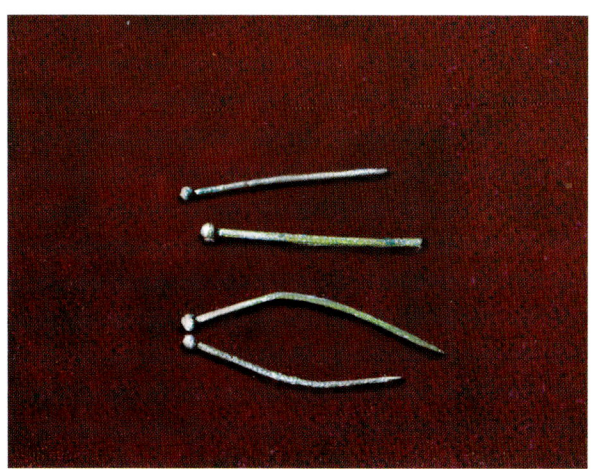

口絵4-2-6③ 針の発掘品　奴隷が使用　パレス・プランテーション出土
長さ（上から）　2.3センチ、2.5センチ、3.2センチ、2.6センチ
Copperas alloy tinで仕上げる
同上所蔵（access number　0093-33AS-54AP）．
筆者撮影　1999年8月17日

口絵4-2-4①　1770年代のウィリアムズバーグで使われていた織機の複製品
Weaving Room, Colonial Willamsburg Foundation, Virginia
筆者撮影　1999年7月27日

口絵4-2-4②　18世紀の布を再現している織物の専門家 Max Hamrick
　　　　　　同上

口絵4-2-5① ウール
Max Hamrick 提供のサンプルからコピー（実物は筆者所蔵）

口絵4-2-5② コットン
Max Hamrick 提供のサンプルからコピー（実物は筆者所蔵）

口絵4-2-5③ ウール
Max Hamrick 提供のサンプルからコピー（実物は筆者所蔵）

口絵4-2-5④ リネン
Max Hamrick 提供のサンプルからコピー（実物は筆者所蔵）

口絵4-2-5⑤ キャンバス
Max Hamrick 提供のサンプルからコピー（実物は筆者所蔵）

口絵4-2-5⑥ リンジー・ウールジー
Max Hamrick 提供のサンプルからコピー（実物は筆者所蔵）

口絵4-2-5⑦ ウール（馬のサドル用）
Max Hamrick 提供のサンプルからコピー（実物は筆者所蔵）

口絵4-3-7 マウント・ヴァーノンのジョージ・ワシントンのマンション
筆者撮影　1999年9月12日

◀口絵4-3-8　マウント・ヴァーノン・プランテーション（復元）
　奴隷監督の部屋　筆者撮影　1999年9月12日
　口絵4-3-9　マウント・ヴァーノン・プランテーション（復元）
　奴隷小屋　筆者撮影　1999年9月12日
　口絵4-3-10　マウント・ヴァーノン・プランテーション（復元）
　紡績部屋　筆者撮影　1999年9月12日

▲口絵4-3-11　マウント・ヴァーノン・プランテーション（復元）
　紡績用の部屋の梳毛具　筆者撮影　1999年9月12日
　口絵4-3-12　マウント・ヴァーノン・プランテーション（復元）
　紡績用の部屋に関する解説　筆者撮影　1999年9月12日

序文

丹 野 郁
埼玉大学名誉教授
国際服飾学会会長
文学博士

　本著の基盤になった「奴隷の服装の社会史的考察」という意表を突くようなテーマは、既存の服飾研究に新たな扉を開いた。というのは、とかく華やかさに目を奪われがちなこれまでの服飾史研究に、光と影の存在を映し出したからで、本著はその影の部分に照射しつつ社会史的な意味づけを行っている点に大きな価値が認められる。
　そもそも、着衣の行為は人類の歴史と共に始まったに違いないが、布による衣服は新石器時代に始まるといわれる。地中海沿岸の温暖な地域に早くから定着した人々の間で織布が始まったことは、古代エジプト、ギリシア、ローマの人々の当時の資料により明らかである。それらの衣服はすべて奴隷の手によるものであったという。古代はいわゆる奴隷制時代で、生産労働はすべて奴隷によるものであった。そのピークはギリシアからローマにかけてのことで、エンゲルスによれば、ギリシアでは一人の貴婦人に何十人もの奴隷がいて、布を織り着せつけもおこなった。また、ローマでは男性の民族服であるトーガの着せつけが上手な奴隷は、高値で取引きされたという。というように古代の衣服文化は奴隷の労働力によって栄えたといえる。しかし、ローマ帝国は、奴隷の供給が欠乏して滅びた。
　その後、ヨーロッパではダイナミックな民族移動のあと、国々が成立するが、その社会構造は階級を基盤とする封建制というピラミッド型のもので、その生産力は、やはり底辺

を形成する農奴で、彼らの労働力が上流社会を支えていた。17世紀のバロック、18世紀のロココという華やかな貴族の文化を花開かせたのである。

　ふと、アメリカ大陸に目を転ずると17世紀前半に早くもアメリカ大陸に奴隷が輸送されていた。またしても奴隷の労働力に依存する上流人の生活が始まる。新大陸の最初の植民地は東部のヴァージニアであった。ここは、イギリスによる最初の恒久的植民地で、著者濱田さんは、この地をフィールド・ワークの舞台として選び、情熱を傾け周辺の方々の暖かい協力も効を奏して、予想以上に第一次史料を入手することができた。資料としては、写真はもとより実物、記録等が見出されたという。それらを詳細に整理し、コンピュータ等の機器を駆使し得たことは客観性を増幅している。今の時代でこそなし得たことであろうと思う。奴隷の衣服がステータスシンボルとしての役割を果たしたことも感動的に伺われる。アメリカの今日の繁栄は膨大な奴隷の労働力に支えられたことも思い知らされる。アメリカの人々にも本書を是非読んでいただきたいと思う。本著書が世界の服飾文化の研究に少なからず資するものと確信し、著者の今後の研鑽を期待しつつ序文に代えさせていただく。（たんの・かおる）

序文

風 間　健
武庫川女子大学名誉教授
工学博士

　「むかしの人はどんな服装をしていたか」という疑問に答えるのは、記録に残る上層階級や話題の服装、例えば軍服であれば、比較的容易である。しかし普通の人が、多くの場合に着ていた服装となると、記録が少なく難しい。まして写真が普及しない250年前、しかも戦乱のアメリカとなると、記録はほとんどなく、答えるに困難を極めるであろう。
　本書の著者、濱田雅子氏は、この問題に真正面から取り組み、記録の収集に絶妙の手法を編み出した。第一は、下層階級の服装を「奴隷の逃亡広告の記録から探る」という優れた着想である。奴隷の逃亡広告とは、奴隷の持ち主が「うちの奴隷が逃げた、こんな服装をしている、見つけてくれたら謝礼進呈」と新聞に掲載した記事である。奴隷の特徴を示す必要があったため、描写は詳細であった。そこに著者は目を付けた。
　第二は、奴隷の記録を現地で集めて回った。多くの奴隷を使ったプランテーションを回り、奴隷の服装はもちろん、奴隷の生活や衣服生産に用いた機器も調べた。また図書館や博物館では、館員と暖かい交流の輪を築き、種々の専門家から献身的な協力を得た。
　こうして多くの記録を手にしたが、その当時と今では衣服の表現が違う。今は使われていない素材名さえある。そこから素材の組成や構造を一語ずつ調べる、気の遠くなるような作業が始まった。しかし筆者のこの努力が、本書のハイライト部を生み出した。それは

250年前のアメリカ衣服素材の事典とも呼べる内容で、本書の価値を押し上げている。

アメリカ独立戦争では、欧州との貿易が途絶えたので、衣服も国内生産に頼らざるを得ない。それは衣服を変えるとともに、奴隷のしごとや身分も変えた。本書は、このように衣服の問題を社会背景とともに扱い、衣服の社会的な意義まで描き出している。

本書は、舞台を奴隷が集められたヴァージニアに置き、独立戦争という印象的な時代を、衣服の側面から活き活きと写し出した楽しい読物である。しかも資料にこだわり、論理に厳しい研究者の目が貫かれていて、斯界における資料的価値が高い。

本書のもとになった学位論文の主査として、衣服の素材に関心を持つ者として、本書の上梓を心から喜んでいる。（かざま・けん）

目　次

付．図表・資料一覧（日本語・英語）

序　文 ……………………………………………………………… 丹野　郁 (1)
序　文 ……………………………………………………………… 風間　健 (3)

序　章 …………………………………………………………………………… 1

　第1節　目的と方法 ……………………………………………………………… 2
　第2節　研　究　史 ……………………………………………………………… 4
　　1．アメリカ服飾史に関する筆者の先行研究 ………………………………… 4
　　2．「逃亡奴隷広告」に基く先行諸研究 ………………………………………… 6
　　3．本研究の位置づけ …………………………………………………………… 8
　第3節　本書の構成―凡例にかえて― ………………………………………… 10

第1章　歴史的背景 …………………………………………………………… 15

　はじめに …………………………………………………………………………… 16
　第1節　アメリカ独立革命と合衆国の成立 …………………………………… 16
　第2節　ヴァージニア植民地の成立 …………………………………………… 20
　第3節　ヴァージニアの「黒人」奴隷制度 …………………………………… 21
　　1．奴隷貿易 ……………………………………………………………………… 21
　　2．白人年季奉公人制度 ………………………………………………………… 22
　　3．「黒人」奴隷制度の成立 …………………………………………………… 24
　　　(1) 白人年季奉公人制度から黒人奴隷制度へ ……………………………… 24
　　　(2) 黒人奴隷制度の特質 ……………………………………………………… 25
　第4節　アメリカ独立革命期の服飾の特徴 …………………………………… 30
　　1．上流階級の服飾 ……………………………………………………………… 30
　　　(1) 男子服 ……………………………………………………………………… 30
　　　　　a．コート (30) ……b．ウェストコート (31) ……c．ブリーチズ (31)
　　　(2) 女子服 ……………………………………………………………………… 31
　　2．中産・下層階級の衣服 ……………………………………………………… 33

第2章　史料としての逃亡奴隷広告　……… 37

第1節　被服描写の史料的価値　……… 38
第2節　被服情報の数量化　……… 40
第3節　被服素材の種類　……… 42

第3章　逃亡奴隷の着装情況―その数量的アプローチ―　……… 65

第1節　奴隷の被服の種類と素材の特徴　……… 66
1. 種類とデザイン　……… 66
2. 奴隷の服装のイメージ　……… 67
3. 逃亡奴隷の被服の素材　……… 70

第2節　男子の逃亡奴隷の着装実態　……… 74
1. 被服の組み合わせ　……… 74
    (1) 対象時期　……… 74
    (2) 被験者　……… 74
    (3) 数量化の手順　……… 77
2. 小　括　……… 95

第3節　ヴァージニア・クロスの特徴　……… 104
1. ヴァージニア・クロスの定義づけ　……… 104
    (1) ヴァージニア・クロス生産のはじまり　……… 104
    (2) ヴァージニア・クロスの定義づけ　……… 104
2. 逃亡奴隷広告に見るヴァージニア・クロス製の被服　……… 105
    (1) 被服の種類について　……… 106
    (2) 色・柄について　……… 106

第4節　対照資料としてのオズナブルグ　……… 108
1. 被服の種類について　……… 109
2. 色について　……… 110

第5節　逃亡奴隷広告に見る被服素材の年次変化　……… 111

第4章　奴隷の被服の支給と生産　……… 117

第1節　先行研究　……… 118
第2節　実物資料の調査　……… 119
1. ヴァージニア・クロス製、男子用スーツ　……… 119
    ―コロニアル・ウィリアムズバーグ振興財団にて―

2．パッチワーク・キルトの実物資料 ……………………………………………… 119
　　　　―Valentine Museumにて―
　　3．18世紀の織物の複製 ……………………………………………………………… 121
　　　　―コロニアル・ウィリアムズバーグ振興財団織物工房にて―
　　4．プランテーションからの出土品 ………………………………………………… 121
　　　　―コロニアル・ウィリアムズバーグ振興財団考古学研究部門にて―
　第3節　プランテーションにおける被服管理 …………………………………………… 123
　　1．カーター家（Carter Family）の場合 …………………………………………… 124
　　　（1）事例1．ランドン・カーター（Landon Carter）の場合 ………………… 126
　　　（2）事例2．ロバート・カーター・オブ・ノミニ・ホール（Robert Carter of Nomini Hall）
　　　　　の場合 ……………………………………………………………………… 134
　　　（3）事例3．ロバート・ウォームレイ・カーター（Robert Wormeley Carter）の場合…… 142
　　2．ジョージ・ワシントンの場合 …………………………………………………… 145
　　　（1）ジョージ・ワシントン（George Washington）の経歴 …………………… 145
　　　（2）奴隷の被服の種類 ……………………………………………………… 146
　　　（3）奴隷用の被服素材の入手方法について ……………………………… 147
　　　（4）奴隷のお仕着せの生産について ……………………………………… 147
　　　（5）奴隷の靴の支給と生産について ……………………………………… 148
　　　（6）奴隷用の衣服素材の生産について …………………………………… 148
　　3．その他の事例 ……………………………………………………………………… 149
　　　（1）ターナー・サウスホール大佐（Turner Southhall）の事例 ……………… 152
　　　（2）カーベル（Cabell）家の事例 …………………………………………… 153

終　章 ……………………………………………………………………………………… 165

　参考文献 ………………………………………………………………………………… 172

付　録　資料編 …………………………………………………………………………… 179
　　1．逃亡奴隷広告の事例 ……………………………………………………………… 180
　　2．John Wily, *A Treatise on the Propagation of Sheep, the Manufacture of Wool,
　　　and the Cultivation and Manufacture of Flax, with Direction for Making
　　　Utencils for the Business,* Williamsburg, 1765. ………………………………… 185
　　3．John Hargrove, *Weavers Draft Book and Clothiers Assistant,* Worcester,
　　　American Antiquary Society, 1979. ……………………………………………… 199

あとがき	211
英文要旨	219
索　引	227

図表・資料一覧

① 本書に掲げた挿図・表および史料について、その表題を章ごとに掲載ページ順に配列し、その掲載ページを併記した。
② 口絵カラー写真については、その表題を、それぞれの写真について言及した本文の掲載ページ順に配列し、その掲載ページ（括弧付き）を併記した。
③ これらの表題の英文表記については、別掲の英文一覧を参照されたい。

【第1章】

口絵 1 – 2 – 1	ジェームズタウン（復元）	(1)
口絵 1 – 3 – 1	カーターズ・グローブ・プランテーション（復元）	(1)
口絵 1 – 3 – 2	カーターズ・グローブ・プランテーション（復元）	(1)
図 1 – 3 – 3	1775年の13植民地とイギリス領①②③	26
口絵 1 – 4 – 1	フル・ドレスまたは宮廷用コート〈フランス製〉（1775〜1810年）	(2)
口絵 1 – 4 – 2	左＝刺繍が施されたドレス・コート（1780年） 右＝縞柄のグリーンのタフタ製のドレス・コート（中産階級用）	(2)〜(3)
口絵 1 – 4 – 3	①②ウェストコート　右半面／正面	(2)
口絵 1 – 4 – 4	①②ブリーチズ　前面／背面	(2)
図 1 – 4 – 5	ブリーチズのパターン	32
口絵 1 – 4 – 6	①②ポロネーズ型ドレス　前面／側面	(3)
口絵 1 – 4 – 7	①②コルセット　前面／側面	(3)
表 1 – 3 – 1	チェサピークにおける成人男子の奴隷の職種の構成比（1733〜1809年）	28
表 1 – 3 – 2	チェサピークにおける成人女子の奴隷の職種の構成比（1733〜1809年）	29
表 1 – 3 – 3	成人男子熟練工黒人奴隷の年齢の構成比（1730〜1810年）	29
表 1 – 3 – 4	ヴァジニアの熟練労働者の逃亡奴隷の年齢別構成比（1732〜1779年）	29
表 1 – 4 – 1	欧米の中産・下層階級の職業着一覧（18世紀）	34

【第2章】

図 2 – 2 – 1	逃亡奴隷広告数と被服情報数［*Virginia Gazette*］（1766〜1789年）	41
口絵 2 – 3 – 1	ブロード・クロスとカルゼ	(4)
口絵 2 – 3 – 2	キャリマンコ	(4)
口絵 2 – 3 – 3	カシミア	(4)
口絵 2 – 3 – 4	コーティング	(4)
口絵 2 – 3 – 5	ダッフィル	(5)
口絵 2 – 3 – 6	デュロイ	(5)
口絵 2 – 3 – 7	エヴァーラスティング	(5)
口絵 2 – 3 – 8	フランネル	(5)
口絵 2 – 3 – 9	フリーズ	(5)
口絵 2 – 3 – 10	プレインズ	(6)
口絵 2 – 3 – 11	プラッシュ	(6)
口絵 2 – 3 – 12	サガスィー	(6)
口絵 2 – 3 – 13	サージ	(6)
口絵 2 – 3 – 14	シャグ	(6)
口絵 2 – 3 – 15	シャルーン	(6)
口絵 2 – 3 – 16	プレード	(7)
口絵 2 – 3 – 17	ベルベット	(7)
口絵 2 – 3 – 18	キャリコ	(7)
口絵 2 – 3 – 19	コットン	(7)

口絵2－3－20	ディミティー	(8)
口絵2－3－21	スィックセットまたはコットン	(8)
口絵2－3－22	ベルブレットまたはコットン	(8)
口絵2－3－23	チェック	(8)
口絵2－3－24	リネン	(8)
表2－3－1	逃亡奴隷広告に見る被服素材一覧	44～53
表2－3－2	逃亡奴隷広告に見る被服素材年次別一覧	54～63

【第3章】

口絵3－1－1	①お仕着せのコート、イギリス製（1790～1800年）	(9)
	②③同ポケットの部分／袖の部分	
口絵3－1－2	マウント・ヴァーノンの奴隷の従僕（1765年）	(9)
図3－1－3	逃亡奴隷広告に見る服種別素材の構成比（1766年）	71
図3－1－4	逃亡奴隷広告に見る服種別素材の構成比（1771年）	71
図3－1－5	逃亡奴隷広告に見る服種別素材の構成比（1776年）	73
図3－1－6	逃亡奴隷広告に見る服種別素材の構成比（1784年）	73
図3－2－2	①AⅠ［upper clothes］＋［lower clothes］＋［head covering］＋［stocking］＋［shoes］	96
	②AⅡ［upper clothes］＋［lower clothes］＋［head covering］＋［shoes］	96
	③AⅢ［upper clothes］＋［lower clothes］＋［stocking］＋［shoes］	97
	④AⅣ［upper clothes］＋［lower clothes］＋［shoes］	97
	⑤BⅠ［upper clothes］＋［lower clothes］＋［head covering］＋［stocking］	98
	⑥BⅡ［upper clothes］＋［lower clothes］＋［head covering］	98
	⑦BⅢ［upper clothes］＋［lower clothes］＋［stocking］	99
	⑧BⅣ［upper clothes］＋［lower clothes］	99
図3－2－3	逃亡奴隷の着装の事例—HarryとWillの場合—	100
図3－2－4	逃亡奴隷広告に見る着装の8パターン	101
図3－3－1	逃亡奴隷広告に見るヴァージニア・クロス製の被服の種類（1766～1789年）	107
図3－3－2	逃亡奴隷広告に見るヴァージニア・クロス製の被服の色・柄の構成比（1766～1789年）	107
図3－3－3	逃亡奴隷広告に見るヴァージニア・クロス製の被服のストライプの種類（1766～1789年）	108
図3－4－1	逃亡奴隷広告に見るオズナブルグ製の被服の種類（1766～1789年）	110
図3－4－2	逃亡奴隷広告に見るオズナブルグ製の被服の色の構成比（1766～1789年）	110
図3－5－1	逃亡奴隷広告に見る輸入品とヴァージニア・クロスの構成比（1766～1789年）	112
史料3－1－1	黒人奴隷用の衣服の支給に関する記載［ランド・ワシントンの会計帳簿から］(1774年)	69
史料3－1－2	家内奴隷用の衣服の支給に関する記載［ランド・ワシントンの会計帳簿から］(1772年)	69
史料3－1－3	職人奴隷用の衣服の支給に関する記載［ランド・ワシントンの会計帳簿から］(1774年)	70
史料3－2－1	*Virginia Gazette*（Dixon & Hunter）January 21, 1775	75
史料3－2－2	*Virginia Gazette*（Purdie & Dixon）November 3, 1768	75
表3－2－1	逃亡奴隷広告に見る男子の逃亡奴隷数	77
表3－2－2	逃亡奴隷の被服の種類	78
	［1767年］	78
	［1768年］	78
	［1769年］	80
	［1770年］	82
	［1776年］	84
	［1777年］	84
	［1778年］	86
	［1779年］	88
表3－2－3	逃亡奴隷広告に見る男子奴隷の被服の組み合わせ	90
	［1767年］	90

	［1768年］	90
	［1769年］	90
	［1770年］	91
	［1776年］	91
	［1777年］	92
	［1778年］	92
	［1779年］	93
表3-2-4	男子逃亡奴隷の被服の組み合わせの8パターン	94
表3-2-5	男子逃亡奴隷の被服の組み合わせ	94
表3-2-6	男子逃亡奴隷の上衣の着用枚数	
	［1767年］	102
	［1768年］	102
	［1769年］	102
	［1770年］	102
	［1776年］	102
	［1777年］	103
	［1778年］	103
	［1779年］	103
表3-2-7	男子逃亡奴隷の上衣の着用枚数年次別一覧	103
表3-2-8	逃亡奴隷広告に見るブリーチズとトラウザーズの数	103
表3-3-1	逃亡奴隷広告に見るヴァージニア・クロスに関する記載	105
表3-3-2	逃亡奴隷広告に見るヴァージニア・クロス製の被服の種類（1766～1789年）	106
表3-3-3	逃亡奴隷広告に見るヴァージニア・クロス製の被服の色・柄（1766～1789年）	106
表3-3-4	逃亡奴隷広告に見るヴァージニア・クロスのストライプの種類（1766～1789年）	106
表3-4-1	逃亡奴隷広告に見るオズナブルグ製の被服の種類（1766～1789年）	109
表3-4-2	逃亡奴隷広告に見るオズナブルグ製の被服の色（1766～1789年）	109
表3-5-1	逃亡奴隷広告に見る輸入品とヴァージニア・クロスの構成比（1766～1789年）	112

【第4章】

口絵4-2-1	①ヴァージニア・クロス製の男子または少年用コート	(10)
	②同　コートの上部	(10)
	③同　前身頃のヴァージニア・クロスの拡大写真	(10)
	④同　衿	(10)
	⑤同　ポケットの部分	(10)
口絵4-2-2	①ヴァージニア・クロス製の男子または少年用ブリーチズ	(11)
	②同　中心から折りたたんだ写真	
	③同　ウェスト部分の内側	
	④同　裾　口	
	⑤同　脇ポケット	
	⑥同　裾口の内側	
口絵4-2-3	①パッチワーク・キルト（1800年頃）	(12)
	②同	
	③同	(13)
	④同	
口絵4-2-4	①1770年代のウィリアムズ・バーグで使われていた織機の複製品	(14)
	②18世紀の布を再現している織物の専門家　Max Hamrick	
口絵4-2-5	①ウール	(15)
	②コットン	
	③ウール	

　　　　　　　　　④リネン
　　　　　　　　　⑤キャンバス
　　　　　　　　　⑥リンジー・ウールジー
　　　　　　　　　⑦ウール（馬のサドル用）
　　口絵4－2－6　①鋏の発掘品（パレス・プランテーション出土）……………………(12)
　　　　　　　　　②指貫の発掘品（パレス・プランテーション出土）…………………(13)
　　　　　　　　　③針の発掘品（パレス・プランテーション出土）……………………(13)
　　図4－3－1　ランドン・カーター大佐　……………………………………………………127
　　図4－3－2　ランドン・カーター大佐の所有地　……………………………………………127
　　図4－3－3　サビーン・ホール　……………………………………………………………130
　　図4－3－4　ロバート・カーター・オブ・ノミニ・ホール　………………………………136
　　図4－3－5　ロバート・カーター・オブ・ノミニ・ホールの所有地　……………………136
　　図4－3－6　ジョージ・ワシントン　………………………………………………………146
　　口絵4－3－7　マウント・ヴァーノン・プランテーション（復元）ジョージ・ワシントンのマンション　…(16)
　　口絵4－3－8　マウント・ヴァーノン・プランテーション（復元）奴隷監督の部屋　…………(16)
　　口絵4－3－9　マウント・ヴァーノン・プランテーション（復元）奴隷小屋　………………(16)
　　口絵4－3－10　マウント・ヴァーノン・プランテーション（復元）紡績部屋　………………(16)
　　口絵4－3－11　マウント・ヴァーノン・プランテーション（復元）紡績用の部屋の紡毛具　…(16)
　　口絵4－3－12　マウント・ヴァーノン・プランテーション（復元）紡績用の部屋に関する解説　…(16)
　　史料4－3－1　17～19世紀のカーター家の主要メンバー系図　………………………124～125
　　史料4－3－2　ランドン・カーターの財産目録における「黒人奴隷のリスト」(1779年2月)……128
　　史料4－3－3　「黒人奴隷ベティによる衣服の裁断」に関する記載［ランドン・カーターの日記］(1763年
　　　　　　　　　11月17日から)　………………………………………………………………132
　　史料4－3－4　「製織工場の設備」に関する記載［ランドン・カーターの財産目録］(1779年2月9日)……133
　　史料4－3－5　ロバート・カーターの奴隷所有数一覧（1773～1791年）…………………135
　　史料4－3－6　黒人奴隷の織工の雇用に関するロバート・カーターとダニエル・サリバンの契約書
　　　　　　　　　(1782年1月1日)　……………………………………………………………137
　　史料4－3－7　ダニエル・サリバンによって提出された紡績および製織費用（1787年9月15日）………139
　　史料4－3－8　ロバート・カーターの奴隷解放の文書（1791年8月1日）………………141
　　史料4－3－9　ロバート・カーター所有の職人と熟練労働者の一覧（1791年）………142
　　史料4－3－10　黒人奴隷用のリネンの購入について［ロバート・ウォームレイ・カーターの日記］
　　　　　　　　　(1766年3月11日から)　…………………………………………………144
　　史料4－3－11　黒人奴隷用の靴の購入について［ロバート・ウォームレイ・カーターの日記］(1769年
　　　　　　　　　12月31日から)　……………………………………………………………144
　　史料4－3－12　1769年にMcKawayによって紡績された糸について［ロバート・ウォームレイ・カーター
　　　　　　　　　の日記］(1769年12月から)　……………………………………………145
　　史料4－3－13　マウント・ヴァーノン・プランテーションにおける製織に関するトーマス・デイヴィスの
　　　　　　　　　会計帳簿（1767年、原本の写し）………………………………………149
　　史料4－3－14　マウント・ヴァーノン・プランテーションにおける製織に関するトーマス・ディヴィスの
　　　　　　　　　会計帳簿（1767年）(タイプ印刷文書) ……………………………………150
　　史料4－3－15　マウント・ヴァーノンの紡績工、編物工および裁断師の一覧表［ジョージ・ワシントン
　　　　　　　　　の奴隷財産目録から］(1799年)　………………………………………154
　　史料4－3－16　ジョージ・ワシントンによる輸入素材と国内産素材のコストの比較（1768年）(原文書／
　　　　　　　　　タイプ印刷) ……………………………………………………………………155
　　史料4－3－17　①②ターナー・サウスホール大佐が黒人奴隷用の衣服に支払った代金の領収書（1777年
　　　　　　　　　12月) ……………………………………………………………………………156
　　史料4－3－18　黒人奴隷の被服に関するカーベル家の覚書（1796年9月27日）………157
　　表4－2－1　ヴァージニア・クロス製のスーツに関する記載事項－情報カードから－　………120

List of Figures, Tables and Historical Documents

① The titles of figures, the tables and the historical documents referred to in each chapter of this book are listed here with the pages where they are presented.
② The titles of the color photographs in the frontispieces are also listed here in order of page where they are mentioned in the text.
③ The pages where the color photographs are presented in the frontispieces are given in paretheses.

【Chapter 1】

Fig. 1－2－1	Jamestown (restoration)	(1)
Fig. 1－3－1	Carter's Grove Plantation (restoration)	(1)
Fig. 1－3－2	Carter's Grove Plantation (restoration)	(1)
Fig. 1－3－3	Thirteen Colonies and Territory of England in 1775 ①②③	26
Fig. 1－4－1	full dress or court dress (made in France) 1775〜1810	(2)
Fig. 1－4－2	left = embroidered dress coat 1780 ……(2)〜(3) right = stripe green taffeta dress coat (for middle class)	
Fig. 1－4－3	waistcoat　right part / front	(2)
Fig. 1－4－4	①②breeches　front / back	(2)
Fig. 1－4－5	pattern of breeches	32
Fig. 1－4－6	①②polonaise dress　front / side	(3)
Fig. 1－4－7	①②corset　front / side	(3)
Table 1－3－1	Occupations of Adult Male Slaves In the Chesapeake 1733〜1809	28
Table 1－3－2	Occupations of Adult Female Slaves In the Chesapeake 1733〜1809	29
Table 1－3－3	Age of Skilled Male Slaves 1730〜1809	29
Table 1－3－4	Age of Runaway Skilled Workers 1732〜1779	29
Table 1－4－1	List of Working Dress in Europe and the Colonial and Revolutionary America (18th century)	34

【Chapter 2】

Fig. 2－2－1	The Number of Runaway Slave Advertisements and Descriptions of Clothes in *Virginia Gazette* 1766〜1789	41
Fig. 2－3－1	broad cloth and kerzey	(4)
Fig. 2－3－2	calimanco	(4)
Fig. 2－3－3	casimer	(4)
Fig. 2－3－4	coating	(4)
Fig. 2－3－5	duffel (duffil, duffle)	(5)
Fig. 2－3－6	duroy	(5)
Fig. 2－3－7	everlasting	(5)
Fig. 2－3－8	flannel (nel)	(5)
Fig. 2－3－9	frieze	(5)
Fig. 2－3－10	plains	(6)
Fig. 2－3－11	plush	(6)
Fig. 2－3－12	sagathy	(6)
Fig. 2－3－13	serge	(6)
Fig. 2－3－14	shag	(6)
Fig. 2－3－15	shalloon	(6)
Fig. 2－3－16	plaid	(7)
Fig. 2－3－17	velvet	(7)
Fig. 2－3－18	calico	(7)

Fig. 2 − 3 − 19	cotton	(7)
Fig. 2 − 3 − 20	dimity	(8)
Fig. 2 − 3 − 21	thickset or cotton	(8)
Fig. 2 − 3 − 22	velveret or cotton	(8)
Fig. 2 − 3 − 23	check	(8)
Fig. 2 − 3 − 24	linen	(8)
Table 2 − 3 − 1	List of Materials of Clothes Extracted from Runaway Slave Advertisements	44〜53
Table 2 − 3 − 2	List of Annual Materials of Clothing Extracted from Runaway Slave Advertisements	54〜63

【Chapter 3】

Fig. 3 − 1 − 1	①livery coat, made in England 1790〜1800	(9)
	②③part of pocket / part of sleeve of the coat	(9)
Fig. 3 − 1 − 2	A Slave Footman in Mount Vernon (1765)	(9)
Fig. 3 − 1 − 3	Ratios of the Materials of each item of Clothes Extracted from Runaway Slave Advertisements 1766	71
Fig. 3 − 1 − 4	Ratios of the Materials of each item of Clothes Extracted from Runaway Slave Advertisements 1771	71
Fig. 3 − 1 − 5	Ratios of the Materials of each item of Clothes Extracted from Runaway Slave Advertisements 1776	73
Fig. 3 − 1 − 6	Ratios of the Materials of each item of Clothes Extracted from Runaway Slave Advertisements 1784	73
Fig. 3 − 2 − 2	①A Ⅰ [upper clothes] + [lower clothes] + [head covering] + [stocking] + [shoes]	96
	②A Ⅱ [upper clothes] + [lower clothes] + [head covering] + [shoes]	96
	③A Ⅲ [upper clothes] + [lower clothes] + [stocking] + [shoes]	97
	④A Ⅳ [upper clothes] + [lower clothes] + [shoes]	97
	⑤B Ⅰ [upper clothes] + [lower clothes] + [head covering] + [stocking]	98
	⑥B Ⅱ [upper clothes] + [lower clothes] + [head covering]	98
	⑦B Ⅲ [upper clothes] + [lower clothes] + [stocking]	99
	⑧B Ⅳ [upper clothes] + [lower clothes]	99
Fig. 3 − 2 − 3	Illustrations of Clothes for Runaway Slaves — Harry and Will —	100
Fig. 3 − 2 − 4	Illustrations of 8 Patterns of the Conbinations of Clothes for Runaway Slaves	101
Fig. 3 − 3 − 1	Types of Virginia Cloth Clothes Extracted from Runaway Slave Advertisements (1766〜1789)	107
Fig. 3 − 3 − 2	Colors and Patterns of Virginia Cloth Extracted from Runaway Slave Advertisements (1766〜1789)	107
Fig. 3 − 3 − 3	Types of Stripes of Virginia Cloth Extracted from Runaway Slave Advertisements (1766〜1789)	108
Fig. 3 − 4 − 1	Types of Osnabrug Clothes Extracted from Runaway Slave Advertisements (1766〜1789)	110
Fig. 3 − 4 − 2	Colors of Osnabrug Clothes Extracted from Runaway Slave Advertisements (1766〜1789)	110
Fig. 3 − 5 − 1	Changes in the Ratios of Imported Cloth and Virginia Cloth Extracted from Runaway Slave Advertisements (1766〜1789)	112
Doc. 3 − 1 − 1	Description of Issue of Clothes for Negroes 1774 (from Lund Washington's Account Books)	69
Doc. 3 − 1 − 2	Description of Issue of Clothes for House Slaves 1772 (from Lund Washington's Account Books)	69
Doc. 3 − 1 − 3	Description of Issue of Clothes for Slave Artisans 1774 (from Lund Washington's Account Books)	70

Doc. 3-2-1	*Virginia Gazette* (Dixon & Hunter) January 21, 1775	75
Doc. 3-2-2	*Virginia Gazette* (Purdie & Dixon) November 2, 1768	75
Table 3-2-1	Number of Male Runaway Slaves Extracted from Runaway Slave Advertisements	77
Table 3-2-2	Types of Clothes for Runaway Slave	78
	[1767]	78
	[1768]	78
	[1769]	80
	[1770]	82
	[1776]	84
	[1777]	84
	[1778]	86
	[1779]	88
Table 3-2-3	Patterns of the Conbinations of Clothes for Male Runaway Slaves Extracted from Runaway Slave Advertisements	90
	[1767]	90
	[1768]	90
	[1769]	90
	[1770]	91
	[1776]	91
	[1777]	92
	[1778]	92
	[1779]	93
Table 3-2-4	8 Patterns of the Conbinations of Clothes for Runaway Slaves	94
Table 3-2-5	Patterns of the Conbinations of Clothes for Male Runaway Slaves	94
Table 3-2-6	Numbers of Upper Clothes worn by Male Runaway Slaves	102
	[1767]	102
	[1768]	102
	[1769]	102
	[1770]	102
	[1776]	102
	[1777]	103
	[1778]	103
	[1779]	103
Table 3-2-7	A List of Numbers of Upper Clothes worn by Male Runaway Slaves	103
Table 3-2-8	Numbers of Breeches and Trousers Extracted from Runaway Slave Advertisements	103
Table 3-3-1	Descriptions of Virginia Cloth Extracted from Runaway Slave Advertisements	105
Table 3-3-2	Types of Virginia Cloth Clothes Extracted From Runaway Slave Advertisements (1766〜1789)	106
Table 3-3-3	Colors and Patterns of Virginia Cloth Extracted from Runaway Slave Advertisements (1766〜1789)	106
Table 3-3-4	Types of Stripes of Virginia Cloth Extracted from Runaway Slave Advertisements (1766〜1789)	106
Table 3-4-1	Types of Osnabrug Clothes Extracted from Runaway Slave Advertisements (1766〜1789)	109
Table 3-4-2	Colors of Osnabrug Clothes Extracted from Runaway Slave Advertisements (1766〜1789)	109
Table 3-5-1	Changes in the Ratios of Imported Cloth and Virginia Cloth Extracted from Runaway Slave Advertisements (1766〜1789)	112

【Chapter 4】

Fig. 4-2-1	①man's or boy's Virginia cloth coat	(10)

	②upper part of the coat	(10)
	③an enlarged photograph of the front body of the coat	(10)
	④a collar of the coat	(10)
	⑤part of pocket of the coat	(10)
Fig. 4 - 2 - 2	①man's or boy's Virginia cloth breeches	(11)
	②a photograph of the folded breeches	(11)
	③inside of waist of the breeches	(11)
	④bottom edge of the breeches	(11)
	⑤side pocket of the breeches	(11)
	⑥inside of the bottom of the breeches	(11)
Fig. 4 - 2 - 3	①patchwork quilt made by slaves c.1800	(12)
	②Ibid.	(12)
	③Ibid.	(13)
	④Ibid.	(13)
Fig. 4 - 2 - 4	①reprica of loom used at Williamsburg in 1770's	(14)
	②Mr. Max Hamrick, a specialist of weaving, is reproducing the 18th century cloth	(14)
Fig. 4 - 2 - 5	①wool	(15)
	②cotton	(15)
	③wool	(15)
	④linen	(15)
	⑤canvas	(15)
	⑥linsey-woolsey	(15)
	⑦wool (for the saddle of horse)	(15)
Fig. 4 - 2 - 6	①scissor (excavated from Palace Plantation)	(12)
	②thimbles (excavated from Palace Plantation)	(13)
	③pins (excavated from Palace Plantation)	(13)
Fig. 4 - 3 - 1	Colonel Landon Carter	127
Fig. 4 - 3 - 2	Property of Colonel Landon Carter	127
Fig. 4 - 3 - 3	Sabine Hall	130
Fig. 4 - 3 - 4	Robert Carter of Nomini Hall	136
Fig. 4 - 3 - 5	Property of Robert Carter of Nomini Hall	136
Fig. 4 - 3 - 6	George Washington	146
Fig. 4 - 3 - 7	Mount Vernon Plantation (restoration) a mansion of George Washington	(16)
Fig. 4 - 3 - 8	Mount Vernon Plantation (restoration) a room of overseer of slave	(16)
Fig. 4 - 3 - 9	Mount Vernon Plantation (restoration) slave quarter	(16)
Fig. 4 - 3 - 10	Mount Vernon Plantation (restoration) weaving room	(16)
Fig. 4 - 3 - 11	Mount Vernon Plantation (restoration) carding comb at the weaving room	(16)
Fig. 4 - 3 - 12	Mount Vernon Plantation (restoration) explanation of the weaving room	(16)
Doc. 4 - 3 - 1	A Genealogy of Carter Family from 17th to 19th century	124〜125
Doc. 4 - 3 - 2	Inventory of the Estate of Landon Carter, Feb. 1779, Page 1 "A list of Negroes……", Sabine Hall Papers (#1959), The Albert and Shirley Small Special Collections Library, University of Virginia Library.	128
Doc. 4 - 3 - 3	"Cut out by Betty", Landon Carter's Diary, Nov. 17, 1763, Sabine Hall Papers (#1959), The Albert and Shirley Small Special Collections Library, University of Virginia Library.	132
Doc. 4 - 3 - 4	Inventory of The Estate of Landon Carter esqr, February 1779. Page5, "In the Weaving Manufactory", Sabine Hall Papers (#1959), The Albert and Shirley Small Special Collections Library, The University of Virginia Library.	133
Doc. 4 - 3 - 5	A List of Numbers of Slaves owned by Robert Carter (1773〜1791), Louis Morton,	

	Robert Carter of Nomini Hall, A Virginia Tabacco Planter of the Eighteenth Century, Williamsburg Restoration Historical Studies No. 2 (Princeton, 1941) ············135
Doc. 4－3－6	Contract of Robert Carter with Daniel Sullivan, overseer, for his negro clothworker, Jan. 1, 1782, MSS1C 2468a 2068, The Virginia Historical Society, Richmond, Virginia.···137
Doc. 4－3－7	Estimates of earnings by Robert Carter's slave spinners and weavers, furnished by Daniel Sullivan, September 15, 1787, MSS1C 2468a 810-816, The Virginia Historical Society, Richmond, Virginia. ············139
Doc. 4－3－8	Document of Emancipation by Robert Carter, Deed of Gift, copied from Robert Carter Day Book, Volume XI(Aug. 1, 1791), pages1-2 MSS. Div., Duke University, Special Collections, John D. Rockefeller, Jr. Library, Colonial Williamsburg Foundation, Williamsburg, Virginia. ············141
Doc. 4－3－9	Artisans and Special Task Workers owned by Robert Carter(1791), John Randolf Barden, *"Flushed with Notions' of Freedom": The Growth and Emancipation of a Virginia Slave Community,* 1732-1812, Dissertation: Degree Date 1993, Duke University, p.465. ············142
Fig. 4－3－10	To Buy Linen for Negroes. The Diary of Robert Wormeley Carter, March 11, 1766, Manuscripts and Rare Books Department, Swem Library, College of William and Mary, Williamsburg, Virginia············144
Doc. 4－3－11	To Buy Shoes for Negroes. The Diary of Robert Wormeley Carter, December 31, 1769, Manuscripts and Rare Books Department, Swem Library, College of William and Mary, Williamsburg, Virginia. ············144
Doc. 4－3－12	The Diary of Robert Wormeley Carter, December 1769, The linen thread spun by McKaway 1769, Manuscripts and Rare Books Department, Swem Library, College of William and Mary, Williamsburg, Virginia. ············145
Doc. 4－3－13	An Account of Weaving Done by Thomas Davis &ca. in the Year 1767(copied from manuscript) George Washington Papers, Series Vol. #6, Library of Congress. ·········149
Doc. 4－3－14	AN ACCOUNT OF WEAVING DONE BY THOMAS DAVIS &CA. IN THE YEAR 1767 ············150
Doc. 4－3－15	John C. Fitzpatrick ed.,*The Writings of George Washington from the Original Manuscript Sources,* vol.37, Washington, United States Government Printing Office, 1931(?), Greenwood Press, Publishers, Westport Connecticut, p.268. ············154
Doc. 4－3－16	A Comparison drawn, between Manufacturing & Importing, George Washington Papers, M-2075, 116, Special Collections, John D. Rockefeller, Jr. Library, Colonial Williamsburg Foundation, Williamsburg, Virginia. ············155
Doc. 4－3－17	①②Turner Southhall Receipt Book 1776～1784, 1Vol.,[73] pp. MS 31.3, Neg # 99-151, 1s CN, Special Collections, John D. Rockefeller, Jr. Library, Colonial Williamsburg Foundation, Williamsburg, Virginia. ············156
Doc. 4－3－18	Memo of Cabell Family Papers 1693～1913, "Memo of shoes, stockings & blankets gave my negroes," 27 Nov., 1796 in Box Ⅲ, folder 10, Manuscripts and Rare Books Department, Swem Library, College of William and Mary, Williamsburg, Virginia ······157
Table 4－2－1	A Description of Virginia Cloth Suit, from Information Card at DeWitt Wallace Gallery of Decorative Art, Colonial Williamsburg, Williamsburg, Virginia ············120

序　章

第1節　目的と方法

　近年のアメリカ学界では計量的研究、社会史、大衆運動史など新しい分野の研究の進展[1]にともない、従来の研究領域も深化し、新たな総合化と展望の必要が急務とされている。

　このような研究動向のもとで、アメリカ独立革命期の奴隷の被服をテーマとする本書は、新しいアメリカ社会史研究の一分野であるいわゆる「マテリアル・カルチャー」の領域の研究として位置づけられる。「マテリアル・カルチャー」とは換言すれば、人間生活に必要な衣服や食べ物や住居やその他の生活物資に関する物質文化を意味している。今日、上流階級の服飾に関する研究は進んでいるが、中産階級や下層階級の被服に関する研究は数少ない。下層階級のそれは、特に僅少である。そこで、本書では「黒人」（以下「」略）奴隷という象徴的な下層階級の人々の被服を種類、素材、および、その支給と生産の実態に着眼して考察することとする。

　考察対象とした時期はアメリカ独立革命期の24年間（1766～1789年）であり、地域はアメリカ最初の植民地であるヴァージニアに限定した。ここで取り上げた「被服」には、厳密に定義するならば、衣服のほかに帽子、靴、靴下などの付属品も含まれる。

　では、なぜ独立革命期のヴァージニアなのか。

　次の一節はあまりにも有名なアメリカ合衆国独立宣言前文の一部である。

> 「我々は以下の事実を自明のものと信じる。すなわち、全ての人間は平等に造られており、創造の神から何人にも譲り渡すことのできない権利を与えられていることを。そしてその権利の中に、生命、自由、幸福の追求が含まれていることを。」

　しかし、1776年7月、大陸会議でジョン・ハンコックがこの前文に続けて合衆国の独立を高らかに宣言した時、この新共和国には40万人を越す黒人奴隷が住んでいたのである。「全ての人間は平等に造られて」いるとし、その信条をナショナル・アイデンティティの一つにまでしたアメリカ合衆国に、なぜ、こんなにも大量の黒人奴隷が存在しえたのであろうか。

　独立13州のうち、実にヴァージニアこそ、この奴隷制と共和制が盾の両面のように一体化しつつ、まことに矛盾した展開をとげたところであった。

　1661年のヴァージニア植民地議会による黒人奴隷制度の法制化とあい前後して、1630年にコネティカット、1641年にマサチューセッツ、1652年にロードアイランド、1663年にニュー・ヨーク、1682年にサウス・カロライナ、1714年にニュー・ハンプシャー、1715年にノース・カロライナ、1721年にデラウェア、1749年にジョージアと、アメリカ植民地の全土にわたって、黒人奴隷制度が法制化された。

　アメリカ合衆国で最初の人口センサス[2]がおこなわれた1790年には、当時の総人口392万9,214人の17パーセントにあたる75万7,208人が黒人であった。そのうち黒人奴隷が69万7,681人で、自由黒人は5万9,527人を数えたにすぎず、しかも、この70万人ちかい黒人奴隷のほとんどが南部諸州に

住んでいた。とりわけ、ヴァージニアの黒人奴隷人口は、29万2,627人と一番多かった[3]。この植民地がマサチューセッツとともに独立革命の先頭を切り、やがては「建国の父祖」たちを輩出させたことはよく知られている。だがしかし、初代大統領のジョージ・ワシントン（George Washington）は、彼の生存中は黒人奴隷制度を廃止することなく、その死後、遺言[4]においてマウント・ヴァーノン・プランテーション（Mount Vernon Plantation）[5]の彼の所有する奴隷を解放したのである。このようなアメリカ独立革命期における黒人奴隷制度存続の問題に真向から取り組んだ研究はわずかしかない[6]。

　以上のような認識から本書では、アメリカ独立革命期のヴァージニアの奴隷制問題を通して、ステイタス・シンボルとしての「被服」に取り組んでみた。次に本書の二つの中心的課題とこれらの課題解明のために採用したそれぞれの方法について述べよう。

　本書の中心的課題の一つは「奴隷の被服をどのようにイメージ化するか」である。

　本書では奴隷の被服のイメージ化にあたって、逃亡奴隷の新聞広告における奴隷の被服描写をヴァージニア・ガゼット（Virginia Gazette）紙（1766～1789年）他から抽出し、まず、被服の種類、素材および男子の奴隷の逃亡時の着装実態を考察した。次に、考察対象を素材にしぼり、逃亡奴隷広告に見られるヴァージニア・クロスの特徴について、また、ヴァージニア・クロス製の衣服の特徴を示す対照資料として、オズナブルグ製の衣服の特徴を被服の種類、色について分類・分析した。さらに、67種の被服素材をあらいだした上で、アメリカ独立革命期の24年間における国内産の素材（ヴァージニア産の布地。総称ヴァージニア・クロス Virginia cloth）の生産の推移について比率検定を行い、その社会的要因を検討した。

　本書のもう一つの中心的課題は「ヴァージニアの有数なプランターであるカーター家（Carter Family）のプランテーションおよびアメリカの初代大統領G．ワシントンが所有していたマウント・ヴァーノンのプランテーションにおいて、ランドン・カーター（Landon Carter）、ロバート・カーター・オブ・ノミニ・ホール（Robert Carter of Nomini Hall）、ロバート・ウォームレイ・カーター（Robert Wormeley Carter）およびG．ワシントンという４人のプランターたちは、彼らの黒人奴隷の衣生活をどのようにして管理・維持していたのか」である。この問題の考察にあたって、筆者はヴァージニア・クロス製の衣服と奴隷の被服および被服生産の道具に関する実物調査を行なった。すなわち、DeWitt Wallace Gallery of Decorative Arts（ヴァージニア州コロニアル・ウィリアムズバーグ所在のコロニアル・ウィリアムズバーグ振興財団の一部門）所蔵のヴァージニア・クロス製の男子用スーツの調査、ヴァージニア州リッチモンドに所在するValentine Museum 所蔵の奴隷が作ったパッチワーク・キルトの実物資料の調査、コロニアル・ウィリアムズバーグ振興財団の織物部門における織物の調査、同財団の考古学研究部門における出土品の調査を行なった。また、ヴァージニアの有数なプランターであるカーター家のプランテーションおよびアメリカの初代大統領G．ワシントンが所有していたマウント・ヴァーノンのプランテーションにおける奴隷の被服生産の実態（18世紀後半）把握のために、プランテーションの記録、商人の記録、プランターの日誌や手紙およびその他の公文書の調査を行なった。

第2節　研究史

本節では、まず、1．アメリカ服飾史に関する筆者の先行研究、および、2．「逃亡奴隷広告」に基く先行諸研究に言及し、これらの研究の目的と方法を比較検討する。そののち3．本研究の位置づけについて述べることとする。

1．アメリカ服飾史に関する筆者の先行研究

わが国における欧米の服飾史研究は、丹野郁氏らの西洋服飾史研究[7]を出発点としている。筆者は丹野郁博士のご指導のもとに、西洋服飾史はもとより、アメリカ服飾史の研究を20年間にわたって行なってきた。

ここでは筆者の先行研究のうち、本書と関連をもつ著書、翻訳書、論文および研究ノートを要約・紹介する。

(1)『アメリカ植民地時代の服飾』(せせらぎ出版、1996年)[8]

本書では、アメリカ植民地時代にヨーロッパの服飾がアメリカ新大陸にいかに移入されたのか、また、それらは移入後、アメリカ植民地の建設過程において、アメリカ新大陸の気候・風土のなかで、いかなる変化・発展を遂げていったのか、という問題を、ヴァージニア、ニュー・イングランドおよびニュー・ネザーランドの場合について、文献資料およびアメリカ合衆国の美術館・博物館における衣服の実物調査より得た資料に基づいて、実証的研究をおこなった。すなわち、第一、二章ではヴァージニア植民地 (1607～1675)、ニュー・イングランド植民地 (1620～1675)、およびニュー・ネザーランド植民地 (1623～1675) を形成した植民者たちが着用していた衣服の形態とその植民地における変化・発展の問題を、それぞれの植民地形成の歴史的背景に照らしながら、男女別、階級別に考察した。また、特に経済史の面から衣服生産の実態、つまり服装の存立基盤としての衣服の素材の問題や家内工業の経営状態を考察し、服飾史と経済史との接点の追究を試みた。第三章では17世紀の最後の四半世紀から18世紀のアメリカ独立革命前夜に至る時期 (1675～1775) の植民地における社会経済的発達にともなうファッションの統一の状況を考察した。

結論として、17世紀初頭からアメリカ独立革命前夜にかけて、ヨーロッパ大陸からアメリカ新大陸に移住した人々の服装は、基本的にヨーロッパの服装の生き写しであり、そこにはあくまでもヨーロッパの伝統を維持していこうとする植民者たちの保守的な姿勢がうかがえることを明らかにした。

しかし、本書では服飾史と経済史との接点の解明が不十分であった。例えば、技術的な問題として、植民の初期から進められていたヴァージニアの亜麻、大麻、羊毛および絹の生産が、独立後発展しなかったのはなぜか、などの問題は解明はされていない。

(2) Peter F. Copeland著、濱田雅子訳『アメリカ史にみる職業着―植民地時代〜独立革命期―』
（せせらぎ出版、1998年10月）

　本書の原題は"Working Dress in Colonial and Revolutionary America, Greenwood Press, Westport, Connecticut, 1977"である。本書には著者自身が描いた200点を越えるイラストと36枚の写真が収録されており、1710年から1810年までの100年間にわたって、欧米で労働に携わっていたと推定される人々の職業着が、歴史的背景とともにビジュアルに描かれている。上流階級の華やかで、きらびやかな衣裳とは趣を異にする、仕事の場面に特有な服装で労働に携わっている様相が、豊富な絵画資料によって再現されている。本書に登場する人物は、船乗り、漁師、農民、商人、呼び売り、フロンティア開拓者、御者、正規兵や民兵、医者、法律家、聖職者、使用人、年季契約奉公人、奴隷、犯罪人、民族諸集団など、合計424人である。これらの人々一人ひとりの仕事に取り組んでいる姿やしぐさや表情や、職種によって異なるさまざまな服装は、18世紀の欧米の中産・下層階級の人々の生活の様相を彷彿とさせてくれる。
　本書はイラストや写真によって、中産・下層階級の職業着をビジュアルに描いた貴重な文献であるが、各州単位の地域史としては不十分である。

(3)「アメリカ独立革命と服飾―スミソニアン・インスティテューションの収蔵品に基づいて―」
（衣生活研究会「衣生活」第31巻第3号、1988年6月）

　スミソニアン協会の国立アメリカ史博物館（National Museum of American History）は、18世紀の男女の体形が、どのように現在の体形と異なっているのかを究明するための研究プログラムを実行し、その成果に基づいて、1985年11月から独立200年を記念して、「独立の後：アメリカの日常生活1780〜1800」（After The Revolution: Everyday Life in America 1780〜1800）と題する展示が行われた。その展示場内に、「Costume Study Gallery」という服飾専門のコーナーが設けられており、1775年頃のイブニング・レセプションで着用されたと思われる男女の衣裳が展示された。筆者は1987年夏、同博物館を訪れ、展示の品や展示の方法を直接見ることができた。同協会では展示しているスーツやガウンを注意深く採寸して分析することにより、それぞれの着用者の、身長とプロポーションとポーズを推測することに成功したのである。また、協会は男女のマネキンを作成し、上流階級人の立ち居振る舞いと、男女の体形の変化及び衣服の構成上の問題を提起した。

(4)「18、19世紀アメリカにおけるショート・ガウンの復元作業を通じての一考察」（国際服飾学会誌No.14, 1998年3月）

　18世紀から19世紀前半のアメリカにおいて、庶民の女性の間で広く着用されていた衣服にショート・ガウン（short gown）がある。本稿ではアメリカのスミソニアン協会のクローディア・キドウェル（Claudia Kidwell）の調査研究に基づいて、シーチングを用いて、3着のショート・ガウンの複製を試み、背景情報、素材、裁断、縫製、デザインおよび運動機能性の観点から分析・考察し、ショート・ガウンの歴史的意義、つまり女子庶民服としての有用性を明らかにした。

タイトルは「復元作業」としているが、「複製」(reproduction)とすべきである。C. キドウェルによれば、ショート・ガウンは庶民の女性の労働着であって、決して装飾的なものではない[9]。
(5)「18世紀ヴァージニアにおけるお仕着せに関する歴史的考察」(国際服飾学会誌No.12, 1995年11月)
　黒人奴隷の衣服を取り上げたアメリカ服飾史の研究書はほとんどない。本研究では1993年8月の国際服飾学会主催の米国服飾学術調査旅行に際して、ヴァージニア州ウィリアムズバーグのDeWitt Wallace Gallery of Decorative Artsで調査の機会を得た白人と黒人の召使いのお仕着せのコートを取りあげ、18世紀アメリカ南部プランテーション奴隷制社会の衣服におけるシンボリズムについて論じた。

　以上のように、筆者はアメリカ植民地時代から独立革命期の衣服文化について、上流階級だけではなく、中産・下層階級の衣服についても模索を続けてきた。

2.「逃亡奴隷広告」に基く先行諸研究

　17、18世紀、北米大陸の13植民地はイギリス第一帝国の重要な構成要素であり、とりわけ南部植民地（メリーランド、ヴァージニア、ノース・カロライナ、サウス・カロライナ、ジョージア）は、主要商品作物（タバコ、米、藍、砂糖などの植民地産の商品向け作物）を産出する帝国の辺境として、不可欠な役割を演じている。その「辺境」で、主要商品作物の生産を担っていたのが、最初は白人年季奉公人、次いで17世紀末から大量に導入された黒人奴隷である。黒人奴隷制プランテーションを基礎におく「人種奴隷制社会」はこうして成立する。集団奴隷反乱の少ない北米大陸において、「逃亡」こそが、黒人奴隷の人間としての抵抗の、端的な証であると考えられたのである。
　さて、この逃亡奴隷について、合衆国における研究史を振り返ってみると、南北戦争前夜の時期を対象としたものは、多くの蓄積がみられるが、植民地時代を対象とした包括的な研究は、比較的新しい。以下、箇条書きにその動向を整理する。

(1) ジェラルド・W. マリン（Gerald W. Mullin）の研究[10]
　G. W. マリンの研究は、ヴァージニア・ガゼット紙に掲載された大量の「逃亡奴隷広告」を数量的に分析し、18世紀ヴァージニアにおける逃亡奴隷の全体像を、初めて浮きぼりにした点で、特筆すべきものである。しかし、衣服や織物については言及がされていない。

(2) ラーサン・A. ウィンドレイ（L. A. Windley）編集の逃亡奴隷広告[11]
　1983年に出版されたL. A. ウィンドレイ編集の『逃亡奴隷広告集―1730年代～1790年―』全4巻は、18世紀南部の諸新聞から逃亡広告のみを抜粋・編集し、史料へのアクセスを極めて容易にした。この史料集を用いた統計的・包括的な逃亡奴隷研究は、合衆国でもいまだ不十分である。

(3) 池本幸三によるG. W. マリンの研究の紹介・分析[12]

わが国においては、植民地時代の逃亡奴隷のまとまった研究としては、池本幸三によるG. マリンの研究の紹介・分析がある。しかし、本書でも衣服や織物については言及されていない。

(4) リンダ・バウムガルテン（Linda Baumgarten）のヴァージニアの奴隷の衣服研究[13]

主として18世紀（一部は19世紀初期についても言及）のヴァージニアの奴隷の衣服の種類やその生産について、歴史的・思想的背景に照らして、ヴァージニア・ガゼット紙や旅行記や日記などを用いて、上流階級の服飾と対比させながら具体的に考察している。しかし、本研究は奴隷の衣服のみを考察対象としたものであり、アメリカ人の立場からアメリカ独立革命史の中に、奴隷制問題をどう位置づけるかという歴史的視点は見られない。

(5) L. バウムガルテンの奴隷の衣服素材（プレインズ Plains，プレイド Plaidおよびコットン Cotton）に関する研究[14]

上述の論文を踏まえて、奴隷の衣服に用いられた三つの素材、すなわち、Plains, PlaidおよびCottonについて、逃亡奴隷広告や植民地の記録を史料に用いて、それらの用途および布地特性を考察している。とりわけ、Cottonという言葉がヘンリー7世の時代からの記録では多種のウール素材を包含していた、という見解が紹介されている。また、L. バウムガルテンは奴隷の衣服描写にあたって、L. A. ウィンドレイ編集の『逃亡奴隷広告集―1730年代～1790年―』から5年間隔で広告を抽出している。

(6) グロリア・M. ウィリアムズ（Gloria. M. Williams）およびキャロル・ケントラッロ（Carol Centrallo）のアフリカン・アメリカンの衣服に関する研究[15]

この研究は、17、18世紀のヴァージニア植民地への植民と植民地の生活条件、植民者の服装、さらに、同様に17、18世紀の植民地（ヴァージニア、サウス・カロライナおよびノース・カロライナ）におけるアフリカン・アメリカンの衣服を簡潔にまとめている。なかでも、L. A. ウィンドレイ編集による『逃亡奴隷広告集―1730年代～1790年―』を用いてデータ分析を行い、奴隷の衣服研究におけるこの史料の有効性と問題点を明快に結論づけている。しかし、本研究ではヴァージニア・ガゼット紙から1736年、1746年、1756年、1766年および1776年という具合に、10年間隔でデータを抽出して、逃亡奴隷の衣服のタイプと素材を一覧表にまとめているため、断片的なデータ紹介に終わっている。

(7) ジョナサン・プルード（Jonathan Prude）の逃亡奴隷広告のなかの衣服研究[16]

本研究は1700年代からアメリカで定期刊行されている下記の新聞14紙に掲載された逃亡奴隷広告やL. A. ウィンドレイ編集『逃亡奴隷広告集―1730年代～1790年―』を駆使して、下層階級の衣服描写の視点について論じている。彼は18世紀後半に逃亡した1,724人のサンプルを、1750年代、

1770年代および1790年代の14紙の逃亡奴隷広告から抽出して、コンピュータによる計量分析を行っている。J. プルードの分析する逃亡奴隷の新聞広告にみる身体的特徴と衣服の有り様は、当時の上流階級のいわゆるエリート層の人びとが、下層階級の人びと（年季奉公人、犯罪人および奴隷）をどう思い、どのように描いたのか、を知る貴重な資料である。

 Boston Gazette
 Connecticut Courant（Hartford）
 Connecticut Gazette（New London）
 Daily Advertiser（New York）
 New-York Mercury
 New-York Gazette
 Weekly Mercury
 New-York Journal
 General Advertiser
 New-York Journal & Patriotic Register
 Pennsylvania Gazette
 Maryland Gazette（Baltimore）
 South Carolina Gazette（Charleston）
 Virginia Gazette（Williamsburg）

(8) ブライヤン・P. ハワード（Bryan Paul Howard）の逃亡奴隷広告にみる年季奉公人と犯罪人の衣服研究[17]

 1774年から1778年のヴァージニア・ガゼット紙に描かれている年季奉公人と犯罪人の衣服についての考察である。技術的な背景を明らかにするために、現存する衣服と考古学的な出土品が、また、衣服の社会的背景を明らかにするために、日記や商人の記録やプランテーションの新聞などの史料が用いられている。さらに、新聞広告に見られる201種の逃亡者の描写を検討・分析した結果に基づいて、逃亡者の服装をグラフィック・イラストに描きだしている。巻末の資料編には、逃亡者のリスト、逃亡者の服装、逃亡地、年齢、性別、季節別の逃亡数、さらに、ヴァージニア・ガゼット紙に見られる逃亡者の衣服の素材50余種に関する用語解説が掲載されている。

 しかし、この研究では、アフリカン・アメリカンではなく、その大半がイギリスから移住してきた、あるいは移住させられた年季奉公人と犯罪人を対象としている。

3. 本研究の位置づけ

 日本における先行研究には逃亡奴隷広告を史料に用いた池本幸三および和田光弘[18]のアメリカ史

研究がある。池本や和田が分析対象としたこれらの史料は被服の研究には用いられていない。

上記の他にも、アメリカでは逃亡奴隷広告を史料に用いた奴隷の衣服研究は、ヴァージニア以外の地域に関しても見られる[19]。しかし地域としてヴァージニアを取りあげ、アメリカ独立革命前夜から革命終息の全期間（1766～1789年）を対象に、奴隷の被服の種類と被服素材に着目して、統計検定によって動態分析した研究は見られない[20]。

L. バウムガルテンの奴隷の衣服やテキスタイルに関する研究は、衣服やテキスタイルの枠にとどまらず、アメリカ史の枠組みの中で、アメリカ人の立場から、これらの問題が論じられるとより有効な問題提起となるのではなかろうか。つまり、衣服学、被服学ないし服飾史学と歴史学をいかに融合させていくか、という問題意識が必要なのではないか、と考える。

またB. P. ハワードの研究をさらに拡大し、アフリカン・アメリカンをも考察対象とすべきであろう。同時に単に独立革命期の5年間だけではなく、アメリカ独立革命史全体の中に位置づけて、年季奉公人や犯罪人や奴隷の衣服およびテキスタイルの動態分析を行なうことにより、より有効な研究になるのではないかと思う。つまり、このような作業を通じて、はじめてアメリカ独立革命期の奴隷制問題の本質が見えてくるものと確信する。筆者は先行研究に対する以上の理解の上に立って、筆者独自の方法と立場で本研究に取り組んだ。

以上に述べてきたことをもう一度整理し、本研究の対象（地域および時期）と方法をどのように限定したのか、について明確にしておこう。

1）対象とする地域をヴァージニアに限定する。

前述のように、1661年、ヴァージニア植民地議会は黒人奴隷制度を法制化した。「1640年には、わずか150人だったヴァージニアの黒人人口は、1670年には2,000人（当時のヴァージニアの総人口は4万人。以下、カッコ内は総人口）、1690年には9,000人（5万3,000人）、と増加したが、18世紀に入って1710年になると2万3,000人（7万8,000人）、1750年には10万2,000人（23万1,000人）を数えるにいたった[21]」。

アメリカ合衆国で最初の人口センサスがおこなわれた1790年には、70万人ちかい黒人奴隷のほとんどが南部諸州に住んでおり、とりわけ、ヴァージニアが他にぬきんでて多く、29万2,627人であった。とくに奴隷所有州としてのヴァージニアの優越は、植民地時代を通じて一般に認められていた。独立13州のうち、実にヴァージニアこそ、この奴隷制と共和制が盾の両面のように一体化しつつ、まことに矛盾した展開をとげたところであった。すなわち、この植民地がマサチューセッツとともに独立革命の先頭を切り、やがては「建国の父祖」たちを輩出させたにもかかわらず、黒人奴隷制度は存続した。アメリカ独立革命期における黒人奴隷制度存続の問題に真向から取り組んだ研究はわずかしかない。そこで、アメリカ独立革命期のヴァージニアの奴隷制問題を通して、ステイタス・シンボルとしての「被服」を取り上げた。

2）対象とする時期をアメリカ独立革命の1766年から1789年とする。

第2章で逃亡奴隷広告に見られる被服素材に関するデータを洗い出した。第3章では、奴隷の被

服の種類と特徴、逃亡広告に見られる被服の素材、男子の逃亡奴隷の逃亡時の着装実態を考察した。次に、第2章で洗い出した被服素材のデータを基に、国内産の素材と輸入素材（主なもののみ）の年次変化を比較・考察した。対象年は1766年から1789年とした。アメリカ新大陸では、1700年代中期まではイギリス本国の「有益な怠慢」政策（Salutary Neglect）がとられており、輸入品が入っていたが、1765年の印紙法の公布を境に、状況は大きく変化していく。「有益な怠慢政策」とは、1721年から20年以上にわたって、イギリスで続いたウォルポール政権時代の政策であった。ウォルポールは植民地の経済発展が本国の利益になることを重視し、植民地に対して宥和政策をとり、植民地人と紛争を起こすことをできるだけ避けようとした。イギリス政府は7年戦争で北アメリカの領土を拡大したのを機会に、北アメリカの植民地に対する統治政策の立てなおしに乗り出し、植民地貿易に新たな規制が加えられ、「有益な怠慢」政策は改められた。

3）奴隷の被服の種類と被服素材を数量的に分析する。

上流階級の衣服の実物は博物館に遺品として所蔵されているが、下層の奴隷の被服の実物はまったくと言っていいほど残っていない。しかし、上流階級の服飾の研究だけに終始していては、衣生活の真髄に触れることはできないと考え、奴隷の被服描写に関する歴史的事実を確認するための情報としての逃亡奴隷広告の史料価値に着目した。L. A. ウィンドレイ編集の『逃亡奴隷広告集—1730年代〜1790年—』は、ウィンドレイも述べているように、逃亡奴隷数を確定することはできないが、奴隷の被服の種類と被服素材の洗い出しをし、数量分析を試みるには有益である。

これらの資料から67種の被服素材を洗い出すことが可能となった。これらの素材は輸入素材と国内産の素材に分類できる。本書の対象時期の社会背景に照らしながら、被服素材の使用量の年次変化を統計的検定を用いて比較した。本書で扱う国内産の素材は、基本的にヴァージニア・クロスをさす。逃亡奴隷広告には繊維の種類に関する具体的な記述は少なく、これらがコットンであるのか、ウールであるのか不明である。とくにヴァージニア・クロスについては僅少である。広告主にとっては、その繊維が何であれ、ヴァージニア製の布地であることが重要であった。L. バウムガルテンとパトリシア・ギブズ（Patricia Gibbs）らもヴァージニア・クロスは国内産の布地を指しているとの見解を示している。

第3節　本書の構成 ——凡例にかえて——

序章をしめくくるにあたって、本書の構成について述べよう。

第1章では歴史的背景を概観する。第1節ではアメリカ独立革命とアメリカ合衆国の成立、第2節ではヴァージニア植民地の成立について、第3節ではヴァージニアの黒人奴隷制度、第4節ではアメリカ独立革命期の服飾の特徴、について述べる。

第2章では史料としての逃亡奴隷広告研究について述べる。第1節では逃亡奴隷広告における被服描写の史料的価値について、第2節では逃亡奴隷広告における被服情報の数量化について述べる。第3節では逃亡奴隷広告に見る被服素材の種類（67種）について述べる。B. P. ハワードの研究やフ

ローレンス・M. モンゴメリー（Florence M. Montgomery）やルイス・ハーミュス（Louis Harmuth）の辞書などを参照している。

　本書の第一の中心部をなす第3章では、逃亡奴隷の着装情況に、数量的にアプローチする。すなわち、第1節では奴隷の被服の種類と素材の特徴について考察し、第2節では男子の逃亡奴隷の逃亡時の着装実態を考察する。第3節では逃亡奴隷広告に見られるヴァージニア・クロスの特徴について、第4節では対照資料としてのオズナブルグの特徴について考察し、第5節では逃亡奴隷の被服素材の年次変化を輸入素材と国内産の素材の比較という観点から考察する。

　次いで、第二の中心部をなす第4章では、ヴァージニアにおける奴隷の被服の支給と生産実態について、現地における実物資料調査と第一次史料の調査結果に基づいて考察する。すなわち、第1節では先行研究について整理し、本章における筆者の研究方法を提示する。第2節では次の順に実物資料調査の結果報告と考察を行なう。

1．DeWitt Wallace Gallery of Decorative Arts に所蔵品されている18世紀のヴァージニア・クロス製の男子のスーツの調査報告。
2．Valentine Museumに所蔵されている18世紀に奴隷が作ったパッチワーク・キルトの実物資料の調査報告。
3．コロニアル・ウィリアムズバーグ振興財団の織物部門における調査からの報告。
4．同財団の考古学研究部門における調査報告。

　第3節では、プランテーションにおける被服管理に関して、カーター家とG．ワシントンのプランテーションの記録、商人の記録やその他の公文書などの第一次史料をもとに考察する。また、その他の事例、例えばターナー・サウスホール大佐（Turner Southhall）が、武器・弾薬の鋳造所建設現場で働く黒人奴隷用の被服のために支払った金額を証明する領収書の事例なども第一次史料に基づいて紹介する。

　終章ではアメリカ独立革命期の奴隷の被服に関する考察結果を全体の流れにそって、次の項目についてまとめる。

1．先行研究から得られた知見とその問題点。
2．本研究の二つの方法と得られた結論。
　(1) 第一の方法について―ヴァージニア・ガゼット紙に掲載された逃亡奴隷広告における被服描写の考察から得られた結論。「奴隷の被服をいかにイメージ化するか」という第2章第2節および第3章の課題にどのような方法で取り組み、どのような結論に至ったか。次の順に述べる。
　　1）逃亡奴隷広告（1766～1789）に登場する67種の被服素材の定義づけと解説。
　　2）逃亡奴隷の被服の種類、形および男子奴隷の着装実態について。
　　3）逃亡奴隷広告に登場する国産の素材について。
　　　① ヴァージニア・クロスの定義、布地の生産の実態、ヴァージニア・クロス製の衣服の特徴（被服の種類、色・柄）。

② オズナブルグ製の被服の特徴（被服の種類、色）―ヴァージニア・クロス製の被服の特徴を示す対照資料として―。
　　③ 逃亡奴隷広告に見られる被服素材の年次変化について―輸入素材と自国産の素材の比較において―。
(2) 第二の方法について
　1) ヴァージニア・クロス製の衣服と奴隷の被服および被服生産の道具に関する実物調査から得られた結論について。
　2) ヴァージニアの有数なプランターであるカーター家のプランテーションおよびアメリカの初代大統領G. ワシントンが所有していたマウント・ヴァーノンのプランテーションにおける調査（プランテーションの記録、商人の記録、プランターの日誌や手紙およびその他の公文書）から得られた結論について。

最後に、「口絵」図版頁の説明、巻末の資料編、索引、本研究に際して利用したソフトウェアー、および本文と資料の用語表記について述べ　序章の結びとすることとする。

1．「口絵」図版頁はすべてカラー図版とし、本文中に口絵1-2-1という具合に表記した。
2．巻末の資料編に次の三種類の資料を掲載した。
　1) 逃亡奴隷広告の事例
　2) John Wily, *A Treatise on the Propagation of Sheep, the Manufacture of Wool, and the Cultivation and Manufacture of Flax, with Direction for Making Utensils for the Business*, Williamsburg, 1765.
　3) John Hargrove, *Weavers Draft book and clothiers Assistant*, Worcester, American Antiquary Society, 1979.

3．索引は人名、地名、素材名、および、その他重要と思われる事項を軸に掲げた。
4．本研究に際して利用したソフトウェアーは次のとおりである。
　1) Omnipage Professional Macintosh版
　2) Excel 97 Windows 98
　3) Word 97 Windows 98版

5．本文および資料の用語表記は、次の原則にしたがった。
　1) 本文中の人名、地名、被服名および素材名については、各章毎に、原則として、初出の訳語の後の（　）内に原語名を表記した。
　　　例．初出　　　　　ロバート・カーター（Robert Carter）
　　　　　2回目以降　　　R. カーター

組織名（博物館名や美術館名）については、原語で表記した。
　　例．DeWitt Wallace Gallery of Decorative Arts
2) 主として、英文の文献に基いて作成した表には、英語の原語を表記した。
3) 出典は原語で文献名を表記した。

[注]

(1) ① ロナルド・タカキ著、富田虎男訳『多文化社会アメリカの歴史―別の鏡に映して―』（明石書房、1995年）。
② 中野勝朗「この慎ましやかな夢―多文化主義とナショナル・ヒストリー」アメリカ研究、第21号、(1998年)、2-10.

(2) Bureau of the Census, Historical Statistics of the United States: Colonial Times to 1970, Washington, D.C., U.S. Government Printing Office, 8, 14.

(3) U. S. Bureau of the Census, Negro Population in the United States, 1790～1915, 57.

(4) John C. Fitzpatrick, (ed.), The Last Will and Testimony of George Washington, an Schedule of his Property to which is appended the Last Will and Testament of Martha Washington, The Mount Vernon Ladies Association of the Union, first edition 1939, sixth edition, revised, (U.S.A., 1992), 2-4.

(5) Mount Vernon Ladies Association, Mount Vernon, ヴァージニア 22121.

(6) 日本のアメリカ研究をリードする学会にアメリカ学会がある。そこから毎年、学会誌『アメリカ研究』が刊行されているが、現在第33号になるその雑誌を第1号から調べてみても革命の原理と奴隷制度の原理との矛盾に真向から取り組んだ論文はない。
アメリカ人の研究には次の博士論文が上梓されている。
John Randolf Barden, "Flushed with Notions' of Freedom": The Growth and emancipation of a Virginia Slave Community, 1732～1812, Dissertation: Degree Date 1993, Duke University.

(7) 丹野郁『西洋服飾発達史―古代・中世編』光正館、1958年。
同『西洋服飾発達史―近世編』（光正館、1960年）。
同『西洋服飾発達史―現代編』（光正館、1965年）。
同『近代西欧服飾発達文化史』（光正館、1973年）。
丹野郁、原田二郎『西洋服飾史』（衣生活研究会、1975年）。
丹野郁『南蛮服飾の研究』（雄山閣、1976年）。
同『服飾の世界史』（白水社、1985年）。
同編『西洋服飾史―増訂版―』（東京堂出版、1999年）。

(8) 本書は筆者の修士論文『アメリカ植民地時代の服飾の歴史的考察―ヴァージニア、ニュー・イングランド、ニュー・ネザーランドの場合―』（武庫川女子大学大学院家政学研究科被服学専攻）の一部を書き改めて出版したものである。

(9) 1998年10月9日付の私信。

(10) Gerald W. Mullin, Flight and Rebellion, Slave Resistance in Eighteenth Century Virginia, Oxford University Press, (New York, 1972).

(11) Lathan A. Windley, (comp.), Runaway Slave Advertisement: A Documentary History from 1730s to 1790, Vol.1 of Vol.4, Greenwood, (Westport, Connecticut, 1983).

(12) 池本幸三『近代奴隷制社会の史的展開―チェサピーク湾ヴァージニア植民地を中心として―』（ミネルヴァ書房、1987年初版第1刷、1999年新装版第1刷）。

(13) Linda Baumgarten," Clothes for the People: Slave Clothing in Early Virginia", Journal of Early Southern Decorative Arts, Vol.14, No.2, (Nov.1988), Museum of Early Southern Decorative Arts, Winston Salem, N.C., 27-70.

(14) Linda Baumgarten, "Plains, Plaid and Cotton: Woolens for Slave Clothing," ARS TEXTRINA 15, (1991), 203-222.

(15) Gloria M. Williams and Carol Centrallo, "Clothing Acquisition and Use by the Colonial African American" (Barbara M. Starke, Lillian O. Holloman, Barbara K. Nordquist, African American Dress and Adornment, A Cultural Respective, Kendall /Hunt Publishing Company, U.S.A. 1990. 所収論文)

(16) Jonathan Prude, "To Look upon the 'Lower Sort': Runaway Ads and the Appearance of Unfree Laborers in America," *The Journal of American History*, (June 1991), 124-159.
(17) Bryan Paul Howard, *Had on and took with him: Runaway Indentured Servant Clothing in Virginia, 1774~1778*, UMI Dissertation Series, Degree Date: 1996, Texas A&M University.
(18) 和田光弘「南部植民地における逃亡奴隷―新聞広告の計量分析―」社会経済史学、第56巻第5号、(1990年12月)、62-76.
(19) Patricia Campbell Warner, "Some Kind of Coarse Clothing": Slave Clothes in Eighteenth-Century America, *The Catalog of The 44th Washington Antiques Show*, January 7-10, (1999), 81-85.
(20) 筆者はヴァージニアの奴隷の衣服に関して、下記の研究発表を行っている。本研究はこれらの研究発表をさらに発展させた研究である。
① 「18世紀から19世紀前半における黒人奴隷の衣服の社会史的考察」アメリカ史研究会第177回例会、1997年11月1日（土）、東京大学アメリカ研究資料センター会議室。発表要旨とコメンテイターのコメントについては、「アメリカ研究」第21号、1998年に次のように報告されている。

濱田雅子氏の報告「18世紀から19世紀前半における黒人奴隷の衣服の社会史的考察」は、合衆国における服飾研究者および歴史研究者による近年の研究業績に基づき、18世紀後半のヴァージニア、アンティベラム期のルイジアナ州およびミシシッピ州を例にした、黒人奴隷の衣服の考察を目的とした。考察にあたり、濱田氏は、以下の三点に特に留意した。第一に、当該時期の北アメリカ黒人奴隷が、どのような衣服を着用し、衣服および衣服材料をどのよう入手していたかに関する考察。第二に、奴隷制社会における、階級差別、人種差別および性差別の手段としての衣服に関する考察。具体的には、上流階級の衣服と黒人奴隷の衣服との比較、奴隷コミュニティーにおける職業別、階層別の衣服の違い、白人奉公人と黒人奴隷との衣服の違い、男女の奴隷の衣服の違い、子供と大人の奴隷の衣服の違いの考察。第三に、奴隷制社会における衣服の役割の考察。以上を踏まえた上で、今後の研究課題として、ステイタス・シンボルとしての衣服と黒人奴隷制度との関係の深さに関する更なる研究、黒人奴隷の実物の衣服を収集する必要性、黒人奴隷の衣服についての地域別の研究の必要性があげられた。

コメンテーターの宮井勢都子氏は、濱田報告を受けて、まず、装いという観点からみた支配者、被支配者の関係を、「支配者が」、自らと被支配者とをどのように表現したかという、支配者の自己認識の問題を論点として指摘した。また、服飾史が、従来の奴隷制社会の歴史的研究に加えうる点として、衣服が支配の手段として使われていったこと、および「装う」ことにおける黒人奴隷たちの主体性の表現とを指摘した。さらに、服飾史と社会史との接点の可能性として、18世紀から19世紀への移行の中での変遷、または普遍であったものを探る必要性について指摘した。

② 「18世紀後半ヴァージニアにおける黒人奴隷の衣服の社会史的考察―Linda Baumgarten氏とJonathan Prude氏の研究に基づいて―」関西アメリカ史研究会第207回例会、1998年5月24日（日）、立命館大学白雲荘にて
(21) 本田創造『アメリカ黒人の歴史　新版』(岩波新書、1991年)、39.

第 1 章

歴史的背景

はじめに

アメリカ独立革命史研究をめぐるアメリカ学界の動向を振り返ると、革新主義史学と「ネオ・ホイッグ」史観の二つの潮流が支配してきた。前者はアメリカ独立革命を政治・社会の民主化運動とみなす立場である。それに対して後者はこの革命はイギリスからの分離であったことを強調する立場である。

アメリカ史の教科書における通説では、アメリカの独立をもたらした植民地人の闘争は「アメリカ革命」(「アメリカ独立革命」ともいう) とよばれ、アメリカ独立革命はたんなる植民地の独立ではなく、一定の普遍的理念をかかげ、それにもとづいて政府を形成しようとした革命であった、とされている[1]。この革命の期間は1763年の7年戦争（フレンチ・アンド・インディアン戦争）の終結後間もない、イギリス本国と北アメリカ植民地との間の紛争の勃発から、1789年のアメリカ合衆国憲法にもとづく政府の発足に至る25年間である。

第1節　アメリカ独立革命と合衆国の成立

本節ではアメリカ独立革命の背景とアメリカ合衆国の成立過程を、通説に拠って、被服との関連において、特にイギリス商品ボイコット運動およびホームスパン運動に焦点を当てて概観しよう。

清水知久、高橋章、富田虎男著『アメリカ史研究入門』（山川出版社）では、アメリカ独立革命はアメリカ帝国の形成の時期も含めて、次のように段階区分されている[2]。

アメリカ独立革命の第1段階（1763〜1775年）
　　第1期（1763〜1766年）……国王宣言、砂糖法、通貨法、印紙法、軍隊宿営法などの一連の諸政策にたいする、印紙法反対運動を頂点とする植民地人の抵抗の段階。
　　第2期（1767〜1770年）……タウンゼンド諸法による外部課税の賦課と行政機能の拡充にたいする、植民地人の撤回運動の段階。
　　第3期（1770〜1773年）……一時的平穏期
　　第4期（1773〜1775年）……ボストン茶会事件を頂点に植民地人の組織的力行使展開、独立＝「革命」への転換開始。

アメリカ独立革命の第2段階（1775〜1829年）
　　第1期（1775〜1783年）……独立戦争
　　第2期（1783〜1788年）……連合時代
　　第3期（1789〜1801年）……フェデラリストの時代

第4期（1801〜1825年）……リパブリカンズの時代
第5期（1825〜1829年）……ジョン・クインシー・アダムズ時代

　植民地北アメリカは、イギリス人のヴァージニアへの入植（1607年）以来、150年にわたってヨーロッパから継承してきた諸制度や生活慣習を変容させ、新社会の基礎を作り出してきた。服飾文化もヨーロッパの文化が移入され、植民地北アメリカの気候・風土に適合すべく、北部・中部・南部というそれぞれの地域の相異なる社会・経済構造に見合った形で変容を遂げていった。こうしたなか北アメリカ東部のイギリス植民地は7年戦争（フレンチ・アンド・インディアン戦争）後の課税問題をめぐってイギリス本国と対立し、1773年のボストン茶会事件を契機に対立は一層深まり、レキシントン・コンコードの戦いにおいて、独立戦争の火ぶたが切られた。この戦争は1789年のアメリカ合衆国憲法にもとづく政府の成立によって終結を見る。
　では独立革命の原因は何であったのか？
　紛争前のイギリス本国の植民地政策は、いわゆる「有益な怠慢」政策である。つまり、イギリス本国は植民地人に大幅な自由を許しており、植民地は重商主義規制にかかわらず、豊かな貿易から恩恵を受けていた。
　ちなみに、イギリスの1773年対北アメリカ植民地の輸出量は、全輸出量の16.1パーセントであり、輸入量は全輸入量の12.5パーセントであった。また、対西インド貿易の輸出量は全輸出量の6.6パーセントであり、輸入量は全輸入量の24.8パーセントであった。このように18世紀後半の第一次イギリス帝国における北アメリカ植民地の経済的地位は高まっていた[3]。
　それでは本国と植民地間の紛争の発端は何に起因していたのか。それは本国の植民地政策の変化にあった。
　1763年に7年戦争（フレンチ・アンド・インディアン戦争）が終結し、イギリスはフランス領カナダ、スペイン領フロリダをも併せた、大西洋岸からミシシッピ川、ハドソン湾からメキシコ湾に至る広大な領土と東インドの支配権を得た。だが、同時に3,000万ポンドの戦時負債を背負った。そこでイギリスは戦後、帝国防衛のため、約1万人の軍隊駐留費用（年間30万ポンド）の一部を植民地に負担させようとした[4]。
　1764年に砂糖法、1765年に印紙法を出し重税を課したため、植民地側は反発し、「代表なければ課税なし」とうたい抵抗した。すなわち、イギリス国民はみずからの代表が同意した税のみを負担するというのがイギリス憲法の原則であり、植民地のイギリス人は本国議会に代表を送っていないので、本国議会の決定によって課税されるのは不当であり、彼らはそれぞれの植民地議会の同意によってのみ、課税されるというのが彼らの主張であった。その結果、印紙法は発効後、半年にして撤廃された。
　1767年には、(1) 茶、ガラス、鉛、塗料、紙への関税という形で、歳入をはかり、(2) ニュー・ヨーク議会を、1765年の軍隊宿営法拒否の罪で停止し、(3) アメリカ関税局を再編・強化するとともに、4市に海事裁判所を置き、「白紙の捜査令状」を発行できるなどのタウンゼンド諸法が発布

された。この結果、航海法規制の効果があがり、植民地史上、はじめて関税収入が徴収税を上回るほどになった[5]。これに対して再び植民地人の反抗運動が起こり、イギリス製品不輸入協定が全国的に実施された。そのため、本国からの輸入は、250万ポンドから163万ポンドへと急落し、イギリス商人は大打撃を受けた。また、植民地ではアメリカ製品愛用運動も展開され、このような背景のもとに、アメリカ国内では繊維工業と製靴業とが急速に工場制手工業の段階へと突入していった。本国は1770年にタウンゼンド諸法を撤廃するに至る[6]。

その後約3年間は、いわゆる「静穏の時期」が続くが、1773年、東インド会社に茶の輸入と販売権を独占的に与えるという茶法が出された。そして、この法律に反対する植民地の急進派（独立を願う人達）が東インド会社の船を襲い、積荷の茶を海中に投げ捨てるという、ボストン茶会事件が起こった。このボストン茶会事件こそ、これまでの植民地人の抵抗運動が独立戦争へと飛躍する転機となった。事件に対し、イギリスはボストン港の閉鎖という報復措置をとった。1774年、植民地側は9月から10月にかけて、フィラデルフィアで第一回大陸会議を開き、本国の圧政と不当な課税に対して抗議した。ここで採択された「宣言と決議」は植民地に対するイギリス議会の立法権を全面的に否定し、全イギリス商品の「不輸入、不輸出、不消費」を決めた大陸通商断絶同盟を結成した。だが、本国政府と国王はとりあわなかった[7]。

戦争[8]はまず、マサチューセッツで始まった。マサチューセッツでは、軍隊に守られた政府と武装した人民に支えられた革命権力とが対立していたためである。革命側はボストンをイギリスにおさえられていたが、農村を基盤として抵抗することができた。多くのタウンやカウンティで抵抗するための軍隊組織が作られた。イギリスはこれらの動きに対して、少数の正規軍で一握りの反逆分子を十分制圧できると考えていた。1775年4月19日、イギリス軍はコンコードに集積されているとみられる武器を押収しようとしたが、レキシントンで民兵の抵抗にあい、さらにコンコードでも民兵と遭遇した。イギリス軍はコンコードでは多数の住民から銃撃され、多くの死傷者をだした。このレキシントン・コンコードの戦いにより、アメリカ独立戦争が開始された。

植民地側は、1775年5月にフィラデルフィアで第二次大陸会議を開き、全植民地の戦争としてイギリスと戦うことを決めた（ジョージアは遅れて同年9月に出席）。多くの植民地では植民会議が革命政権となった。6月には、ヴァージニアのジョージ・ワシントンを植民地軍全体の総指令官とした。しかし、植民地人の立場が完全に一致していたわけではなく、官吏や大地主・大商人は王に忠誠であり、また中立の立場をとった者も多かった。1776年1月にトマス・ペインにより独立の必要と共和政について述べた「コモン・センス」が発行され、独立戦争を盛り上げた。アメリカ人を独立と「新しい自由な共和国の建設」へ向かわせる役割を果たした。独立支持の急進派はマサチューセッツとヴァージニアで、ヴァージニアは13植民地の中心にある最大の植民地でもあり、多くの指導力のある政治家を出したことから植民地全体の動向に大きな影響を与えた。他方、中部植民地のニュー・ヨーク、ペンシルヴェニア、ニュー・ジャージーは独立を戦争目的にすることに最も慎重だった。1776年7月4日、13植民地の代表はフィラデルフィアで独立宣言を発表した。トマス・ジェファソンらが起草し、人間の自由・平等や圧政に対する反乱の正当性を主張した。

独立軍ははじめ武器・食料の不足などで苦戦したが、1777年サラトガの戦いでイギリス軍は大敗、降伏し、独立軍は勝利を得た。一方、フィラデルフィアではG.ワシントンが率いる革命軍が大敗した。駐仏大使のフランクリンがフランスの植民地の独立支持をとりつけるという動きもあって、1778年にフランスが参戦し、翌年にスペイン、またオランダも参戦した。さらに、イギリスの中立船舶の捕獲宣言に対抗して、ロシア皇帝エカチェリーナ2世の提唱する武装中立同盟がロシア・プロイセン・ポルトガル・スウェーデン・デンマークによって結成されると、イギリスは国際的に孤立し、独立軍の士気は高まった。1777年に連合規約が成立した。この規約は「ユナイテッド・ステイツ・オブ・アメリカ」を独立・自由・主権を有する諸州の永久的同盟と規定し、外交使節の交換や条約の締結など対外関係に関する権限を連合会議に与えた。1781年ヨークタウンの戦いでイギリス軍は大敗し、植民地側では1777年に成立した連合規約が発効した。1783年のパリ条約においてイギリスはアメリカ合衆国の独立を承認し、アメリカにミシシッピ川以東のルイジアナを譲った。

　独立後、兵士たちはもとの職に戻った。橋や運河の建設が行われ、宗教の自由も許された。しかし、独立したものの合衆国は13の州の連合体を意味するに過ぎず、中央権力が弱かったため、政治的・経済的に混乱が続いた。アメリカは重商主義の世界の中で独立国になったため、諸大国の重商主義の壁に突き当たり、アメリカ経済は不況に陥った。アメリカ人は独立後もイギリスの船舶と商品をアメリカの港に受け入れる代りに、アメリカの船舶と商品もイギリスの港にいれることを期待したが、イギリスはアメリカに対して厳しい態度をとった。イギリスはアメリカ船をイギリス領西インド諸島から締め出した。アメリカ産の魚の塩漬け・塩肉の輸入を禁止し、鯨油には重い関税を課した。フランスやスペインとの貿易もアメリカが期待したほどの伸びはなかった。アメリカはオランダ・スウェーデン・プロシアなどの国と通商関係を結び、特にオランダとの貿易は発展したが、イギリス市場への輸出や海運収入の減少の十分な埋め合わせにはならなかった。また、戦争によって生じた負債の埋め合わせのために紙幣を大量に発行したことから、インフレとなった。この混乱期において大きな利益を得た人もいた。州は財政が困難になると公然たる忠誠派の財産を没収して競売にかけ、収入源にした。革命側に立って権力を得た人もいれば、大商人や大地主の中にはイギリス側についたために権力と財産を失い、アメリカを去る人もかなりいた。

　問題を解決するためには、中央政府の樹立が必要だという運動が高まり、1787年にフィラデルフィアでG.ワシントンを議長として憲法制定会議が開かれ、合衆国憲法が作られた。この憲法は共和政の民主主義を土台とし、各州に大幅な自治を認めながらも、中央政府の権限を従来より強化する連邦主義を採用し、さらに、行政・立法・司法の三権分立を基本原理とした。モンテスキューの「法の精神」の影響が大きいと思われる。合衆国の行政権は大統領の率いる政府が握り、立法権は各州の代表からなる上院と人民を代表する下院にあり、司法権は最高裁判所が行使した。

　1787年までには、フランスやスペインによる貿易の規制が緩められたことと、オランダやその他の国との貿易が拡大したことなどのため輸出量が増大し、アメリカの景気は上向きになった。

　1789年、この憲法にもとづく連邦政府が発足し、G.ワシントンが初代大統領に就任し、合衆国が成立した。

第2節　ヴァージニア植民地の成立

　本節では、第1節で言及した13植民地の中から、本書の舞台であるヴァージニア植民地を取り上げ、その成立の背景について述べよう[9]。

　チェサピーク湾地域に発展したヴァージニアは、イギリスの北アメリカ植民地の中で最も古い植民地で、独立当時の13州の一つである。ヴァージニアの名称は「処女王」(Virgin Queen) として知られたイギリス女王エリザベスの名誉のために、廷臣ウォルター・ローリー (Sir Walter Raleigh) によって名付けられたものである。エリザベス朝の内政の整備はやがて海外発展を促し、イギリスは北アメリカ植民地に着眼するに至った。ヴァージニア植民地に恩恵をもたらしたものはタバコ栽培である。エリザベスの廷臣ギルバートがエリザベス女王より特許状を得て新大陸に植民地を作ろうとして失敗し、その異母弟ローリーが1584年に最初の遠征隊を送ったが、スペインとの間の国際情勢が悪く、1591年これを断念した。しかし、このとき初めてタバコがイギリスにもたらされている。次いで、1606年にはロンドンに設立されたヴァージニア会社がジェームズ一世より特許状を得、翌年、百余人の最初の移民を送った。彼らはロンドン・カンパニーのグッドスピード号、サラーコンスタント号、ディスカバリー号の3隻によって、1606年12月20日、ロンドンを出発、1607年5月6日、チェサピーク湾に入った。彼らは上陸した土地を国王ジェームズの名に因んでジェームズタウンと名付けた。

　1609年から1616年までの8年間に、ヴァージニアに送られた入植者は1,650人であったが、そのうち1,000人近くが死亡し、約300人が帰国して、1616年には351人を数えるのみであった。移住者のほとんどは年季奉公人制度下で社有地で耕作に従事したが、1614年には最初の移住者の7年年季があけ、「農民」ないし「小作人」と呼ばれる半ば自由な労働者と彼等の「私有地」が出現した。これ以後、土地の私有化はジョン・ロルフ (John Rolf 1585～1622) によって改良されたタバコ栽培（口絵1-2-1）と結びついて急速に広がり、社有制の建て前はくずれていった。

　1609年および1612年の特許状で、植民地統治権は王より会社に与えられ、1618年には自治憲法とも呼ばれるものの制定に発展し、1619年にはジェームズタウンには新大陸最初の議会が設けられた。これはイギリス式の議会政治の移入として注目すべきものである。1622年インディアンによる大虐殺があって後、1624年、ヴァージニア会社による特許植民地の王領植民地には変化は見られなかった。

　1619年にはジェームズタウンに、はじめて黒人がオランダ船により移入されたのであるが、当時の文書によれば、これは奴隷ではなく、一定の年限をつとめれば解放される年季契約労働者としてであった。しかし白人契約労働者が契約年季を終了するとともに独立経営者に変わったのに反し、黒人は年季終了後も依然として奴隷的地位にとどまり、この慣例は後の奴隷制に発展した。

　さて、入植地ヴァージニアの気候・風土はイギリス人にとっていかなるものであったであろうか。ジョン・スミス (John Smith, 1580～1631) は1624年にロンドンで出版された『ヴァージニア、ニューイングランドおよびサマー諸島の一般史、1584～1624』の一節で、1606年に植民した当時のこ

の地域の気温について、次のように記している。

「この Country の気温は、いったんこの地に馴れてしまえば、イギリス人の体質に良く合っていた。そのため、多くの場合、イギリス人たちは病気にかかりはしたが、ほとんど大事に至ることなく回復して、健康を維持していた。もっとも、他の大きな原因が彼らをただ病気にしてしまうばかりか、その命さえ奪ってしまう場合もありはしたが。

夏はスペイン同様に暑く、冬はフランスやイギリスにおけるように寒い。夏の高温は6月、7月および8月であるが、一般に涼風は激しい高温を和らげてくれた。冬の盛りは12月後半から1月、2月、3月の半ばにかけてである。寒さは極めて厳しくはある。だが、どんなことも極端なことは長くは続かない、という諺は真実である[10]」。

第3節　ヴァージニアの「黒人」奴隷制度

本節では18世紀ヴァージニアの黒人奴隷制度の成立の背景とこの制度の特質を考察する。この制度の成立について語るには、奴隷貿易のはじまりから述べなければならない。

1．奴隷貿易

ヨーロッパ人によるアフリカ人奴隷貿易は、誰が何時頃はじめたのか[11]。

それはアフリカに進出したポルトガル人であり、15世紀のことである。コロンブスが大西洋を横断するちょうど半世紀前の1441年、アンタン・ゴンサルヴェスを船長とするカラヴェル船がモーリタニア北部のリオ・デ・オロに上陸し、12名のアゼネゲ人をいけどりにして、ラゴスに連れ帰った。アゼネゲ人はベルベル系の一種族で、いわゆる黒人種ではない。この種族は当時西サハラからモーリタニアにかけて居住していた。ポルトガルのアフリカ、アジア進出の中心人物であったエンリケ航海王子は、当地のアゼネゲ社会ではサハラ以南の地から連れてこられた黒人が奴隷として使役されていることを、彼らから聞き及んだ。

また、1444年にはランサローテ・デ・フレイタスが6隻の船で、さらに南のアルギン礁に出向き、235人を捕虜とした。彼らの大半はアゼネゲ人であったが、黒人種も含まれていた。これらの捕虜のうち5分の1はエンリケ航海王子に献上され、残りはラゴス郊外で競売にかけられた。

1517年、スペインの植民地宣教師ラス・カサスは植民地に来住するスペイン人に黒人奴隷12人の所有を認める提案をした。西半球のヨーロッパ人植民地が発展した17世紀になると、多数の奴隷が西半球に持ち込まれた。西インド諸島、ブラジル、イギリス領北アメリカなどが急速に発達した18世紀は、奴隷貿易の最盛期であった。

大西洋奴隷貿易の全期間を通算すると、イギリス領北アメリカの輸入奴隷数は40万人であった。奴隷化されたアフリカ人は、ヨーロッパ人がしばしば思い込んだような原始的未開人ではなく、かなり発達した農耕文化をもっていた。このような文化的背景により、奴隷たちは短期間で白人社会

における有用な労働力となり、単純労働以上の仕事をこなすようになった。

2．白人年季奉公人制度

　第2節で述べたように、現在のヴァージニア州に植民地建設が開始されたのは1607年のことである。当初は疫病と飢餓によって入植者の死亡率が異常に高く、植民地経営の安定には時間を要した。その安定をもたらした主要な要因は、植民者個人への土地の分与と自営農民制度の導入が行なわれたこと、および、タバコという主要作物の栽培に成功したことである。王領植民地となる1623年には、人口は1,300人となり、前途有望な植民地としての足場が固められた。

　問題は労働力の担い手である。タバコ・プランテーションでの労働力の主たる担い手は黒人奴隷ではなく、白人年季奉公人（Indentured Servant）であった。イギリス人の植民者たちは、スペイン人の先例にならって、最初は原住民の奴隷化を試みた。しかし、インディアンは狩猟民で農耕に適しておらず、諸種族の抵抗があり、逃亡援助が繰り返されて、地理的に詳しい彼らを1箇所に縛り付けることは困難で、うまくいかなかった。それでもインディアンの奴隷化は熱心に進められた。例えば、サウス・カロライナの場合には、1706年の総人口9,580人のうち1,400人がインディアン奴隷だった[12]。

　このような状況下で成立したのが、白人年季奉公人制度である。ここで、植民地での年季奉公人制度の起源について述べたいと思う[13]。この問題には次の二つの側面がある。一つには植民地で新たに形成された制度という側面である。もう一つはイギリス本国にもともと存在した制度という側面である。まず、後者の側面について説明しよう。

　結論から言えば、イギリスの年季の限られた奉公人は、「任意の召使い」あるいは「強制された召使い」であり、その大半が未成年層からなる若い集団であった。彼らはどちらかと言えば貧民層の出身の人々であり、識字率は低く、職業教育も充分に受けておらず、記載すべき職業もない社会的に独立していない若者であった。

　イギリス社会の習わしとして、彼らは10代で一定期間、他人の家庭でサーヴァントとして仕え、何年間かそこで過ごしたのち、結婚して独立の所帯をもった。彼らは「ライフスタイル・サーヴァント」と呼ばれ、「サーヴァントというものは、15歳から24歳までの人口の、じつに60％前後を占めていた[14]」と推計されている。彼らは通常、農業サーヴァントや家事サーヴァントや徒弟サーヴァントから成っていた。なかでも重要な労働力であったのは、農業サーヴァントであり、原則として年季は1年であった。彼らの調達は、人的なつながりを通じて、あるいはもっと一般的には奴隷の競売や馬の市を思わせる「雇用市」において行なわれた。

　年季という通過点を通過した若者は、通常結婚して独立の世帯をもって、一定の職業に就いた。だが、なかには失業者や浮浪者になる者もいた。彼らは職につけず、植民地で年季奉公人にならざるをえなくなるのである。このため彼らは「任意の召使い」と称された。また、犯罪を犯した囚人が死刑を執行される代わりに、植民地で年季奉公人として働くように強制されて植民地へ送られるケースもあった。

以上のように、イギリス本国に制度的起源をもつ年季奉公人制度は、北アメリカ植民地に移植され、黒人奴隷制度成立以前に、あるいはそれと並行して、新世界における強制労働制度として定着していったのである。

以降、この制度は植民地において、三つの点において変質していく。第一には年季の長期化、第二には主人の奉公人に対する日常的権力の強化、第三には年季期間中は奉公人を自由に売買できたことにおいてである。

植民地に渡った白人年季奉公人の数は、植民地時代にアメリカへ移住した人々の3分の2にも達し、総数30万人とも40万人ともいわれている。本国の農業サーヴァントの年季は通常1年であったが、任意の年季奉公人の場合は、渡航費が高かったため、その年季は4年であった。その他にもっと非合法的なやり方、たとえば誘拐や略奪によるものもあった。「数千人のひとびとが、わけもなくイギリスの諸都市の路上で殴り倒され、残忍な紐にひきずられて[15]」無理矢理に植民地におくりこまれた、という。それ以外に、政治犯や刑事犯にとらわれ、死刑その他の有罪判決を受けた後に恩赦の措置を通じて、強制的に植民地に送りこまれて、不自由労働に服したものもいた。当時、イギリスでは浮浪行為も刑事犯をなしたので、浮浪者や物ごいもこれに含まれた。彼らの年季は、犯罪の軽重に応じて7年ないしは14年であった。総数はおよそ5万人と推定されている。

17世紀のチェサピーク湾地域（ヴァージニア、メリーランド、ノース・カロライナ北部）には、このような年季奉公人が13万人から15万人送られてきたといわれている[16]。たとえば、ヴァージニアでは、1625年にはその総人口1,200人のうち500人たらずが、1670年には4万人のうち6,000人が白人年季奉公人で、この後者の場合は、当時のヴァージニアの黒人奴隷2,000人の3倍にあたる[17]。

年季奉公人は17世紀の第3四半期まではタバコ生産の重要な労働力であった。白人年季奉公人制度の特質は、その強制労働としての側面にある。植民地での年季奉公人の日常生活の状態は、場所によって、また主人によって、多少の違いはあるが、年季中の結婚は厳禁しており、酒を買ったり、ものを売ったりすることもできなかった。奉公人が逃亡したり、彼らを匿ったり、隠れて雇ったりすることに対して厳罰が課された。鞭で打たれたうえ、焼印を押されたりすることもあった。処罰としては大幅な年季延長が中心であった。また、奉公人は、年季契約期間中、主人の裁量で自由に売買できる対象であった。それゆえ、彼らはしばしば年季奴隷とよばれた。

しかし、年季奉公人制度にはもう一つの特質があった。彼らは「白人」であり、「年季の限られた奉公人」であった。年季があけると、自由人として生活するために、解放給付（Freedom dues）を受けた。1705年のヴァージニアの奉公人・奴隷法第13条には、従来、とうもろこしや衣類を慣習として給付してきたが、それらが次のように条文化されている[18]。

　男子奉公人ひとりにつき、とうもろこし、10ブッシェル、貨幣30シリング、もしくはそれに相当する物品、および最低20シリングの価値をもったしっかりとした小銃または導火線（fuzee=fusee）。

　女子奉公人ひとりにつき、とうもろこし15ブッシェルと、貨幣40シリング、もしくはそれに相

当するとうもろこし。

　主人がそれらの給付を拒否したばあい、当該奉公人は裁判所に訴えることができる。

ときには50エーカーほどの土地をもらうこともあった。ただし、1660年以降は年季明けの奉公人たちが、土地を確保して小プランターになれる可能性は次第に少なくなっていった。後述する1676年のベーコンの反乱もヴァージニアの元奉公人の不満が爆発したものと見ることができる。

3．「黒人」奴隷制度の成立

(1) 白人年季奉公人制度から黒人奴隷制度へ[19]

　前述のように、17世紀半ばまでのイギリス領植民地の労働力の主力は白人年季奉公人であった。だが、17世紀も終わりに近づくにつれて、ヴァージニアやメリーランドではタバコ栽培（口絵1-3-1、1-3-2）が急激に発展し、さらに18世紀に入って、サウス・カロライナやジョージアでは米、続いて藍の栽培が促進され、生産が増大していく。それにともなって、従来の白人年季奉公人制度から黒人奴隷制度への移行をみることになる。

　ヴァージニアにおける白人年季奉公人制度から黒人奴隷制度への移行の要因として、次の三つが挙げられる。第一の要因は年季奉公人がヴァージニアで土地を所有する機会が減少したことにある。年季奉公人の年季中の生活はきわめて劣悪で、労働時間は1週6日、1日10～14時間労働であり、年季中は売却可能であった。また、逃亡すると年季延長を含む厳重な処罰が待ち受けていた。体罰も加えられた。だが、1640年代、50年代には彼らは年季が明けると少なくとも10年以内には土地を獲得し、政治にも参加できた。

　ところが、1660年以降は年季が明けた年季奉公人によるこのような土地獲得の機会は急速に減少していった。その背景をなしたのは、プランターたちが17世紀の半ば頃から土地を大量に購入し、土地価格が高騰したことにある。年季が明けたばかりの自由民には手が届かない価格であった。土地を手に入れることのできない彼らには、二つの選択肢があった。一つはプランターの下で地代を払って小作人となる道である。もう一つは西部のフロンティアへ移住して土地を入手する道である。1676年に起きた「ベーコンの反乱」は、1673年にイギリスからやってきたばかりの青年プランターのナザニエル・ベーコン（Nathaniei Bacon）が指導者であり、近隣のインディアンの奴隷化、彼らからの土地の略奪を目指す反乱であった。この反乱には土地を求める多くの白人奉公人の出の人々が加わったのである。反乱を機にプランターは、タバコ・プランテーションの労働力をもっと安全だと思われていた黒人奴隷に切り替えていく傾向が強くなってきた。

　白人年季奉公人制度から黒人奴隷制度への移行の第二の要因は、年季が明けると独立生産者として去っていく労働力を常時、手元に維持しておくことが難しかった点にある。そのうえ、白人年季奉公人は黒人奴隷に比べると経費が高くついた。年季の長さにもよるが、最初の購入費で約10ポンドから20ポンド、次に年季中の諸経費、最後に解放給付を支払わなければならなかった。

　黒人奴隷の場合は、最初の購入費は白人年季奉公人よりも高くついた。奴隷価格は、例えば1650

年には20ポンド、1700年には25ポンド、1740年には30ポンドであった[20]。だが、彼らは一生涯奴隷であり、その維持費は白人年季奉公人より安くついた。子どもができれば、購入費は要らず、維持費だけで済んだのである。

　白人年季奉公人制度から黒人奴隷制度への移行の第三の要因は、黒人側の事情にあった。すなわち、第一に、黒人たちが熱帯および亜熱帯での労働に適していたこと。第二に、インディアンとは異なり、すでに農業がかなり発達した社会に住んでいたこと。第三に、皮膚の色が黒く逃亡してもすぐに見分けがついたこと。第四に、黒人には白人が尊重しなければならない法律上の権利は一切与えなくてもよかったこと…など、白人優越主義者の側から挙げられる黒人奴隷化の理由である。

　以上の三つの要因を集約すると、結局、南部において黒人奴隷制度への転換をもたらした基本的な理由は、当時の北アメリカ植民地において、南部のプランターたちが、タバコその他の主要商品作物の生産量をより高めるために、白人年季奉公人にかわる、より安定性のある、より安価な労働力を絶えず確保しておく必要があったことにある。

　他方、北部では大商人や船主たちが黒人奴隷貿易からの収益を期待し、これをきわめて有利な「職業」としようとしていた。これらは、とりもなおさず、イギリス重商主義の一環としての対北アメリカ植民地政策であった。

　フィリップ・D.モーガン（Philip D. Morgan）は著書 "*Slave Counterpoint, Black Culture in the Eighteenth-Century Chesapeake & Lowcountry*"[21] に、1775年から1790年のヴァージニアにおける黒人奴隷の分布図（図1-3-3②③）を掲載している。図1-3-3①は1775年の13植民地とその他のイギリス領を示す地図であり、斜線の部分が図1-3-3②③のヴァージニアに当たる。これらの分布図からヴァージニアの黒人奴隷数が著しい増加傾向を示していることが一目瞭然である。

(2) 黒人奴隷制度の特質

　奴隷の労働のあり方について述べるに当って、ディヴッド・ガレンソン（David W. Galenson）の説を看過するわけにはいかない。彼の説は、一口で言えば、白人年季奉公人制度から黒人奴隷制度への移行についての「労働力移行の二段階説」である。それによると、「西インドでは砂糖、チェサピーク湾地域ではタバコ、サウス・カロライナでは米やインディゴというように、三地域内のそれぞれのプランテーションでは、第一段階として非熟練分野、つまり野外耕作労働において、労働主体が黒人奴隷に移り、熟練労働のみが白人奉公人に委ねられる。ついで黒人奴隷がさまざまな技術を修得するにつれ、熟練労働の分野においても、白人奉公人に取って代るようになる第二段階へ移行した[22]」という。

　ガレンソンのいう第二段階においては、黒人奴隷の身分は労働形態により、3つの階層、すなわち、プランターの側仕えの上級の奴隷（馬車を引く人、召使い、給仕など）、技術を持った職人奴隷、および農園で働く耕作奴隷に区分されていた。

　それでは、黒人奴隷が修得した熟練労働とはどのような仕事であったのか。

　森杲はD.ガレンソンと共通の立場から、「チェサピーク湾岸のタバコ・プランテーションの黒人

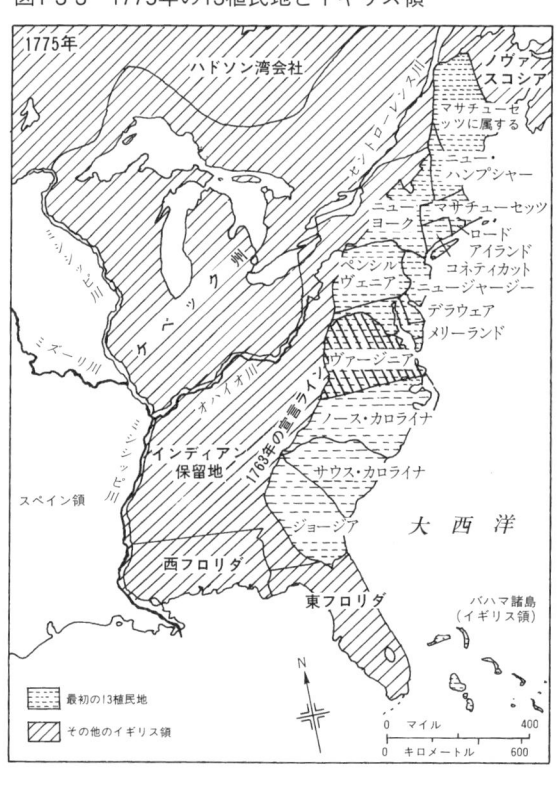

図1-3-3　1775年の13植民地とイギリス領

参考図：R.H., フェレル著、猿谷要監修『図説　アメリカ歴史地図』原書房　1994年、p.174

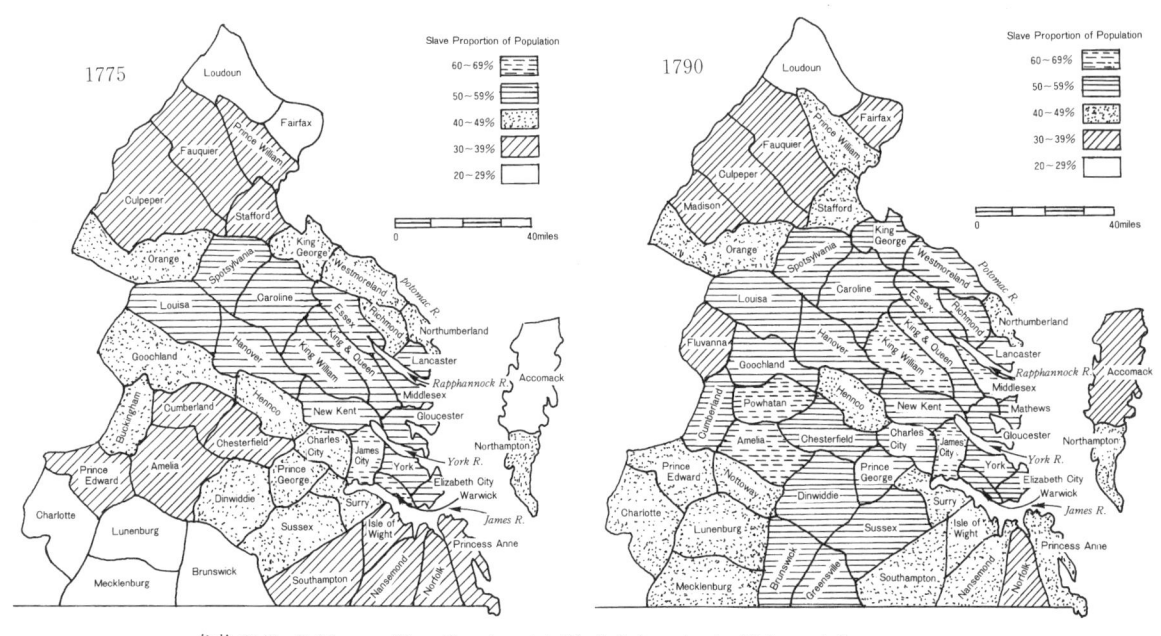

参考: Philip D. Morgan, *Slave Counterpoint, Black Culture in the Eighteenth-Century Chesapeake & Lowcountry*, The University of North Carolina Press, Chapel Hill & London, 1998, p.99.

がどのような職人的な仕事を仕込まれていたのか」という問題について、下記のような具体的な見解を述べている。

「黒人にやらせた最もてっとり早い職人仕事は、樽つくりである。タバコをはじめ作物を入れる容器としてさまざまの形状の樽の需要は莫大で、大プランターなら複数の製樽工を常時かかえているのがふつうだった。黒人はまずこれの技能を仕込まれ、さらには農具や家具の製作、鍛冶、革なめしや靴つくり、製粉などもこなすようになっていた。家族もちの黒人の場合には、一部の子供が早くから特定の職人仕事を教えこまれた。また夫人がフルタイムの縫製の仕事にたずさわった例も多い。そうした技能を誰が仕込むのかというと、それはときに奴隷所有者のプランターであり――独立自営農民の場合に似て、多くのプランターが自ら万能的な職人技能を身につけていた――、あるいはプランテーションに雇われている職人である。こうして彼らがつくった製品が、プランテーション内の需要をまかなうだけでなく、しばしば商品として市場にだされ取引された[23]」

南部植民地の大きな特徴として、このような専門職人も含めて、労働において黒人奴隷が担う割合がかなり高かった[24]。

ここに挙げられている以外にも、チェサピークとサウス・カロライナの黒人奴隷の職人について、P.D. モーガンは詳しい考察を行なっている。モーガンは彼らの職種として、仕立て屋（taylor）、大工（carpenter）、ろくろ細工師（turner）、車大工（wheelwright）、織工（weaver）、塗装工（painter）、木挽き工（sawyer）、医者（doctor）、御者（driver）、樵（woodworker）、屠殺業者（butcher）、鉄骨組み立て職人（iron worker）などを挙げている[25]。

表1-3-1 は1733～1809年のチェサピークにおける成人男子の奴隷の職種の構成比に関するものである。18世紀後半から、熟練工の増加が見られる。

表1-3-2 は1757～1809年のヴァージニアの大プランテーションにおける成人女子の奴隷の職種の構成比に関するものである。1780年代から家内の酪農関係の仕事や裁縫に携わる女性が増えている。

表1-3-3 は1730～1809年のチェサピークの奴隷の職人の年齢構成比に関するものである。1770年代から1790年代にかけて、20代から30代の職人が増加していることが明らかである

表1-3-4 は1732～1779年のヴァージニアの技能労働者の逃亡奴隷の年齢別構成比である。20代から30代の逃亡者が多いことが、明らかである。

次に、ヴァージニアの農園の奴隷の労働のあり方を考察しよう[26]。

タバコの生産過程は数多くの作業からなっている。すなわち、「盛土、畦切り、藩種と植え付け、摘茎・摘枝による盛育止め、吸枝除去、除草、下葉の刈り取り、タバコ葉の摘み取りまたは枝取り

表1-3-1　チェサピークにおける成人男子の奴隷の職種の構成比（1733～1809年）

年度　　　職種	a 1733（%）	b 1733（%）	c 1744（%）	d 1757～1775（%）	e 1784～1809（%）
農業	*95*	*86*	*92*	*70*	*65*
耕作奴隷	90	69	82	70	60
組頭	2	17	4	*	1
その他	3	0	6	0	4
熟練工	*4*	*12*	*5*	*21*	*21*
大工と樽職人	4	7	3	9	10
樵	0	4	0	2	0
その他	0	1	2	10	11
半熟練工	*0*	*2*	*1*	*3*	*4*
車力	0	*	*	3	3
船頭	0	2	*	*	1
召使い	*1*	*	*1*	*4*	*10*
家内	1	*	1	2	6
その他	0	*	0	2	4

＊は5%以下　　総数　a = 1,323，b = 243，c = 2,037，d = 409，e = 382

出典：Philip Morgan, *Slave Counterpoint, Black Culture in the Eighteenth-Century Chesapeake Lowcountry*, The University of North Carolina Press, Chapel Hill, London, 1988, p.211. より作成

［Morganの注］

a,c　Allan Kulikoff, *Tobacco and Slaves: The Development of Southern Cultures in the Chesapeake, 1680～1800*, Chapel Hill, N.C.,1986 p.385, p.400.

b　Inventory of estate of Robert Carter, November 1733, Virginia Historical Society.

d　List of Negroes belonging to Hon. William Byrd, July1757, Misc, MSS Collection, Library of Congress; List of tithables belonging to George Washington. June 4, 1761, Papers of George Washington, 5th Ser., Financial Papers, microfilm, Library of Congress;

　　Lists of slaves belonging to Colonel Custis, 1771, Custis Papers, Virginia Historical Society;

　　List of Thomas Jefferson's slaves, 1774, Edwin Morris Betts, ed., *Thomas Jefferson's Farm Book, with Commentary and Relevant Extracts from Other Writings*, American Philosophical Society; Memoirs, XXXV(Princeton, N.J., 1953), pp.15-18; Inventory of Philip Ludwell's estate, 1774～1775, Lee-Ludwell Papers, Virginia Historical Society.

e　List of Negroes belonging to Edmund Randolph in Charlotte County, Sept. 25, 1784. microfilm, Colonial Williamsburg; List of slaves belonging to George Washington, Feb. 18, 1786, in Donald Jackson and Dorothy Twohig, eds., *The Diaries of George Washington* (Charlottesville, Va., 1976～1979), IV, pp.277-283;

　　List of slaves belonging to Robert Carter of Nomini Hall, 1971, Robert Carter Letter Book, XI, pp.1-15, Duke;

　　Appraisement of the estate of Benjamin Harrison, July 1791, Brock Collection, microfilm, Colonial Williamsburg;

　　A list of John Tayloe's slaves, Jan.1, 1809, in Richard S. Dunn, "A Tale of Two Plantations: Slave Life at Mesopotamia in Jamaica and Mount Airy in Virginia, 1799 to 1828," *William and Mary Quarterly*, 3d Ser., XXIV (1977), p.52.

表1-3-2　チェサピークにおける成人女子の奴隷の職種の構成比（1733～1809年）

職種＼年	a 1757～1775（％）	b 1784～1809（％）
農業	89	76
召使い	10	10
家内の召使い	9	4
洗濯女	＊	2
料理人	＊	1
その他	0	3
家事	2	14
酪農	1	2
裁縫師	1	12

＊は5％以下。　総数　a＝322, b＝313
出典：Philip Morgan, *ibid.*, p.245.

表1-3-3　成人男子熟練工黒人奴隷の年齢の構成比（1730～1810年）

年齢＼年代	a 1730～1769（％）	b 1770s.1791（％）	c 1810（％）
15-19	1	12	9
20-29	6	30	31
30-39	6	22	30
40-49	10	16	24
50-59	10	16	14
60＋	3	0	0

出典：Philip Morgan, *ibid.*, p.217.
［Morganの注］
a　Kulikoff, *Tobacco and Slaves*, p.404.
b　Carroll Account Book, 1773～1774, Maryland Historical Society, Baltimore;
　　List of Robert Carter's slaves, 1791, Carter Letterbook, XI, pp.1-15, Duke.
c　Slaves belonging to William Fitzhugh, 1810.

表1-3-4　ヴァージニアの熟練労働者の逃亡奴隷の年齢別構成比（1732～1779年）

職種＼年齢	15-19（％）	20-29（％）	30-39（％）	40-49（％）	50-59（％）
指物師	6	45	23	22	4
その他の熟練工	12	35	45	5	3
船頭	9	46	37	9	0
召使い	28	43	23	6	0

出典：Philip Morgan, *ibid.*, p.213.
［Morganの注］
Charleston Library Society, *South Carolina Newspapers*, 1732～1782, microfilm;
Lathan A.Windley, ed., *Runaway Slave Advertisements : A Documentary History from the 1730's to 1790*. Vol.I, Westport, Connecticut, 1983.

による根ごとの収穫、乾燥のための吊架、熱乾燥、徐茎、樽づめなど[27]」である。このような労働は「組制度」という集団管理制度の下で行なわれた。奴隷監督（boss）、追い立て人（driver）、組頭（foreman）、監視人（overseer）の監視下で、10ないし30～40人単位で「組」を組まされた奴隷は共同作業を強いられた。作業内容はタバコの需要の増大にともなって、厳しさを増していった。例えば、茎からむしり取られた葉は、束にまとめられ樽につめられた。「樽づめ作業は梃子を利用して数人がかりで、葉を圧搾しながら[28]」行なわれた。

奴隷の日常生活は衣食住のどの分野もプランターの一存ですべてが決定されていた。このような労働の激しさは、農園の奴隷の衣服の形と素材のあり方を決定したものと推察される。労働のあり方と衣服との関りについては、第3章で考察する。

18世紀の奴隷の身分と労働形態は、19世紀の南北戦争前夜とは異なっており、その違いが衣服にも反映されているのではないかと思われる。

第4節　アメリカ独立革命期の服飾の特徴

1．上流階級の服飾

(1) 男子服

17、18世紀にヨーロッパから移入された服飾は、植民地において独自の変化・発展をとげる。アメリカ独立革命前夜の男子服は、18世紀の大半を通じて着用されたスリー・ピース・スーツであり、コート、ウェストコートおよびブリーチズから構成されていた[29]。これらの服装は、古着ではあるが、男子の黒人奴隷の衣服でもあった。そこで、これら三つのアイテムのデザインと裁断の特徴を考察する。

a．コート

ヨーロッパでは、18世紀を通じて、コートのスタイルは多くの変化を遂げた[30]。ロココ調のコートの前身頃には、沢山のボタンが付いており、袖には大きなカフスがあしらわれていた。ボタンやブレードやブロケードが装飾に用いられた。1700年代の初期のコートは衿なしであったが、やがて短いスタンドカラーが付けられるようになり、フロック・コートと呼ばれた。フォーマルの場合には、アメリカでもまだ、ロココ調の優雅な装いは保持されており、豪華に装飾されたフランスのフロックが用いられた[31]（口絵1-4-1）。

アメリカではコートのスタイルは1750～1800年のファッションの展開過程で中庸になっていく。初期のコートよりも裾が狭くなり、身体にぴったりと裁断されるようになる[32]。

ヨーロッパ製のコート（口絵1-4-2の左)[33]は、後部の低い位置にあるアームホールは衣服の胸部を広くして、背中が狭く裁断されていた。また、当時の男性はアームホールを"C"の形にカーブ

させたしぐさを期待されていたため、袖は肘の部分で曲げて裁断されていた[34]。

b．ウェストコート

ヨーロッパのウェストコートは、コートの下に用いられた上着で、部屋ではコートを脱いで部屋着として用いられた。1750年代のウェストコートはもも丈で、袖付きであった。だが、やがて袖なしのベスト状となる[35]。アメリカのウェストコートは、ヨーロッパのものと用い方には変わりはなかった[36]。

口絵1-4-3の刺繍を施した絹のウェストコートは、マサチューセッツ州ケンブリッジのFrancis Danaに合うように作られていた。着用の時期は1775年から1785年である。このウェストコートはコートのように、着用者の肩を後に反らせて歩く訓練の効果を高めるために、口絵1-4-3の右に見られるように、アームホールが後部になるように裁断されていた[37]。

c．ブリーチズ

17世紀から18世紀のヨーロッパの貴族たちは、脚線にぴったりとそうように仕立てられた半ズボンのブリーチズを粋にはきこなしていた。ブリーチズはアメリカにも輸入され、上流階級の男性だけではなく、中産・下層階級の男性によって用いられていた。

口絵1-4-4はフィラデルフィアの Bayard Smith 家のメンバーが着用していたと言われているブリーチズ（1760～1775年）である[38]。この膝丈のブリーチズはパターン（図1-4-5）[39]に見られるように、背部にゆとりをもって作られ、きついウェストバンドの部分でギャザーが寄せられていた。脚部はふくらはぎまでフィットしており、両サイドにボタンやリボン結びが施されていた。

ブリーチズは元来、上流階級の男子の衣服であり、プランテーションでの労働には不適切な衣服であった。そのため、なめし皮製の伸縮性のあるブリーチズが用いられる場合もあった。この種のブリーチズは、18世紀を通じて、英国の紳士の乗馬用の日常着として好まれていた。L．バウムガルテンによると、逃亡奴隷の脚衣には「長ズボンは8人のうち、約1人に見られた[40]」という。長ズボンは後に流行のスタイルとなり、労働者の衣類となる。さらに種々のスタイルで男性によって、今日にいたるまで、着用され続けている。長ズボンの着用はアメリカ独立革命後、増加していく。

以上の考察から明らかなように、アメリカ独立革命前夜に上流階級の男性が着用していたスリーピース・スーツには、次の共通した特徴が見られる。すなわち、男性のスリーピース・スーツは、子供の頃からヒップから身体を曲げて、ヒップから足を踏み出すようにしつけられていた男性のために、構成上の工夫がこらされていた。これは着用者が教えられてきた立ち居振る舞いのための不可欠要素であった。上流階級人らしい「感じのいい」風采に見せることが必要だったのである。

18世紀のヴァージニアの黒人奴隷もコートやウェストコートやブリーチズを支給されていた。これらの衣服は決して動きやすい衣服ではなかった。プランターや奴隷たちは衣服の運動機能性の問題にいかに対処したのであろうか。この問題は、第3章で考察する。

(2) 女子服

図1-4-5　ブリーチズのパターン

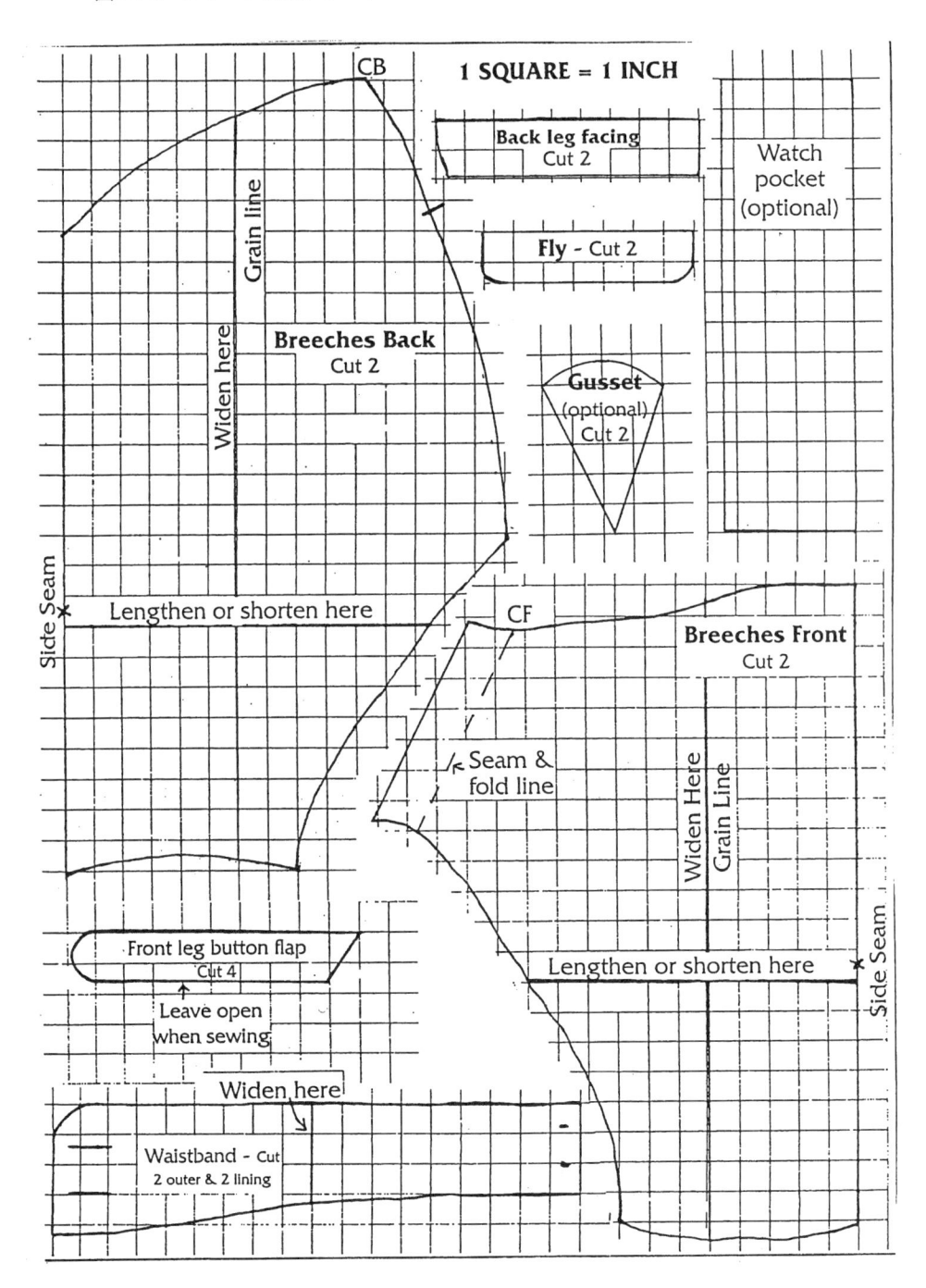

出典: Beth Gilgun, *Tidings from the 18th Century*, Rebel Publishing Co., Inc Texarkana, Texas, 1993, p.91.

口絵1-4-6のポロネーズ型のガウンは、Mrs. Margart Ogilivieのブロケードの絹のガウンである[41]。フランスからもたらされたもので、アメリカ独立革命前後の時期に、大変、人気のあった衣裳である。このガウンはぴったりと締められたコルセットの上に着用され、上流階級人らしい女性の体型に形作っていた。この衣裳の型紙は、男性のコートやウェストコートと同じように、肩を後に反らせて振る舞うように作られていた。18世紀の婦人たちは、その上体を逆円錐形に形づくるために、入念にフィットさせたコルセット（口絵1-4-7）を付けていた。

　Philip Vickers Fithianは、1774年10月のある日のこと、ヴァージニアのプランターの妻のロバート・カーター（Robert Carter）婦人が、コルセットを着用していない姿を見て、驚きのあまり、日記にこう書き記したという。「驚いたことに、コルセットを着用していないカーター婦人を見た！[42]」と。彼女は胸が痛くて、コルセットをはずしていたのである。コルセットは上流人のステイタス・シンボルであり、その着用は上流階級の女性のたしなみであった。

　だが、家内の召使いの女奴隷は白人の召使いと同じような衣服をあてがわれ、彼女たちのなかには、コルセットを携行して逃亡したものもいた。逃亡奴隷広告にはアグネスやアギーという名の白黒混血の奴隷は、青色のリボンで縁取りされたコルセットを付けて、ノーフォークから逃亡したと記録されている[43]。コルセットを装用した奴隷に関する記録は少ないが、この記事から家内の女奴隷は、コルセットを支給されていたものと推察される。

2．中産・下層階級の衣服

　アメリカ植民地時代と独立革命期の中産・下層階級の衣服に関する代表的な研究は、ピーター・F.コープランド（Peter F. Copeland）の職業着に関する研究である[44]。表1-4-1は彼の研究に基いて、筆者が作成した「欧米の中産・下層階級の職業着一覧」である。上流階級の華やかで、きらびやかな衣裳とは趣を異にする、仕事の場面に特有な服装で労働に携わっている様相が、豊富な絵画資料によって再現されている。本書に登場する人物は、船乗り、漁師、農民、商人、呼び売り、フロンティア開拓者、御者、正規兵や民兵、医者、法律家、聖職者、使用人、年季奉公人、奴隷、犯罪人、民族諸集団など、合計424人である。これらの人々一人ひとりの仕事に取り組んでいる姿やしぐさや表情や、職種によって異なるさまざまな服装は、18世紀の欧米の中産・下層階級の人々の生活の様相を彷彿とさせてくれる。本書は筆者の奴隷の被服研究の動機づけとなった研究書である。

　P.F.コープランドは本書で奴隷の衣服についての章を設けて、イラストによって奴隷の衣服をイメージ化している。本書ではこの、P.F.コープランドの著書も参考に、ヴァージニアに限定してさらに詳しい考察を行なった。

[注]
(1)「こうして達成されたアメリカ合衆国の独立は、アメリカ社会にとっては市民革命の意味をもっている。もともと北アメリカ植民地には封建制がないためヨーロッパの市民革命とは様相がことなるが……」（『新世界史　世界史B』山川出版社、1996年、217）。
　「もともとアメリカには、ヨーロッパに成立したような封建制はなかったが、イギリスの重商主義政策や、それと結びついた

表1-4-1　欧米の中産・下層階級の職業着一覧（18世紀）

	職種	性別又は職種の区分	服腫
1	船乗り		ボディー・シャツ、ウェストコート、ジャケット、大型コート、シュルトゥー、ブリーチズ、幅広のズボン（silvers, slops, petticoat trousers)、帽子、靴（バックル付き）、ネッカチーフ、手袋
	漁師	男	ジャケット、ズボン、ペティコート・トラウザーズ、レギンス、帽子、手袋、シー・ブーツ、スカーフ、バーベル（粗悪な革製エプロン）
		女	コルセット・ボディス、ジャケット、ブラウス、スカート、ペティコート、ずきん、鍔ひろでクラウンが高い平らな帽子、縁なし帽、モブ・キャップ、サボ（木製）、パトン（木製）、靴（短い皮革製）、スカーフ、エプロン
2	農民と地方労働者	男	ウェストコート、スモック、フロック・コート、ブリーチズ、ズボン、スキルト、フェルト帽、フリジア帽、革製の靴、モカシン
		女	コルセット・ボディス、ブラウス、ジャケット、男ものの外套、シュルトゥー、ペティコート、スカート、麦わら帽子、円い縁付きのフェルト帽（バリーコック）、パトン、スカーフ、ネッカチーフ、エプロン
3	職人と都市労働者		シャツ（襞飾り付き）、コート、帽子、靴（バックル付き）、スカーフ、エプロン
4	商人と行商人	宿屋の主人　煙突掃除夫　路上の商売人	ジャケット、ベルト付きジャケット、短いコート、ブリーチズ、縁なし帽、エプロン、※ヨーロッパの資料による
		肉屋	シャツ、ウェストコート（白と赤の縞）、コート、ブリーチズ、帽子、ベルト、エプロン
5	辺境地の住民と開拓者	猟師　商人　罠猟師	ボディー・シャツ、狩猟用のシャツ、ブランケット・コート、ブランケット、レギンス、帽子（縁なし帽）、帽子（ガラガラヘビの皮）、フェルト帽、モカシン、小物入れ、ナイフ
		女	上衣、シュミーズ、ブランケット、スカート、フェルト帽、モカシン、靴下、ショール、スカーフ、エプロン
6	輸送労働者		シャツ（亜麻布）、スモック、ジャケット、狩猟用シャツ、大型コート、ジャックブーツ、制服、ボブ・ウィッグ（鬘）、ブリーチズ（なめし革）、帽子、手袋、サッシュ（緋色）、
7	公僕	消防士	ジャケット、ブリーチズ、ヘルメット、ブーツ
		夜警	ジャケット、シュルトゥー・コート、帽子、提灯、棍棒
		護衛と御者	制服のコート、帽子（花形帽章付き）、騎手用のブーツ
		騎馬郵便配達人	コート、大型外套（ロクロール）、ブリーチズ、ヘルメット
		墓掘り女	ウェストコート、コート
8	正規軍と民兵		※軍服なし、狩猟用シャツ、インディアンのレギンス、制服、モカシン、ブリーチズ
9	知的職業人	医者	シャツ（襞飾り付きの白い亜麻布製）、スーツ（黒など）、鬘（医者用）、帽子（鍔が巻き上げられている）、靴（銀製のバックル付き）、杖、刀剣、※田舎医者—暮し向きの良い農民の服装
		裁判官	緋色のガウン
		弁護士	黒のローブ
		下級判事	ぼろぼろのバンヤン
		聖職者	スーツ（地味な黒）、バンヤン
10	使用人	小世帯	通常の職業着
		大世帯の従僕、御者、左馬御者	仕着せ—ウェストコート、コート、オーバー・コート、シュルトゥー・コート（ラップ・ラスカル）、ブリーチズ、帽子
		上層の召使い	主人の衣服に類似した紳士の衣裳、制服
		女の召使い	※家族の階層に従った服装
		下級の召使（少年馬丁、馬丁助手、馬丁）	簡素なジャケット、丈の短い上衣、ウェストコート、ブリーチズ、円い縁付きの帽子、縁なし帽、ゲートル
11	年季奉公人と奴隷		※つましい恰好、シャツ、ジャケット、ウェストコート、コート、ブリーチズ、ニグロ・クロスやニグロ・コットン製の衣服
12	犯罪者	追いはぎ	※上流階級の最上のファッション、ジャケット、ブリーチズ、ウェストコート、コート、帽子、ブーツ、ベール
13	民族に固有の服装		民族服

特権的植民地の支配を打破したという点で、アメリカ合衆国の独立は市民革命としての意義をもった」(『世界史B』東京書籍、1996年、221)。
(2) 清水知久、高橋章、富田虎男『アメリカ史研究入門』(山川出版社、1980年)、47-71.
有賀貞・大下尚一・志邨晃佑・平野孝編『世界歴史大系 アメリカ史1―17世紀～1877年―』(山川出版社、1994年)、111-191.
(3) 有賀貞、大下尚一編『新版 概説アメリカ史』(有斐閣選書、1994年)、43.
(4) 同上、44.
(5) 同上、46.
アメリカ学会編『原典アメリカ史 第2巻―革命と建国―』(岩波書店、1951年)、105-108.
メアリー・ベス・ノートン他著、本田創造監修、白井洋子、戸田徹子訳『アメリカの歴史 ①新世界への挑戦 15世紀―18世紀』(三省堂、1996年)、202-203.
(6) 有賀貞、大下尚一編『同上書』46.
メアリー・ベス・ノートン他『同上書』204-208.
(7) 有賀貞、大下尚一編『同上書』46-47.
メアリー・ベス・ノートン他『同上書』215-220.
(8) メアリー・ベス・ノートン他『同上書』225-325.
有賀貞、大下尚一、志邨晃佑、平野孝編『前掲書』125-198.
紀平英作編『世界各国史24 アメリカ史』(山川出版社、1999年)、72-88.
(9) 池本幸三著『近代奴隷制社会の史的展開―チェサピーク湾ヴァージニア植民地を中心として―』(ミネルヴァ書房、1987年初版第1刷、1999年新装版第1刷)、164-184, 212-234.
(10) John Smith, *The General Historie of Virginia, New England and Summer Iles.*, Ann Arbor[reprinted 1966] (Original ed., 1624), 21.
(11) 池本幸三・布留川正博・下山晃『近代世界と奴隷制―太平洋システムの中で―』(人文書院、1995年)、93.
本田創造『アメリカ黒人の歴史 新版』(岩波新書、1991年)、24-25.
(12) 本田創造『同上書』32.
(13) 池本幸三他『前掲書』75-78.
(14) 川北 稔『民衆の大英帝国』(岩波書店、1990年)、53-54. (Kussmaul, *Servants in husbandery in early modern England*, 1981, 3から引用)
(15) 本田創造『前掲書』33.
(16) 池本幸三他『前掲書』74.
(17) 本田創造『前掲書』33-34.
(18) 池本幸三『前掲書』424.
(19) 池本幸三他『前掲書』81-85
本田創造『前掲書』34-40.
(20) 本田創造『同上書』43.
(21) Philip D. Morgan, *Slave Counterpoint, Black Culture in the Eighteenth-Century Chesapeake & Lowcountry*, University of North Carolina Press, (Chapel Hill & London, 1998), 98-99.
(22) 池本幸三『前掲書』212. David W. Galenson, "White Servitude and the Growth of Black Slavery in Colonial America", *Journal of Economic History* Vol. XLI, No.1, March 1981, 39-49.
(23) 森 杲『アメリカ職人の仕事史』中公新書、(中央公論社刊、1996年)、31-32.
(24) 『同上書』32.
(25) Philip Morgan, *op. cit.*, 204-218.
(26) 池本幸三『前掲書』228-229.
(27) 『同上書』228.
(28) 『同上書』229.
(29) Edward Warwick, Henry C. Pitz and Alexander Wyckoff, *Early American Dress, The Colonial and Revolutionary*

　　　 Periods, Bonanza Books, New York, 1965, 213.
(30) 丹野郁『服飾の世界史』(白水社、1985年)、288-290.
(31) Linda Baumgarten, *Eighteenth-Century Clothing* at Williamsburg, The Colonial Williamsburg Foundation, (Colonial Williamsburg, Virginia,1986), 54-56.
(32) National Museum of American History: "Getting Dressed: Fashionable Appearance, 1750～1800," Smithsonian Institution, (Washington, DC.1985). 濱田雅子「アメリカ独立革命と服飾－スミソニアン・インスティテューションの収蔵品に基づいて－」(衣生活研究会「衣生活」第31巻第3号、1988年6月)、52-53.
(33) Carl Köhler, *A History of Costume*, Dover Publisher, (New York, 1928, reprint 1968), 356.
(34) National Museum of American History, ibid　濱田雅子「前掲」53.
(35) 丹野郁『前掲書』292-293.
(36) Edward Warwick et al., *op. cit.*, 154-155, 214.
(37) National Museum of American History, ibid.　濱田雅子「前掲」52.
(38) Ibid.「同上」51.
(39) 「このパターンはNorah Waugh, *The Cut of Men's Clothes*に拠っている。William Brown　所有のブリーチズの実物を手にとって研究できたのは大変、幸運である」とBeth Gilgun は述べている (Beth Gilgun, *Tidings from the 18th Century*, Rebel Publishing Co., Inc. Texarkana, Texas, 1993, 90.)
(40) Linda Baumgarten, "Clothes for the People: Slave Clothing in Early Virginia," *Journal of Early Southern Decorative Arts*, Vol. 14, No.2, (Nov.1988), Museum of Early Southern Decorative Arts, Winston Salem, N.C., 52-53.
(41) National Museum of American History, op. cit.　濱田雅子「前掲」53.
(42) Linda Baumgarten, op. cit., 30.
(43) *Virginia Gazette*, Purdie & Dixon, 25 Apr. 1766(L. A. Windley, (comp.), *Runaway Slave Advertisement: A Documentary History from 1730s to 1790*, Vol.1 of Vol.4, Greenwood, (Westport, Connecticut, 1983), 40.
(44) Peter F. Copeland著、濱田雅子訳『アメリカ史にみる職業着－植民地時代～独立革命期－』(せせらぎ出版、1998年)。本書の原題は "*Working Dress in Colonial and Revolutionary America*", Greenwood Press, (Westport, Connecticut, 1977)。

第 2 章

史料としての逃亡奴隷広告

第1節　被服描写の史料的価値

　本節ではヴァージニア・ガゼット紙に掲載された逃亡奴隷広告の具体的事例を挙げて、広告の内容、目的、広告主に言及しながら、当該広告における奴隷の被服描写の史料的価値について述べることとしよう。

Virginia Gazette（Purdie & Dixon），March 5, 1772[1]
　ディンウィディー（Dinwiddie）の広告主のもとから、2月16日日曜日、ヴァージニア生まれと思われる白黒混血の男が逃亡した。名前はディック（Dick）。30歳位でよく太っている。背丈は5フィート7～8インチで、目はグレーである。短いカールしたヘアーが額にぴったりとくっついている。とても大きな黒い顎鬚をたくわえており、右足には傷がある。靴職人でどんな仕事でもとてもよくこなせる。この男は読み書きができるので、自由人として通ることをもくろんでいるようである。この男は明るい色のダッフィル（Duffil）製の大型外套とニグロ・コットン（Negro Cotton）製のダブルの打ち合わせのショートコートと同じくニグロ・コットン製の深紅色に染めたブリーチズと赤いフリーズ（Frieze）製の折り返った衿の付いたウェストコート—これはこの男にはちょっと大きすぎるのだが—、1枚の白い亜麻布製のIWと印されたシャツとビーバー・コーティング（Beaver Coating）製のポンパドゥール色のショートコートを着用している。このコートは大幅に作り替えられ、スラッシュ入りのポケットが付けられ、ダブルの打ち合わせで、シャルーン（Shalloon）の裏が付けられている。この男は3～4年位前に逃亡し、ウァンノーク（Wyanoke）のハーウッド（Harwood）氏の元で留まっていた。この男にはプリンス・ジョージ（Prince George）のデイビッド・スコット（David Scott）氏が所有している兄弟がいる。この兄弟は1～2年の間、逃亡していたことがあり、パマンキー川（Pamunkey River）の川辺に住むインディアンと住んでいて、そこから何度も連れ戻された。彼らはきっと2人で組んで行動を起こしたのであろう。あるいはまた、彼らは2人ともミル（Mill）氏の黒人と知り合いなので、アーバンナ（Urbanna）へと逃亡した可能性もある。私はあらゆる船主に上記の奴隷を雇ったり、この奴隷を植民地から連れ戻すことを禁じる。私がこの奴隷を捕獲できるようにしてくれる人には法が認めている報償金のほかに上記の報償金を与える。彼は法益を剥奪されている。

　　　　　　　　　　　　　　　　　　　　　　　　　　ジェームズ　ウォーカー

　通常、逃亡広告のなかに含まれている情報は、広告日、逃亡の日付、住所、奴隷の人種、名前、身長、年齢、職種・技能、容貌・特徴、服装、逃亡理由・目的、英語能力の有無、推定逃亡場所、賞金額、広告主（プランター）名、などである。広告文は長いものもごく短いものもある。
　逃亡奴隷広告に見られる被服とは、どのような被服なのか。この点については第3章第1節で言

及する。

次に誰が、何の目的でこのような広告を出したのか、という点について考察しよう[2]。

この記事から、この広告の目的は、逃亡者の救済にあるのではないということは明らかである。奴隷の労働力はプランターにとって貴重なものであった。報償金を出してまでも確保しなければならない必要な労働力であった。つまり、奴隷の逃亡を阻止し、引き戻すことも、重要な事業の１つであった。広告を出すには、当然のことながら広告料がかかった。それゆえ、広告料をかけてまで、逃亡奴隷の捕獲・返還を達成し、奴隷労働力から高利益を生むだけの財力のあるプランターが広告を出したものと考えられる。

また、このように奴隷制度が高利益を生むようになると、労働力を確保するために、奴隷の誘拐が行われた、という記事もある。

以上のことから、広告を出す第一の目的はプランターの経済目的であったことが明らかである。

印刷所が近いプランテーションの主人が広告を出したという見方もある[3]。この点は広告を出す経費と時間の問題を考えるなら、なるほどと思える見方である。

また、政治的批判を恐れて広告を出さないケースもあった[4]。ジョージ・ワシントンは自己の所有するマウント・ヴァーノン（Mount Vernon）のプランテーションの奴隷が逃亡しても、いくつかの新聞に対しては広告を出さなかった事実があるという。このようなケースは奴隷制擁護と反対の双方の見地から見て興味深い。G.ワシントンは奴隷制反対論者からの社会的批判を警戒したのである。

逃亡奴隷広告における被服情報は、あくまでも奴隷所有者が描いた被服情報である。奴隷制という社会秩序のもとで、広告主が逃亡した奴隷を見下して、服装やふるまいを描くことも想定される。それゆえ、この情報の内容には例えば、盗んではいないのに衣服を盗んで着ているというように、バイヤスがかけられているのではないか、という疑問が当然、出てくる。

広告が出された背景から考えると、バイヤスがかけられている強い可能性は確かにある。しかし、広告の目的はあくまでも逃亡奴隷の捕獲・返還にあった。それゆえに、主人はできるだけ正確な逃亡奴隷の被服描写に努めたといえるのではないだろうか。つまり、奴隷の主人がエリートの立場からバイヤスをかけて描写したのは、逃亡奴隷の被服ではなく、彼らのキャラクターや振舞い方であったといえるのではなかろうか。奴隷主は年に一度、奴隷に衣服を支給する際に、衣服に番号を付け、支給した衣服に関する情報を記録したという事実も判明している。奴隷制度をマテリアル・カルチャーの面から研究しているロレーナ・S. ウォルシュ（Lorena S. Walsh）は、奴隷に支給された衣服について、次のように述べている[5]。

「カーター家の信書控帳および財産目録もまた、1730年代のマーチャント・ハンドレッド・プランテーション（Merchant's Hundred Plantation）[6]における衣類などの状態について、何らかの示唆をしてくれる。各々の奴隷は、年に一度、冬用の新しいスーツと夏用のもっと軽い衣服を支給された。男にはシャツとファスチャンのジャケットとリネンのブリーチズが、女にはシフトと

ペティコートとエプロンが支給された。子供はフロックだけをもらった。大人たちはかれらの身支度をすっかり整えるために、輸入ものの靴1足とアイルランド製の靴下1足、あるいは格子縞の靴下（Plaid hose）1足とキルマーノック産の縁なし帽（Kilmarnock milled caps）を支給された。シーツ（Bed rugs）と毛布、あるいは枕カバー（Hair Coverlet）は最初に支給されたものがすっかり擦り切れてしまった時にだけ交換してもらった。カーター家の人々は新しい寝具を「めいめいのニグロが付けられた名前」を付けて、奴隷小屋に支給した。マーチャント・ハンドレッド・プランテーションの奴隷監督人は、フェアーフィールド（Fairfield）で毎年、秋に冬用の衣服を調達し、品物全部に問題がないかどうかを調べるために、包みをチェックしてから、一人一人の名前のラベルを付けた衣服を配給したものと思われる。」

奴隷に対する衣服の支給のこのような慣行は、L.S.ウォルシュが取り上げている1720～30年代以降も続けられた。

奴隷に対する衣服の支給がこのように厳密に管理されたこともあり、逃亡奴隷広告における逃亡奴隷の被服描写は、かれらの被服描写に関する歴史的事実を確認するための信頼性の高い史料であることが認められるであろう。

第2節　被服情報の数量化

本節では逃亡奴隷広告に見られる被服情報の分析方法について述べることとしよう。

対象としたサンプルは基本的には、ラーサン・A.ウィンドレイ（Lathan A.Windley）編集の"*Runaway Slave Advertisement: A Documentary History from 1730s to 1790*, Vol. 4"掲載の逃亡広告のなかのヴァージニア・ガゼット（*Virginia Gazette*）紙（1766～1789年発行）[7]におけるサンプル1069点である。L.A.ウィンドレイはヴァージニア・ガゼット紙を次のように出版人[8]別に分類して掲載している。

Virginia Gazette（Parks）1739～1750

Virginia Gazette（Hunter; Royle; Purdie & Dixon; Dixon & Hunter）1751～1778

Virginia Gazette（Dixon & Nicolson）1779～1780

Virginia Gazette or Weekly Advertiser（Nicolson & Prentis; Nicolson）1781～1790

Virginia Gazette（Purdie; Clarkson & Davis）1775～1780

Virginia Gazette（Rind; Pinkney）1766～1776

Virginia Gazette or American Advertiser（Hayes）1781～1786

上記に掲載された逃亡広告1,069点のうち、逃亡奴隷が逃亡時に着用していた衣服や靴や靴下な

どの被服情報が記載されている広告数は、合計545すなわち、51パーセントである。年度別の逃亡広告数と被服情報数の相関関係を表すグラフと元のデータを図2-2-1に表した。ここでいう被服情報とは、第1節の冒頭で紹介した逃亡奴隷広告を例に挙げると、「この男は明るい色のダッフィル（Duffil）製の大型外套と……シャルーン（Shalloon）の裏が付けられている」という逃亡奴隷が逃亡時に着用ないし携行していた被服を描写した部分を指す。このように逃亡奴隷広告に逃亡奴隷がひとりだけ登場し、その奴隷が着用ないし携行した被服の描写が広告中に見られる場合には、被服情報1と数えた。逃亡広告に逃亡奴隷が複数登場し、1人ひとりについて、被服描写が行なわれている場合もある。被服情報の記載が見られない広告もある。一つの広告に2人の逃亡奴隷の被服の描写が、それぞれ別々の文で記載されている場合は、被服情報数を2と数えた。被服情報の記載が見られない場合は、被服情報を0と数えた。

図2-2-1　逃亡奴隷広告数と被服情報数［*Virginia Gazette*］（1766～1789年）

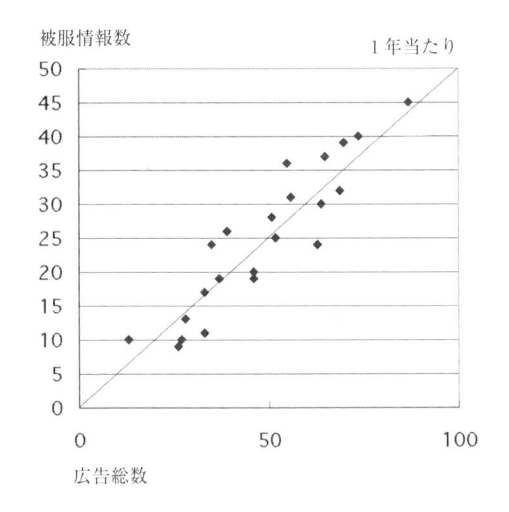

	逃亡広告数	被服情報数	構成比（％）
1766	39	26	67
1767	27	10	37
1768	51	28	55
1769	52	25	48
1770	55	36	65
1771	69	32	46
1772	65	37	57
1773	56	31	55
1774	70	39	56
1775	74	40	54
1776	35	24	69
1777	87	45	52
1778	46	20	43
1779	64	30	47
1782	33	11	33
1783	46	19	41
1784	63	24	38
1785	37	19	51
1786	26	9	35
1787	13	10	77
1788	23	17	52
1789	28	13	46
合計	1069	545	51

第3節　被服素材の種類

　衣服を研究しようとすれば、必ず織物を理解する必要がある。逃亡奴隷が着用ないし携行していた被服にはどのような素材が見られたのか。また、それらのうち自国産の素材はどの素材か。次にこの点について述べる。

　逃亡奴隷広告に見られる素材の種類は後掲表2-3-1に示す67種である。この表では、67種の素材を繊維別、すなわち、(1) ウール (wool)、(2) ウール (wool) とコットン (cotton)、(3) シルク (silk) とウール (wool) とコットン (cotton)、(4) コットン (cotton)、(5) コットン (cotton) とシルク (silk)、(6) コットン (cotton) とリネン (linen)、(7) リネン (linen)、(8) シルク (silk)、(9) その他、および (10) 国産品、に分類し、それらの特徴を概要、組成（糸と織組織）、仕上げ、色・柄、および、逃亡奴隷広告における用途について解説する[9]。残念なことに、考古学的・博物館学的見地から見て、織物は残存率が非常に低い。18世紀から残されている織物は比較的わずかしかない。ヴァージニアで調査した結果、コロニアル・ウィリアムズバーグの考古学研究部門の収蔵品には、1760年代のものと特定できる綾織毛布があるが、この生地は奴隷の被服の素材ではない。複製でない織物の最も有用な情報源は、現存する18世紀の生地見本に関する文献である。デラウェアー州のウィンターザー（Winterthur）美術館のフローレンス・M.モンゴメリー（Florence M. Montgomery）は、同著 "Textiles in America, 1650〜1870: A Dictionary Based on Original Documents, Prints and Paintings, Commercial Records, American Merchant' Papers, Shopkeepers' Advertisements and Pattern Books with Original Swatches of Cloth, Norton, New York, 1984" に生地見本の写真複写を掲載している。そこで、本節で解説する一部の素材は、本書口絵に生地見本の写真を収録し、そのキャプションの記号ないし番号（口絵2-3-1〜2-3-24）を、これらの表の右欄に掲載した。

　表2-3-2は、1766年から1789年の逃亡奴隷広告に見られる被服素材の年次別一覧である。例えば、"Virginia cloth waistcoat and breeches" という記載は、Viriginia clothが2回登場したものとして数えている。また、これらの表は67種の素材を上記の繊維別に分類して、一覧表に作成した。これらの表は第3章で活用する。

【注】

(1) Lathan A. Windley, (comp.), *Runaway Slave Advertisement: A Documentary History from 1730s to 1790*, Vol.4, Greenwood, (Westport, Connecticut, 1983), 109-110.

> RUN away from the Subscriber, in Dinwiddie, on Sunday the 16th of February, a likely Virginia born Mulatto Fellow named DICK, about thirty Years of Age, a thick well made Fellow, five Feet seven or eight Inches high, with gray Eyes, short Hair curled close to his Head, a very large black Beard, and a Sore on his right Leg; he is a Shoemaker by Trade, and very handy about any other Business. He may probably attempt to pass for a Freeman, as he can read and write; he wore, or carried with him, a light coloured Duffil great coat, a Negro Cotton double-breasted short Coat, died purple

Breeches of the same, a red Frieze Waistcoat lapelled, which is rather too large for him, a white Linen Shirt marked I W, a Beaver Coating short Coat, of the Pompadour Colour, but much altered, with slash Pockets, double breasted, and lined with Shalloon. He ran away about three or four Years ago, and then harboured about Mr. Harwood's, at Wyanoke; he has a Brother belonging to Mr. David Scott of Prince George, who has been run away for a Year or two, and was several Times brought from among the Indians on Pamunkey River; they probably may make that Way together, or to Urbanna, as they are both acquainted with Mr. Mills's Negroes. I hereby forewarn all Masters of Vessels from employing the said Slave, or carrying him out of the Colony. I will give the above Reward, besides what the Law allows, to any Person that will secure him so that I may get him again. He is outlawed.

JAMES WALKER.

(2) Bryan Paul Howard, *Had on and took with him: Runaway Indentured Servant Clothing in Virginia, 1774〜1778*, UMI Dissertation Series, Degree Date: 1996, 8.

(3) *Ibid.*, 8-9.

(4) *Ibid.*, 8.

(5) Lorena S. Walsh, *From Calabar to Carter's Grove, The History of a Virginia Slave Community*, University Press of Virginia,(Charlottesville and London, 1997), 89.

(6) ロバート「キング」カーター（Robert "King" Carter）が息子のロバート・カーター（Robert Carter）のために購入したジェイムズ・シティ・カウンティ（James City County）のプランテーション *op.cit.*, 37-411.

(7) L. A. Windley,（comp.）*op.cit.*

(8) *Virginia Gazette* 紙の出版人を年代順に列記すると次のようである。
　William Parks, 1736〜50
　William Hunter, 1751〜61
　Joseph Royle, 1761〜65
　Alexander Purdie & Co., 1765〜66
　Alexander Purdie & John Dixon, 1766〜75
　William Rind, 1766〜73
　Clementina Rind, 1773〜74
　Dixon & William Hunter（Jr.）, 1775〜78
　John Pinkney, 1774〜76
　Alexander Purdie, 1775〜79
　Dixon & Thomas Nicolson, 1779〜Apr., 1780
　John Clarkson & Augustine Davis, 1779〜Dec., 1780
　（Lester J. Cappon and Stella F. Duff, *Virginia Gazette* Index 1736〜1780, Vol.I, The Institute of Early American History and Culture, Williamsburg, Virginia, 1950, vi）

(9) 解説作成に当って、次の文献を参照した。
　・『増訂織物染色辞典』（織物染色文化研究所編集発行、1954年）.
　・吉川和志『新しい繊維の知識』（鎌倉書房、1974年）.
　・一見輝彦『繊維素材辞典』（ファッション教育社、1995年第1刷、1999年第3刷）.
　・現代ファブリック事典刊行会編『現代ファブリック事典』（相川書房、1981年）.
　・JIS繊維用語（繊維部門）JISL0206-1976（1984確認）、1976年2月1日改正
　・P.F.コープランド著、濱田雅子訳『アメリカ史に見る職業着—植民地時代〜独立革命期—』（せせらぎ出版、1998年）、209-215.
　・Louis Harmuth, *Dictionary of Textiles*, The Third Enlarged Edition, Fairchild Publishing Company,（New York, 1924）
　・Bryan Paul Howard, *Had on and took with him: Runaway Indentured Servant Clothing in Virginia, 1774〜1778*, UMI Dissertation Series, Degree Date: 1996. 231-257.
　・Dorothy F. McCombs, *Virginia cloth: Early Textiles in Virginia Particularly in the Backcountry Between the Bluc*

表2-3-1　逃亡奴隷広告に見る被服素材一覧

(1) ウール（Wool）

	素材名〈和〉	素材名〈英〉	概要	組成（糸と織組織）
1	バース・コーティング	Bath coating	長い毛羽のある毛織物の一種。	
2	ベア・スキン	Bearskin	動物の皮ではないが、粗くて、厚い丈夫な毛織物。	よこ糸に短毛。綾織。
3	ビーバー・コーティング	Beaver coating	ビーバーの毛皮に似た毛織物。	綾織、五面サテン、四面破れ、綾織。
4	ブロード・クロス	Broadcloth	紡毛織物の一種。幅は137～154センチ。	たて糸に紡毛糸または梳毛糸、よこ糸に紡毛糸を用いた二重織。表面を平織、裏面を綾織。
5	バックスキン	Buckskin	なめされたシカ皮。	
6	キャリマンコ	Calimanco	梳毛織物の一種。	一重または二重織。
7	カムレット	Camlet	梳毛織物の一種。駱駝毛とアンゴラ山羊毛から得た糸から織られた。	アンゴラ山羊毛の糸を用いた平織。
8	カシミア	Casimer	ヤギの毛を使用した毛織物の一種。	カシミア梳毛糸を用いた綾織（おもに2/2または2/1）。
9	カスター	Castor	ブロードクロスの厚手の毛織物。	
10	クロス	Cloth	広義には織物または布の意。狭義には縮絨された毛織物の総称。	綾織、梳毛織、平綾。
11	コーティング	Coating	梳毛織物の一種。	たてよことも梳毛撚糸を用いた種々の綾織。
12	ドラブ	Drab	イングランド産の厚手で丈夫な毛織物の外套地。	
13	ラシア・ドラブ	Russia drab		
14	ダッフィル	Duffil	目の粗い毛織物。	2/2の綾織。
	ダッフェル	Duffel	ベルギー産。	
15	デュロイ	Duroy	18世紀イギリス製の梳毛織物。	
16	エルクスキン	Elkskin	ヘラジカの皮。	
17	エヴァー・ラスティング	Everlasting	梳毛織物の一種。	二重または三重のたて糸と単独のよこ糸を用いたサテン織または綾織。
18	フィアノート	Fearnought	梳毛織物の一種。カーセーと類似の紡毛織物。	
		Fearnaught		
	ドレッドノート	Dreadnaught		
	ファーナッシング	Farnothing		

仕上げ	色・柄	用途	口絵写真番号
厚手の二重に毛羽立ったベーズ。	すべての色。	コート、ウェストコート	2-3-4
粗毛の毛羽あり。	こげ茶と黒。	コート、ウェストコート ジャケット、大型外套	
縮絨され、パイル糸が生地面から立ちあがる。	土色がかった赤や茶。明るい青や灰色。	コート、ショートコート スーツ	
充分の仕上げを施され表面は均一に短く、揃った毛端でおおわれ、手触りが柔らかく、滑らかで光沢あり。	白、灰色、青、紫、赤、黒と明色から暗色にわたる。	コート、ウェストコート ブリーチズ、ジャケット	2-3-1
	茶	ブリーチズ	
表面に光沢あり。	すべての色。無地物、縞模様、花の模様、透かし模様など種々の細工が施されたもの。	ペティコート	2-3-2
		ウェストコート	
	すべての色。	コート、ジャケット、ブリーチズ	2-3-3
縮絨され、艶がある。厚地で丈夫。		縁付き帽	
		コート、ブリーチズ ジャケット、マーケット・コート	
長い毛羽あり。	無地および縞物。	コート	2-3-4
	くすんだ茶色、黄色または灰色、ベージュ。	コート、ベスト、アンダー・ベスト	
縮絨され、毛羽がある。	青、赤	コート、ブリーチズ	2-3-5
なめらかなオープン・フェイス。		コート	3-3-6
	茶		
緻密に織られ、密度の高い仕上がり。	ツートンカラー、黒、その他規則的な紋様に菱形、正方形、長方形または十字形などの幾何学的紋様入り。	ブリーチズ	2-3-7
地合は厚く、手触りが粗くて、硬い。		ウェストコート ジャケット、大型外套	

	素材名〈和〉	素材名〈英〉	概要	組成（糸と織組織）
19	フランネル	Flannel	毛織物の一種。 ネルともいう。	メリノ種の羊毛あるいは羊毛と綿花の混合原料を紡ぎ、製して、たてには比較的撚りが強く、よこには撚甘の紡毛糸あるいはたてに梳毛糸、よこに紡毛糸を用い、粗く平織または綾織に組織。
20	フリーズ	Frieze	紡毛織物の一種。 13世紀の頃、オランダのフリーズランドにて製造されたことに由来。アイルランドを生産地とする。	仔羊毛または特に粗くて細く、縮みの多い、弾力に富む羊毛からなる太い紡毛糸を用いる。平織または綾織。
21	ハーフスィックス	Half-thicks	粗悪な毛織物の一種。	綾織。
22	ホームスパン	Homespun	手で紡いだ太い糸を使って、平織または綾織にし、縮絨しないで仕上げた紡毛織物。	平織または綾織。
23	カルゼ カーセー	Kerzey	紡毛織物の一種。	たてよこともに粗い紡毛糸を用いた普通の綾織。
24	プレインズ	Plains	目の粗い毛織物の一種。	梳毛のたて糸と紡毛のよこ糸を用いた平織。
25	プラッシュ	Plush	ビロード織の一種 一部紡毛で、一部ヤギの毛のもの、麻とヤギの毛のもの、全体が絹のものあり。	一本の紡毛のよこ糸と紡毛とヤギかラクダの毛を撚り合わせたたて糸を用いる。梳毛だけのものも動物の毛だけのものもある。
26	ラックーン	Rackoon	あらいぐまの皮。	
27	サガスィー	Sagathy	薄手の毛織物の一種。	たては白、よこは色糸で四綜絖織。
28	サージ	Serge	毛織物の一種。	たて糸もよこ糸も梳毛を用いたものが一般的。たてに梳毛糸よこに紡毛糸を用いたものもある。2/2綾織が普通であり、2/1綾織あるいは繻子の組織を応用したものもある。たて糸は多くの場合24〜52番の単糸または双糸を用いる。
29	シャグ	Shag	目の粗い動物の毛に似た外観をもつ毛織物の一種。	梳毛と動物の毛のもの、紡毛と亜麻のものもあり。
30	シャルーン	Shalloon	梳毛織物の一種。	一本たて糸。 綾織。

仕上げ	色・柄	用途	口絵写真番号
軽い縮絨を施す。あるいは両面起毛を行う。柔軟で弾力あり。	無地物、縞物。	ウェストコート、ジャケット、シャツ、ペティコートの裏	2-3-8
2メートル42センチに織り上げ、1メートル70センチから1メートル67センチまで縮絨し、起毛を行なう。表面は縮れた不揃いの長い毛羽におおわれる。粗い地厚な織物。	各種の色あり。霜降りがもっとも多い。	コート、ウェストコート	2-3-9
	青、緑、紫、赤	コート、ブリーチズ ペティコート	
縮絨しないで仕上げる。			
充分、縮絨と起毛を行なったあと、短く剪毛した厚地紡毛織物。	紺、黒、赤、緑	コート、ジャケット ウェストコート、ブリーチズ、シュルトゥー・コート	2-3-4
わずかに縮絨される。	白、鉛色、青	コート、ジャケット、ウェストコート、ブリーチズ、ペティコート	2-3-10
ビロードより毛脚が長く、ループを全部切り放ってある。毛羽立っている。	青、黒、赤、白	ジャケット、ブリーチズ	2-3-11
		帽子	
	白、青	コート、ジャケット、ウェストコート、ブリーチズ	2-3-12
軽く縮絨を施し、表裏に少し毛羽を出したものと、毛羽のないものあり。地合にも厚薄あり。	紺地が多い。黒地、白無地、縞物などあり。	コート、ブリーチズ ウェストコート、ジャケット、ヴェスト	2-3-13
長い粗毛の毛羽あり。	広範囲の色彩。縞物あり。	ブリーチズ	2-3-14
なめらかな仕上がりを出すために、光沢出しや加熱圧縮されることが多い。	広範囲の色彩。	コートの裏地用 ガウン	2-3-15

	素材名〈和〉	素材名〈英〉	概要	組成（糸と織組織）
31	スワンスキン	Swanskin	軽いFlannelに似た紡毛織物。	梳毛のたて糸と紡毛のよこ糸を用いる。
32	タミー	Tammy	上質の紡毛織物の一種。	1本たて糸。綾織。
33	ウィルトン	Wilton	梳毛織物の一種。	
34	ウーレン	Woolen	主として紡毛糸を使用した織物。	紡毛糸を用いる。木綿との混紡あり。

(2) ウール（Wool）とコットン（Cotton）

	素材名〈和〉	素材名〈英〉	概要	組成（糸と織組織）
35	プレード プレーディング	Plaid Plaiding	スコットランド産の紡毛織物。	

(3) シルク（Silk）とウール（Wool）とコットン（Cotton）

	素材名〈和〉	素材名〈英〉	概要	組成（糸と織組織）
36	ベルベット	Velvet	添毛織物の一種。	たて糸ビロードとよこ糸ビロードの2種あり。平織。ふつうは毛たて糸に絹糸または紡績絹糸などを用い、地たて糸およびよこ糸に綿糸を用いる。

(4) コットン（Cotton）

	素材名〈和〉	素材名〈英〉	概要	組成（糸と織組織）
37	キャリコ	Calico	元来、インドから輸入された木綿織物。すべての綿織物に対して使われるようになる。	たて糸は31番以上、よこ糸は36番内外の綿糸を使用するものが多い。平織
38	コーデュロイ	Corduroy	添毛織の一種。木綿織物。よこ糸ビロード織。	たて糸1組とよこ糸2組を用いる。1組のよこ糸はたて糸を組織して、地を織る地織である。もう1組のよこ糸は毛よこに用いる。浮いた毛よこを押さえる点をたて方向に大体一直線に配列、ちょうど畳表のように織上げる。下地は平織、綾織あり。
39 40	コットン ケンダル・コットン	Cotton Kedall Cotton	17、18世紀には動物性の紡毛織物と植物性の木綿の二義があった。逃亡奴隷広告におけるCottonは、通常、紡毛織物である。18世紀末から19世紀に木綿と紡毛の混紡が生産された。	
41	ディミティー	Dimity	畝織の木綿織物の一種。ギリシャ語のdimitosに由来する。双糸または2本引きそろえのたて糸を意味する。軽量で薄い。	地糸と同じ番手の単糸を2本から3本、またはそれ以上の本数ずつ引きそろえにしたところをインチ間に6〜8個所作り、布面にたて畝の縞を現したり、たて畝とよこ畝とで格子を織り現す平織

仕上げ	色・柄	用途	口絵写真番号
		ウェストコート、衣服の裏地	
充分な仕上げが施される。		ペティコート、ドレスコートの裏地	
		コート、ウェストコートジャケット	
		ストッキング	
	無地物、格子柄	コート、ウェストコートジャケット、ブリーチズ	2-3-16
毛足が短く、目が粗い柔らかい毛羽でおおわれる。	黒、赤、茶	ウェストコート、ケープブリーチズ、シュルトゥーコート、ジャケット、アンダー・ジャケット、縁なし帽	2-3-17
大部分は織り上げ後、晒し仕上げを施す。		フロック・コート、ガウン、ショート・ガウン、サック	2-3-18
浮いた毛よこを浮いた中央部で真っ直ぐに突き切ると列をなして毛が立ち、立毛でよこの畝ができる。		ブリーチズ	
		ジャケット、ウェストコート、ブリーチズ、レギンス、シャツ、シフト、ストッキング	2-3-19
手触りはこわめで、柔らい光沢がある。	必ず、たて縞か格子状に平たい畝目が織り込まれている。目の細かい鳥目織から大型の装飾模様、ストライプ柄まで、多種多様。	ウェストコート	2-3-20

	素材名〈和〉	素材名〈英〉	概要	組成（糸と織組織）
42	ガーゼ	Gauze	薄い織物の総称。ガーゼの名は昔、このような薄い織物を織っていた町、すなわちパレスチナのガーザ（Gaza）に由来すると言われる。	甘撚りの糸で、平織に織る。
43	ナンキーン	Nankeen	中国産綿織物の一種。中国の南京地方で産出するので、この名がつけられる。地厚。	黄褐色を帯びた20から30番の綿糸を用いて、平織に組織。
44	スィックセット	Thickset	畝織の木綿織物の一種Corduroyあるいは Fustianに分類されることもある。	
45	ベルブレット	Velveret	通常、絹に似せて作られた幅広の木綿のVelvet。	よこ糸は、通常、2本のたて糸を同時に渡る。畝織。

(5) コットン（Cotton）とウール（Wool）

	素材名〈和〉	素材名〈英〉	概要	組成（糸と織組織）
46	スタッフ	Stuff	織物の総称。Cotton stuff、Silk stuffと記述。	

(6) コットン（Cotton）とリネン（Linen）

	素材名〈和〉	素材名〈英〉	概要	組成（糸と織組織）
47	ファスチャン	Fustian	木綿または木綿とリネンの混紡の目の粗い織物。Corduroyに類似。	綾織の厚くて、緻密な綿布の片面または両面に毛を掻き出したもの。
48	ジーンズ ジェーンズ	Jeans Janes	細綾木綿。綿織物の一種。単に細綾ともいう。リネンとの混紡もあり。	通常、たて糸に20〜24番、よこ糸に18〜20番の綿単糸を用いる。幅90センチ内外。綾織。
49 50	ニグロ・クロス ニグロ・コットン	Negro cloth Negro cotton	アメリカ独立革命前の奴隷用の高価でない輸入毛織物の一種。亜麻や木綿も用いられる。	

(7) リネン（Linen）

	素材名〈和〉	素材名〈英〉	概要	組成（糸と織組織）
51	キャンバス （ダック）	Canvas (Duck)	麻織物、綿織物の二種あり。一般には帆布に使用する麻織物を指し、これには黄麻糸製のものと亜麻糸製がある。	通常、10番の撚糸を用いて、蜜に平織に織る。糸は厚さに応じて、10番の撚糸程度の糸を厚さに応じて、1本から2〜8本撚り合わせる。
52	チェック	Check	縞柄の名で、たてよこに縞を表した柄を指すが、この柄の布地も指す。亜麻のもの、亜麻、木綿混紡もの多い。	平織。
53	クロッカス	Crocus	サフランで黄色に染められたリネン。目の粗いズックやバーラップのような袋地。召使いや奴隷用の織物。	

仕上げ	色・柄	用途	口絵写真番号
晒したあと、無のりに仕上げたもの。		縁なし帽	
	黄褐色、白、濃紺、黒	コート、ウェストコート、ブリーチズ	
仕上げの難しさのために生産に適していない。	目の細かい畝を生み出す。花模様付きのものもあり。	コート	2－3－21
	畝織あるいはプリント模様。	ウェストコート	2－3－22
		ガウン、ジャケット	
		コート、ジャケット、ズボン	
生または晒のものの大部分が含まれる。織上後、毛羽焼、糊抜き、シルケット処理を施す。黒染めが主であり、その他各種の色合いに染めることもある。張り仕上げと光沢仕上げあり。	白、暗色	コート、ウェストコート、ブリーチズ	
		コート、ジャケット、ブリーチズ、ウェストコート、アンダー・ジャケット	
		帆、ズボン、エプロン、ジャケット、シャツ、ウェストコート	
	あらゆる色柄。青、茶、赤の組み合わせが一般的。白地の一色。一色の濃淡。多色もの。	ズボン、シャツ、エプロン、ブリーチズ	2－3－23
		シャツ、ズボン、ブリーチズ	

	素材名〈和〉	素材名〈英〉	概要	組成（糸と織組織）
54	ダウラス	Dowlas	厚手の目の粗い亜麻布。労働者用の織物。	
55 56	オランダ アイリッシュ・オランダ	Holland Irish Holland	目の細かい亜麻織物の一種。オランダ産と特定はできない。イングランド産もある。	平織
57	リネン	Linen	亜麻糸を用いて織った麻布の総称。品質には細かいもの、粗いもの、厚いもの、薄いものと種々ある。	平地が一般的で斜文織、紋織および生リネン、晒リネン等あり。
58	オズナブルグ オズナブリグ	Osnabrug Osnabrig Oznabrug Oznabrig	安価で粗目であるが、丈夫な亜麻布で、元はドイツのオズナブリュグで作られていた。下層階級によって用いられた。	現在は8〜12番の太番の綿糸をたてよこに用いて疎く織る。
59	ロールズ	Rolls	目の粗い亜麻布の一種。巻かれた布。	

(8) シルク（Silk）

	素材名〈和〉	素材名〈英〉	概要	組成（糸と織組織）
60	シルク	Silk	絹織物	

(9) その他

	素材名〈和〉	素材名〈英〉	概要	組成（糸と織組織）
61	フェルト	Felt	反毛（繊維の糸くずを再製した羊毛）などを縮絨させて、シート状にしたもの。紡毛織物を縮絨、起毛してフェルト状にした織フェルトもあり。	
62	ニット	Knit	編まれたもの。	
63	レザー	Leather	なめし皮	
64	スレッド	Thread	木綿やシルクや亜麻の糸。	
65	ヤーン	Yarn	紡ぎ糸	

(10) 国産品

	素材名〈和〉	素材名〈英〉	概要	組成（糸と織組織）
66	カントリー・クロス	Country cloth	国産の織物。	
67	ヴァージニア・クロス	Virginia cloth	ヴァージニア産の織物。	

仕上げ	色・柄	用途	口絵写真番号
半分晒してある。		シャツ	
	白、自然の茶色、格子柄、縞模様。	シャツ、ズボン、コート、ウェストコート	
生地のもの、漂泊したもの、染めたものあり。		ウェストコート、ジャケットコート、ブリーチズ、ズボン、ペティコート、シャツ	2-3-24
無漂白で、染色されていない。	自然の茶色（18世紀）19世紀の間に青、白、茶のストライプやチェック、色物が見られるようになる。	シャツ、袋、ジャケットブリーチズ、ズボン、ペティコート	
無漂白	無漂白の茶色。	ブリーチズ、ズボン	

仕上げ	色・柄	用途	口絵写真番号
精錬を施したもの。精錬していないもの。	黒、赤、白他	ハンカチ、ストッキング	

仕上げ	色・柄	用途	口絵写真番号
		帽子	
		ストッキング	
		ブリーチズ	
		ストッキング、シャツ	
		ストッキング	

仕上げ	色・柄	用途	口絵写真番号
		ウェストコート、ジャケットコート、ブリーチズ、シャツペティコート	
		ウェストコート、ジャケットコート、ブリーチズ、シャツペティコート	

表2-3-2　逃亡奴隷広告に見る被服素材年次別一覧

	1	2	3	4	5	6	7
	Bath coating	Bearskin	Beaver coating	Broadcloth	Buckskin	Calimanco	Camlet
1766	0	0	0	1	0	0	0
1767	0	2	0	3	2	0	0
1768	0	0	0	1	0	0	0
1769	0	0	0	1	1	0	0
1770	0	0	0	4	1	0	0
1771	0	1	0	2	0	0	0
1772	0	2	1	1	0	0	0
1773	0	2	1	0	1	0	0
1774	0	0	1	5	0	1	0
1775	2	0	1	1	0	0	0
1776	0	1	0	1	2	0	0
1777	0	0	0	7	1	0	1
1778	0	0	0	0	0	0	0
1779	0	0	0	3	0	1	0
1780	0	0	0	0	1	0	0
1781	0	0	0	0	0	0	0
1782	0	0	0	0	0	0	0
1783	3	0	0	2	1	0	0
1784	0	0	0	0	1	0	0
1785	0	0	0	0	0	0	0
1786	0	0	0	4	0	0	0
1787	0	0	0	5	0	0	0
1788	0	0	0	2	1	0	0
1789	0	0	0	0	0	0	0
total	5	8	4	43	12	2	1

8	9	10	11	12	13	14	
Casimer	Castor	Cloth	Coating	Drab	Russia drab	Duffil	
0	0	1	0	0	0	0	1766
0	0	2	0	0	0	2	1767
0	0	1	0	0	0	0	1768
0	0	3	0	0	3	4	1769
0	0	4	0	0	1	1	1770
0	0	4	0	0	1	0	1771
0	0	4	0	1	6	2	1772
0	0	5	0	0	3	4	1773
0	1	6	0	1	5	6	1774
0	0	8	0	0	2	0	1775
0	0	5	0	2	1	2	1776
0	0	10	0	2	1	2	1777
0	0	9	0	1	1	0	1778
0	0	8	0	0	0	0	1779
0	0	0	0	0	0	0	1780
0	0	0	0	0	0	0	1781
0	0	0	0	0	0	0	1782
0	0	5	2	0	0	1	1783
0	0	2	0	0	0	0	1784
0	0	12	0	1	0	0	1785
0	0	0	2	1	0	0	1786
1	0	0	2	1	0	2	1787
1	1	1	1	0	0	0	1788
0	0	0	1	1	0	1	1789
2	2	90	8	11	24	27	total

	15	16	17	18	19	20	21
	Duroy	Elk skin	Everlasting	Fearnought	Flannel	Frieze	Half-thicks
1766	0	0	0	1	0	0	0
1767	0	0	0	1	0	1	0
1768	1	0	1	1	0	0	0
1769	1	0	0	1	0	1	0
1770	0	0	0	1	4	1	0
1771	0	0	0	0	0	2	1
1772	0	0	1	4	0	1	0
1773	0	0	0	0	1	0	0
1774	0	0	0	5	0	0	1
1775	0	1	0	1	0	0	0
1776	0	0	0	4	0	0	0
1777	1	0	0	4	0	1	0
1778	0	0	0	0	2	1	0
1779	0	0	0	0	0	0	0
1780	0	0	0	0	0	0	0
1781	0	0	0	0	0	0	0
1782	0	0	0	0	0	0	0
1783	1	0	0	0	0	0	0
1784	0	0	0	0	1	0	1
1785	0	0	0	0	0	0	0
1786	1	0	0	0	0	0	0
1787	0	0	0	1	0	0	0
1788	1	0	0	0	0	0	0
1789	0	0	0	0	0	0	0
total	6	1	2	24	8	8	3

22	23	24	25	26	27	28	
Homespun	Kerzey	Plains	Plush	Rackoon	Sagathy	Serge	
0	1	0	0	0	0	1	1766
0	1	0	0	0	0	1	1767
0	0	0	0	0	0	0	1768
0	3	2	0	0	0	0	1769
0	0	3	0	1	0	0	1770
0	0	5	0	0	0	0	1771
0	3	1	1	0	0	0	1772
0	1	1	0	0	0	2	1773
0	0	4	1	0	0	0	1774
0	2	1	1	0	0	0	1775
0	2	0	0	0	0	1	1776
1	2	0	0	0	0	1	1777
0	1	2	0	1	0	0	1778
0	0	0	0	0	0	2	1779
0	0	0	0	0	0	0	1780
0	0	0	0	0	0	0	1781
1	0	0	0	0	0	0	1782
0	0	0	0	0	0	0	1783
2	0	1	1	1	0	1	1784
0	0	2	0	0	0	1	1785
0	0	3	0	0	0	0	1786
0	0	1	0	0	0	0	1787
0	0	5	0	0	1	0	1788
0	0	0	0	0	0	0	1789
4	16	31	4	3	1	10	total

	29	30	31	32	33	34	35
	Shag	Shalloon	Swanskin	Tammy	Wilton	Woolen	Plaid
1766	0	0	0	0	0	0	1
1767	0	1	0	1	0	0	0
1768	0	0	0	0	0	0	0
1769	1	0	0	0	1	0	5
1770	0	0	0	0	0	1	1
1771	1	0	1	0	0	2	1
1772	0	1	1	0	0	0	1
1773	0	1	0	0	0	1	2
1774	0	0	0	0	0	1	1
1775	0	0	0	0	1	0	1
1776	1	1	0	0	0	0	0
1777	0	1	1	0	0	3	0
1778	0	0	0	0	1	2	0
1779	0	2	0	0	0	0	0
1780	0	0	0	0	0	0	0
1781	0	0	0	0	0	0	0
1782	0	0	0	0	0	0	0
1783	0	0	0	0	0	3	0
1784	0	0	0	0	0	0	0
1785	0	0	0	0	0	0	0
1786	0	0	0	0	0	0	0
1787	0	0	0	0	0	0	0
1788	0	0	0	0	0	0	0
1789	0	0	0	0	0	2	0
total	3	7	3	1	3	15	13

36	37	38	39	40	41	42	
Velvet	Calico	Corduroy	Cotton	Kendall cotton	Dimity	Gauze	
0	0	0	33	0	0	0	1766
3	1	0	8	0	0	0	1767
2	0	0	9	0	0	0	1768
0	0	0	16	0	0	0	1769
0	0	0	15	0	0	0	1770
0	0	0	16	0	0	1	1771
1	0	0	16	0	0	0	1772
1	1	0	12	0	0	0	1773
1	0	0	16	2	0	0	1774
0	0	0	10	1	0	0	1775
0	0	0	6	0	0	0	1776
1	2	0	19	0	0	0	1777
0	0	0	8	0	0	0	1778
1	0	0	12	0	0	0	1779
0	0	0	0	0	0	0	1780
0	0	0	0	0	0	0	1781
0	1	0	1	0	0	0	1782
1	0	0	4	1	0	0	1783
0	1	0	6	0	0	0	1784
0	0	1	3	0	0	0	1785
0	0	1	1	0	0	0	1786
0	0	0	0	0	0	0	1787
1	0	1	3	0	2	0	1788
1	1	1	0	0	1	0	1789
13	7	4	214	4	3	1	total

	43	44	45	46	47	48	49
	Nankeen	Thickset	Velveret	Stuff	Fustian	Jeans	Negro cloth
1766	0	0	0	0	0	0	0
1767	0	0	0	0	0	0	0
1768	1	0	0	0	0	0	0
1769	1	0	0	0	1	0	0
1770	0	0	0	0	1	0	5
1771	0	0	0	1	0	0	0
1772	0	0	0	0	0	0	0
1773	0	1	0	1	0	3	1
1774	0	0	1	0	0	0	0
1775	0	0	0	0	0	0	0
1776	0	0	1	0	0	0	0
1777	0	1	0	1	0	0	0
1778	0	0	0	0	0	1	0
1779	1	0	0	0	0	0	0
1780	0	0	0	0	0	0	0
1781	0	0	0	0	0	0	0
1782	0	0	0	0	0	0	1
1783	0	0	0	1	0	0	0
1784	0	0	0	0	0	0	0
1785	0	0	0	0	0	0	0
1786	0	0	0	0	1	0	0
1787	0	0	0	0	0	0	0
1788	1	0	0	0	0	0	0
1789	0	0	0	0	0	0	0
total	4	2	2	4	3	4	7

50	51	52	53	54	55	56	
Negro cotton	Canvas	Check	Crocus	Dowlas	Holland	Irish Holland	
6	0	0	0	0	0	0	1766
1	1	0	1	0	2	1	1767
3	0	1	0	0	0	0	1768
0	0	1	0	0	0	0	1769
6	1	1	0	0	0	0	1770
1	0	2	0	0	0	0	1771
6	1	3	0	1	0	0	1772
4	0	3	1	0	0	0	1773
6	1	0	0	0	3	0	1774
7	0	2	0	2	0	0	1775
3	0	0	0	1	0	0	1776
0	1	2	0	2	1	0	1777
0	0	1	0	0	0	0	1778
0	1	1	0	0	0	0	1779
0	0	0	0	0	0	2	1780
0	0	0	0	0	0	0	1781
0	0	0	0	0	0	0	1782
2	0	0	0	0	0	0	1783
3	0	1	0	0	0	0	1784
2	0	0	0	0	0	0	1785
0	0	0	0	0	0	0	1786
2	0	0	0	0	0	0	1787
5	0	0	1	0	0	0	1788
1	0	0	0	0	0	0	1789
58	6	18	3	6	6	3	total

	57	58	59	60	61	62	63
	Linen	Osnabrug	Rolls	Silk	Felt	Knit	Leather
1766	5	20	1	0	2	0	4
1767	1	0	0	0	1	0	0
1768	1	1	2	0	2	0	0
1769	1	6	3	0	3	0	2
1770	2	27	1	0	8	0	2
1771	5	19	0	0	7	0	2
1772	5	22	2	0	5	1	4
1773	4	14	5	1	4	0	3
1774	6	14	7	0	5	0	2
1775	4	13	5	0	3	0	7
1776	10	2	0	0	4	2	7
1777	9	5	0	1	4	0	7
1778	5	1	0	0	2	0	1
1779	3	2	0	2	0	0	5
1780	1	0	0	1	0	0	0
1781	0	0	0	0	0	0	0
1782	0	0	0	0	0	0	1
1783	2	4	0	0	0	0	3
1784	2	8	0	1	4	0	0
1785	1	1	0	0	1	0	2
1786	2	6	0	0	2	0	1
1787	1	2	0	0	0	0	1
1788	1	4	1	0	4	0	1
1789	0	3	0	0	2	0	0
total	71	174	27	6	63	3	55

64	65	66	67	
Thread	Yarn	Country cloth	Virginia cloth	
0	2	0	1	1766
0	0	0	7	1767
0	0	0	6	1768
0	2	0	4	1769
0	1	0	5	1770
0	4	0	4	1771
0	4	0	12	1772
0	3	1	4	1773
0	7	3	7	1774
1	5	2	6	1775
0	6	1	11	1776
1	6	5	23	1777
1	6	0	10	1778
2	6	0	6	1779
0	0	0	1	1780
0	0	0	0	1781
0	0	0	5	1782
0	2	4	9	1783
0	4	1	7	1784
0	4	0	6	1785
0	0	0	0	1786
0	1	0	1	1787
0	3	0	3	1788
0	0	0	2	1789
5	66	17	140	total

Ridge and Allegheny Mountain until 1830. Unpublished Master's Thesis, Department of History, Virginia Polytechnic Institute, Blacksburg, (Virginia, 1976), 139-141.
- Florence Montgomery, *Textiles in America, 1650-1870: A Dictionary Based on Original Documents, Prints and Paintings, Commercial Records, American Merchant' Papers, Shopkeepers' Advertisements and Pattern Books with Original Swatches of Cloth,* Norton, New Papers, Shopkeepers' Advertisements and Pattern Books with Original Swatches of Cloth, (Norton, New York, 1984).
- Linda Baumgarten, "'Clothes for the People': Slave Clothing in Early Virginia," *Journal of Early Southern Decorative Arts* Vol. 14, No.2 (Nov. 1988), 62-66.
- Linda Baumgarten, Plains, Plaid and Cotton: Woolens for Slave Clothing, *ARS TEXTRINA* 15, (1991), 203-222.

第 3 章

逃亡奴隷の着装情況

―その数量的アプローチ―

第1節　奴隷の被服の種類と素材の特徴

1．種類とデザイン

　逃亡奴隷広告には種々の被服が登場する。そこで、まず奴隷が支給された基本的な被服の種類とデザインの特徴を整理しておこう[1]。男女ともに用いられた被服もあるため、あえて男子服と女子服の区分はしない。

（1）ジャケット［ジャックコート］（jacket, jackcoat）……18世紀を通じて、あらゆるタイプの労働者たちが、外着用ジャケットや下着用ジャケットを着用した。18世紀初期にはほとんどが膝丈であった。世紀が進むにつれて丈が短くなり、1800年には腰丈となる。打ち合わせはシングルのものもダブルのものもあった。袖付きの場合も、袖なしの場合もあった。男女ともに用いた。

（2）ウェストコート（waistcoat）……18世紀を通じて男性に用いられたアンダー・ジャケット。18世紀初期には、ほぼ膝丈に達する裾布付きであったが、18世紀後半には丈が短くなった。袖付きの場合も、袖なしの場合もあった。ベストと同義。

（3）シャツ（shirt）……長方形の布地を肩の部分で二つ折りにして、折り目に頭が通るだけの開きを作り、袖を付けたシンプルな衣服。丈は長く、幅広である。ネックの開きや袖口に襞飾りがあしらわれているものもあった。

（4）コート（coat）……三つ揃えのスーツの一番上から着られた袖付きの丈長の上着。大型外套は防寒の目的で着用されたオーバーコート。

（5）フロック（frock）……ワンピース形式の子供服。大人向けのスモック風の外着。

（6）ブリーチズ（breeches）……半ズボン。ウェストと膝にボタンがけされ、ボタンの下の膝の部分にはバックルが取り付けられていた。紐で結ばれているものもあった。素材は多様。男性用。

（7）ズボン（trousers）……ウェストからくるぶしまでおおう衣服。裁断は現代の長ズボンによく似ている。多種多様な素材で作られた。労働者や船乗りに用いられた。

（8）オーバーオール（overall）……長ズボンの一種。ズボンの上にはくゆったりした上履きズボン、上からきゃはんを巻いて用いるぴったりした長ズボン、などがある。

（9）ガウン（gown）……丈の長いゆったりした上着。男女ともに用いた。

（10）サック（sack）……丈の短い、女性用のジャケット風の上着。

（11）ショート・ガウン（short gown）……短い裾布の付いた女性用のガウン。肩縫い目はなく、袖は身頃から一続きに裁断された。丈や幅が不足する場合は布を接ぎ足す工夫が凝らされた。労働者用の衣服。

（12）ペティコート（petticoat）……ウェストがぴったりした女性用のスカート。ドレスやガウンと合わせて用いる場合には、ペティコートの素材もガウンと共布であった。コートともいう。

（13）シフト（shift）……植民地時代の女性用の亜麻布製のアンダー・シャツ、またはシュミーズ。

(14) ステイズ（stays）……コルセット
(15) エプロン（apron）……一般に目の粗い亜麻布（linen）やキャンバス（canvas）やベーズ（baize）製で、男女に用いられた。
(16) ハット（hat）……縁付きの帽子。後ろあるいは片方が巻き上げられたもの、3ヶ所で巻き上げられ、ループで固定されているものなど、さまざまな形に巻き上げられていた。労働者にとって、必ずしも実用的であったとは言えない。
(17) キャップ（cap）……小さな縁のないぴったりした被り物。
(18) ボンネット（bonnet）……男女に用いられた小さな被り物で、通常、鍔は付いていない。
(19) ストッキング（stocking）……長靴下。
(20) 靴（shoes）……奴隷は靴をはいていないこともあった。また、足に合わないサイズや形の靴に悩まされていたという記録も多い。

2．奴隷の服装のイメージ

　上述の被服の種類を黒人奴隷がどのように着用していたのか。いわば奴隷の服装のイメージを考えるにあたっては、第1章第3節で言及したヴァージニアの黒人奴隷制度の特質を思い起こさなければならない。すなわち、ヴァージニアやサウス・カロライナなどの北アメリカ南部のプランテーションでは、奴隷の労働形態によって身分の違いがあり、プランターの側仕えの上級家内奴隷（馬車を引く人、召使い、給仕など）、技術を持った職人奴隷（樽職人、仕立て屋、鍛冶屋、靴屋など）、および農園で働く奴隷という三つの階層に区分されていた。そして「奴隷に与えられた衣服のスタイルと質は身分や職業によって異なっていた[2]。」

　上級の召使いである黒人奴隷には、主人のお古やお仕着せがあてがわれた。「お仕着せは中世からヨーロッパの慣習であったが、植民地で広く使用され、アメリカでもジョージ・ワシントン（George Washington）やロバート・カーター（Robert Carter）のような富裕なヴァージニア人によって進んで採用されていた[3]。」G.ワシントンは召使いの黒人奴隷に緋色と白のお仕着せを着せていた。これらの色は、彼の家族の紋章に見られた色であった[4]。口絵3-1-1はコロニアル・ウィリアムズバーグ振興財団 DeWitt Wallace Gallery of Decoarative Arts 所蔵のイギリス製のお仕着せのコートである。ヴァージニアにもたらされ、御者など上級の白人の召使いと黒人の召使いによって着用されていた[5]、と考証されている。このコートは主人のものと形は変わらないが、興味深いことに、そこには、召使いであることを象徴するいくつかの装飾的要素が見られるのである。上質のウール（wool）製で、召使いの主人の紋章の色である緑と赤の2色使いで粋に配色されており、裏は綾織のウーステッド（worsted）製である。緑のブロード・クロス（broadcloth）地に赤の衿とカフスが付けられ、金糸や銀糸で織られた入念な縁取りが施されている[6]。

　家内奴隷のなかには、主人に気に入られた者もいた。そのような奴隷たちは、主人のお下がりの古着を着たり、主人の遺言によって付与された衣服を着用していた。だが、このような慣習は奴隷全体の人口のほんの数パーセントにしか適用されなかった。それはヴァージニアの大プランテーシ

ョンで働いている何千人もの奴隷に支給するものがなかったためだけではない。このような衣服は外で働くための衣服としては、形と素材の面で、不適切であったためである。女の召使いの家内奴隷は、白人の召使いのような恰好をしていた。第1章の上流階級の女子服の項目でも触たが、コルセットを装用した奴隷もいた。

　熟練を要する職業や工芸に従事する奴隷は、白人の年季奉公人と同じ服装であった。彼らは一般に、上流人と同じような構成の衣服を着ていた。すなわち、男性の職人奴隷の衣服はコート、ウェストコート、ジャケット、シャツおよびブリーチズという構成が基本であった。これは特殊な技能が重要視されていたことを示している。また、このような衣服が最も入手しやすかったこともある。逃亡奴隷には、この種の服装が多かった。例えば、ヴァージニア生まれのジョージ・アメリカ（George America）という名前の黒人奴隷は、腕利きの靴職人で、家を作る大工仕事もできたのだが、逃亡時には、コットン（cotton）製のウェストコートとブリーチズ、オズナブルグ（osnabrug）のシャツおよびヤーン（yarn）製の靴下を着用していた[7]。

　農園の奴隷は「クロップ・ニグロ」（crop negro）と呼ばれ、安価な素材の制服を着用していることもあった[8]。逃亡奴隷広告によると、農園の奴隷の一般的な衣服はオズナブルグのシャツ、コットンのジャケットとズボン、格子縞の靴下およびヴァージニア製の靴であった。夏服は目の粗いリネン（linen）のブリーチズ、または長ズボン、およびリネンのシャツである。冬服は目の粗いオズナブルグのシャツ、ウールのジャケットおよびブリーチズである。通常、これらの服装は逃亡奴隷広告では「黒人奴隷が一般に着用していた衣服」"such clothes as crop Negroes usually wear"と記されていた。また、女の奴隷の衣服は、夏用はリネンのワンピースやショート・ガウンと呼ばれたゆるやかなガウン、ぴったりしたウェストコートやジャケットとやや厚手のリネンのペティコートといった貧しい婦人の典型的な服装であった。

　筆者は、これら奴隷の被服の実物資料を求めて、ヴァージニア州の博物館やコロニアル・ウィリアムズバーグ振興財団考古学研究部門をたずねたが、ヴァージニア製の奴隷の被服の実物は1枚も残存しておらず、布の断片も残存していないのが実状であった。したがって、当時の奴隷の服装のイメージの把握はイラストに拠らざるをえない。この点でピーター・F. コープランド（Peter F. Copeland）が描いている黒人奴隷のイラストは、彼らの服装のイメージを捉える格好の資料である。

　口絵3-1-2は、G. ワシントンのマウント・ヴァーノンのプランテーションで働いていた奴隷の従僕である。ワシントン家の紋章の緋色と白のお仕着せを着用している。

　筆者は第2章でロレーナ・S. ウォルシュ（Lorena S. Walsh）に拠って、1730年代のカーター家（Carter Family）のマーチャント・ハンドレッド・プランテーションの「各々の奴隷は、年に一度、冬用の新しいスーツと夏用のもっと軽い衣服を支給された。男にはシャツとファスチャンのジャケットとリネンのブリーチズが、女にはシフトとペティコートとエプロンが支給された。子供はフロックだけをもらった。大人たちはかれらの身支度をすっかり整えるために、輸入ものの靴1足とアイルランド製の靴下1足、あるいは格子縞の靴下（Plaid hose）1足とキルマーノック産の縁なし帽（Kilmarnock milled caps）を支給された[9]」と述べた。G.ワシントンのいとこのランド・ワシントン

史料3-1-1　黒人奴隷用の衣服の支給に関する記載
　（1774年）[ランド・ワシントンの会計帳簿から]

```
        D.r River Plantation for Workmens Wages, & other
                    Expenses &c.
                              1
1774    To Cloaths for Negro men, viz. Frederick
         2      3      4    5     6    7   8
        Will, Abram, Natt, Ben, Essex, Nap, George
         9    10    11      12    13
        Ned, George, Boombs Robin, Arlington, a
        Jacket, a pair breeches, 2 Shirts a pair
        Stookings, 1 p. Shoes each a

        To D° for 2 boys, Peter & Adam D°. a

         1    2    3    4
        To D° for Women viz Ruth, Peg, Daphne,
         4    5    6    7    8    9    10
        Francis, Kate, Doll, Led, Suck, Mariane,
          10    11    12   13    14    15
        Milly, Ester, Nelly Cloe, Judy, Hanna,
         16    17
        Judy, Nancy - a Pettycoat, Jackett, 2
        Shifts 1 p Stookings 1 p Shoes each, a

        To a Machine for thrashing wheat (Mr Hobdays)

1775
Janry 1  To Smiths work pr acco.t in Smiths ledger }
          folo Since August 1st 1774 to date      } 7. 15. 4
```

Mount Vernon Ladies' Association of the Union, Lund Washington's Account Books 1772-1787.

史料3-1-2　家内奴隷用の衣服の支給に関する記載
　（1772年）[ランド・ワシントンの会計帳簿から]

```
                Altering 1 pr Velvet &
                  1 pr Colt Breech              :4. 6
        23      D°. 3 pair stocking d°          4.--
                Making 4 pair drawers           4.
                Mending your Sourtout Coat      2.
                Making 3 pair of drawrs
                  for Hercules                  4. 6
                Mendg 4 pair of Breeches
                  for Will                      4.
        John Custis Esqr.
                Making 1 waistcoat for
                  Jullia  1S                    2. 6
        Do      Mending 1 pair Buckskin
                  breeches 1S                   1.
                making 1 close bodied
                  Coat     1S                  15.--
        Lund Washington
                Mending 1 pr Breeches & 1
                  Coat for Aaron                2.
        D°.     Making a Coat for Aaron 1S      7.
                for mendg 6 froeks &
        30.       waistcoats & 5 pair of    }  15.
                  Breeches                   }
        febry 10  6 pair drilling breeches      1. 4.
        20      Mending 3 pair breeches
                  for brechy                    3. -
                Waistcoats 25.pr.Breeches       7. -
                Mending 1 pr Breeches for
                  breohy                         .6
        March 16 D° 3 pr D° Frank, H. & D°      3. -
                Covering 3 books                3. -
                Making 22 waistcoats &
                  25 p Breech                   2. -.-
        Colo George Willm Fairfax
                  altering a Coat  17           2. -
        John Parke Custis Esq.
                  altering 1 waistcoat
                  & Breeches     1S             1. 6
        Lund Washington
                  Mending 4 pair breeches 1S    4. -
        James Boyles
                  Making 1 Coat & waistcoat    15. -
                         17
        16      Lund Washington
        26        Making 1 duroy Coat  1S      10. -
                                              ─────
                                              23. 5. 2
        Debits & Credits Carried to 19
```

Mount Vernon Ladies' Association of the Union, Lund Washington's Account Books 1772-1787.

（Lund Washington）の会計帳簿（account book）[10]には、大半のプランテーションでは1774年に、男の奴隷にはジャケット1着、ブリーチズ1本、シャツ2枚、靴下および靴各1足がめいめいに支給された、と記されている。また、女の奴隷はペティコート1着とジャケット1着とシフト2枚と靴下と靴各1足を受け取った（史料3-1-1）、と記されている。さらに、この会計帳簿には、家内奴隷はもっと沢山受け取ったという多くの証拠がある。例えば、ヘルクレス（Hercules）のために、1772年にスーツ1着と下着用ズボン3着を作らせ、ウィル（Will）には繕われたブリーチズ4本を用意した（史料3-1-2）。ウィルはG.ワシントンの側仕えの召使いの奴隷であった。また、年季奉公人で煉瓦職人のジョン・ノールズ（John Knowles）のために、1774年にウェストコート1着とブリーチズ1本を作らせた（史料3-1-3）、と記録されている。

　こうした実例によって、農園の奴隷よりも家内奴隷の方が多くの衣服を支給されていたことが裏付けられよう。また、逃亡奴隷広告に見られる奴隷の被服の種類と、上述のカーター家およびG.ワシントン家のプランテーション内で奴隷に支給されていた被服の種類に整合性を見出すこともで

きる。

以上の考察から、奴隷の被服の特徴は次のように小括できる。

（1）上級の黒人奴隷は上等ではあるが、奴隷の身分を示す縁取り装飾が施された主人の紋章の色を配したお仕着せをあてがわれていた。
（2）女の召使いの家内奴隷は、白人の召使いのような恰好をしていた。コルセットを支給されていた場合もあった。
（3）家内の職人奴隷は年季奉公人と同じ服種をあてがわれていた。
（4）農園の奴隷よりも家内奴隷の方が多くの衣服を支給されていた。
（5）農園の奴隷はオズナブルグのシャツや未晒しのニグロ・クロスのブリーチズやズボンという粗末な服装であった。
（6）女の奴隷の服装は貧しい婦人の典型的な服装であった。
（7）この時代には家内奴隷も農園の奴隷もブリーチズをあてがわれている

史料3-1-3　職人奴隷用の衣服の支給に関する記載（1774年）［ランド・ワシントンの会計帳簿から］

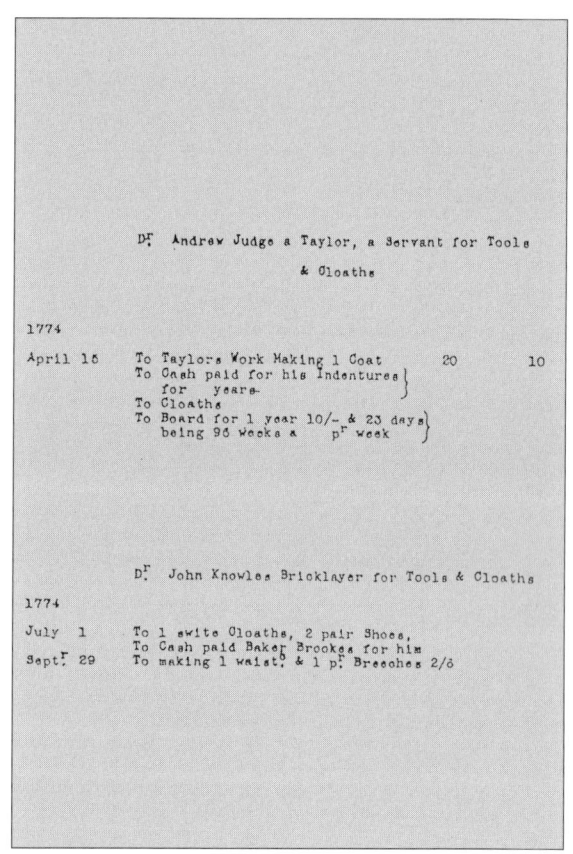

```
D.r  Andrew Judge a Taylor, a Servant for Tools
                                     & Cloaths
1774
April 15   To Taylors Work Making 1 Coat      20    10
           To Cash paid for his Indentures }
              for    years.               }
           To Cloaths                     }
           To Board for 1 year 10/- & 23 days}
              being 96 weeks a    p.r week  }


           D.r  John Knowles Bricklayer for Tools & Cloaths
1774
July   1   To 1 suite Cloaths, 2 pair Shoes,
           To Cash paid Baker Brookes for him
Sept.r 29  To making 1 waist.t & 1 p.r Breeches 2/6
```

Mount Vernon Ladies' Association of the Union, Lund Washington's Account Books 1772～1787.

ことが多い。ブリーチズは元来、上流階級の男子の衣服であった。この脚衣は第1章第4節で触れたように、きわめて動きにくい、機能性に乏しい衣服であった。プランテーションでの労働には不適切な衣服であったであろう。だが、なかにはなめし皮製の伸縮性のあるブリーチズも用いられていた。我々は以上のまとめから、ステイタス・シンボルとしての被服の役割をはっきりと見ることができる。

3．逃亡奴隷の被服の素材

次に、逃亡奴隷の被服の素材について考察するために、年度毎にその傾向を分析し図3-1-3から図3-1-6を作成した。

1766年（図3-1-3）においては、コットン（cotton）がジャケットに60パーセント、ブリーチズに56.3パーセント、ウェストコートに58.3パーセントといった具合に、約6割を占めている。その他の素材としてはジャケットにリネン（linen）とカルゼ（kerzey）がそれぞれ10パーセントを占めて

第 3 章　逃亡奴隷の着装情況―その数量的アプローチ―　　71

図3-1-3　逃亡奴隷広告に見る服種別素材の構成比（1766年）

jacket
- ④ 20.0%
- ③ 10.0%
- ② 10.0%
- ① 60.0%

① cotton
② linen
③ kerzey
④ その他

breeches
- ⑤ 12.5%
- ④ 6.3%
- ③ 6.3%
- ② 18.8%
- ① 56.3%

① cotton
② leather
③ Negro cotton
④ rolls
⑤ その他

waistcoat
- ③ 33.3%
- ② 8.3%
- ① 58.3%

① cotton
② fearnought
③ その他

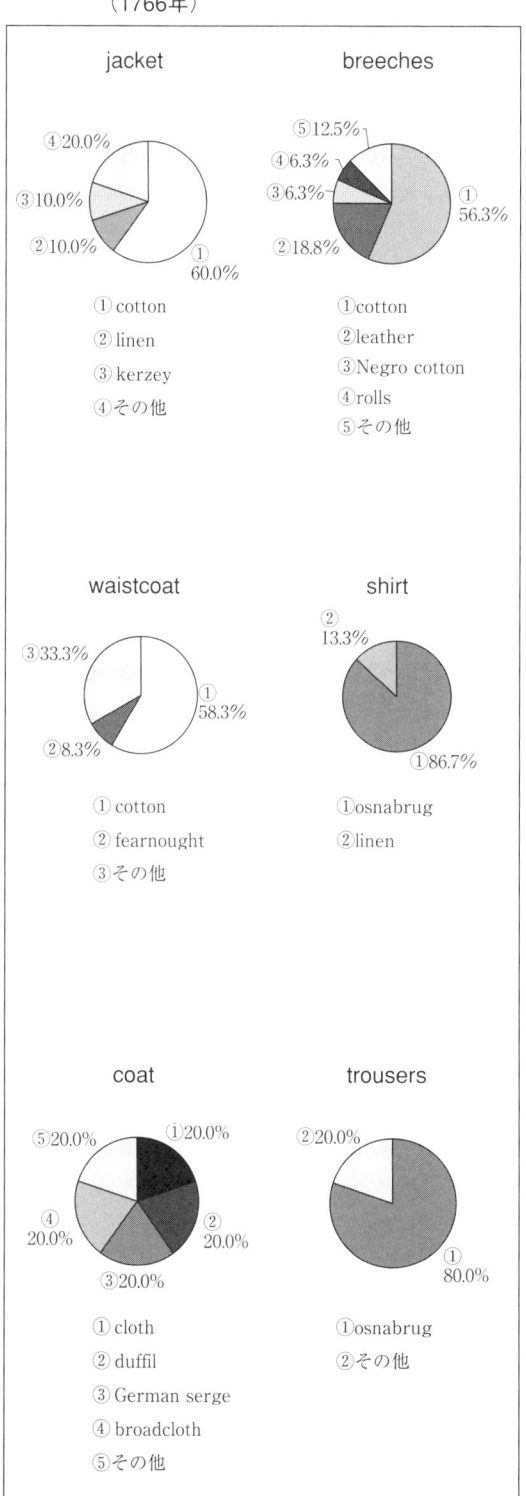

shirt
- ② 13.3%
- ① 86.7%

① osnabrug
② linen

coat
- ⑤ 20.0%
- ④ 20.0%
- ③ 20.0%
- ② 20.0%
- ① 20.0%

① cloth
② duffil
③ German serge
④ broadcloth
⑤ その他

trousers
- ② 20.0%
- ① 80.0%

① osnabrug
② その他

図3-1-4　逃亡奴隷広告に見る服種別素材の構成比（1771年）

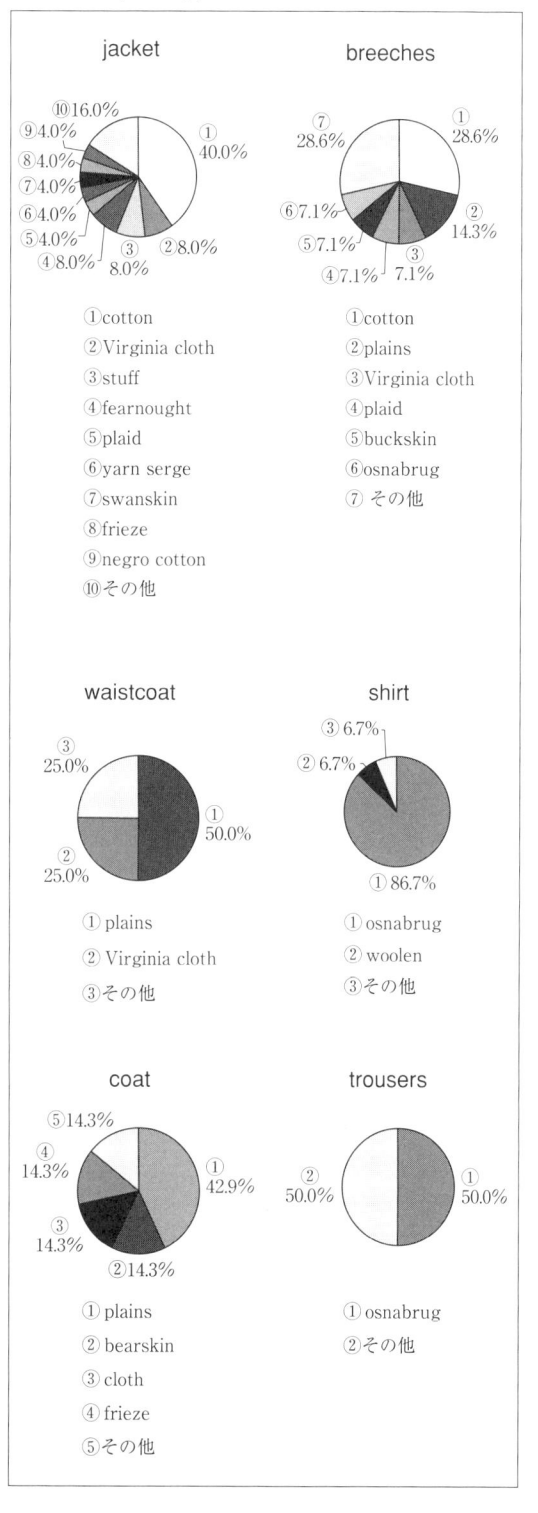

jacket
- ⑩ 16.0%
- ⑨ 4.0%
- ⑧ 4.0%
- ⑦ 4.0%
- ⑥ 4.0%
- ⑤ 4.0%
- ④ 8.0%
- ③ 8.0%
- ② 8.0%
- ① 40.0%

① cotton
② Virginia cloth
③ stuff
④ fearnought
⑤ plaid
⑥ yarn serge
⑦ swanskin
⑧ frieze
⑨ negro cotton
⑩ その他

breeches
- ⑦ 28.6%
- ⑥ 7.1%
- ⑤ 7.1%
- ④ 7.1%
- ③ 7.1%
- ② 14.3%
- ① 28.6%

① cotton
② plains
③ Virginia cloth
④ plaid
⑤ buckskin
⑥ osnabrug
⑦ その他

waistcoat
- ③ 25.0%
- ② 25.0%
- ① 50.0%

① plains
② Virginia cloth
③ その他

shirt
- ③ 6.7%
- ② 6.7%
- ① 86.7%

① osnabrug
② woolen
③ その他

coat
- ⑤ 14.3%
- ④ 14.3%
- ③ 14.3%
- ② 14.3%
- ① 42.9%

① plains
② bearskin
③ cloth
④ frieze
⑤ その他

trousers
- ② 50.0%
- ① 50.0%

① osnabrug
② その他

いる。また、オズナブルグ（osnabrug）がシャツに86.7パーセント、長ズボンに80パーセントを占めている。コートにはクロス（cloth）、ダッフィル（duffil）、ジャーマン・サージ（German serge）およびブロード・クロス（broadcloth）がそれぞれ20パーセントを占めている。

　1771年（図3-1-4）になると、ジャケットに用いられた素材の種類が、1766年の3種類に比べて、9種類にものぼっているのが特徴である。すなわち、コットンが4割を占め、その他にヴァージニア・クロス（Virginia cloth）、スタッフ（stuff）、フィアノート（fearnought）、プレード（plaid）、ヤーン・サージ（yarn serge）、スワンスキン（swanskin）、フリーズ（frieze）およびニグロ・コットン（negro cotton）が用いられている。国内産のヴァージニア・クロスが見られるようになった点に注目したい。

　ブリーチズについても1766年においてはコットンが56.3パーセント、その他になめし皮（leather）、ニグロ・コットンおよびロールズ（rolls）という構成であったのが、1771年においてはコットンが3割、その他にプレインズ（plains）、ヴァージニア・クロス、プレード、バックスキン（buckskin）およびオズナブルグという構成になり、素材の内容が大幅に変化している。

　ウェストコートにもプレインズが50パーセント、ヴァージニア・クロスが25パーセントという具合に、1766年とは素材における変化が見られる。やはり国内産のヴァージニア・クロスが見られるようになった点に注目したい。

　シャツと長ズボンには、オズナブルグが86.7パーセントと50パーセント用いられている。

　コートにはプレインズが42.9パーセント、ベア・スキン（bearskin）、クロスおよびフリーズ（frieze）がそれぞれ14.3パーセントというように羊毛および皮革が用いられている。

　さらに1776年（図3-1-5）になると、どの服種にもヴァージニア・クロスが用いられている。ジャケットにはヴァージニア・クロスが25パーセント、コットン、ウールン（woolen）とコットンの混紡、カルゼおよびプレインズが12.5パーセントを占めている。

　ブリーチズにはヴァージニア・クロスとバックスキンが18.2パーセント、コットン、ウールンとコットンの混紡、リネンおよびカルゼが9.1パーセントを占めており、多様な素材が用いられている。

　ウェストコートにはヴァージニア・クロスが25パーセント、クロス、ダッフィル、ベア・スキン、カルゼおよびニグロ・コットンが12.5パーセントを占めている。

　シャツにもヴァージニア・クロスが33.3パーセントを占めており、オズナブルグ、コットン、コットンと亜麻（flax）の混紡、ダウラス（dowlas）、ロールズおよびリネンがそれぞれ11.1パーセントを占めており、多様な素材が用いられている。

　コートには、やはりクロス、ブロードクロス、サージ（serge）、ニグロ・コットン、ラシア・ドラブ（Russia drab）、フィアノートおよびヴァージニア・クロスが10パーセントを占めており、多様な素材が用いられている。

　総じて、1776年の逃亡奴隷広告に見られる被服には、多様な素材が用いられ、ヴァージニア・クロスの使用がどの服種にも顕著になっている。

第3章　逃亡奴隷の着装情況—その数量的アプローチ—　　73

図3-1-5　逃亡奴隷広告に見る服種別素材の構成比
（1776年）

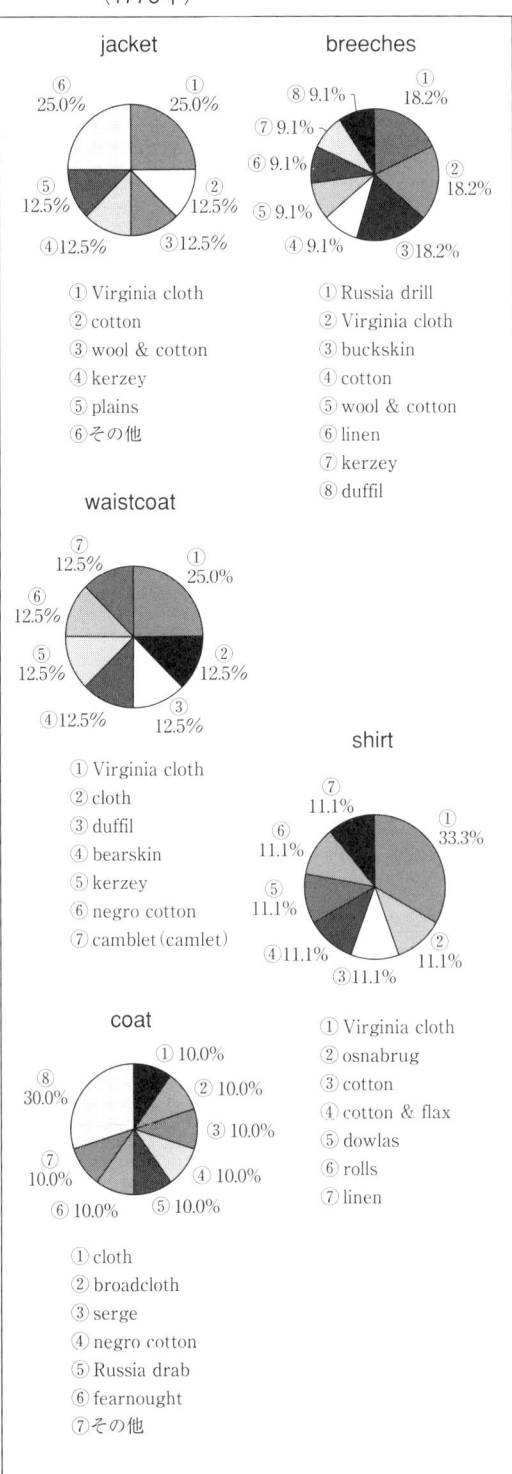

jacket
⑥ 25.0%
① 25.0%
⑤ 12.5%
② 12.5%
④ 12.5%
③ 12.5%

① Virginia cloth
② cotton
③ wool & cotton
④ kerzey
⑤ plains
⑥ その他

breeches
⑧ 9.1%
① 18.2%
⑦ 9.1%
⑥ 9.1%
② 18.2%
⑤ 9.1%
④ 9.1%
③ 18.2%

① Russia drill
② Virginia cloth
③ buckskin
④ cotton
⑤ wool & cotton
⑥ linen
⑦ kerzey
⑧ duffil

waistcoat
⑦ 12.5%
① 25.0%
⑥ 12.5%
⑤ 12.5%
② 12.5%
④ 12.5%
③ 12.5%

① Virginia cloth
② cloth
③ duffil
④ bearskin
⑤ kerzey
⑥ negro cotton
⑦ camblet (camlet)

shirt
⑦ 11.1%
① 33.3%
⑥ 11.1%
⑤ 11.1%
④ 11.1%
② 11.1%
③ 11.1%

① Virginia cloth
② osnabrug
③ cotton
④ cotton & flax
⑤ dowlas
⑥ rolls
⑦ linen

coat
① 10.0%
⑧ 30.0%
② 10.0%
③ 10.0%
⑦ 10.0%
④ 10.0%
⑥ 10.0%
⑤ 10.0%

① cloth
② broadcloth
③ serge
④ negro cotton
⑤ Russia drab
⑥ fearnought
⑦ その他

図3-1-6　逃亡奴隷広告に見る服種別素材の構成比
（1784年）

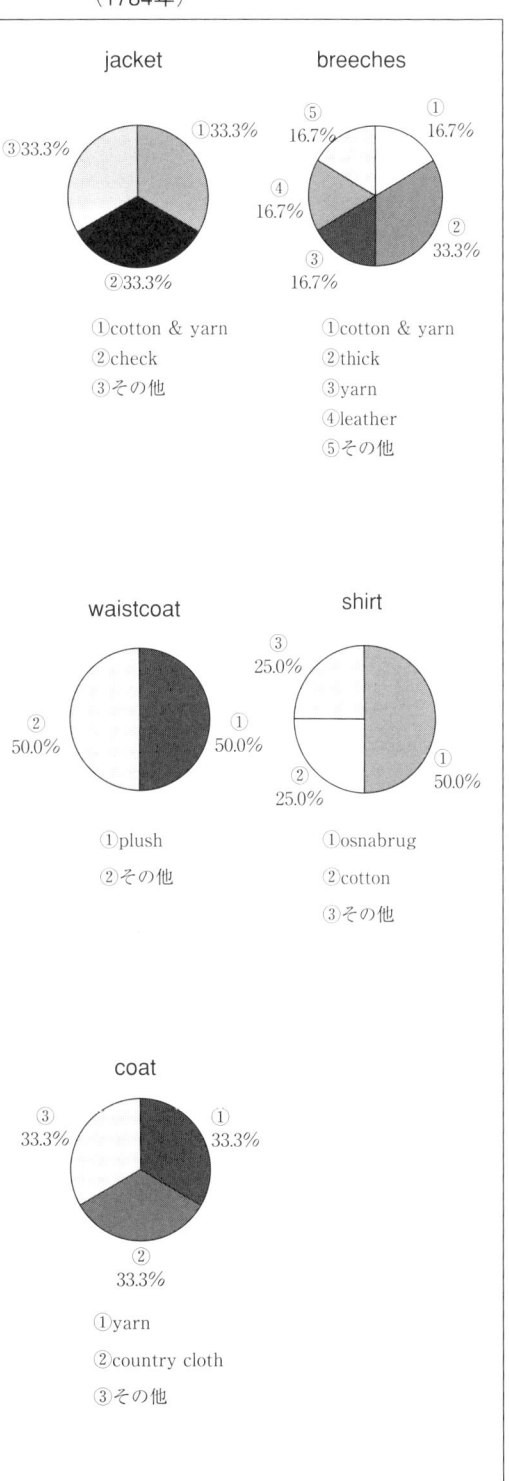

jacket
③ 33.3%
① 33.3%
② 33.3%

① cotton & yarn
② check
③ その他

breeches
⑤ 16.7%
① 16.7%
④ 16.7%
② 33.3%
③ 16.7%

① cotton & yarn
② thick
③ yarn
④ leather
⑤ その他

waistcoat
② 50.0%
① 50.0%

① plush
② その他

shirt
③ 25.0%
① 50.0%
② 25.0%

① osnabrug
② cotton
③ その他

coat
③ 33.3%
① 33.3%
② 33.3%

① yarn
② country cloth
③ その他

最後に、1784年（図3-1-6）においては、ヴァージニア・クロスが全く見られず、ジャケットにはコットンとヤーン（yarn）の混紡が33.3パーセント、チェック（check）が33.3パーセント、ブリーチズにはスィック（thick）が33.3パーセント、コットンおよびなめし皮がそれぞれ16.7パーセントを占めている。

シャツにはオズナブルグが50パーセント、コットンが25パーセントを占めている。

ウェストコートにはプラッシュ（plush）が50パーセントを占めている。コートにはヤーンが33.3パーセント、カントリー・クロス（country cloth）が33.3パーセントを占めている。

総じて、1784年においては、ヴァージニア・クロスが全く見られなくなっているが、コートには国内産のカントリー・クロスが用いられている。

以上、1766年、1771年、1776年および1784年の逃亡奴隷広告に見る被服素材の構成比について、年度毎にまとめてみた。

第2章に掲載した「逃亡奴隷広告に見る被服素材一覧」（表2-3-1、2-3-2）に記したように、17、18世紀にはコットンには動物性の紡毛織物と植物性の木綿の二義があった。逃亡奴隷広告におけるコットンは、通常、紡毛織物である。

第2節　男子の逃亡奴隷の着装実態

1．被服の組み合わせ

(1)　対象時期

本節では、男子の逃亡奴隷の逃亡時の着装実態を、Lathan A. Windley 編集の*Runaway Slave Advertisement: A Documentary History from 1730s to 1790*, Vol.4, Greenwood, Westport, Connecticut, 1983.（『逃亡奴隷広告集―1730年代～1790年―』）を資料に用いて、数量的に分析してみよう。

対象とした時期は、1767年から1770年と1776年から1779年である。前者はアメリカ独立革命期の独立戦争前の時期である。この時期はタウンゼンド諸法による外部課税の賦課と行政機能の拡充にたいする植民地人の撤回運動の段階である。後者は1776年1月にトマス・ペインの「コモン・センス」が発行され、引き続いて、7月4日に、トマス・ジェファーソン（Thomas Jefferson）起草になる独立宣言が公布されてからの4年弱の期間である。

(2) 被験者

被験者は、逃亡奴隷広告に被服情報が掲載されている男子の逃亡奴隷のうち、被服の着用情報が記載されている人に限定した。

ここで、逃亡奴隷広告における被服情報の具体例を挙げると、次の3つのケースに整理される。

史料3-2-1　*Virginia Gazette*（Dixon & Hunter）, January 21, 1775, Neg. #99-155,4S CN.

> It is expected he will make for *Wilmington*, in *North Carolina*, as he has a Brother's Widow living there, who moved from *Virginia* some Time since.　　　　　　　　　JOHN COCKBURN.
>
> ## THREE POUNDS REWARD.
>
> RAN away from the Subscriber, on the 1st of *January*, a middling dark Mulatto named STEPHEN, about 21 Years of Age, and thick made; had on, when he went off, a Negro Cotton Waistcoat and Breeches, an Osnabrug Shirt, and Negro made Shoes, with Pegs drove in the Soals; his Hair is cut off the Top of his Head, and but little remains at the Sides. He carried with him a white Mulatto Woman Slave named PHEBE, whose Hair is long, straight, and black; she had on a blue Waistcoat and Petticoat, and took with her two new Osnabrug Shirts, and a Suit of striped *Virginia* Cloth; she is about 21 Years of Age. They also carried off two Osnabrug Shirts, 6 or 7 Ells of Rolls, a new *Dutch* Blanket, and one about Half worn. It is imagined they will make for *Carolina*, and endeavour to pass for free People. All Persons are forewarned from harbouring them, at their Peril. Whoever brings them to me, or secures them in any Gaol, so that I may get them again, shall have the above Reward.
>
> 　　　　　　　　　　　　　　　HENRY HARDAWAY.
>
> ## TWENTY SHILLINGS REWARD.

Special Collections, John D. Rockefeller, Jr. Library, Colonial Williamsburg Foundation, Williamsburg, Virginia（写真の原本は筆者所蔵）

史料3-2-2　*Virginia Gazette*（Purdie & Dixon）, November.3, 1768, Neg.# 99-154,2S CN.

> above may view the same by applying to Mr. *Benjamin Fambrough*, who lives on the premises, any time before the day of sale, or the subscriber in *New Kent*.
>
> 　　　　　　　RICHARD CHAMBERLAYNE.
>
> RUN away from the subscriber in *Chesterfield*, about the end of *August* last, a middle sized Negro man named WILL, about 30 years old, of a yellowish complexion, very much marked on his face, arms, and breast, his country fashion, speaks very broken, and can hardly tell his master's name; had on when he went away a new osnabrugs shirt, *Virginia* linen short trousers, old cotton jacket, and felt hat, with part of the brim burnt off. He has made three attempts, as he said, to get to his country, but was apprehended. All masters of vessels are hereby forewarned from carrying the said slave out of the colony. Whoever apprehends him, and brings him to me, shall have 20 s. reward, besides what the law allows.　　JORDAN ANDERSON.
>
> COMMITTED to the publick gaol of *Princess Anne* county, by order of court, a yellow complexioned mulatto, who calls himself TOM WHEELER, about

Special Collections, John D. Rockefeller, Jr. Library, Colonial Williamsburg Foundation, Williamsburg, Virginia（写真の原本は筆者所蔵）

(a) 被服の着用情報が記載されている場合（史料3-2-1・2）
Virginia Gazette（Dixon & Hunter）, January 21, 1775.[11]

THREE POUNDS REWARD.
　RAN away from the Subscriber, on the 1st of January, a middling dark Mulatto named STEPHEN, about 21 Years of Age, and thick made; <u>had on, when he went off</u>, a Negro Cotton Waistcoat and Breeches, an Osnabrug Shirt, and Negro made Shoes,

この事例には　had on, when he went off（下線筆者）とあるが、これは被服を着用していた場合の表現である。その他に、he wore……、his clothes was……といった表現が見られる。

(b) 被服の携行情報が記載されている場合
Virginia Gazette（Purdie & Dixon）, March 22, 1770.[12]

Five Pounds Reward.
　RUN away from the subscriber's plantation in Chesterfield county, in July last, a Negro man named STERLING, about 6 feet high, who has a large body, though small legs and thighs, stoops very much when he walks, not of a very black complexion, has a blemish in one eye (or rather squints) and the other a large full eye; <u>he carried with him two cotton waistcoats</u>, two osnabrug shirts, two pair of breeches (one of Negro cotton, the other of osnabrugs) two striped Virginia cloth waistcoats, and a Dutch blanket. He is an African born, talks very bad, and hard to be understood by those not well acquainted with him, though very sensible. Whoever brings the said Negro to me shall have the above reward.
　CREED HASKINS.

この事例には he carried with him two cotton waistcoats（下線筆者）とあるが、これは被服を携行していた場合の表現である。

(c) 被服情報が不備な人
Virginia Gazette（Dixon & Hunter）, April 24, 1778.[13]

TWENTY DOLLARS REWARD.
　RUN away from Mr. Robert Donald's plantation in Prince Edward, two Negro fellows, GEORGE and HARRY. <u>George is about 35 years old, stout made and stoops a little; he had on a light coloured cloth jacket, and a great coat made of a duffle blanket</u>. As he has a wife at Mrs. Floyd's in Charles City, I suspect he is in that neighbourhood; he is an old offender, and is branded on both cheeks R. Harry is a tall, straight, well made fellow, of a yellowish

表3-2-1　逃亡奴隷広告に見る男子の逃亡奴隷数

	A	B	C	A-B-C	total
1767	11	1	5	5	
1768	17	0	1	16	61
1769	35	3	4	18	
1770	30	4	4	22	
1776	23	0	2	21	
1777	42	0	7	35	88
1778	21	0	4	17	
1779	18	1	2	15	
total	197	9	29	149	149

・被服情報が記載されている男子の逃亡奴隷数(A)
・「被服を携行していた」(carried with their clothes)と記載されている男子の逃亡奴隷数(B)
・被服情報が不明瞭な男子の逃亡奴隷数(C)
・「被服を着用していた」(had on their clothes)と記載されている男子の逃亡奴隷数(A-B-C)

complexion, about 27 years of age, his dress I cannot describe; he was bought of Mr. William Noble of Prince George county, where he has many connections, and I imagine he will make for that quarter. Whoever will bring the said Negroes to Mr. Robert Donald in Warwick, to whom they belong, shall receive the above reward, or ten dollars for each.
MICHAEL COULTER.

　Georgeの被服情報には下線部（筆者）に見られるように、ズボンの記載が見られない。裸で逃亡したとは考えられない。

　以上から、(b)と(c)に該当する逃亡奴隷は被験者に含めない方針とした。被験者の数は**表3-2-1**のとおりである。

(3)　数量化の手順
　以上を前提として、逃亡奴隷の被服の組み合わせパターンを8通りに分類する。そのための基礎作業として、マイクロソフトのExcelを用いて、表3-2-2を作成した。作成手順は以下の通り。
（1）対象年（1767～1770、1776～1779）の*Virginia Gazette*紙に登場する逃亡奴隷の被服情報を新聞発行人、発行年月日、逃亡奴隷の名前、年齢、職業、着用していた被服の種類と枚数、その他の被服情報（盗んで着替えた、とか、携行していた被服の種類と数）を逃亡広告から抽出し、年度毎に時系列に沿い、一覧表を作成した。
（2）次に、これらの表をもとに男子の逃亡奴隷の被服の組み合わせを年度別に一覧表にした（**表3-2-3**）。
（3）次に、上記の表（表3-2-3）をもとに男子の逃亡奴隷の被服の組み合わせパターンを8通りに分類した（表3-2-4）。
　A　グループは靴の記載がある逃亡奴隷であり、着用している被服の組み合わせによって、次の

表3-2-2　逃亡奴隷の被服の種類
[1767年]

Date of Publish	name of slave	age	trade	upper clothes				lower clothes		suit
				jacket	waistcoat	shirt	coat	breeches	trousers	
PD1767-1-8	Peter				1		1	1		
R1767-3-12	Moses				1		1	1		
PD1767-3-19	Jack	28		(2)		(2)	(1)	(2)		
PD1767-4-2	Frank	20		2						
PD1767-4-16	Bob	26		1				1		
PD1767-5-7	David Grantenread				(2)	(1)		(1)		
PD1767-5-28	Jack	30								
PD1767-7-9	Jack				1(1)	1(1)	(1)	1(1)		
R1767-7-23	Johney or John Brooks						1			
PD1767-9-10	Senewer	26				2	1			
PD1767-9-24	Will	28		1	1	1(1)	1	1	(1)	
PD1767-10-1	Jupiter	35		1		1	1			
	Robin	25	preacher							
PD1767-11-26	Pysant	25	sailor							
total				5(2)	4(3)	5(5)	6(2)	5(4)	(1)	

PD=Purdie & Dixon、R=Rind. 新聞発行人を省略表記した。
1767-1-8→1767年1月8日を示す。
(1)は1枚着用していたことを、(2)は2枚携帯していたことを示す。逃亡奴隷広告には、着用していた場合には、he had on, he

[1768年]

Date of Publish	name of slave	age	trade	upper clothes				lower clothes		suit
				jacket	waistcoat	shirt	coat	breeches	trousers	
PD1768-1-28	Tom	24								
PD1768-2-11	Johnny									
PD1768-2-11	Frank	20		1				1		
R1768-3-3	Ben	27								
R1768-3-24	Harry	24-25								
PD1768-3-31	Charles	15-16		1		1		1		
R1768-5-12	Sam				1		1	1		
PD1768-6-23	Adam	40		2		1		1		
	Sterling	30		1		1		1		
PD1768-6-23	Dick	35								
PD1768-6-30	Harry	22								
R1768-6-30	Solomon	19		1			1	1		
R1768-7-14	Will			1		1		1		
PD1768-8-4	Billy		ship carpenter	1		2			1(1)	
R1768-8-25	Jack			1(1)		1(1)			1	
PD1768-9-1	Tom	20		1		1		1		
PD1768-9-8	George			1(1)				1(1)		
PD1768-9-15	Frederick	16					1	1		
PD1768-9-15	Gaby	40								
R1768-9-22	Peter Deadfoot	22	shoemaker							
			butcher							
			ploughman							
			carter							
			sawyer							
			waterman							
PD1768-9-29	Dick		blacksmith							
R1768-9-29	Cyrus			1		1			1	

第3章　逃亡奴隷の着装情況―その数量的アプローチ―

head covering		stockings		foot wear			apron	others
hat	cap	stockings	hose	shoes	boots	pumps		
1		1		1				
	1		1					
(1)		(2)		(1)				
(1)								brown cut wig, several old clothes
								stole many clothes
	(1)	(1)		(1)				
								many good clothes
			1			1		
1		1(1)		1				
								variety of cloth
								variety of cloth
								well clothed
2(2)	1(1)	2(4)	2	2(2)		1		

wore、携行していた場合には、he had, he carried withと記載されている。

head covering		stockings		foot wear			others
hat	cap	stockings	hose	shoes	boots	pumps	
							clothing of labouring Negroes
							uncertain
1							
							variety of other clothes
							his clothes are worn out or changed
							sundry other clothes
							clothing of labouring Negroes
							cotton clothes
	1			2			plated buckles
1							
1			1			1	other clothes
							winter clothing of corn field Negroes
							he is fond of dress
							very good clothing
	1						

Date	name of slave	age	trade							
R1768-9-29	Will			1		1		1		
PD1768-10-20	Will	30		1		1			1	
PD1768-11-3	Ned									
PD1768-11-3	Solomon Haynes		pilot			1		1		
R1768-11-17	Sam									
R1768-11-17	Jem	45-50		1		1		1		
total				15(2)	2	12(1)	4	12(1)	4(1)	0

[1769年]

Date of Publish	name of slave	age	trade	upper clothes				lower clothes		suit
				jacket	waistcoat	shirt	coat	breeches	trousers	
PD1769-1-26	Frank			1(1)			(2)	1(1)		
PD1769-2-9	Peter	27				1				
	Jemboy	20				1				
	Harry	21				1				
R1769-2-9	Billie	30	ship carpenter	1			1			
R1769-2-9	Daniel		pilot	1	1		1			
R1769-2-23	Peter			1						
	Manel			1						
R1769-2-23	Dublin									
PD1769-3-9	Tom	38								
PD1769-4-13	Frank									
PD1769-5-4	Peter	44			(1)					
R1769-5-11	Harry	27			(1)	(3)	(1)	(3)		
PD1769-5-18	York			2						
R1769-6-6	Billy	16				1		1	1	
	David Randolph		cooper			1		1	1	
R1769-6-15	Sam					1		1		
	Jack			1		1		1		
PD1769-6-29	Humphrey	12-14			1	1		1		
R1769-7-13	Will					1	1		1	
	Roman					1	1		1	
	George					1			1	
PD1769-7-27	Bob	27		1						
PD1769-8-3	Ned	20				(several)	(1)	(2)		
PD1769-8-17	Joe		waitingman	1		1(several)	1(2)	1		
			shoemaker							
PD1769-9-21	Julius	17-18				1	1		1	
PD1769-9-21	George	20			1		1	1		
R1769-10-5	William Hanover	40	carpenter				(1)			
			joiner							
R1769-10-13	William Hood	16				1			1	
PD1769-11-9	Dick	25								(1)
	Moses									
PD1769-11-9	Caesar						1	1		
PD1769-11-9	Joe			1			1	1		
PD1769-11-23	Charles	22					(2)			
PD1769-12-7	Frank					1		1		
PD1769-12-7	unknown	40		1	1	1			1	
	unknown					1	1		1	

hat	cap	stockings	hose	shoes	boots	pumps	others
					1		
1							
							cannot describe his clothing
							many other kinds of clothes
							usual cloathing for labouring Negroes
1							
5	2	0	1	2		2	

head covering		stockings		foot wear			others
hat	cap	stockings	hose	shoes	boots	pumps	
		several	1	(2)			he may change them
		1		1			carried away other clothes
		1		1			carried away other clothes
		1		1			carried away other clothes
		1		1			sundry other sorts of clothes
							many other clothes
							he was cloathed as usual
							variety of clothes
							carried with him several suits
							such as crop Negroes usually wear
							carried with him sundry clothes
1		1		1			
							had other clothes
1							
							his other clothes are unknown
							clothing of field Negroes
		(several)					
1		1(several)		1			
							wearing clothes he carried with him
1							
		(1)		(1)			
							variety of clothes
1							
		1					
			1	1			
1							
1							

				sawyer	2					
				carpenter						
				cooper						
total					14(1)	7(2)	15(many)	11(9)	11(6)	7	(1)

[1770年]

Date of Publish	name of slave	age	trade	upper clothes				lower clothes		suit
				jacket	waistcoat	shirt	coat	breeches	trousers	
PD1770-2-22	Jack	22								
	Joshua	22								
PD1770-3-22	Ben	35	Carpenter							
			Cooper							
PD1770-3-22				(4)	(2)		(2)			
PD1770-4-19	Ned	21			1	1		1		
	Frank	30				1				
PD1770-4-19	Dick				2			1		
PD1770-4-19	Frank	25				1		1		
R1770-4-19			servant	1			1	1		
R1770-4-19	Sam	35		1	1	1		1		
R1770-4-19	Emanuel	middle	sawyer							
R1770-5-31	Peter	22			1		1	1		
PD1770-6-7	Harry									
PD1770-6-7	Ned	27			1	1				
R1770-7-12	Adam			1		1		1		
PD1770-7-19	Joe	20		1			1		1	
R1770-8-2	James	40								
PD1770-8-16	Windsor	14		1						
PD1770-8-16	Milford	22				1			1	
	Mingo	40								
PD1770-8-16	Mingo	35			1	1				
PD1770-9-6	Davy	28			1	1		1		
PD1770-9-6										
PD1770-9-27	Jack				1		1	1		
PD1770-9-27	Will Morris	40			1				1	
PD1770-10-4	Cuffey	25		1			1	1		
PD1770-10-18	Nick	22					(1)	(1)		
PD1770-10-25	Jack			1		1			1	
	Sam			1		1			1	
PD1770-10-25	Sam									
PD1770-11-1	Daniel		Cooper							
			Shoemaker							
R1770-11-1	America	40		1		1		1		
PD1770-11-1	Chelter	25		(1)		(3)	(1)			
PD1770-11-8						1			1	
PD1770-11-8	Tom									
R1770-11-8	Tony	50								
R1770-11-15	Will	34	carpenter		(2)	1	(2)	(1)	1	
			cooper							
			turner							
PD1770-12-13	John Wilson	34		(2)		(1)	(1)	(1)	(1)	
PD1770-12-13		28		1		1		1		

第3章　逃亡奴隷の着装情況—その数量的アプローチ—

7	0	7(many)	2	7(3)	0	0	

head covering		stockings		foot wear			others
hat	cap	stockings	hose	shoes	boots	pumps	
							they are clothed in the usual manner for Negroes
							he has many clothes
1		1		1			unknown other clothes
1	1						muffs
1					1		he had other clothes
							a bundle of other clothes
1							
							sundry clothes
							usual clothing of crop Negro
1							
1							
							old cotton winter clothes
							his clothing such as Negroes usually have
				1			
1							
							have a pass by the name of Thomas Scott
1		1		1			
1				1			
							many other good clothes
1							
							unknown apparel
							very well dressed
(2)							sundry other clothes
1							
							clothed in the usual negro dress
							old blue cotton
1				1			
		(1)		(1)			
				1			in the common dress of field slaves

Date of Publish	name of slave	age	trade	jacket	waistcoat	shirt	coat	breeches	trousers	suit
		28		1		1		1		
		26		1		1		1		
R1770-12-13	Frank									1
total				12(3)	10(6)	17(6)	5(4)	14(5)	7(1)	1

[1776年]

Date of Publish	name of slave	age	trade	upper clothes				lower clothes		suit
				jacket	waistcoat	shirt	coat	breeches	trousers	
DH1776-1-13	Solomon				1	1		1		
P1776-3-8	Jack	26			1	(2)	1	1		
P1776-3-15	Will	35		1				1		
DH1776-3-23	Quash	21		1		1		1		
DH1776-3-30	Jacob	30	Farmer		1	1	2	1		
P1776-4-5	Phill					1		1		
DH1776-4-6	Daniel	35					1	1		
P1776-5-10	Appleby		Weaver	1		1	1	1		
P1776-5-24	Peter	30		1		1		1		
P1776-5-31	Anthony	12-13								
DH1776-6-8	Esther	16		1			1			
P1776-6-21	Jamie	15					1	2		
	Toby	15					1	2		
P1776-7-5	Billy	25								
	Kitt	17-18								
DH1776-7-20	Bagley	20				1	1	1		
P1776-9-6-1	Billy	24-25					1	1		
P1776-9-6-2	John Bibbin				1	1		1		
DH1776-10-11	Joe					1		1		
DH1776-11-1	Elijan	23	Blacksmith		1	1		1		
DH1776-11-8	Quash	30								
P1776-11-8	John			1(1)		1(1)	1	1(1)		
P1776-12-13	Stephen			1					1	
DH1776-12-27	Joe			1			1	1		
total				8	7	11(2)	10	19	1	0

[1777年]

Date of Publish	name of slave	age	trade	upper clothes				lower clothes		suit
				jacket	waistcoat	shirt	coat	breeches	trousers	
P1777-1-3	Joe	46				1		1		
P1777-1-17	Harry(Hal)	15			1	1	1		1	
P1777-2-21	Austin	30		1		2		1(1)		
DH1777-3-7	Josse		waiting man				1	1		
DH1777-3-14-1	Sam	30		1				1		
DH1777-3-14-2	Will		Carpenter	1		1(1)	1	1(1)		
DH1777-3-21	Sam	26		1		1		1		
DH1777-4-11	John Towpence					1				
P1777-4-11	Marcus	35				1	2	1		
DH1777-4-18-1	Bob				1	1	1	1		
DH1777-4-18-2	Will	17								
	James	16								
DH1777-5-2-1	Moses	45					1		1	
DH1777-5-2-1	Simon	20				1	2	1		

第3章　逃亡奴隷の着装情況―その数量的アプローチ―

				1			
				1			
12(2)	1	2(1)		8(1)	1		

head covering		stockings		foot wear			others
hat	cap	stockings	hose	shoes	boots	pumps	
		1		1			
(1)							
				1			
1		1		1			
1		1		1			several shirts
		1					
				1			
	1						he is dressed in Virginia cloth
	1						they went off in their work clothes
							they went off in their work clothes
	1						
	1						
							sundry other clothes
		1				1	
		1		1			
		1		1			
2(1)	4	7	0	7	0	1	

head covering		stockings		foot wear			others
hat	cap	stockings	hose	shoes	boots	pumps	
				1			he had other clothes
		1		1			several other clothes
		1		1			
		1		1			had several other things
		1		1			
1				1			
1							
							sundry other Negroes clothing
1							
							Clothing Virginia cloth
							old light coloured cloth clothing
	1						

Date of Publish	name of slave	age	trade	jacket	waistcoat	shirt	coat	breeches	trousers	suit
P1777-5-2	Gardner	40			1	1		1		
DH1777-5-9	Arthur	35-40								
DH1777-5-9	Ben	25-30								
P1777-5-9	Sam	28	Carpenter Cooper	1		1	1	1		
P1777-5-9	Jack						1(2)	1		
DH1777-5-23	Abraham									
DH1777-6-6	Sam	40					1		1	
P1777-6-13	Will	40		1				1		
DH1777-6-20	Pompey	40					1	1		
P1777-6-20	George	21		1			1			
DH1777-6-27	Leiw					1	1			
P1777-7-18	Sam	25		1		1	1(1)	1(1)		
P1777-7-25	Baker Hazard			1		1		1		
DH1777-9-1	Kenter	30		1(1)						
P1777-9-12	Joe	21				1		1		
P1777-9-19	Lewis					1	1			
	Prince			1		1	1			
DH1777-10-3	Jem					1	1			(1)
DH1777-10-10	Adam		Shoemaker	1			1	1		
P1777-10-17	Peter			1		1	1			
P1777-10-17	Jacob			1		1	1			
DH1777-10-31	Jack	21								
DH1777-11-7	Glass	40		1	1(1)	(1)	1(1)			
DH1777-11-7	Joe	22		1		1	1			
P1777-11-21	Caleb			1						
DH1777-12-5		35	Blacksmith				1			
DH1777-12-12	Joe	20								
	Tom	18								
	James	10		1				1		
DH1777-12-12	Charles	35		1		1	1			
DH1777-12-19	Peter		Waggoner	(1)		(4)	(4-5)			(2)
DH1777-12-19	John Goodwin	19				2		1		
DH1777-12-19	Harry	23		1		1	1			
total				19(2)	7	23(6)	19(4)	25(8-9)	7	(3)

[1778年]

| Date of Publish | name of slave | age | trade | upper clothes | | | | lower clothes | | suit |
				jacket	waistcoat	shirt	coat	breeches	trousers	
DH1778-1-23	Ayre	35								
DH1778-4-24	George	33		1			1			
P1778-5-1	Ben									(1)
P1778-5-1	Jack			1				1		
P1778-5-29	Colas	40		1				1		
P1778-6-5	Tom	18			1	1				
P1778-6-5	Sam	21		1			1	1		
P1778-6-12	Ishmael	27 or 28		1		1			1	
P1778-6-19	Will or Billy	30				1				
P1778-6-19	Sam	35		(1)			1	1		
	Tom	18-19		1(2)			1(2)	1		
P1778-7-10	Joe	35		1(1)				1		

hat	cap	stockings	hose	shoes	boots	pumps	others
1							
							carried a variety of clothes which stole
							his clothes I can not describe
		1		1			sundry other clothes
							I do not know how to describe his clothes
	1						
1		1					
1							
1		1(2)		1			
							his clothes I do not remember
1							
1							
							dressed tolerably well
		1		1			
							had a variety of clothes
		1(1)		1			
							had a several changes of clothes
1				1			
							Country made clothing
							Country made coating
1							
(1)	(1)			(3)			
1							
12(1)	2(1)	9(3)		11(3)			

head covering		stockings		foot wear			others
hat	cap	stockings	hose	shoes	boots	pumps	
1				1			apparel of striped country cloth
1							several other clothes
	1						
1		1					jackcoat
		1		1			several other clothes
		1		1			

Date of Publish	name of slave	age							
P1778-7-10	Dick	36	1			1			
DH1778-7-10	Caesar	36							
DH1778-7-17		25	1		1(1)	1		1(1)	
P1778-8-21	Sam	27			1	1	1		
P1778-8-21	Tom	23		1	1		1		
P1778-8-21	Cupid	35		1	1		1		
P1778-8-21	Prince	18	1		1		1		
DH1778-10-9	Cyrus								
DH1778-10-19	Will							1	
DH1778-11-27	Daniel					1	1	1	
total			10(4)	3	8(1)	7(2)	12	4(1)	(1)

[1779年]

Date of Publish	name of slave	age	trade	upper clothes				lower clothes		suit
				jacket	waistcoat	shirt	coat	breeches	trousers	
DN1779-2-12	Tom	19		1				1		
DN1779-2-26	Tom			1		1		1		
DN1779-2-26		20								
DN1779-2-26		30-35								
DN1779-3-12	Will	23-24	cooper							
DN1779-3-19	Charles				2	1		1		
DN1779-4-2	Matt	25		1			1	1		
DN1779-4-2	Sufferer	31				1	1	1		
DN1779-5-1	Emanuel			1		1(1)	1	1		
	George	20				1(1)		1		
DN1779-5-22	Jack	34					1	1		
DN1779-5-22	George	19					1			
DN1779-6-12	Conner		sailor?	1		1			1	
DN1779-7-24	Frank	25				(1)				
P1779-7-3	Frank	40		(1)		1(2)	1(1)	(1)	1	
P1779-8-28		21				1	1	1		
P1779-10-30	Tom	40				1	1		1	
DN1779-10-9	Isaac			1		1	1	1		
DN1779-11-27	James	21					1			
P1779-11-27	Caesar									
DN1779-12-18	Phill				1		1	1		
DN1779-12-25	Francis		sailor				1	1(1)		
total				6(1)	3	10(5)	12(1)	12(2)	3	

							other clothes
							sundry clothes
1							
	1						other clothes
							other clothes, stole clothes
							his clothing I cannot describe
							Country made clothing
1		1		1			
5	2	4		4			

head covering		stockings		foot wear			others
hat	cap	stockings	hose	shoes	boots	pumps	
							some very good clothes
1							
							sundry other clothes
1				1			
	1			1			
							sundry other clothes
		(1)					
1		(1)					
1					1		
	1						
		2					
							homespun clothes such as Negroes usually wear in summer
1		1		1			
		1		1			
5	2	4(2)		4	1		

表3-2-3 逃亡奴隷広告に見る男子奴隷の被服の組み合わせ

[1767年]

	upper clothes				lower clothes		head covering		stocking		shoes		
	jacket	waistcoat	shirt	coat	breeches	trousers	hat	cap	stocking	hose	shoes	boots	pumps
1	1	1	1	1	1		1		1		1		
2		1		1	1		1		1		1		
3		1		1	1			1		1			
4		1	1		1								
5			1		1		1						
total	1	4	3	3	5	0	3	1	2	1	2		

[1768年]

	upper clothes				lower clothes		head covering		stocking		shoes		
	jacket	waistcoat	shirt	coat	breeches	trousers	hat	cap	stocking	hose	shoes	boots	pumps
1			1		1		1			1			1
2	1		1		1								1
3	1		2			1		1			2		
4	1				1		1						
5	1		1			1	1						
6	1		1			1	1						
7	1		1			1		1					
8	2		1		1								
9	1		1		1								
10	1		1		1								
11	1		1		1								
12	1		1		1								
13	1		1		1								
14	1			1	1								
15		1		1	1								
16	1				1								
total	15	1	12	3	12	4	4	2	0	1	2	0	2

[1769年]

	upper clothes				lower clothes		head covering		stocking		shoes		
	jacket	waistcoat	shirt	coat	breeches	trousers	hat	cap	stocking	hose	shoes	boots	pumps
1			1		1					1	1		
2	1			1	1				1				
3	1				1					1			
4	1		1	1	1		1	1					
5		1	1		1		1						
6		1	1			1	1						
7			1			1	1						
8			1			1	1						
9	1	1	1			1	1						
10				1	1		1						
11	1		1		1								
12			1		1								
13			1	1		1							
14			1	1		1							
15			1			1							
16		1		1	1								
17		1		1	1								

第3章　逃亡奴隷の着装情況―その数量的アプローチ―

18		1		1	1							
total	5	6	12	8	11	7	7	1	1	2	1	0	0

[1770年]

	upper clothes				lower clothes		head covering		stocking		shoes		
	jacket	waistcoat	shirt	coat	breeches	trousers	hat	cap	stocking	hose	shoes	boots	pumps
1		1	1		1		1		1		1		
2		1				1	1		1		1		
3	1		1	1	1		1				1		
4			1			1	1				1		
5			1		1		1					1	
6	1		1		1						1		
7	1		1		1						1		
8	1		1		1						1		
9	1	1			1		1						
10		1	1		1								
11	1		1			1	1						
12	1		1		1		1						
13			1			1	1						
14		2			1								
15	1			1	1								
16	1			1	1								
17	1		1		1								
18	1		1		1								
19		1		1	1								
20		1		1	1								
21					1								
22		1			1								
total	11	8	15	5	14	8	10	0	2	0	7	1	0

[1776年]

	upper clothes				lower clothes		head covering		stocking		shoes		
	jacket	waistcoat	shirt	coat	breeches	trousers	hat	cap	stocking	hose	shoes	boots	pumps
1		1	1	2	1		1		1		1		
2	1		1		1		1		1		1		
3		1	1		1				1		1		
4	1			1	1				1		1		
5	1					1			1		1		
6	1		1	1	1						1		
7	1				1						1		
8	1		1	1	1				1				1
9			1	1					1				
10			1	1	1								
11		1	1		1			1					
12	1		1		1								
13			1	2									
14			1	2									
15			1	2									
16			1	2									
17		1	1	1									
18		1		1									
19		1		1									

	jacket	waistcoat	shirt	coat	breeches	trousers	hat	cap	stocking	hose	shoes	boots	pumps
20		1		1	1								
21				1	1								
total	7	7	13	20	13	1	2	1	7	0	7	0	1

[1777年]

	upper clothes				lower clothes		head covering		stocking		shoes		
	jacket	waistcoat	shirt	coat	breeches	trousers	hat	cap	stocking	hose	shoes	boots	pumps
1			1	1	1		1		1		1		
2	1		2		1				1		1		
3	1				1				1		1		
4		1	1		1				1		1		
5		1	1	1		1			1		1		
6				1	1				1		1		
7				1	1				1		1		
8				1	1				1		1		
9	1		1	1	1		1				1		
10			1		1						1		
11	1			1		1			1				
12		1	1	1	1		1						
13		1	1		1		1						
14	1		1		1		1						
15	1		1		1		1						
16	1		1			1	1						
17			1		1		1						
18			1		1		1						
19			1		1		1						
20				1		1		1					
21	1		1		1								
22	1		1	1	1								
23	1		1		1								
24			1			1							
25			1			1							
26			1		1								
27		1		2	1								
28		1		2	1								
29	1			1	1								
30			2			1							
31	1				1								
32				1	1								
33				1	1								
total	13	6	23	17	25	8	10	1	9	0	10	0	0

[1778年]

	upper clothes				lower clothes		head covering		stocking		shoes		
	jacket	waistcoat	shirt	coat	breeches	trousers	hat	cap	stocking	hose	shoes	boots	pumps
1				1	1				1		1		
2	1			1	1				1		1		
3				1	1	1	1		1		1		
4	1		1	1			1						
5	1		1	1		1	1						
6	1		1		1								
7		1	1		1								

	jacket	waistcoat	shirt	coat	breeches	trousers	hat	cap	stocking	hose	shoes	boots	pumps
8		1	1		1								
9	1		1			1							
10	1			1	1								
11					1								
12	1				1								
13	1				1								
14	1				1		1						
15		1			1								
16		1		1	1			1					
17	1				1								
total	10	2	8	7	13	4	3	2	3	0	3	0	0

[1779年]

	upper clothes				lower clothes		head covering		stocking		shoes		
	jacket	waistcoat	shirt	coat	breeches	trousers	hat	cap	stocking	hose	shoes	boots	pumps
1			1	1	1		1					1	
2		1		1	1		1		1		1		
3			1		1				1		1		
4		1			1		1				1		
5			1		1			1			1		
6	1		1	1	1				2				
7			1	1		1	1						
8		2	1		1		1						
9	1		1	1	1								
10			1	1	1								
11	1		1			1							
12	1		1		1								
13			1	1			1	1					
14	1			1	1								
15	1				1								
total	6	3	10	10	12	3	5	2	4	0	4	1	0

表3-2-4　男子逃亡奴隷の被服の組み合わせの8パターン

	上衣	下衣	被り物	靴下	靴
AⅠ	■	■	■	■	■
AⅡ	■	■	■		■
AⅢ	■	■		■	■
AⅣ	■	■			■
BⅠ	■	■	■	■	
BⅡ	■	■	■		
BⅢ	■	■		■	
BⅣ	■	■			

表3-2-5　男子逃亡奴隷の被服の組み合わせ
（Aタイプの集計結果人数）

	AⅠ	AⅡ	AⅢ	AⅣ	total
1767-1770	5	5	1	4	15
1776-1779	5	4	13	3	25
total	10	9	14	7	40

（Aタイプの集計結果　％）

	AⅠ	AⅡ	AⅢ	AⅣ	total
1767-1770	8	8	2	7	25
1776-1779	6	5	15	3	29
total	7	6	9	5	27

（Bタイプの集計結果人数）

	BⅠ	BⅡ	BⅢ	BⅣ	total
1767-1770	2	14	2	27	45
1776-1779	0	16	1	47	64
total	2	30	3	74	109

（Bタイプの集計結果　％）

	BⅠ	BⅡ	BⅢ	BⅣ	total
1767-1770	3	23	3	45	74
1776-1779		18	1	53	72
total	1	20	2	50	73

4グループに分類した。
   Ⅰ　上衣＋下衣＋被り物＋靴下＋靴
   Ⅱ　上衣＋下衣＋被り物＋靴下
   Ⅲ　上衣＋下衣＋被り物＋靴
   Ⅳ　上衣＋下衣＋靴

　Ｂ　グループは靴の記載がない逃亡奴隷であり、着用している被服の組み合わせによって、次の4グループに分類した。
   Ⅰ　上衣＋下衣＋被り物＋靴下
   Ⅱ　上衣＋下衣＋被り物
   Ⅲ　上衣＋下衣＋靴下
   Ⅳ　上衣＋下衣

　ＡグループとＢグループの集計結果は、人数とパーセンテージに分けて、表3-2-5の一覧表にまとめた。これらのデータの分析は、本節の総括において、一括して行なう。
　次に、図3-2-2①から図3-2-2⑧は、上記のAⅠからAⅣ、およびBⅠからBⅣに属する男子の逃亡奴隷の服装を逃亡広告における被服描写に基づいて、筆者の下絵を基に、橋本裕佳子さんに描いてもらったイラストである。この描写の基礎資料である逃亡広告を併記した。また、被験者数と該当の奴隷数および被験者全体に占める割合を表に示した。
　また、図3-2-3では、今後の考察を容易にするために、これらのイラストから2体を選んで衣服名を示した。図3-2-4はＡグループとＢグループのイラストを比較するためにひとまとめにしたものである。
　次に表3-2-6は逃亡時に着用していた上衣の枚数を示したものである。また、表3-2-7は、上衣の着用枚数の集計結果を示している。
　最後にブリーチズ（breeches）とトラウザーズ（trousers）の割合は、表3-2-8に見るように、3対1である。

2．小　括

　以上により、男子の黒人奴隷が逃亡時に着用していた被服の種類の組み合わせの実態が明らかとなった。これらのデータ分析から次の点を指摘しておきたい。
（1）ＡⅠ（帽子から靴までそろっているタイプ）は149人中10人（6.7％）と極めて少ない。
（2）逃亡奴隷広告の逃亡者の被服の記載に靴の記載があるケースは、149人中40人（26.8％）、つまり4分の1強である。その要因として、a．靴をもっていない、b．靴が痛くてはけない、c．靴が古くなってはけない、という三つのケースが考えられる。奴隷の靴の形、はきごこち、素材、耐久性は今後の研究課題である。

図3-2-2①A Ⅰ ［upper clothes］＋［lower clothes］＋［head covering］＋［stocking］＋［shoes］

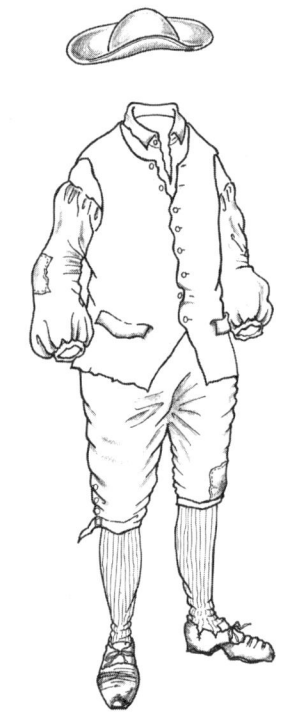

Virginia Gazette (Purdie & Dixon), April 19, 1770.

₤.20 Reward.

RUN away from the subscriber, on Monday night the 9th instant, three Negro men, two of them slaves, viz. NED, about 5 feet 8 inches high, 21 years of age, of a yellow complexion, a likely well made fellow; <u>his usual clothing an osnabrug shirt, dark gray fearnought waistcoat, cotton breeches, coarse yarn stockings, bad shoes, and a felt hat. He also took other clothes, but what not yet known.</u> FRANK, a foreign Negro, a very good cook, says he was born in the Spanish West Indies, speaks bad English, as also French, Spanish, and some Dutch, near the same height of Ned, about 30 years of age, of a yellow complexion, with little or no beard, and has several remarkable wounds on his body, and a large one near his throat; he is clothed in blue plains, osnabrug shirt, and felt hat, as also a pair of red flannel muffs, and a red cap. HENRY COOKE, a free Negro, born in Gloucester county . . . It is thought they took with them a Negro fellow belonging to the estate of the late Major William Tate, middle aged, about 5 feet 6 inches high, well set, bow legged, of a dark copper complexion, an old offender in this way, and a few years past advertised in the Maryland and Pennsylvania Gazettes by William Tate, deceased, by virtue of which he was taken up near the head of the bay, within a few miles of the Pennsylvania government. They took with them a yawl of about 18 feet keel, London clinch work, painted white to her gunwales, two good sails, rudder, and two new pine oars. The 20 l. reward, or 5 l. for each, will be paid if taken in any other colony; but if taken in Virginia only 12 l. or 3 l. for each.

WILLIAM FLOOD.

WESTMORELAND,
April 12, 1770.

	numbers	total	%
1767-1770	5	60	8.3
1776-1779	5	89	5.6
total	10	149	6.7

Windley, *op. cit.*, 80-81

図3-2-2②A Ⅱ ［upper clothes］＋［lower clothes］＋［head covering］＋［shoes］

Virginia Gazette (Dixon & Hunter), March 14, 1777.

HANOVER, March 1, 1777.

RUN away from the Subscriber on the 3d of February, at Night, WILL, a Negro Man, by Trade a Carpenter, of a yellow Complexion, middle Statute, well set, flat nosed, and has lost one of his upper fore Teeth; <u>had on when he went away white Virginia Jacket and Breeches, Country made Linen Shirt, striped Virginia Cloth Wrappers, common Negro Shoes, old Beaver Hat, with a small Brim, and carried with him a Dutch Blanket almost new, a Pair of old black Lasting Breeches, and a Shirt of the same Linen of the one he had on.</u> I expect he is either lurking about Mr. Braxton Bird's in King and Queen, of whom I purchased him, or Mr. Corbin's in Middlesex, where his Mother lives. He is a cunning sensible Fellow, well acquainted in many Parts of the Country, and is very capable of telling a plausible Story. I will give 5 l. Reward to any Person who will secure the said Slave, so that I get him again, and reasonable Expenses if brought Home.

DANIEL TRUEHEART.

	numbers	total	%
1767-1770	5	60	8.3
1776-1779	4	89	5.6
total	9	149	6.7

Windley, *op. cit.*, 181

図3-2-2③AⅢ ［upper clothes］＋［lower clothes］＋［stocking］＋［shoes］

Virginia Gazette (Purdie), January 17, 1777.

RUN away from the subscriber, near Bevil's bridge in Amelia county, the 27th of August last, a Virrginia /sic/ born negro lad named HARRY, but is usually called HAL. He is about 15 years old, and is slightly pitted with the smallpox. He took with him a light coloured frieze coat, striped waistcoat, trousers of tow and cotton, a shirt of cotton, and several other clothes, shoes, stockings, &c. He is capable of being a complete waiting man, both as attendant in a house, and a manager of horses, to which employment he has been put for some time, at mr. Wright's store in Cumberland county, and at mr. James Cooke's ordinary (of whom I bought him) in Amelia. I have reason to expect that he is with mr. John Chambers in Buckingham county, and that he will use every effort in his power to detain him from me. Whoever will bring the said lad to me shall have 3 l. reward; and I do hereby forewarn the said Chambers, and all others, from entertaining the said negro.

JOHN FORD.

	numbers	total	%
1767-1770	1	60	1.7
1776-1779	13	89	14.6
total	14	149	9.4

Windley, op. cit., 255-256

図3-2-2④AⅣ ［upper clothes］＋［lower clothes］＋［shoes］

Virginia Gazette (Rind), September 29, 1768.

RUN away from the subscriber, living in Culpeper, the 12th of September, a Negro fellow named WILL, about 25 years of age, 5 feet 6 inches high, and a little bow legged; he is very cunning, and will pretend he is a freeman, as he attempted the same thing about 3 years ago. He had on when he went away, a yellowish colour'd Negro cotton jacket, country linen shirt and breeches, and a pair of new pumps. As he will likely offer himself to some vessel, all masters of ships are cautioned not to take him. Whoever conveys him to me in Culpeper, or to Mr. Joseph Holladay, inspector in Fredericksburg, shall receive TWO POUNDS reward.

THOMAS GRAVES.

	numbers	total	%
1767-1770	4	60	6.7
1776-1779	3	89	3.4
total	7	149	4.7

Windley, op. cit., 291

図3-2-2⑤B I ［upper clothes］＋［lower clothes］＋［head covering］＋［stocking］

Virginia Gazette (Rind), March 12, 1767.

ON the 13th of February, run away from the Subscriber, a Negro Boy named MOSES. <u>He had on an old Claret coloured Coat, with a brown Cape and Cuffs, a brown Waistcoat, Cotton Breeches, Plaid hose, and a Jocky Cap.</u> He carried away with him, a black horse about four Feet five Inches high, a Bridle and Saddle, a Male Pillion, a Portmanteau, and 3 Pair of old Breeches in it. Whoever contrives me the said Boy to Aylett's Warehouses, shall have a Reward of FORTY SHILLINGS.
JOHN AYLETT.

	numbers	total	%
1767-1770	2	60	3.3
1776-1779	0	89	0
total	2	149	1.3

Windley, op. cit., 283

図3-2-2⑥B II ［upper clothes］＋［lower clothes］＋［head covering］

Virginia Gazette (Dixon & Hunter), November 1, 1776.

Five Pounds Reward.

RUN away from Mr. Peter Le Poole, in Charlestown, South Carolina, in June last, a NEGRO FELLOW named <u>ELIJAH</u>, of a yellow Complexion, is Virginia born, about 5 Feet 10 or 11 Inches high, and about 22 or 23 Years of Age, by Trade a Blacksmith, and an excellent Workman at that Business. <u>He had on, when he went away, a Scarlet Camblet Waistcoat, Buckskin Breeches almost new, an Osnabrug Shirt, and a Leather Jockey Cap.</u> It is supposed, as he is an artful sensible Fellow, that he will endeavour to pass for a free Man; but all Persons are hereby forbid to harbour him on any Pretence whatsoever, as any Person so offending may depend on the severest Prosecution. The above Reward of FIVE POUNDS Currency will be given to any Person that will apprehend and deliver the said Fellow to the

Subscriber, in Hanover.
RICHARD BURNLEY.

	numbers	total	%
1767-1770	14	60	23.3
1776-1779	16	89	18.0
total	30	149	20.1

Windley, op. cit., 178-179

図3-2-2⑦BⅢ ［upper clothes］＋［lower clothes］＋「stocking］

Virginia Gazette (Purdie & Dixon), November 9, 1769.

　RUN away from the subscriber in Chesterfield county, a mulatto man, about 17 years old, very well grown, named JOE, but since his departure has changed his name to NED SCOTT, and passes for a freeman; had on when he went away an old Virginia cloth coat, of a bluish colour, nankeen breeches, white yarn stockings, and the hair on the top of his head cut very close, but very long about the neck, and one of his legs full of knots. Whoever takes up the said slave, and brings him to me, shall receive TEN POUNDS reward paid by

JOHN COBBS.

　N.B. Whoever takes up the said slave is desired to secure him very well, or else he will make his escape.

	numbers	total	%
1767-1770	2	60	3.3
1776-1779	1	89	1.1
total	3	149	2.0

Windley, *op. cit.*, 75

図3-2-2⑧BⅣ ［upper clothes］＋［lower clothes］

Virginia Gazette (Purdie), August 21, 1778.

　RUN away from the Richmond ropewalk, in May last, a negro man named Prince, about 18 years of age, five feet eight inches high, very black, has holes in his ears, a wart behind his left ear, and has had a cut on his left great toe. He was clothed with a coarse linen shirt, cotton breeches and coarse yarn jacket. He was taken by one Mr. Francis Ross in Elizabeth City county, and got away from the person that was bringing him home, last Friday week, at Richardson's ordinary, in New Kent county, and it is supposed he took the Newcastle road. He took with him a brass barrelled holster pistol from thence. I will give thirty dollars reward for securing him in any jail in this state, or I will pay what the law allows for bringing him to this place, likewise five dollars reward for delivering me the said holster pistol.

JAMES MARSDEN.

	numbers	total	%
1767-1770	27	60	45.0
1776-1779	47	89	52.8
total	74	149	49.7

Windley, *op. cit.*, 276

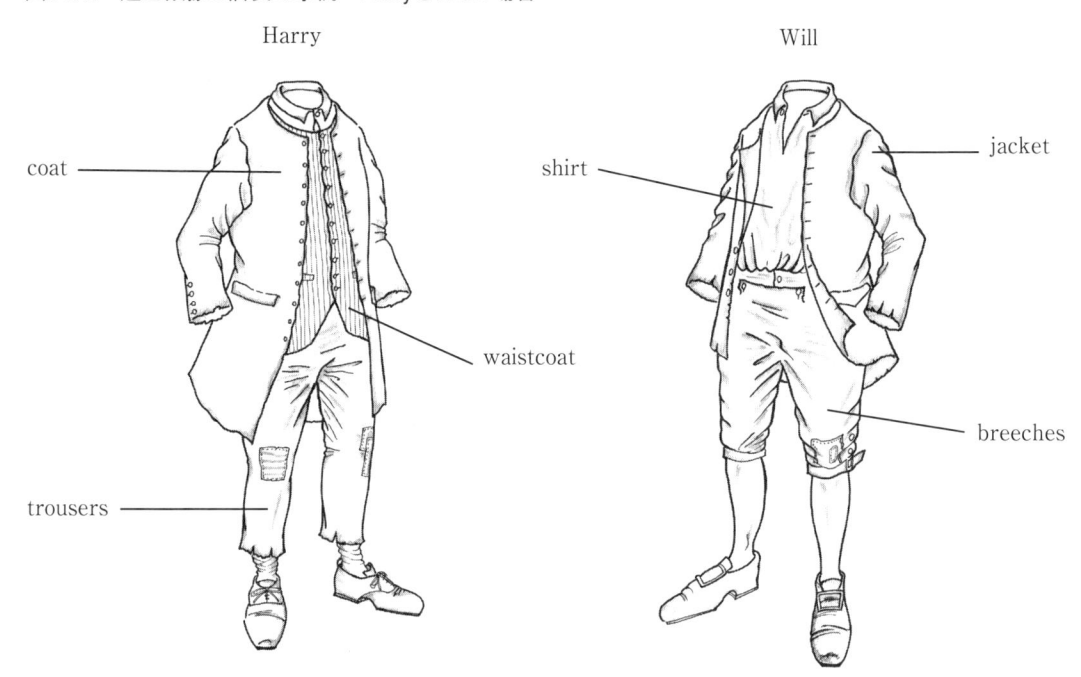

図3-2-3　逃亡奴隷の着装の事例—HarryとWillの場合—

(3) BⅡ（上衣と下衣を着て、帽子を被っている）は149人中30人（21.6％）、つまり5分の1である。

(4) BⅣ（上衣と下衣のみを着ている）は149人中74人（49.7％）である。しかも逃亡時に着用していた上衣の枚数が2枚以下の逃亡奴隷は、1767年から1770年、および、1776年から1779年の8年間に逃亡した被験者の80パーセントを占めていることが明らかとなった。プランターが奴隷に年1回、衣服を支給していたが、逃亡奴隷は支給された最低限の衣服を着用して逃亡するか、プランテーションで衣服を盗んで携行するか、盗んだ衣服に着替えて逃亡するか、のいずれかであった。逃亡広告にはこのような情報が大変多く記載されている。

(5) 下衣については、ブリーチズ（breeches）とトラウザーズ（trousers）の着用の割合が3対1であることが明らかとなった。この時代には家内奴隷も農園の奴隷もきわめて動きにくい、機能性に乏しいブリーチズをあてがわれていることが多かった。リンダ・バウムガルテン（Linda Baumgarten）によると、ズボンは8人のうち、約1人に見られたというが、本研究では4人に1人が長ズボンをはいていたとの結果がでた。さらに、期間を広げて逃亡奴隷広告を調べるべきである。長ズボンの着用はアメリカ独立革命後、増加していくのであるが、その具体的様相の考察は今後の研究課題である。

第3章　逃亡奴隷の着装情況—その数量的アプローチ—　　101

図3-2-4　逃亡奴隷広告に見る着装の8パターン

AⅠ　　　　　AⅡ　　　　　AⅢ　　　　　AⅣ

BⅠ　　　　　BⅡ　　　　　BⅢ　　　　　BⅣ

表3-2-6 男子逃亡奴隷の上衣の着用枚数

[1767年]

1767	upper clothes				total
	jacket	waistcoat	shirt	coat	
1	1	1	1	1	4
2		1	1		2
3			1		1
4		1		1	2
5		1		1	2
total	1	4	3	3	

[1768年]

1768	upper clothes				total
	jacket	waistcoat	shirt	coat	
1	1		1		2
2	1		1		2
3	1		1		2
4	1		1		2
5	1		1		2
6	1		1		2
7	1		1		2
8	1		1		2
9	1		1		2
10	2		1		3
11	1		2		3
12	1				1
13	1			1	2
14	1				1
15				1	1
16		1		1	2
total	15	1	12	3	

[1769年]

1768	upper clothes				total
	jacket	waistcoat	shirt	coat	
1	1	1	1		3
2	1		1	1	3
3	1		1		2
4		1	1		2
5		1	1		2
6			1		1
7			1		1
8			1		1
9			1		1
10			1	1	2
11			1	1	2
12			1		1
13	1			1	2
14	1				1
15		1		1	2
16		1		1	2
17		1		1	2
18				1	1
total	5	6	12	8	

[1770年]

1770	upper clothes				total
	jacket	waistcoat	shirt	coat	
1	1	1	1		3
2	1		1	1	3
3	1		1		2
4	1		1		2
5	1		1		2
6	1		1		2
7	1		1		2
8	1		1		2
9	1		1		2
10		1	1		2
11		1	1		2
12			1		1
13			1		1
14			1		1
15			1		1
16	1			1	2
17	1			1	2
18		1			1
19		1		1	2
20		1		1	2
21		2			2
22					
total	11	8	15	5	

[1776年]

1776	upper clothes				total
	jacket	waistcoat	shirt	coat	
1	1		1		2
2	1		1	1	3
3	1		1	1	3
4	1		1		2
5		1	1	2	4
6		1	1		2
7		1	1		2
8		1	1	1	3
9			1	1	2
10			1	2	3
11			1	2	3
12			1	2	3
13			1	2	3
14	1			1	2
15	1				1
16	1				1
17		1		1	2
18		1		1	2
19		1		1	2

				1	1
20				1	1
21				1	1
total	7	7	13	20	

[1777年]

1777	upper clothes				total
	jacket	waistcoat	shirt	coat	
1	1		1	1	3
2	1		1	1	3
3	1		1		2
4	1		1		2
5	1		1		2
6	1		1		2
7	1		1	1	3
8	1		1		2
9		1	1		2
10		1	1	1	3
11		1	1	1	3
12		1	1		2
13			1		1
14			1		1
15			1		1
16			1		1
17			1		1
18			1		1
19			1		1
20	1		2		3
21			2		2
22	1				1
23	1			1	2
24	1			1	2
25	1				1
26			1		1
27		1		2	3
28		1		2	3
29				1	1
30				1	1
31				1	1
32				1	1
33				1	1
total	13	6	23	17	

[1778年]

1778	upper clothes				total
	jacket	waistcoat	shirt	coat	
1				1	1
2	1			1	2
3				1	1
4	1		1	1	3
5	1		1	1	3
6			1	1	2
7		1	1		2
8		1	1		2
9	1		1		2
10	1			1	2
11					
12	1				1
13	1				1
14	1				1
15			1		1
16			1	1	2
17					
total	10	2	8	7	

[1779年]

1779	upper clothes				total
	jacket	waistcoat	shirt	coat	
1	1		1	1	3
2	1		1	1	3
3	1		1		2
4	1		1		2
5		2	1		3
6			1	1	2
7			1		1
8			1	1	2
9			1	1	2
10			1	1	2
11	1			1	2
12	1				1
13		1		1	2
14				1	1
15				1	1
total	6	3	10	10	

表3-2-7 男子逃亡奴隷の上衣の着用枚数年次別一覧

	1 piece	2 pieces	3 pieces	4 pieces
1767	1	3	0	1
1768	3	11	2	0
1769	7	9	2	0
1770	4	11	2	0
1776	4	8	7	1
1777	15	10	8	0
1778	7	7	2	0
1779	4	8	3	0
total	45	67	26	2
%	32	48	19	1

表3-2-8 逃亡奴隷広告に見るブリーチズとトラウザーズの数

	breeches	trousers
1767	5	0
1768	12	4
1769	11	7
1770	14	8
1776	13	1
1777	25	8
1778	13	4
1779	12	3
total	105	35

第3節　ヴァージニア・クロスの特徴[14]

1．ヴァージニア・クロスの定義づけ

(1) ヴァージニア・クロス生産のはじまり

　ヴァージニア・クロスは革命期の逃亡した使用人や奴隷や職業放棄者の記述に頻繁に登場する。また、18世紀の旅行日誌には、この布地の生産に関する記録が見られる。本項では先行研究や織物に関する文献および18世紀の旅行日誌に基づいて、ヴァージニア・クロスの生産がいつ頃から、どのようにして行なわれていたのか、という問題の考察を通じて、ヴァージニア・クロスの定義づけを行なう。布の内地生産は1763年の航海法や1760年代の様々な税法の施行後は特に愛国者や立法団体によって、国内の様々な地域で推進されていた。

　ヴァージニアの布地製造は17世紀に遡る。1750年代までには、ヴァージニア・クロスという用語は確実に用いられるようになっていた。それを裏付ける記録はヴァージニアを訪れたアンドリュー・バーナビー（Andrew Burnaby）牧師の1759年の旅行日誌に見られる。彼は日誌の中で、ここの住民は「一般に自分達で着用する衣服用の一種のコットン布を作っており、彼等の地名からその名前をつけている[15]」と述べている。

　ドロシー・F.マッコム（Dorothy F. McCombs）によれば、18世紀にはヴァージニア・クロスは、「主にコットン製であるが、山岳地帯の西では、僅かにウールやリネンを混ぜることもあった[16]」という。

　しかし、ヴァージニア・クロスに関する多くの記録に記述された繊維のなかでは、コットンが目立つ。例えばジョン・ハロワー（John Harrower）は、1775年12月6日の書面で「私の思い通りに、お前と私の子供達が今なお、別々に着れるようにと願い、綿布を[17]」織るのにコットンを紡がせるため、代金を奴隷の女に支払ったと記録している。

　また J. ハロワーは1776年2月23日の日誌で、プランテーションの二人の奴隷がコットンとウールの両方を「31日間の労働で6ポンドのウールと8.5ポンドのコットンをポンド当り約5ヤードの長さで紡いだ[18]」と記録している。

(2) ヴァージニア・クロスの定義づけ

　これらの資料からも裏付けられるように、ヴァージニア・クロスはその繊維が何であれ、ヴァージニアで生産されていた布地を指すものと見なすことができる。アメリカの服飾研究者もヴァージニアで生産されていた国内産の布地は、その繊維がコットンであれ、ウールであれ、亜麻であれ、ヴァージニア・クロスと呼ばれていた、との同一見解である[19]。

　以上の考察から、ヴァージニア・クロスは輸入織物と区別するために、ヴァージニアで製造された織物であると定義づけることができる。

表3-3-1 逃亡奴隷広告に見るヴァージニア・クロスに関する記載

年 Year	新聞〈発行者〉 Newspaper(Publisher)	日付 Date	ヴァージニア・クロスに関する記載 Description of Virginia cloth
1767	VG(P)	19-Mar	・two Virginia cotton shirts
		10-Sep	・a Virginia cotton shirt
		19-Mar	・two pair of Virginia yarn stockings
		19-Mar	・pair of Virginia copperas breeches
		28-May	・a pair of Virginia cotton sheets
1776	VG(D&H)	08-Nov	・2 Virginia Linen Shirts, one of them very coarse
		27-Dec	・Virginia knit Stockings
	VG(P)	02-Feb	・they are clad chiefly [sic] in Virginia cloth
		05-Apr	・he has his new waistcoat and breeches, they were of Virginia wool and cotton cloth of kersey weaving
		10-May	・a Virginia cotton shirt, striped Virginia cloth jacket and breeches, striped Virginia cloth wrappers
		31-May	・and is dressed in Virginia cloth
		21-Jun	・their upper and under coats of Virginia cloth, striped with black wool.
		06-Sep	・blue Virginia cloth breeches
		08-Nov	・a black Virginia cloth jacket
1785	VG & WA (N&P, N) VG or AA (H)	28-May	・a Virginia cloth suit, single wove, mixed with blue
		20-Aug	・a Virginia cloth coat of an olive colour, with red cape and cuffs
		16-Apr	・pair of breeches of fine dark mixed plain wove Virginia cloth
		09-Jul	・a pair of dark coloured Virginia cloth breeches, patched on the knees
		09-Jul	・a pair of Virginia cloth breeches
		15-Sep	・two Virginia cloth jacket and petticoats

VG=*Virginia Gazette*, WA=*Weekly Advertiser*, AA=*American Advertiser*, P=Purdie, DH=Dixon&Hunter
N=Nicolson, P=Prentis, H=Hays

2. 逃亡奴隷広告に見るヴァージニア・クロス製の被服

　逃亡奴隷広告における被服描写が、彼らの被服着用に関する歴史事実を確認するための信頼性の高い史料であることは、第2章で述べた。この点を踏まえて、1766年から1789年の時期の逃亡奴隷広告に見るヴァージニア・クロス製、つまりヴァージニアで製造された織物製の被服の事例のなかから、1767年、1776年および1785年のデータを抽出し一覧表（表3-3-1）にした。表3-3-1作成の目的は、1761年、1776年および1785年にはVirginia clothの登場回数が比較的多いことにある。、その社会背景については第5節で述べることとしよう。ヴァージニア・クロスとはどのような用途に用いられた、どのような特性を備えた素材であるのか。このような疑問をいだきつつ、逃亡奴隷広告に忠実に考察を進めよう。

　はじめに、1766年から1789年にわたるヴァージニア・クロス製の被服の全事例をもとに被服の種類（表3-3-2）および色・柄（表3-3-3、表3-3-4）について分類し、一覧表にした。色の項目には柄もの（ストライプおよびチェック）は含まれていない。被服の種類についてはそれぞれの被服が全体に占める割合を、構成比の項目にパーセントで表した。

　その結果、次のことが明らかとなった。

表3-3-2 逃亡奴隷広告に見るヴァージニア・クロス製の被服の種類（1766～1789年）

服種 Type of Clothes	着数 Number of Items	構成比(%) Ratio (%)
breeches	30	20.1
jacket	27	18.1
coat	26	17.4
waistcoat	19	12.8
shirts	13	8.7
suit	7	4.7
petticoat	6	4.0
stockings	5	3.4
trousers	2	1.3
gown	2	1.3
wrapper	2	1.3
jackcoat	1	0.7
その他 / others	9	6.0

表3-3-3 逃亡奴隷広告に見るヴァージニア・クロス製の被服の色・柄（1766～1789年）

色 Color	件数 Number of Items	構成比(%) Ratio (%)
stripe	27	42.2
white	10	15.6
dark	5	7.8
blue(bluish), pale blue	4	6.3
brown	4	6.3
copperas	2	3.1
check	2	3.1
blue & white mixed	2	3.1
black	1	1.6
darkish gray	1	1.6
purple	1	1.6
lightish colour	1	1.6
green	1	1.6
white mixed	1	1.6
snuff colour	1	1.6
olive colour	1	1.6

表3-3-4 逃亡奴隷広告に見るヴァージニア・クロスのストライプの種類（1766～1789年）

ストライプの種類 Type of Stripe	件数 Number of Items	構成比(%) Ratio (%)
striped	17	60.7
narrow striped	3	10.7
white striped	2	7.1
copperas & white stripe	1	3.6
striped with black yarn	1	3.6
striped with black wool	1	3.6
striped with copperas & wool	1	3.6
black striped	1	3.6
striped with blue	1	3.6

（1）被服の種類について（表3-3-2、図3-3-1）

被服の種類の表3-3-2に見るように、男子服においてはヴァージニア・クロス製の服種の20.1パーセントがブリーチズ（半ズボン）、18.1パーセントがジャケット、17.4パーセントがコート、12.8パーセントがウェストコート、8.7パーセントがシャツという順であり、17.4パーセントがその他の服種に占められている。

女子服においては、ヴァージニア・クロス製の服種の4.0パーセントがペティコート、1.3パーセントがガウンという状態である。もっとも逃亡奴隷数としては、女性は男性よりもはるかに少ないため、女子服のデータは男子服に比べて、ずっと少ない。女子服のアイテムの代表的なものは、ジャケットやショート・ガウン、ペティコート、サック、ガウンである。ズボンや半ズボンは支給されていない点は注目したい。

（2）色・柄について（表3-3-3、表3-3-4、図3-3-2、図3-3-3）

色については、約55パーセントが無地またはミックス・カラーであり、約42パーセントがストライプである。チェックが3パーセントで2件見られる。ス

第3章　逃亡奴隷の着装情況―その数量的アプローチ―　　107

図3-3-1　逃亡奴隷広告に見るヴァージニア・クロス製の被服の種類（1766～1789年）

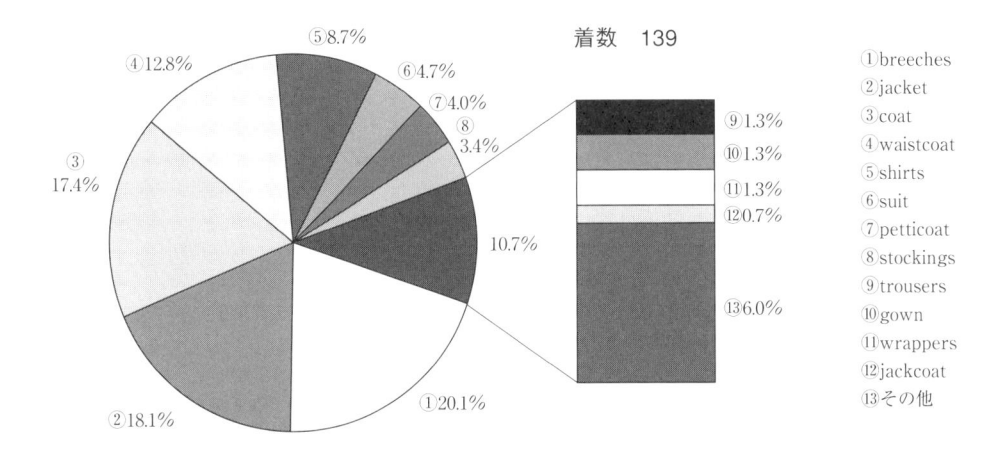

着数　139

⑤8.7%
⑥4.7%
⑦4.0%
⑧3.4%
⑨1.3%
⑩1.3%
⑪1.3%
⑫0.7%
⑬6.0%
④12.8%
③17.4%
②18.1%
①20.1%
⑬10.7%

①breeches
②jacket
③coat
④waistcoat
⑤shirts
⑥suit
⑦petticoat
⑧stockings
⑨trousers
⑩gown
⑪wrappers
⑫jackcoat
⑬その他

図3-3-2　逃亡奴隷広告に見るヴァージニア・クロス製の被服の色・柄の構成比（1766～1789年）

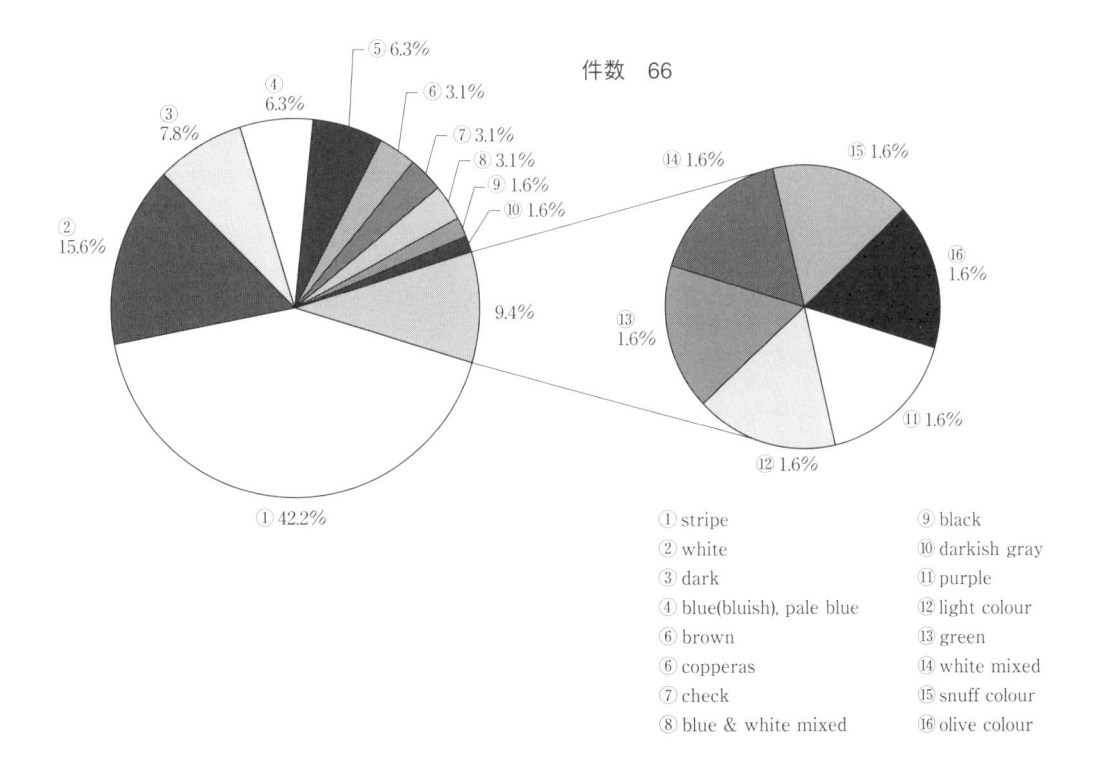

件数　66

⑤6.3%
④6.3%
⑥3.1%
⑦3.1%
⑧3.1%
⑨1.6%
⑩1.6%
③7.8%
②15.6%
①42.2%
⑨9.4%
⑭1.6%
⑮1.6%
⑬1.6%
⑯1.6%
⑪1.6%
⑫1.6%

①stripe
②white
③dark
④blue(bluish), pale blue
⑤brown
⑥copperas
⑦check
⑧blue & white mixed
⑨black
⑩darkish gray
⑪purple
⑫light colour
⑬green
⑭white mixed
⑮snuff colour
⑯olive colour

図3-3-3　逃亡奴隷広告に見るヴァージニア・クロス製の被服のストライプの種類（1766～1789年）

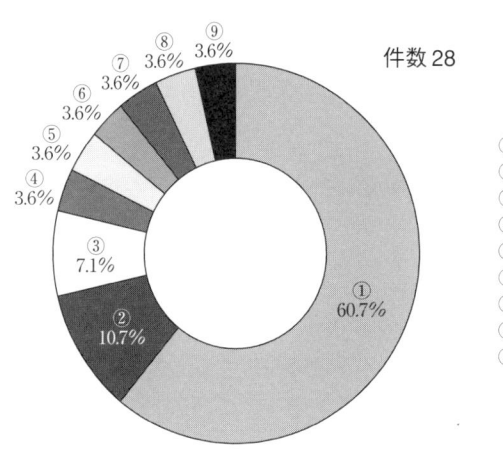

件数 28

① striped　60.7%
② narrow striped　10.7%
③ white striped　7.1%
④ copperas & white stripe　3.6%
⑤ striped with black yarn　3.6%
⑥ striped with black wool　3.6%
⑦ striped with copperas & wool　3.6%
⑧ black striped　3.6%
⑨ striped with blue　3.6%

トライプには幅と色の組み合わせに多様性が見られる。

以上の統計を念頭において、次に逃亡奴隷広告における逃亡奴隷の被服描写から、ヴァージニア・クロス製の被服を着用して逃亡した具体的な事例を二つ挙げる。

Virginia Gazette（Purdie），May 10, 1776. Supplement.[20]
　彼の衣服はヴァージニア・コットンのシャツ、ストライプのヴァージニア・クロスのジャケットとブリーチズ、ヴァージニア・クロスの部屋着および古びた靴である。

Virginia Gazette（Rind），November 19, 1772.[21]
　ミラという名の黒人の女は、丈の短いストライプのヴァージニア・クロス製のガウンとペティコートとオズナブルグ製のシフトを着て、ボンネットをかぶっていた。

さて、以上の考察からヴァージニア・クロスの用途と色・柄の特徴が具体的となり、素材をイメージすることがある程度、可能となってきた。

第4節　対照資料としてのオズナブルグ

そこで、次に上記のヴァージニア・クロスの特徴を示すために、1766年から1789年の逃亡奴隷広告に見られるオズナブルグ製の被服を対照資料としてとりあげ、その描写から、被服の種類、色について分類・分析する。オズナブルグは安価で粗目であるが、丈夫な亜麻布で、下層階級によって

表3-4-1 逃亡奴隷広告に見るオズナブルグ製の被服の種類
（1766〜1789年）

服種 Type of Clothes	着数 Number of Items	構成比(%) Ratio(%)
shirt	114	69.9
trousers	19	11.7
shift	8	4.9
breeches	7	4.3
jacket	3	1.8
petticoat	3	1.8
coat	2	1.2
frock	1	0.6
overall	1	0.6
suit	1	0.6
bonnet	1	0.6
その他/others	3	1.8

表3-4-2 逃亡奴隷広告に見るオズナブルグ製の被服の色
（1766〜1789年）

色 Color	件数 Number of Items	構成比(%) Ratio(%)
white	6	4.0
No Descriptions	157	96.0

用いられた素材である。元はドイツのオズナブリュグで作られていた。逃亡奴隷広告ではコットンに次いで頻出している。表2-3-2ではコットン（214回）、オズナブルグ（174回）、ヴァージニア・クロス（140回）の順となっている。そのようなわけで、オズナブルグをヴァージニア・クロスの対照資料にした。

当該の広告から抽出したオズナブルグ製の被服のデータを種類（表3-4-1）および色（表3-4-2）について分類し、一覧表に表した。被服の種類については、それぞれの種類が全体に占める割合を構成比の項目に、パーセント（%）で表した。

その結果、次のことが明らかとなった。

1. 被服の種類について （表3-4-1、図3-4-1）

表3-4-1に見るように、男子服においてはオズナブルグ製の被服の種類の69.9パーセントがシャツであり、長ズボンがわずか11.7パーセント、ブリーチズはさらに少なく、4.3パーセントである。ジャケットは1.8パーセント、スーツ、フロックおよびオーバーオールは、いずれも0.6パーセントと僅少である。女子服においてはシフトが4.9パーセント、ペティコートが1.8パーセント、ボンネットが0.6パーセントである。

ヴァージニア・クロスはブリーチズやジャケット、コート、ウェストコート、シャツといった奴隷に支給された基本的な服種全般に用いられていたのに対して、オズナブルグは主としてシャツに多用されていたことが明白である。

図 3-4-1　逃亡奴隷広告に見るオズナブルグ製の被服の種類（1766 〜 1789 年）

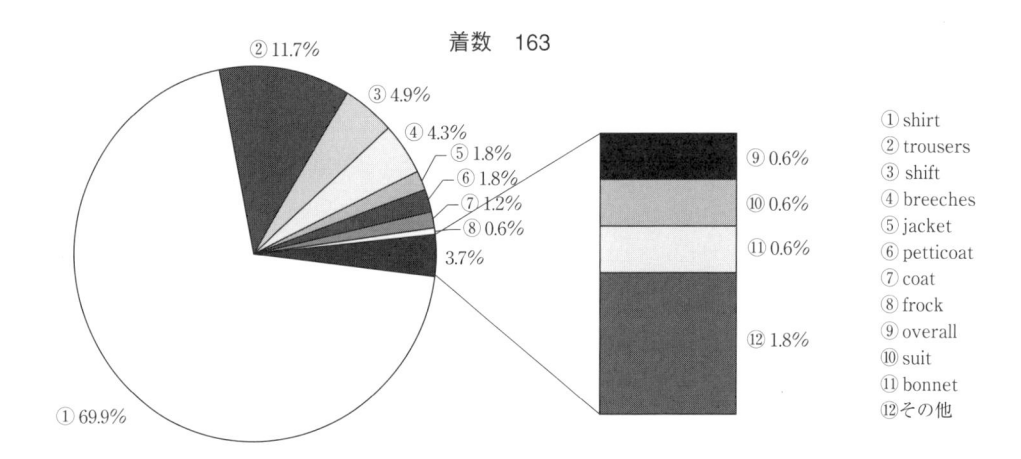

着数　163

① 69.9%
② 11.7%
③ 4.9%
④ 4.3%
⑤ 1.8%
⑥ 1.8%
⑦ 1.2%
⑧ 0.6%
⑨ 0.6%
⑩ 0.6%
⑪ 0.6%
⑫ 1.8%
3.7%

① shirt
② trousers
③ shift
④ breeches
⑤ jacket
⑥ petticoat
⑦ coat
⑧ frock
⑨ overall
⑩ suit
⑪ bonnet
⑫ その他

図 3-4-2　逃亡奴隷広告に見るオズナブルグ製の被服の色の構成比（1766 〜 1789 年）

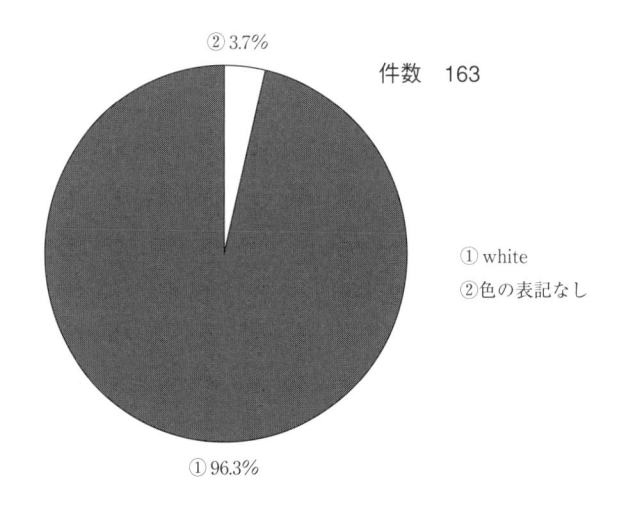

件数　163

① 96.3%
② 3.7%

① white
② 色の表記なし

2. 色について（表3-4-2、図3-4-2）

　逃亡奴隷広告に見られるオズナブルグの色は96パーセントは表記がない。残りの4パーセントは白である。色についても多様な色合いのヴァージニア・クロスとは対照的である。ブライヤン・P.ハワード（Bryan Paul Howard）はオズナブルグについて「アメリカ植民地で見られるオズナブルグの大半は、文献では、無漂白で、染色されず、自然の茶色の、目の粗いリネンか麻の布と一般に捉えられている[22]」と述べている。色の表記がない96パーセントのオズナブルグはこの種のリネンではないかと推察される。

　以上のオズナブルグに関するデータの分析結果はヴァージニア・クロスの場合とは全く対照的で

第5節　逃亡奴隷広告に見る被服素材の年次変化

　逃亡奴隷広告には67種の被服素材が登場する（表2-3-1、表2-3-2）。表3-5-1は逃亡奴隷広告（1766～1785）に見られる被服素材のうち、上位6種を輸入品（Cotton, Osnabrug, Cloth, Linen, Felt）とヴァージニア・クロス（Virginia cloth）に区分し、A項目には登場アイテム数を年度別に示し、B項目には輸入品とヴァージニア・クロスの比率を示したものである。

　素材名は広告に記載されている表記をそのまま採用していることをお断りしておく。

　上記の素材のうちクロス（Cloth）は、今日では布という概念が一般的であるが、B. P. ハワードによると、「逃亡奴隷広告に見られるClothという用語は、その生地が実はウール地と考えられていた[23]」とのことである。

　図3-5-1は輸入品との比率を棒グラフで表したものである。

　図3-5-1では、1766年からヴァージニア・クロスの生産量が伸び、1767年にはピークとなり、それ以降は下り坂となる。その後、1775年から上り坂となり1779年にやや下って、1782年はピークとなり、再び下がる。そこで、このような生産量の変化の原因を第1章で述べた歴史的背景を振り返りながらさぐってみたいと思う。

　1765年は印紙法が出され、重税が課された年である。植民地人は「代表なければ課税なし」とうたい抵抗した。その結果、印紙税法は発効後、半年にして撤回された。1767年にはタウンゼンド諸法が発布された。この結果、航海法規制の効果があがり、植民地史上、はじめて関税収入が徴収税を上回るほどになった。これに対して再び植民地人の反抗運動が起こり、イギリス製品不輸入協定が全国的に実施された。そのため、本国からの輸入は、250万ポンドから163万ポンドへと急落し、イギリス商人は大打撃を受けた。また、植民地ではアメリカ製品愛用運動も展開された。このような背景のもとに、繊維工業と製靴業とが急速に工場制手工業の段階へと突入していった。1769年、ヴァージニア議会はヴァージニア・クロスの生産を奨励する。本国は1770年にタウンゼンド諸法を撤廃するに至る。

　その後約3年間は、いわゆる「静穏の時期」が続く。1773年、東インド会社に茶の輸入と販売権を独占的に与えるという茶法が出された。そして、この法律に反対する植民地の急進派（独立を願う人達）が東インド会社の船を襲い、積荷の茶を海中に投げ捨てるという、ボストン茶会事件が起こった。このボストン茶会事件こそ、これまでのイギリス帝国内の抵抗運動が独立戦争へと飛躍する転機となった。この事件に対し、イギリスはボストン港の閉鎖という報復措置をとった。1774年、植民地側は9月から10月にかけて、フィラデルフィアで第一回大陸会議を開き、本国の圧政と不当な課税に対して抗議した。ここで採択された「宣言と決議」は植民地に対するイギリス議会の立法権を全面的に否定し、全イギリス商品の「不輸入」、「不消費」およびイギリスへの「不輸出」を決

表3-5-1 逃亡奴隷広告に見る輸入品とヴァージニア・クロスの構成比（1766～1789年）

	A（件数）						B（%）	
	輸入品					ヴァージニア・クロス	構成比	
	Cotton	Osnabrug	Cloth	Linen	Felt	Virginia Cloth	輸入品	Virginia Cloth
1766	33	20	1	5	2	1	98.4	1.6
1767	8	0	2	1	1	7	63.2	36.8
1768	9	1	1	1	2	6	70.0	30.0
1769	16	6	3	1	3	4	87.9	12.1
1770	15	27	4	2	8	5	91.8	8.2
1771	16	19	4	5	7	4	92.7	7.3
1772	16	22	4	5	5	12	81.2	18.8
1773	12	14	5	4	4	4	90.7	9.3
1774	16	14	6	6	5	7	87.0	13.0
1775	10	13	8	4	3	6	86.4	13.6
1776	6	2	5	10	4	11	71.1	28.9
1777	19	5	10	9	4	23	67.2	32.8
1778	8	1	9	5	2	10	71.4	28.6
1779	12	2	8	3	0	6	80.6	19.4
1782	1	0	0	0	0	5	16.7	83.3
1783	4	4	5	2	0	9	62.5	37.5
1784	6	8	2	2	4	7	75.9	24.1
1785	3	1	12	1	2	6	76.0	24.0
1786	1	6	0	2	2	0	100.0	0.0
1787	0	2	0	1	0	1	75.0	25.0
1788	3	4	1	1	4	3	81.2	18.8
1789	0	3	0	0	2	2	71.4	28.6

図3-5-1 逃亡奴隷広告に見る輸入品とヴァージニア・クロスの構成比（1766～1789年）

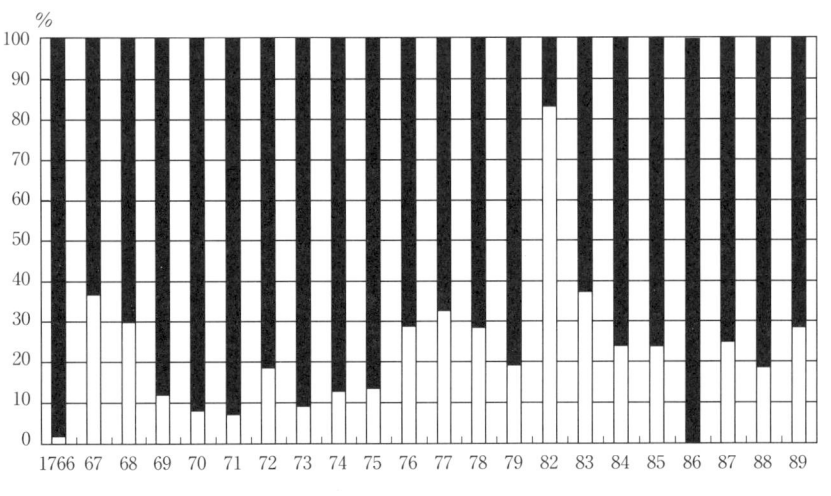

□ヴァージニア・クロス（Virginia Cloth）　■輸入品（Imported Cloth）

めた大陸通商断絶同盟を結成した。だが、本国政府と国王はとりあわなかった[24]。

1775年4月19日、イギリス軍はコンコードに集積されているとみられる武器を押収しようとしたが、レキシントンで民兵の抵抗にあい、さらにコンコードでも民兵と遭遇した。イギリス軍はコンコードで多数の住民から銃撃され、多くの死傷者をだした。このレキシントン・コンコードの戦いにより、アメリカ独立戦争が開始された[25]。

上述の経過を念頭において再び図3-5-1を見ると、戦争の開始を背景として、1775年から1776年を境にヴァージニア・クロスの登場件数に変化が見られる。すなわち1775年から再びヴァージニア・クロスが伸びていることが読み取れる。この時期は、ヴァージニアの有数なプランターのロバート・カーター（Robert Carter of Nomini Hall）が、自ら工場を設立し、ウールやオズナブルグなどの生産に着手した年（1775年）に対応している。さらに彼は、1776年にはコットン、リネンおよびウールの生産にも拡充した。このヴァージニアのプランテーションにおける布の生産については、第4章で考察する。

1782年はデータ数が少なく、信頼性が低いが、その後の生産の状態は実際はどうだったのか。この問題の解明を、ヴァージニア・ガゼット他の新聞を史料として考察するのは困難である。

パトリシア・ギブズ（Patricia Gibbs）によると「布生産はアメリカ独立革命期を通じて続けられた。戦争中は輸入品はわずかしか入手できなかったが、輸入品が市場に再登場すると多くの中産階級から上流階級の人々は、再び輸入品を購入するようになった。だが、輸入品を入手しにくい地域に住んでいた少数の中産階級および上流階級の人々と大半の下層階級のヴァージニア人は、布の生産を続けた[26]」という。また、1791年に財務長官のアレグザンダー・ハミルトン（Alexander Hamilton）に提出されたヴァージニアの製造業に関する報告によると、「ヴァージニアの各地で種々の原料が布の生産に使用されていた[27]」とのことである。この問題の詳細の検討は今後の課題とする。

ここで、上述のヴァージニア・クロスの生産量の伸びを数量的に裏づけるために、1766年から1785年を対象に比率の検定を行っておこう。

比率の検定の公式

$$p = \frac{k_1 + k_2}{n_1 + n_2}$$

$$q = 1 - P$$

$$z = \frac{\frac{k_1}{n_1} - \frac{k_2}{n_2}}{\sqrt{p \times q \times \left(\frac{1}{n_1} + \frac{1}{m_2}\right)}}$$

1766年から1785年の各都市の生産量を1年毎に加算して、上述の公式に当てはめて比率の検定を行った。その結果1766年および1770年から1779年に至る計11年間の正規分布の値zは、次の表のようになり、危険率1％であるzの2.58を越えた。したがって、これらの11年間のヴァージニア・クロスと輸入品の比率は、これら以外の年との間に有意な差があることが、1％の危険率で立証された。

ヴァージニア・クロスの素材の特徴は、さらに実際に実物資料による検証がなされなければならない。この点については、第4章で考察する。

年度	国産品	輸入品	k1	k2	n1	n2	k1/n1	k2/n2	z	国産比率
1766	1	61	1	132	62	651	0.02	0.20	3.60	0.02
1767	7	12	8	125	81	632	0.10	0.20	2.15	0.37
1768	6	14	14	119	101	612	0.14	0.19	1.33	0.30
1769	4	29	18	115	134	579	0.13	0.20	1.72	0.12
1770	5	56	23	110	195	518	0.12	0.21	2.88	0.08
1771	4	51	27	106	250	463	0.11	0.23	3.96	0.07
1772	12	52	39	94	314	399	0.12	0.24	3.79	0.19
1773	4	39	43	90	357	356	0.12	0.25	4.54	0.09
1774	7	47	50	83	411	302	0.12	0.27	5.19	0.13
1775	6	38	56	77	455	258	0.12	0.30	5.78	0.14
1776	11	27	67	66	493	220	0.14	0.30	5.20	0.29
1777	23	47	90	43	563	150	0.16	0.29	3.54	0.33
1778	10	25	100	33	598	115	0.17	0.29	3.02	0.29
1779	6	25	106	27	629	84	0.17	0.32	3.38	0.19
1782	5	1	111	22	635	78	0.17	0.28	2.29	0.83
1783	9	15	120	13	659	54	0.18	0.24	1.06	0.38
1784	7	22	127	6	688	25	0.18	0.24	0.70	0.24
1785	6	19	133	0	713	0	0.19			0.24
	133	580								0.19

　以上、第3節および第4節の考察からヴァージニア・クロスの定義と特徴および社会史的意味は、次のようにまとめることができる。

（1）ヴァージニア・クロスはヴァージニアで製造された織物であり、この用語は一般に輸入素材と区別するために用いられた。ヴァージニアの布地製造は17世紀に遡り、1750年代までにはこの布地は、ヴァージニア・クロスという名前で知られていた。これは当時、ヴァージニアを訪れたバーナビー牧師の旅行日誌から明らかである。

（2）ヴァージニア・クロスに関する多くの記録に記述された繊維のなかでは、コットンが目立つ。だが、コットンにウールが紡ぎ込まれたり、亜麻が紡ぎ込まれたりした織糸を用いた事例もある。コットンにウールが紡ぎ込まれた事例は、第4章で考察するDeWitt Wallace Gallery of Decorative Arts 所蔵の男子のコートである。

　以上から、アメリカ植民地時代と独立革命期にヴァージニアで生産されていたヴァージニア・クロスの繊維の種類の代表的なものはコットン、ウールおよび亜麻であったと結論づけられる。

（3）ヴァージニア・クロスの用途は逃亡奴隷広告（1766～1789）に見られる限りでは、奴隷に支給された基本的な衣服（ブリーチズ、コート、ウェストコート、シャツ、ペティコート）である。シャツに多用されたオズナブルグとは対照的である。

　色・柄については、約55パーセントが無地で、約42パーセントがストライプで、3パーセントがチェックであり、ストライプの幅と色の組み合わせは多様であった。

（4）ヴァージニア・クロス生産はどのような社会史的意味を持っていたのか。

　ヴァージニア・クロスの生産は、確かにプランテーションでの衣服の需要に役立った。この点ではヴァージニア植民地の人々にとっての国内産布地の役割は評価できる。だが、輸入品と比べて、価格および布質の点でどうだったのか。さらに、ヴァージニア・クロス生産の社会史的意味を語るには、これらの問題の解明を待たなければならない。

[注]

（1）・P.F.コープランド著、濱田雅子訳『アメリカ史に見る職業着―植民地時代〜独立革命期―』(せせらぎ出版, 1998)、209-215.
・Linda Baumgarten, "Clothes for the People, Slave Clothing in Early Virginia," *Journal of Early Southern Decorative Arts*, Vol XIV, No.2, (November 1988), Museum of Early Southern Decorative Arts, (Winston-Salem, North Carolina), 62-66.

（2）・Philip D. Morgan, *Slave Counterpoint, Black Culture in the Eighteenth-Century Chesapeake & Lowcountry*, University of North Carolina Press, (Chapel IIill & London), 1998,
・Linda Baumgarten, ibid, 38.

（3）・P. F. コープランド著、濱田雅子訳『前掲書』(せせらぎ出版、1998年10月)、167.
本書の原題は "*Working Dress in Colonial and Revolutionary America*, Greenwood Press, Westport, Connecticut, 1977"
・Linda Baumgarten, ibid., 35.

（4）・濱田雅子「18世紀ヴァージニアにおけるお仕着せに関する歴史的考察」(国際服飾学会誌、No.12, 1995年11月)、114-129.
・L. Baumgarten, ibid.

（5）Ibid., 34.

（6）Ibid., 35.

（7）*Virginia Gazette* (Purdie), April 11, 1766.

（8）Linda Baumgarten, op. cit., 40.

（9）Lorena S. Walsh, *From Calabar to Carter's Grove, The History of a Virginia Slave Community*, University Press of Virginia, (Charlottesville and London, 1997), 89.

（10）Mount Vernon Ladies' Association of the Union. Photocopies of George Washington's Account Books, Farm Ledgers, Cash Memoranda, and Weekly Reports.

（11）L.A.Windley, comp., *Runaway Slave Advertisement: A Documentary History from 1730s to 1790*, Vol.1 of Vol.4, Greenwood, (Westport, Connecticut, 1983), 160.

（12）*Ibid.*, 79.

（13）*Ibid.*, 192.

（14）濱田雅子「ヴァージニア・クロスに関する社会史的考察―逃亡奴隷広告および遺品に基づいて―」(国際服飾学会誌、No.17, 2000年5月)、53-80.

（15）Andrew Burnaby, *Travels Through the Middle Settlement in North-America, in the Years 1759 and 1760: with Observations upon the State of the Colonies*, originally published, T. Payne, 1775. Reprint, Great Seal Books, (Ithaca, New York 1960), 12-13.

（16）Dorothy F. McCombs, *Virginia cloth: Early Textiles in Virginia Particularly in the Backcountry Between the Blue Ridge and Allegheny Mountain until 1830*. Unpublished Master's Thesis, Department of History, Virginia Polytechnic Institute, Blacksburg, (Virginia, 1976), 24

（17）John Harrower, *Journal of John Harrower, an Indentured Servant in the Colony of Virginia, 1773〜1776*, edited, with an Introduction, by Edward Miles Riley, (Williamsburg, Virginia, New York, 1993), 76.

（18）*Ibid.*, 138.

（19）Linda BaumgartenおよびPatricia Gibbsと筆者とのパーソナルコミュニュケーション（1999年7月）

（20）L. A. Windley, *op. cit.*, 251.

（21）*Ibid.*, 319.

（22）Bryan Paul Howard, *Had on and took with him: Runaway Indentured Servant Clothing in Virginia, 1774〜1778*, UMI Dissertation Series, Degree Date: 1996, 249.

（23）*Ibid.*, 235.

（24）・有賀貞、大下尚一編『新版　概説アメリカ史』(有斐閣選書、1994年)、46-47.
・メアリー・ベス・ノートン他著、本田創造監修、白井洋子、戸田徹子訳『アメリカの歴史　①新世界への挑戦　15世紀－18世紀』(三省堂、1996年)、215-220.

（25）・メアリー・ベス・ノートン他『同上書』225-325. 有賀貞、人下尚一、志邨晃佑、平野孝編『世界歴史大系　アメリカ史

17世紀—1877年』(山川出版社、1994年)、125-198.

・紀平英作編『世界各国史24 アメリカ史』(山川出版社、1999年)、72-88.

(26) Patricia Gibbs, *Cloth Production in Virginia to 1800*, Research Department, Colonial Williamsburg Foundation, (Colonial Williamsburg, Virginia, March, 1978), 22.

(27) *Ibid.*, 23.

第 4 章

奴隷の被服の支給と生産

第1節　先行研究

　わが国では、ヴァージニア植民地における布の生産に関する研究は皆無である。ここではアメリカの代表的な二つの研究を挙げておこう。

1．Dorothy F. McCombs, *Virginia Cloth: Early Textiles in Virginia, Particularly in the Backcountry Between the Blue Ridge and Allegheny Mountain until 1830.*[1]

　ヴァージニアの植民地時代から独立革命を経て、1830年に至る時期のヴァージニア・クロス（Virginia cloth）の生産に関する研究である。地域としては、ブルー・リッジ（Blue Ridge）とアルゲニー山脈（Allegheny Mountain）の間の奥地を考察対象に据え、史料としては、当時の公文書、新聞、手紙および回想録を参照している。ドロシー・F. マッコム（D. F. McCombs）は広範なデータの収集・分析を試みており、ヴァージニア・クロスの生産を裏付ける有力な研究である。だが、原史料の実物や織物や衣服の実物の写真がないのは弱点である。とはいえ、織物の解説と文献目録は、筆者のヴァージニア・クロスの研究に大変、役立つ資料である。

2．Patricia Gibbs, *Cloth Production in Virginia to 1800*[2]

　本研究ではヴァージニア・クロスの生産について、ヨーク・カウンティ財産目録をはじめとして、ヴァージニア議会の法令やカーター家（Carter Family）などのヴァージニアの有数なプランターたちの日誌や手紙、ヴァージニア・ガゼット（*Virginia Gazette*）紙などの新聞、旅行記、George Washington Papers, Thomas Jefferson Papers, Alexander Hamilton Papers などの第一次史料を丹念に紐解いて、社会経済史的な観点から非常に克明にまとめられている。巻末には織物生産関連の膨大な資料が Appendix として掲載されている。確かに利用者にとっては大変、便利な資料ではある。しかし、これらの資料のなかには、例えばデニス・ディドロー（Denis Diderot）の百科全書における織物関連の資料のようなヨーロッパのものが多く、アメリカ人研究者としてアメリカ側からの資料分析が行なわれていない。ヴァージニアにおける布の生産に関する研究である限り、ヴァージニア史との接点を保った資料分析がなされるべきであろう。さらに、第一次史料のすべてが記録に基づく史料であり、布や被服や生産用具の実物資料の調査は行なわれていない。

　また、議会の法令や新聞記事やプランターの財産目録や日記や手紙などの第一次史料のオリジナルの写真がまったく掲載されていないなどの問題点がある。

　これらの問題点があるとはいえ、本研究は筆者の奴隷の被服に関する研究において、資料面およびヴァージニアにおける布の生産の事実関係を把握する上で、示唆するところが大であった。

第2節　実物資料の調査

1．ヴァージニア・クロス製、男子用スーツ
　——コロニアル・ウィリアムズバーグ振興財団 DeWitt Wallace Gallery of Decorative Arts にて——

　前章でも触れたが、18世紀の奴隷の被服の調査のため、筆者は、ヴァージニア州内の博物館やコロニアル・ウィリアムズバーグ振興財団考古学研究部門をたずねた。しかし奴隷の被服の実物は1枚も残存しておらず、布の断片も残存していないのが実状であった。ここに紹介するのは奴隷の衣服ではないということだが、ヴァージニア・クロス製という点で、大変貴重な実物資料である。

　写真のスーツ[3]（口絵4-2-1①～⑤）は、コロニアル・ウィリアムズバーグ振興財団 DeWitt Wallace Gallery of Decorative Arts（ヴァージニア州ウィリアムズバーグ）所蔵のスーツである。同資料の情報カードの記載事項を表4-2-1に示しておこう。

　情報カードによると、この資料はアメリカ独立戦争時に、ヴァージニアのグーチランド・カウンティ（Goochland County）またはアイル・オブ・ワイト・カウンティ（Isle of Wight County）に住んでいた、アスキュー（Askew）家あるいはプリューデント（Prudent）家の大人の男性あるいは若い男子がユニホームとして着用していたヴァージニア・クロス製のスーツである。

　コートの素材は、ホームスパンのコットンのたて糸（ナチュラル・カラー）と、茶色の羊毛のくず再生毛である短繊維（ノイル）の節の多く見られる天然のコットンをよこ糸とするタビー織（平織）である。

　スーツの素材は、最初、コットンだけだと考えられていたが、その後の検査で、コットンにウールが紡ぎ込まれた織糸であることが判明した[4]。この追加は糸により強度を持たせるためになされたのであろう。

　ブリーチズ（口絵4-2-2①～⑥）もコートと同じ素材で作られているが、よこ糸には節のないコットンが用いられている。

2．パッチワーク・キルトの実物資料　——Valentine Museumにて——

　口絵4-2-3に示したパッチワーク・キルト（V.50.127.1）は、ヴァージニア州リッチモンドの Valentine Museum の所蔵品である。寄贈者はDr. & Mrs. Emmett H. Terrellで、彼女の考証によると制作者は不明であるが、ハノーバー・カウンティー（Hanover County）のビーバー・ダム・プランテーション（Beaver Dam Plantation）において、1800年頃、奴隷によって作られたパッチワーク・キルトである。

　このキルトに付けられたカード（図4-2-3②）には、「90×80インチ」とサイズが記載されている。織物は多種多様な縞柄と格子柄およびプリントが巧みに組み合わされ、色は藍と赤味を帯びた茶系の濃淡から構成されている。学芸員のコリーン・カラハン（Colleen Callahan）によると、インディ

表4-2-1 ヴァージニア・クロス製のスーツに関する
記載事項—情報カードから—

件名	衣服：男子あるいは少年用スーツ（コートおよびブリーチズ）
素材	a. コットン ＋ ウール b. コットン 　（おそらく　ヴァージニア・クロス）
国名	北アメリカ、ヴァージニア州 （グーチランド・カウンティ　あるいは　アイル・オブ・ワイト・カウンティ）
年代	1780～90年
寸法	コート 　丈：　　　　47.5インチ 　後肩幅：　　14.5インチ ブリーチズ 　丈：　　　　27インチ 　ウェスト：　27インチ
状態	良好。傷みは少ないが、汚れがひどく、色褪せている。
説明	織物：ホームスパンのコットンのたて糸（ナチュラル・カラー）と、茶色の短繊維（ノイル）の節の多く見られる天然のコットンのよこ糸を、タビー織にしたもの（コート素材のみ）。ブリーチズも同じ素材で作られているが、よこ糸に節がない。 コート：折り返された衿。前身頃に8個のボタン（1個とれている）。9個のボタンホールのうち、1個だけ（上から2番目）穴があけられている。フラップ付きの脇ポケット2個。ベンツ仕立てのオープン・カフスで、ボタンはなし。丈長のほぼまっすぐの裾布は深いベンツに仕立てられ、後ろ中央で襞取りされ、飾りボタンが付いている。 ブリーチズ：細身仕立てで、座りやすくするために調節可能なウェスト・バンドに幅広のギャザーが寄せられ、後ろ中央で紐締めし、3個のボタンで留め合わせるようになっている。前垂れ蓋布付き。ヒップ・ポケット2個。膝の部分に4個のボタンとバックル・ストラップ。
歴史	アメリカ独立戦争時に、Askew家あるいはPrudent家の者によって着用された（私的な）ユニホームであったといわれている。

ゴや茜によって染色されているということである[5]。カラハンはまた、このパッチワーク・キルトについて、次のようにも述べている[6]。

「正方形と三角形と長方形のこの複雑な配列が、中央部分のバランスの良い手の込んだレイアウトを生み出している。このキルトのダイヤモンド形の中心部分にある8角の星は、三角形と正方形の布の巧みな扱いによって、いかに独創的な形が生み出されているかを示しているという点で、特に注目に値する。これと同様な星形の模様は、今日でも依然として人気がある。

このキルトの最も珍しい特徴は、現存する1700年代末のパッチワーク・キルトに一般的に見られる高価な輸入品のプリント織物の代わりに用いられている……今ではひどく色褪せてしまっているが、かつては生き生きとしていたであろうストライプのティッキング、チェック、格子縞、無地の……織物にある。このキルトに見られるわずかなブロック・プリント織物（**口絵4-2-3③**）は、プリントが未熟で、デザインも単純であり、これらは、18世紀のアメリカでプリントされた織物の希少な例であろうと思われる。寄贈者の履歴は、プランテーションの奴隷の織り手がこのキルトに用いられている織物のいくつかを制作したかもしれないということ、また奴隷の縫い子たちがこのキルトの制作に参加した可能性もあるということ、を示している。」

C. カラハンによる明快な解説は、この実物資料の歴史的価値を高く評価している。

第3章第5節で考察したヴァージニア・クロスの特徴は、このキルトの織物にも、実に明白に見られる。すなわち、このキルトに見られる多様なストライプ（口絵4-2-3①③④）とその色彩は、ヴァージニア・ガゼット紙掲載の逃亡奴隷広告に見られるヴァージニア・クロスの描写と見事に重なりあっている。このキルトについて、これ以上の考証は難しいが、奴隷の衣服の実物資料が残存していないだけに、素材の面からみても、本研究にとっての有用な実物資料である。

3．18世紀の織物の複製
― コロニアル・ウィリアムズバーグ振興財団織物工房にて ―

製織の専門家のマックス・ハムリック（Max Hamrick）は、1770年にウィリアムズバーグで用いられていた織機のレプリカ（口絵4-2-4①②）を用いて織物の複製を行なっている[7]。

18世紀の織物の複製に当って、M. ハムリックが使用しているマニュアル本は、1792年にアメリカで初めて印刷された織工用の織の設計書、すなわち、John Hargrove[8], *The Weavers Draft Book and Clothiers Assistant*（Baltimore: Hagerty, 1792）の復刻版である[9]。この手引書は、当時、メリーランドで使用されていた。

上記のマニュアルの原本の出版よりも27年前の1765年に、ウィリアムズバーグの出版人のJ. ロイル（Joseph Royle）がカロライン・カウンティ（Caroline County）に住むJ. ウィリー（John Wily）のパンフレット、*A Treatise on the Propaganda of Sheep, the Manufacture of Wool, and the Cultivation and Manufacture of Flax, with Directions for making Several Utensils for the Business.* を出版している[10]。この本がヴァージニアでは、織工向けの手引書として用いられていたと推察される。

口絵4-2-5-1①〜⑦はM. ハムリックによって複製された布のサンプルである。

4．プランテーションからの出土品
― コロニアル・ウィリアムズバーグ振興財団考古学研究部門にて ―

1998年5月から8月にかけて、カーターズ・グローブ・プランテーション（Carter's Grove Plantation）、リッチ・ネック・プランテーション（Rich Neck Plantation）およびパレス・プランテーション（Palace Plantation）から発掘された出土品の中から、奴隷が使用していたツール（指貫、針）や使用者不明の鋏、およびボタンを調査した[11]。

本節では、これらの出土品の中から、奴隷の衣服の生産に関わる出土品3種類（鋏、指貫および針）を紹介する（口絵4-2-6①〜③）。

コロニアル・ウィリアムズバーグ振興財団の観光センターの発掘に関する中間報告[12]によると、発掘の背景は次のようである。

1998年5月から8月にかけて、奴隷小屋（サイト44WB90）の大規模な発掘が、M. フランクリン博士（Dr. Maria Franklin）の指揮下で、コロニアル・ウィリアムズバーグ振興財団とウィリアム・メアリ大学共催の archaeological field school の学生たちによって行なわれた。このサイトの発掘

は、1999年の夏にもオースティンのテキサス大学の学生によって続行される。文献に基づく研究では、サイト44WB90は最終的には総督公邸（Governor's Palace）の財産に吸収された35エーカーに当るという。そもそもこの土地は、1760年にマシュー・ムーディー（Mathew Moody）によってフォクイエル総督（Francis Fauquier、在任：1759～1767）に売却されている。M. ムーディーはカピタル・ランディング（Capital Landing）の渡船の番人で、活発な通商とタバコの船積みをする場所で居酒屋を経営していた。フォクイエル総督は8年後に亡くなるまで、この区画を87エーカーにまで増やした。植民地議会は彼の財産からこの区画を購入し、後任のボティチュール総督（Norborne Berkeley Botetourt、在任：1768～1770）あるいはダンモア総督（John Murray Dunmore、在任：1771～1775）が保有している間に、全体で364エーカーに至った。18世紀の文献ではこの土地は「Park」と言われており、1781年のデザンドゥルアン（Desandrouin）の地図には、牧草地、あるいは耕作地と記されている。

1998年以前の発掘によるサイト44WB90関連の出土資料と、この文献資料の記載とが合致し、1998年夏の考古学者による、このサイトの徹底的な調査へと導いたのである。

新たに発掘された資料は、奴隷化されたヴァージニア人がここに住んでいたことを明らかに示している。大量の良く保存された金属製品が掘り起こされ、それらの中には、鋏と指貫（大人用と子ども用）、および多くの銅製のまっすぐな針が含まれていた。また、少なくとも40個のすばらしいボタンも含まれていた。

さて、以上の発掘の背景を踏まえて、次に、パレス・プランテーションから出土した資料を紹介しよう。

口絵4-2-6①は、鋏である。学芸員のケリー・ラッド（Kelly Ladd）によると、これが誰によって用いられていたかは不明であるという。握りの部分は一部、欠損している。サイズは8.7センチである。口絵4-2-6②は、同プランテーションの奴隷小屋から出土した大、小の指貫である。前者は直径1.4センチであり、後者は直径1.1センチである。K. ラッドによると、いずれも奴隷によって用いられていたという。その精巧さは写真からも推察されるであろうが、指貫の表面には穴が繊細に細工され、センスを感じさせる美しい形状は目を見張るものがある。

最後に、口絵4-2-6③は同プランテーションの奴隷小屋から出土した針である。大量に出土した銅製の針の中から、4本、無作為に抽出した。これらも奴隷によって用いられていたという。

これらの資料から、18世紀ヴァージニアのプランテーションの奴隷小屋において、奴隷によって衣服生産が行なわれていたことが実証できる。

筆者のヴァージニアにおける実物資料調査では、奴隷の衣服の実物はもとより、布の断片も残存していないことが判明し、下層階級の人々の被服のイメージ表現がいかに困難であるかを切実に考えさせられた。だが、本節で考察したヴァージニア・クロス製の男子用スーツとパッチワーク・キルトから、第3章で逃亡奴隷広告に拠って考察したヴァージニア・クロスの特徴が、具体的に明らかになった。すなわち、前者のスーツのコートの素材は、コットンにウールが紡ぎ込まれた事例であり、後者はストライプや縞柄のヴァージニア・クロスの実物の事例である。

また、製織の専門家M. ハムリック提供の布地のサンプルは、18世紀に用いられていたマニュアル本を使って再現された粗悪な布地のサンプルという点で、下層階級の衣服の研究にとって有用な複製資料である。

最後に、ウィリアムズバーグのパレス・プランテーションから出土した鋏、針および指貫は、このプランテーションの奴隷の居住地区において、奴隷の手で衣服生産が行なわれていたことを裏付け、また、18世紀には黒人奴隷の中に、技術者がいたことを裏付ける実物資料であることを指摘しておこう。

以上を念頭において第3節では、ヴァージニアにおける奴隷の被服の支給と生産実態について考察する。

第3節　プランテーションにおける被服管理

既述のように、イギリス本国が植民地に公布した砂糖法（1764年）、印紙法（1765年）およびタウンゼンド諸法に抗して、植民地内では、1767年にボストンおよびヴァージニアを拠点として、布の内地生産が植民初期の生産量を上回る勢いで促進されていく。これは植民地人の本国に対する抵抗運動であり、イギリス商品ボイコット運動の一環であった。女性たちも「自由の娘たち」を名乗って立ち上がり、イギリス製布地への依存を断つために、人前で糸紡ぎをして、他の女性たちにも手織り布地を作るように勧めたとされる。

ヴァージニア議会がヴァージニアにおける布の生産を公に承認し、奨励したのは1769年のことである。ヴァージニア・ガゼット（*Virginia Gazette*）紙, 14 December 1769（発行人 Rind）[13]には、ヴァージニア議会の下院によってボティチュール総督に議事堂で開催された舞踏会が、次のように報じられている。

「最近の事件に際して紳士たちの連帯を生み出すもとになったのと同じ愛国心が、今回、ホームスパンのガウン姿で参加された100人近い数の婦人たちのドレスに最も適切に現れていたということを読者に知らせることができるのは、我々の最大の喜びとするところである。これは、自分たちの国の真のかつ重要な関心事がなんであるかということについての、彼らの暗黙の了承、同意を如実に示している顕著な一例である。公益事業と個人経済とが非常にうまく結びついたこのような例が、アメリカの婦人たちのあらゆる集まりにおいて示されることが望まれる。」

上記は上流人の衣裳の国内生産を奨励する記事であるが、中産・下層階級の被服も当然国内生産が促進されていた。被服の生産様式は、(1) 家内生産（Home Production）、(2) プランテーション生産（Plantation Production）、および (3) 工場生産（Factory Production）の三つのカテゴリーに分けることができる[14]。そこで、本節ではヴァージニアの有数なプランターであるカーター家

史料4-3-1　17〜19世紀のカーター家の主要メンバー系図

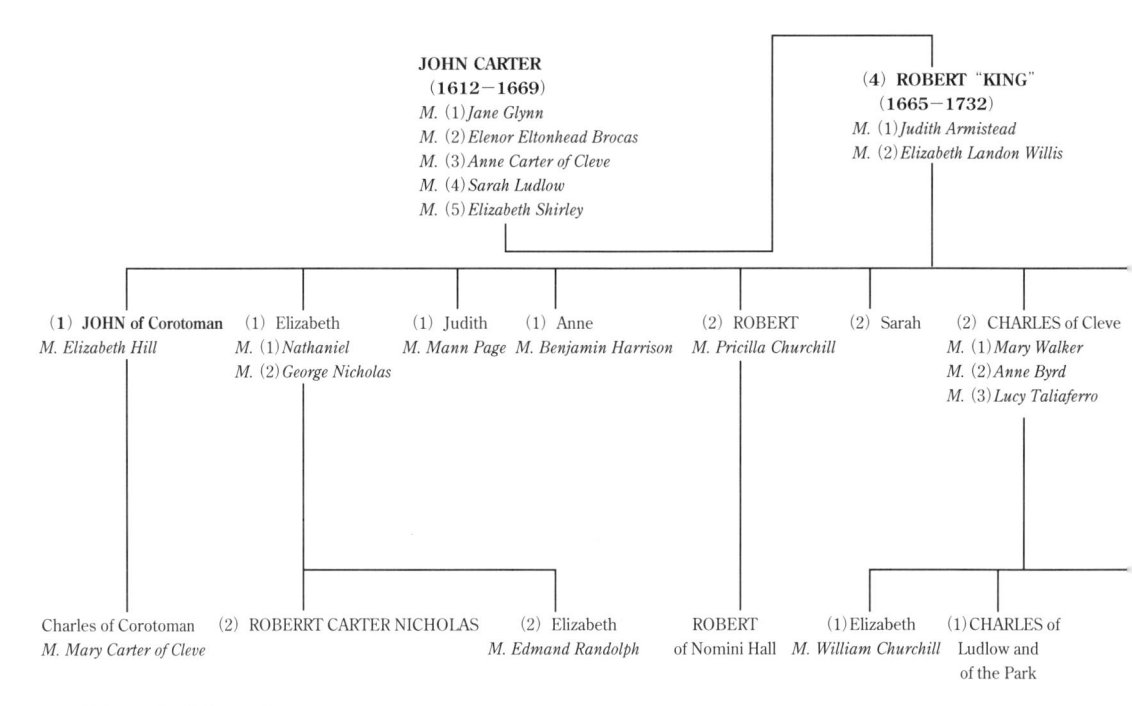

```
                    JOHN CARTER                          (4) ROBERT "KING"
                    (1612-1669)                              (1665-1732)
                    M.(1)Jane Glynn                          M.(1)Judith Armistead
                    M.(2)Elenor Eltonhead Brocas             M.(2)Elizabeth Landon Willis
                    M.(3)Anne Carter of Cleve
                    M.(4)Sarah Ludlow
                    M.(5)Elizabeth Shirley
```

(1) JOHN of Corotoman	(1) Elizabeth	(1) Judith	(1) Anne	(2) ROBERT	(2) Sarah	(2) CHARLES of Cleve
M. Elizabeth Hill	M.(1)Nathaniel M.(2)George Nicholas	M. Mann Page	M. Benjamin Harrison	M. Pricilla Churchill		M.(1)Mary Walker M.(2)Anne Byrd M.(3)Lucy Taliaferro

Charles of Corotoman	(2) ROBERRT CARTER NICHOLAS	(2) Elizabeth		ROBERT	(1)Elizabeth	(1)CHARLES of
M. Mary Carter of Cleve		M. Edmand Randolph		of Nomini Hall	M. William Churchill	Ludlow and of the Park

出典：Paul P. Hoffman ed., *Guide to the Microfilm Edition of the Carter Family Papers, 1659-1797*, in the Sabine Hall Collection, Microfilm Publication, University of Virginia Library, Number Three, 1967, p. 7.

（Carter Family）のプランテーションおよびアメリカの初代大統領ジョージ・ワシントン（George Washington）が所有していたマウント・ヴァーノンのプランテーションにおいて、奴隷の被服の支給および生産が、どのようにして行なわれていたのか、誰によって行なわれていたのか、という問題を、プランテーションの記録、商人の記録、プランターの日誌や手紙およびその他の公文書に基づいて考察する。

1．カーター家（Carter Family）の場合

まずカーター家の背景と3人のプランター、すなわち、ランドン・カーター（Landon Carter）、ロバート・カーター・オブ・ノミニ・ホール（Robert Carter of Nomini Hall）および、ロバート・ウォームレイ・カーター（Robert Wormeley Carter）の経歴をルイ・モートン（Louis Morton）[15]の研究に基づいて把握しておこう。彼ら一人ひとりの事績を把握することによって、ヴァージニアにおけるプランテーションの発展の真相や、プランテーションにおける布および被服生産の実態を明らかにすることが可能になると思われるからである。

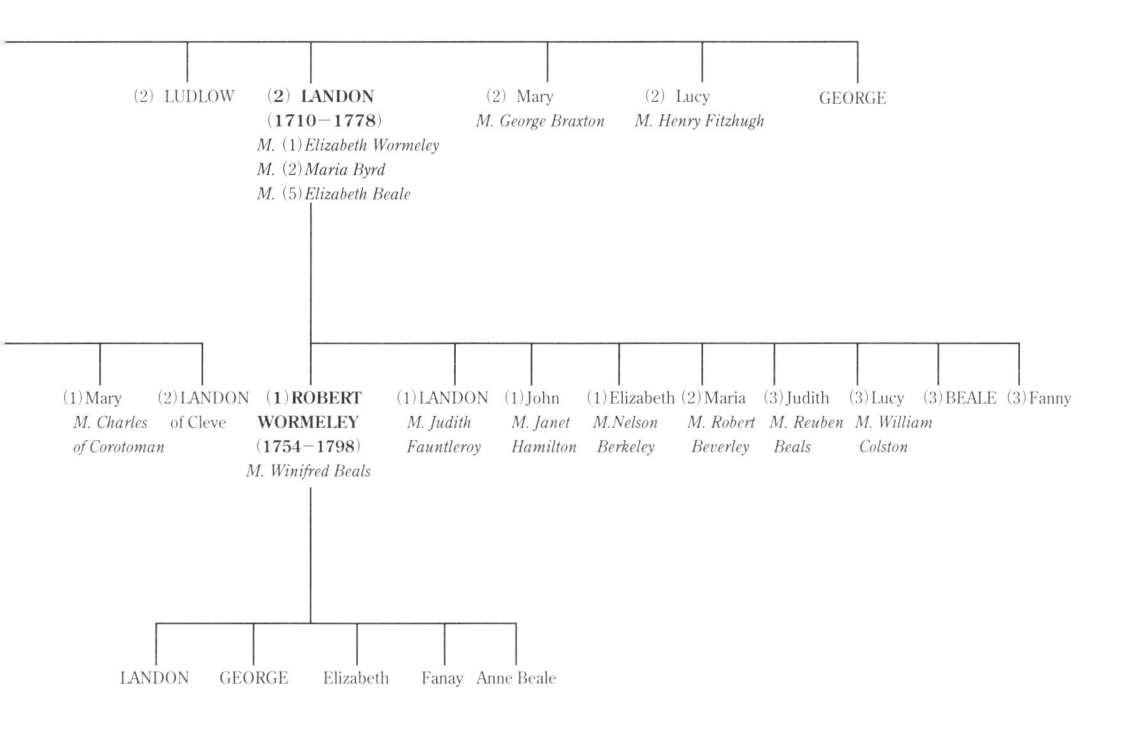

```
(2) LUDLOW    (2) LANDON         (2) Mary             (2) Lucy            GEORGE
              (1710－1778)        M. George Braxton   M. Henry Fitzhugh
              M. (1) Elizabeth Wormeley
              M. (2) Maria Byrd
              M. (5) Elizabeth Beale
```

```
(1)Mary       (2)LANDON    (1)ROBERT        (1)LANDON   (1)John      (1)Elizabeth  (2)Maria     (3)Judith    (3)Lucy      (3)BEALE  (3)Fanny
M. Charles    of Cleve     WORMELEY         M. Judith   M. Janet     M.Nelson      M. Robert    M. Reuben    M. William
of Corotoman               (1754－1798)      Fauntleroy  Hamilton     Berkeley      Beverley     Beals        Colston
                           M. Winifred Beals
```

```
LANDON    GEORGE    Elizabeth    Fanay    Anne Beale
```

系図[16]（史料4-3-1）に見るように、ランドン・カーターの祖父であり、ロバート・カーター・オブ・ノミニ・ホールの曾祖父であるジョン・カーター（John Carter, 1612～1669）は、英国のチャールズ1世（Charles I）が処刑されたとき（1649年）に、不安定で政治的紛争が渦巻いていたイギリスからヴァージニアへと移住してきた。彼の出身地や祖先についてはまったく知られておらず、移住の理由も不明であるが、政治的・宗教的諸困難を逃れるため、あるいは彼の生活条件を向上させるために移住してきたものと推察される[17]。

移住後はアパー・ノーフォーク（Upper Norfolk／今日のナンスモンド・カウンティ Nansemond County）の植民地代議会員を経て、1654年にはノーザン・ネック（Northern Neck）のランカスター・カウンティー（Lancaster County）の植民地代議会員をつとめる。1660年から1669年にかけて、総督府参議会員をつとめ、その間に財産の基礎を築いた。

1665年10月、彼はイギリスから植民地に80人の年季奉公人を輸送したことに対して、4,000エーカーを譲与される。当時の法律はヴァージニアに移住者を連れてきた人に、移住者1人につき55エーカーのヘッドライトを賦与したのである。さらにジョン・カーターは息子のジョン・カーターJr.

と共に、18,500エーカー以上もの公有地を譲渡されている。彼の死亡時の財産目録には、個人的財産だけでも、£2,250..10..6（2,250ポンド10シリング6ペンス）と見積もられており、当時としてはかなりの財産であった。

ジョン・カーターの息子のロバート・カーター（Robert Carter）[18]は「キング」カーター（"King" Carter、1665〜1732）と称され、ヴァージニアきっての富豪として、また最も影響力の強い人物として活躍した。彼は父親からコロトマン川（Corotoman River）の支流の土地1,000エーカーと父の私有財産の3分の1、約1,000ポンドを相続した。1724年には89,937エーカー、1724年から1730年には彼と家族は、父からの相続分とノーザン・ネックおよびブルー・リッジ（Blue Ridge）の西側の土地を合わせて、30万エーカーの土地と700人の奴隷を所有していた。家畜は100頭を越える馬、2,000頭を越える牛と豚、数百頭の羊がいた。これらの財産は子孫に世襲された。

彼は英国で6年間教育を受け、ヴァージニアに帰ってからの政治的活躍ぶりは大変めざましい。1691年から1692年にかけてランカスター・カウンティーを代表して、植民地議会代議会員を務めた。その後、種々の役職を経て、1726年には総督府参議会員（President of Council）となり、1732年に死去した。

「キング」カーターには12人の子供がいたが、次々と死去し、ランドン・カーター（1710〜1778）は父親から莫大な財産を相続し、プランテーションの維持・発展のために活躍した。ヴァージニアのプランテーションで布の生産工場も経営していた。

「キング」カーターの孫であるロバート・カーターは、ロバート・カーター・オブ・ノミニ・ホールとして、知名度の高いプランターである。とくに、鉄と織物および塩の生産工場の設立と奴隷解放を実施したことで名高い。筆者が彼を取り上げる理由も彼のこのような活躍ぶりにある。

最後にランドン・カーターの息子のロバート・ウォームレイ・カーター（1754〜1798）はG. ワシントンとともに布の内地生産の実験を行なったプランターである。筆者はこの点に注目し、彼を取り上げた。

(1) 事例1．ランドン・カーター（Landon Carter）の場合

「キング」・カーターの息子のランドン・カーター（図4-3-1）は、父親から次のプランテーションから成る莫大な財産を相続した（図4-3-2）[19]。すなわち、
- ヨーク（York）川沿いの2つのプランテーション……リングズ・ネック（Ring's Neck）、リポン・ホール（Ripon Hall）
- リッチモンド・カウンティ（Richmond County）の3つのプランテーション……サビーン・ホール（Sabine Hall）、ザ・フォークス（The Forks）、モンゴリーク（Mangorike）
- ノーサンプトン・カウンティー（Northampton County）のプランテーション
- プリンス・ウィリアム（Prince William）の広大な土地

などがそれである。彼の死後、1779年2月に作成されたランドン・カーターの財産目録[20]には、リッチモンド・カウンティー（Richmond County）に所有していた黒人奴隷数181人、総黒人奴隷数

図4-3-1　ランドン・カーター大佐
出典： Jack Greene ed., *The Diary of Colonel Landon Carter of Sabine Hall, 1752～1778*, Charlottesville, 1965, Vol. I.

図4-3-2　ランドン・カーター大佐の所有地
出典：Jack Greene ed., *ibid.*

史料4-3-2 ランドン・カーターの財産目録における「黒人奴隷のリスト」(1779年2月)

出典: Inventory of the Estate of Landon Carter, Feb. 1779, Page 1 " A list of Negroes……", Sabine Hall Papers (#1959), The Albert and Shirley Small Special Collections Library, University of Virginia Library.

401人と記載されている。史料4-3-2はこの財産目録に記載されているリッチモンド・カウンティーに所有していた181人の黒人奴隷の名簿である。年季奉公人から黒人奴隷労働力への転換はランドン・カーターにとって、なかなか深刻な課題であった。彼の日誌[21]から、奴隷の被服および奴隷の紡績工と織工に関する記述を仔細に抽出してみたが、これらの記述から、厳格で仕事の失敗を恐れるランドン・カーターは、黒人奴隷が監督の目を逃れて怠けたり、逃亡したりすること、彼らの仕事の能率が悪いことに不満を抱いていたことがわかる。当時の製織事業の困難さが読み取れるであろう。以下は織工の逃亡の事例である。

　　ハリソン（Harrison）大佐の織工が逃亡し、ジュディ（Judy）の綿糸（Cotton）は、製織されぬまま放置されて12ヶ月近くになる。こんなふうに一家から織工が逃亡すると、その工場での生産は少しも進まない。多くの人々がどんな工場からも大した利益が得られないのは、まったく、このためだと思う[22]。

黒人奴隷をいかに効率よく働かせるかは、ひとりランドン・カーターだけではなく、当時のプランターたちに共通する問題であった。

奴隷の被服の支給は、奴隷の健康を管理し、効率よく働かせるためにもプランターの重要な仕事の一つであった。それは次の事実からも明らかである。すなわち、ヴァージニアきっての知識人プランターであったウィリアム・バード二世（William Byrd II, 1674〜1744）は「病気にかかった奴隷を、1日に1度は必ず、疫病のときには2度も見舞うのが普通であった。奴隷は経営の成否を左右する鍵であったから、その健康は、彼にとって重要な関心事であった[23]」という。ランドン・カーターの日誌には、奴隷の衣服や靴や衣服用の布の注文に関する記録が多く見られる。特に靴に関する記録が頻出する。

　　1763年12月12日（月）
　　　ロンドンの商人　D.カンベル（D. Cambell）氏が来ている。彼はとても親切で、私が欲しいものは何でも提供してくれる。私は彼に次の注文書を書いた[24]。

この注文書の中に、お仕着せの注文が見られる。

　　3 livery suits middling men（中くらいの大きさの男子用の3着のお仕着せ）
　　3 silver laced hats for ditto（同じ男子が被る銀糸の紐が巻かれた縁付き帽3個）

プランテーションの奴隷は家内の召使と職人と野良仕事に携わる奴隷という3つの階層に分けられていた。階層により、衣服にも違いが見られた。ランドン・カーターのこの日の注文書に見られるお仕着せと縁付き帽は、家内の召使用の被服である。

図4-3-3 サビーン・ホール

出典： Jack Greene ed., *ibid.*

1764年11月11日（日）
　プランテーションの御者のサム（Sam）に、プランテーションの黒人奴隷用の上記70足の靴を届けてもらう際の渡船料として3シリング9ペンス与えた[25]。

1767年2月19日（木）
　私は数年前に、黒人奴隷用の靴を作らせるために、彼［Allanson］の使用人を買った[26]。

グリーンの脚注[27]によると、W.アランソン（William Allanson）はヴァージニアのファルマウス（Falmouth）の商人であった。

1770年7月12日（木）
　ルーシー（Lucy）は私の使用人用の亜麻糸（linen）と綿糸（cotton）の代金として、約1,500ポンドのタバコをブレア（Blare）の店に払いに出かけた[28]。

グリーンの脚注[29]によると、ブレア（Blare）はWestmoreland Co.の小商人であり、ノミニ（Nomini）に店を構えていた。ルーシー（Lucy）はランドン・カーターの娘である。

次に、布の生産および衣服生産へのランドン・カーターの取り組みについて、労働力と設備の面から考察しよう。

年季奉公人は年季があけると独立して、離れていってしまうにもかかわらず、彼は、1757年に織工を雇い、サビーン・ホール（Sabine Hall, 図4-3-3）で布を生産した。また、彼の奴隷を紡績工や織工や裁縫師として使っていた。1763年11月25日（木）の日誌（史料4-3-3）[30]には、奴隷のベティー（Bettey）がこの日に裁断した奴隷の少年（Boys）と男（Men）と女（Women）のためのスーツの着数が、

1763年11月25日（木）
　ベティが裁断
　　少年用スーツ　　　　　　　10
　　男性用スーツ　｝
　　女性用スーツ　｝　　　　　40

と記録されている。奴隷の男の子のスーツを10着、男性用と女性用を合わせて40着を、一日で裁断するのはかなりの仕事量であったものと推察される。

彼は大陸連盟（Continental Association）が、1774年12月1日をもって大英帝国とアイルランドからのすべての商品を輸入しないことを呼びかけたときの推進者でもある。ヴァージニアにおける布の生産は1770年代の半ばにピークに達する[31]。

ランドン・カーターの1779年の財産目録（史料 4-3-4）[32]には、製織工場で布を生産するための設備が次のように記載されている。

　　　　　　　製織工場
　織機および付属装置　　　　　2台
　管巻車　　　　　　　　　　　1台
　綿繰機　　　　　　　　　　　1台
　サクソニー紡車　　　　　　　4台
　大紡車　　　　　　　　　　　5台
　コットン用カード機（梳綿機）　7台
　ウール用カード機（梳毛機）　　5台
　スレー　　　　　　　　　　　6台
　ハックリング機（櫛梳機）　　　1台
　トウ（短繊維）用カード機　　　2台

史料4-3-3 「黒人奴隷ベティによる衣服の裁断」に関する記載[ランドン・カーターの日記
（1763年11月17日から）]

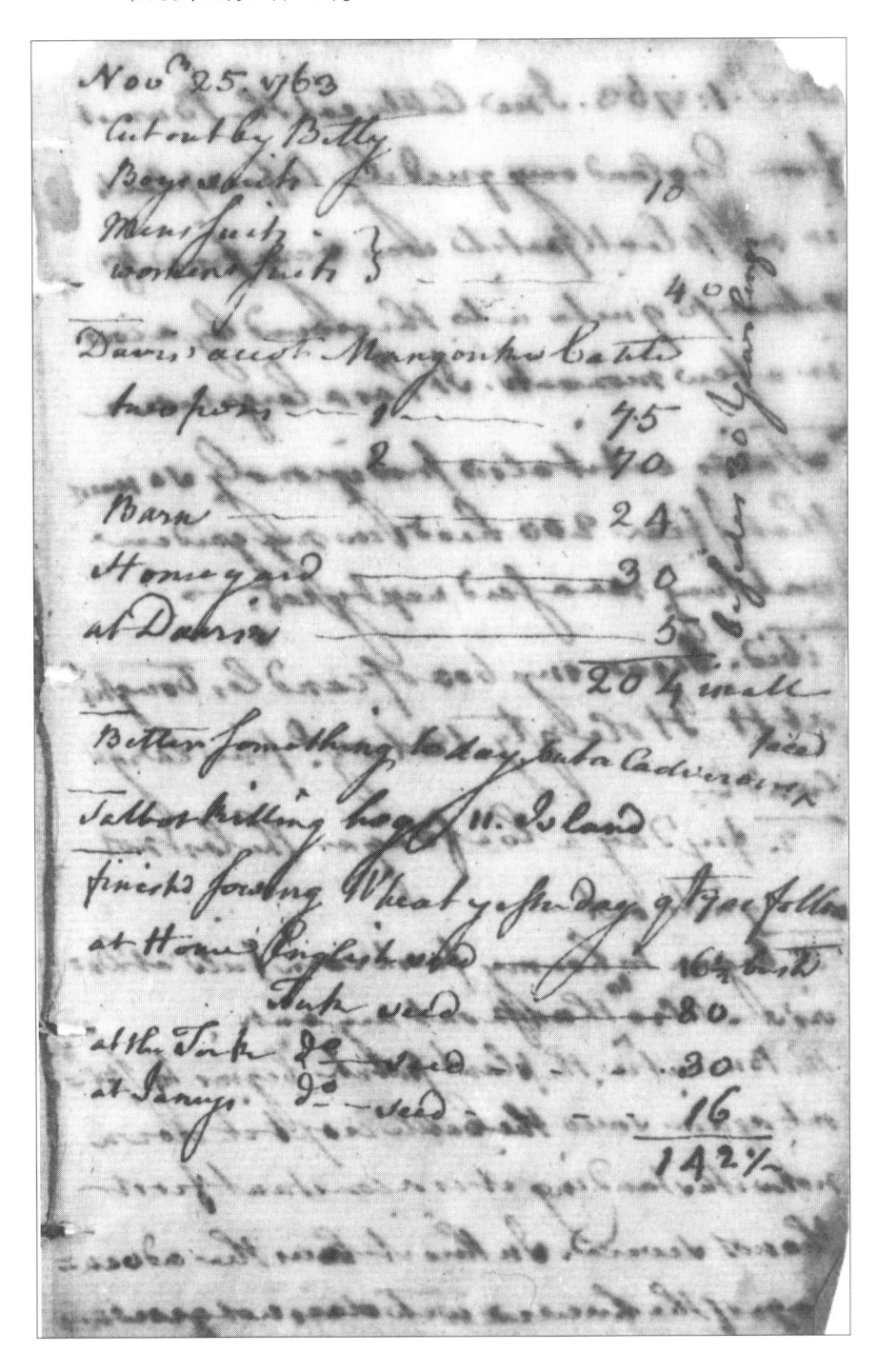

Landon Carter's Diary, Nov. 17, 1763, Sabine Hall Papers (#1959), The Albert and Shirley Small Special collections Library, University of Virginia Library.

史料4-3-4 「製織工場の設備」に関する記載 [ランドン・カーターの財産目録(1779年2月9日から)]

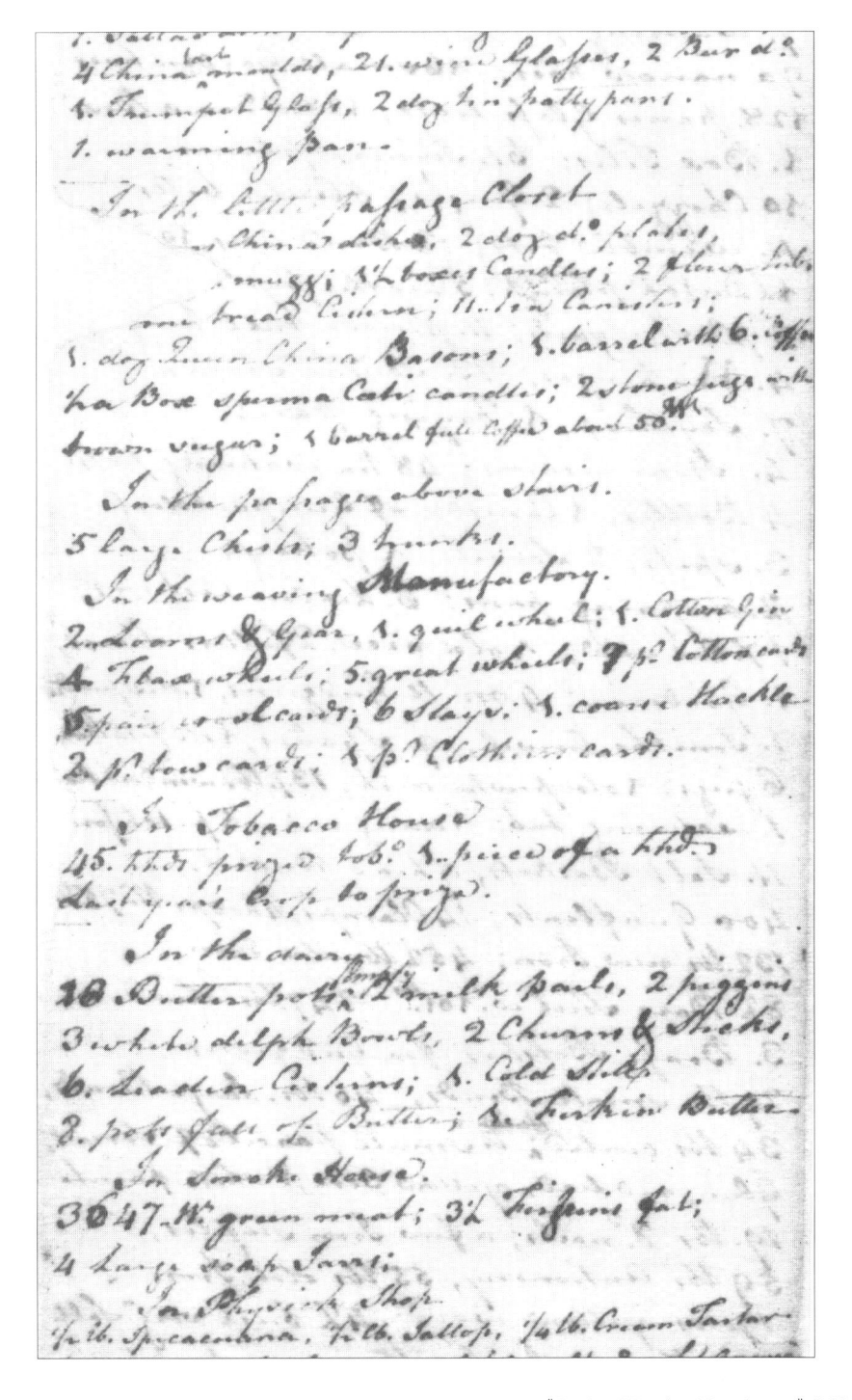

Inventory of The Estate of Landon Carter esqr, February 1779. Page5, " In the Weaving Manufactory", Sabine Hall Papers (#1959), The Albert and Shirley Small Special collections Library, The University of Virginia Library.

　　　　クロージア・カード機　　　　　　　1台
　P.ギブズは「この設備はおそらくヴァージニアのプランテーションにおける布の生産工場の代表的なものであった[33]」と評価している。

　以上の事例から、アメリカ独立革命期におけるランドン・カーターの織物の国内生産への取り組みが、いかに積極的に行なわれたか、その状況を窺い知ることができる。特に黒人奴隷労働力の生産性と生産設備の向上が彼の重要な課題であった。

　さて、これらの課題に対するヴァージニアのプランターたちのその後の経過をロバート・カーター・オブ・ノミニ・ホールのヴァージニアにおける工場生産について調査した。

(2) 事例2．ロバート・カーター・オブ・ノミニ・ホール（Robert Carter of Nomini Hall）の場合[34]
　史料4-3-5は1773～1791年のロバート・カーターの奴隷所有数の一覧[35]である。

　ロバート・カーター（図4-3-4）はノミニ・ホール（図4-3-5）に布の生産工場を設立したが、これはプランテーションにおける最も大きく最も長く続いた布の生産工場であった。彼の工場は当初は彼の多くのプランテーションの需要を満たすために操業していたのであり、工場運営というよりも、むしろプランテーション内部の運営のために機能していた。1760年代および1770年代に織工を雇っていた多くの仲間のプランターとは異なり、ロバート・カーターは大英帝国との貿易が停止されるようになるまで、工場の操業を始めなかった。彼は1775年2月、彼の財産管理人のW.テイラー（William Taylor）に次のように書いた。

　　「奴隷とプランテーションを所有しているすべての人々が、彼らの黒人奴隷と家族のための食料品と同様に、衣服を作らなければならない時がやってきた。今やアメリカ大陸のいくつかの政府が大英帝国との通商を停止されている[36]」と。

　ロバート・カーターは10人の最もすぐれた紡績工を紡績のためにだけ働かせるべく計画し、タバコ小屋を紡績用の部屋に改造し、4ヶ月以内に、8人がこの小屋で羊毛を紡ぐようになった。2人はノミニ・ホールで羊毛を紡いだ。

　ロバート・カーターは最初の紡績工場を始めて間もなく、彼のルードン・カウンティー（Loudoun County）のプランテーションで、さらにもう一つの紡績工場を作った。7月に奴隷監督に「私の若い黒人奴隷の女性と年をとった体の弱い黒人奴隷たちを糸を紡ぐために確保しておくつもりだ。……そして、私はあなたの住居の隣りに建っているタバコ小屋を紡績工場にするように、また、そこに2本の煙突を立て、煙突の周りと先にラスを張り、土とモルタルを詰め、根太をふやして、その上に厚板の床を張るように……この作業はただちに行なわれなければならない。[37]」と書いた。

　次年度のはじめにロバート・カーターはさらに奴隷監督に「2種類のリネン（linen）、すなわち、サッキング・クロス（sacking cloth）とオズナブルグ（osnabrug）を作るための糸を紡ぎなさい。上に述べた布の生産は、トゥ（tow）から作りなさい。あなたの亜麻（flax）と大麻（hemp）を使って

史料4-3-5　ロバート・カーターの奴隷所有数一覧（1773〜1791年）

COUNTY	PLANTATIONS	1773	1780	1782	1784	1785	1788	1791
Westmoreland	Nomini Hall	155	87	77	80	77	110	114
	Aries			22	38	37	34	42
	Old Ordinary		51	49	54	58	—	44
	Taurus		108	47	42	55	20	21
	Gemini			43	44	46	15	14
	Forest Quarter		—	29	27	27	15	21
	Coles Point		16	21	28	38	29	31
	Tenements		—	—	46	—	—	—
Richmond	Dickerson's	—	—	6	5	7	—	—
	Billingsgate	—	—	—	37	—	—	—
	John Peck	—	—	—	11	—	—	3
	Rob't Mitchell	—	—	—	—	—	—	3
	Cancer	—	—	9	—	12	8	9
Prince William	Cancer	—	—	—	—	26	25	23
Loudon	Leo	29	—	—	34	36	42	40
	Hired out		—	—	—	—	—	8
Frederick	Aquarius	—	—	—	—	—	14	14
	Scorpio	—	—	—	—	—	25	26
	Capricorn	—	—	—	—	—	20	24
	Libra	—	—	—	—	—	23	25
	Virgo	—	—	—	—	—	25	29
	Sagittarius	—	—	—	—	—	17	18
	Totals	184	262	303	410	466	422	509

Louis Morton, *Robert Carter of Nomini Hall, A Virginia Tabacco Planter of the Eighteenth Century*, Williamsburg Restoration Historical Studies No.2 (Princeton, 1941)

図4-3-4　ロバート・カーター・オブ・ノミニ・ホール　　図4-3-5　ロバート・カーター・オブ・ノミニ・ホールの所有地

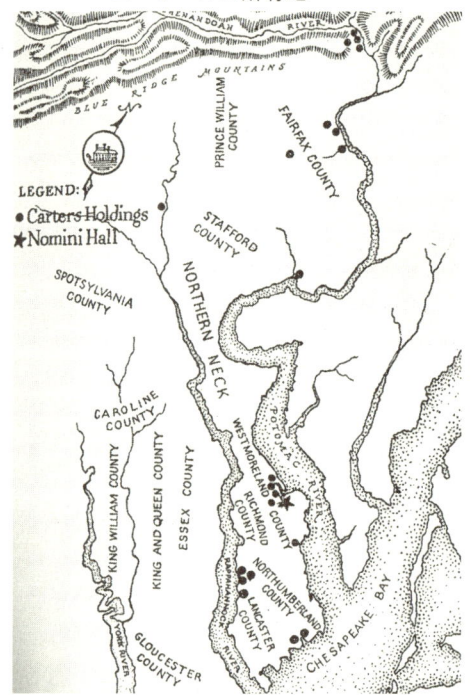

出典：Louis Morton, *Robert Carter of Nomini Hall, A Virginia Tabacco Planter of the Eighteenth Century*, Williamsburg Restoration Historical Studies No.2 (Princeton, 1941)

出典：Louis Morton, *op.cit.*

作ったトゥが、プリンス・ウィリアム・カウンティー（Prince William County）とルードン・カウンティー（Loudoun County）にいる老若を含めて、私の黒人奴隷たちに衣服を着せるのに十分でない場合には、予備の亜麻と大麻を使って紡がせなさい。[38]」と指示を下している。

　ロバート・カーターは1776年、コットン、リネンおよび紡毛織物（woolen cloth）の生産にまで彼の仕事を拡張する[39]。当初3台の織機による操業を白人に行なわせようと計画し、糸の提供、すべての生産物の購入を交渉するが断わられた。そこで、翌年の夏、Giles Higson and Companyを買収し、従業員にアメリカの他の場所と同一の賃金を支払うこと、アリーズ（Aries）に新たに工場を建て、すべての製品を引きとることなどを契約した。8月には織工のG.ヒグソン（Giles Higson）と彼の息子のジョン（John）およびW.ペイトン（William Paton）が女性の黒人奴隷の紡績工を使って布の生産を始めた。アリーズの工場は、アメリカ独立革命後も操業を続けた。1782年には、ダニエ

史料4-3-6　黒人奴隷の織工の雇用に関するロバート・カーターとダニエル・サリバンの契約書（1782年1月1日）

Contract of Robert Carter with Daniel Sullivan, overseer, for his negro clothworker, Jan. 1, 1782, MSS1C 2468a 2068, The Virginia Historical Society, Richmond, Virginia.

ル・サリバン（Daniel Sullivan）マネージャーの下に、6人の男性の黒人奴隷の織工と4人の女性の紡績工がいた。

史料4-3-6[40]は、1782年1月1日のカーターとダニエル・サリバンの契約書の実物の写真である。

 Nominy Hallにて、西暦1782年1月1日
 織工のダニエル・サリバンは、ウェストモアランド・カウンティー（Westmoreland County）のロバート・カーターの所有する紡毛織物およびリネン織物の工場において、6人の黒人奴隷織工……19歳位のGeorge、18歳位のRalph、17歳位のJeremiah、17歳位のDennis、13歳位のPrince、13歳位のWilliam……および4人の黒人糸巻き工……すなわち、65歳位のKate、16歳位のSally、15歳位のAlice、14歳位のMary……の面倒を見、その管理をするものとする。
 上記のダニエル・サリバンには1782年1月1日から12月31日までの1年間の作業に対する全報酬として、金貨または銀貨12ポンド、あるいは、従前の売値で計算したこれに相当する額の地元産物、さらに12バレルのトウモロコシと、400ポンドの豚肉と15ポンドの摘み綿を支給するものとする。これを証するため、私は頭記の年月日にこれに署名する。

                    Daniel Sullivan（署名）
 証人 Geo. Gordon

史料4-3-7[41]は、1787年9月15日、ダニエル・サリバンによって提出された紡績および製織費用に関する史料である。

 ダニエル・サリバンによって提出された紡績および製織費用、1787年9月15日

 拝啓
 来年の紡績・製織事業について、私は、紡績工および製織工たちが幸いにも1年を通じて1日たりとも病気をしないものと仮定して、来年、紡績工場の操業によってどれだけの利益があがるか、また、織工たちがどれだけ稼ぐかを、私にわかる範囲で計算いたしました。お目通しいただければ幸いと存じます。

                      敬具
                      Daniel Sullivan

 紡績単価については
  ブラウン・ロール糸 ……………………… 4シリング
  オズナブルグ糸 …………………………… 1シリング
  袋地用糸 …………………………………… 6ペンス

史料4-3-7　ダニエル・サリバンによって提出された紡績および製織費用（1787年9月15日）

Estimates of earnings by Robert Carter's slave spinners and weavers, furnished by Daniel Sullivan, September 15, 1787, MSS1C 2468a 810-816, The Virginia Historical Society, Richmond, Virginia.

下等の亜麻用糸 …………………… 1シリング3ペンス
　　　下等の紡毛織物用の綿の経糸 …………2シリング（ポンド当たり）
　　　靴下用の下等の紡毛糸 …………………1シリング3ペンス
　　　靴下用の上等の紡毛糸 …………………1シリング6ペンス
　　　下等のトゥ（短繊維）……………………4ペンス
　　　上等のトゥ（短繊維）……………………6ペンス

製織単価は、
　　　ブラウン・ロール ……………………… 4ペンス
　　　オズナブルグ …………………………… 4ペンス
　　　袋地 ……………………………………… 4ペンス
　　　下等の亜麻 ……………………………… 6ペンス
　　　綿の経糸を使用した下等の紡毛織物 …… 4ペンス
　　　上等の毛織物 …………………………… 1シリング
　　　下等の綿布 ……………………………… 4ペンス
　　　17人の紡績工 …………………………… 1人当たり7ポンド16シリング；計　132ポンド12シリング
　　　4人の職工 ……………………………… 1人当たり[　　　　　]；計　110ポンド

　アリーズの工場の生産物は、初期の頃と同じように、粗悪な糸と布であった。生産は白人の助けを借りずに行なわれていた。1787年には利益が急速に減少し、その後3年間、状況が悪化したため、1790年末、ロバート・カーターは工場を貸し出すことにした。借主は工場の土地1,063エーカーに対する税金を支払い、32人の奴隷のうち、16人が年間、65ポンドの賃金を受け取る手はずが整えられる。さらに、すべての黒人奴隷に相応の衣服と食料が提供され、十分な健康管理がなされるべきことが条件として約定された[42]。

　ロバート・カーターは、彼の死までアリーズの工場を所有し続けた。だが、独立戦争中と戦後の時期に経験したような繁栄を見ることは、二度となかった。工場の多くは借主によって管理されており、カーター家の需要を満たすだけの生産が行なわれるにとどまった。

　ここでロバート・カーターが行なった奴隷解放について、是非とも言及しなければならない。

　ロバート・カーターは1791年8月1日、**史料4-3-8**の奴隷解放の文書[43]を公布した。当時、彼は511人の奴隷を所有していた。この文書ではこれらの奴隷を1782年のヴァージニア植民地議会で制定された"An Act to Authorize the Manumission of Slaves"に基づいて、毎年15人ずつ10年かけて解放するとうたっている。南北戦争中、リンカーンが奴隷解放宣言を公布するまで、このように大規模な奴隷解放は例を見ない。奴隷解放問題は本書の直接の目的ではないが、布や被服生産の労働力の観点から見て、本書にも深い関りがある。**史料4-3-9**[44]は1791年にロバート・カーターのプランテーションで働いていた「職人と熟練労働者」の一覧である。紡績工がノミニ・ホールに2

史料4-3-8　ロバート・カーターの奴隷解放の文書（1791年8月1日）

DEED OF GIFT.

  Whereas I Robert Carter of Nomony-Hall in the County of Westmorland and Comon Wealth of Virginia am possessed as my absolute property, off, in and to many Negroe and Mulatto Slaves whose number, Names, Situations and ages will fully appear by a Schedule hereunto annexed: And whereas I have for some time past been convinced that to retain them in Slavery is contrary to the true Principles of Religion and Justice, and that therefor it was my Duty to Manumit them if it could be accomplished without infringing the Laws of my Country, and without being of Disadvantage to my Neighbours and the Community at Large: AND whereas the General Assembly for the Common-Wealth of Virginia did in the Year 1782 enact a Law entitled "An Act to authorize the Manumission of Slaves" now be it remembered that I the said Robert Carter do under the said Act for my-self my Heirs Executors and Administrators emancipate from Slavery all such of my Slaves enumerated in the afore said Schedule (as are under the Age of 45 Years) but in the Manner as herein after particularly mentioned and Set forth, that is to say: that forasmuch as I have with great Care and Attention endeavoured to discover that Mode of Manumission from Slavery which can be effected consonant to Law and with the Least possible Disadvantage to my fellow Citizens I have determined to discharge myself from this Act of Justice and Duty by declaring that my Slaves shall not receive an immediate but a gradual Emancipation in the following Manner - Viz; Fifteen of my Slaves under the Age of 45 beginning at the Oldest and descending according to their Age, are hereby emancipated and Set free on the 2d day of January 1792: And Fifteen more of my Slaves shall be Liberated and Set free on the 1st day of January 1793 and so annually in every Year upon the sd day of January (unless when that happens on a Sunday and then on the next succeeding Day) until the Year 1801 inclusive by which Means, 150 of my Slaves within the Age restricted by the Act aforesaid will be manumitted; Regard still being had in all the Subsequent Manumissions that the Oldest of my Slaves be the first Emancipated: And

whereas it will be found from the Schedule aforesaid that a Large number of my Male and Female Slaves are at present under the Ages of 21 and 18 Years I do hereby declare that such and every of the Male Negroes shall be emancipated and Set free when he or they shall attain the Age of 21 Years, and such and every of the Females when she or they shall have attained to the age of 18 years respectively according to the said Schedule and the aforesaid Act of Assembly: In Witness whereof I have hereunto set my Hand and Affixed my Seal this 1st Day of August 1791 -
Robt Carter

(SEAL)

  And whereas sundry Female Slaves mentioned in the annexed Schedule have been delivered of Children since the 1st Day of January 1791 - which Children are considered as Slaves in the Commonwealth aforesaid - And to provide for the Children that may be so born I do now declare that all the Males and Females that may be born of the aforesaid Women in the course of the present Year 1791 - shall be free - that is to say the Males in the year 1812 Females in the year 1809 or as many of them as may be then living - As witness my hand and Seal the day and Year above written.

Robt Carter.

(SEAL)

Deed of Gift, Robert Carter Day Book, Volume XI(Aug. 1, 1791), pages1-2 MSS. Div., Duke Universityからのコピー。John D. Rockefeller, Jr. Library所蔵。

史料4-3-9　ロバート・カーター所有の職人と熟練労働者の一覧（1791年）

```
B.  Artisans and Special Task Workers

                          At.Nomony Hall     Elsewhere
        Carpenters              12           1--Gemini
        Spinners                 2          10--Aries
                                             1--Old Ord.
        Coopers                  2           1--Forest
                                             1--Leo
                                             1--Virgo
        Weavers                  0           3--Aries
                                             1--Leo
                                             1--Scorpio
        Blacksmiths              3           1--Leo
        Cart drivers             1           1--Coles Point
                                             1--Old Ord.
        Sailors                  3
        Tailor and seamstresses  3
        Livestock herders        1           1--Scorpio
        Fishermen                0           1--Coles Point
                                             1--Old Ord.
        Gardeners                2
        Milkmaids                1           1--Old Ord.
        Woodcutter               0           1--Aries
        Bricklayer               1
        Hatter                   1
        Butcher                  1
        Tanner                   1
        Shoemaker                1
        Miller                   1
                                ──           ──
                                36           28

 Sources:  Deed of Emancipation, August 1, 1791, Robert
Carter Papers (Vol. 11), Perkins Library, Duke University;
"2d Book of Miscellanies," 1788-1790, Robert Carter Papers,
Library of Congress.
```

John Randolf Barden, " *Flushed with Notions' of Freedom": The Growth and Emancipation of a Virginia Slave Community*, 1732-1812, Dissertation: Degree Date 1993, Duke University, p.465.

人、アリーズに10人、オールド・オーチャード（Old Orchard）に１人、織工がアリーズに３人、レオ（Leo）に１人雇われていたことが示されている。

(3) 事例３．ロバート・ウォームレイ・カーター（Robert Wormeley Carter）[45]の場合

　ロバート・ウォームレイ・カーター（1754～1798）はランドン・カーターの末の息子であり、ロバート・キング・カーター（Robert "King" Carter）の孫であった。彼は1765年、印紙条例に反対し、1766年２月27日、リードタウン（Leedtown）で可決されたウェストモアランド決議（Westmoreland Resolution）に署名した。彼の政治家としての活躍は、1767年に郡裁判所の治安判事（Justice of Peace）に任命されたときから始まった。２年後にはリッチモンド・カウンティ（Richmond County）を代表して植民地議会代議会員に任命され（1769～1776）、植民地に対するイギリスの課税に反対し

た。1779年、1781年および1782年にも植民地議会代議会員を務めた。それ以降は公的な生活を引退し、プランテーションの管理に専念した。

ロバート・ウォームレイ・カーターはタバコやとうもろこしや小麦などの穀物を栽培したり、家畜を飼育したりして、家族や奴隷の衣食住をまかなった。また、シェナンドー渓谷（Shenandoah Valley）の借地人に土地を貸し出した。このようなプランテーション管理の傍ら、仲間のプランターたちとギャンブルに興じたという。

1766年3月11日[46]　（史料4-3-10）
　Backwoodsmenの私の黒人奴隷用のリネンを買ってくれるよう、D.トムソン（Dekar Thomson）氏に手紙を書くことを忘れぬこと。

1769年12月31日[47]　（史料4-3-11）
　バル（Ball）氏は私のために黒人奴隷用の靴30足を、1シリング3ペンスで作ってくれたと私に言った。

1769年にMcKawayによって紡績された糸[48]　（史料4-3-12）
　　R. Beverley に売却（済）　……………11.1/4ポンド（11ポンド4オンス）
　　　　Thos Wyld　………………………16ポンド
　済　W. Brockenbrough………………10ポンド
　　　　WmSon Ball　……………………3ポンド9オンス
　済　R. W. Carter　………………………1ポンド14オンス
　済　George Garland　……………………1ポンド8オンス
　済　Mary Garland　………………………1ポンド8オンス
　　　　William Buckland　………………1ポンド
　　　　William Beale　……………………2ポンド
　　　　………………………………………48ポンド2オンス

　　48ポンド2オンス　ポンド当り　2シリング4ペンス　6ポンド3 3/4 ペンス
　　　　　　　　　　　　　　　　　　　　　　　　　12ポンド13シリング1 3/4 ペンス
　　　　　　　　　　　　　　　　　　　　　　　　　18ポンド13シリング5 1/2 ペンス

　上記により、1769年に私の織工は18ポンド13シリング5 1/2 ペンスを稼ぎ出したことが分かるが、ここから彼の被服費、維持費、税金および Hemp（麻）の代金をださなければならず、総計額は大幅に少なくなる。下等および上等の布を5ペンスで織っても何の利益にもならないということは、私にはよく分かっている。従って、今後は私自身のものを作らせることだけを目

史料4-3-10　黒人奴隷用のリネンの購入について［ロバート・ウォームレイ・カーターの日記］
（1766年3月11日から）

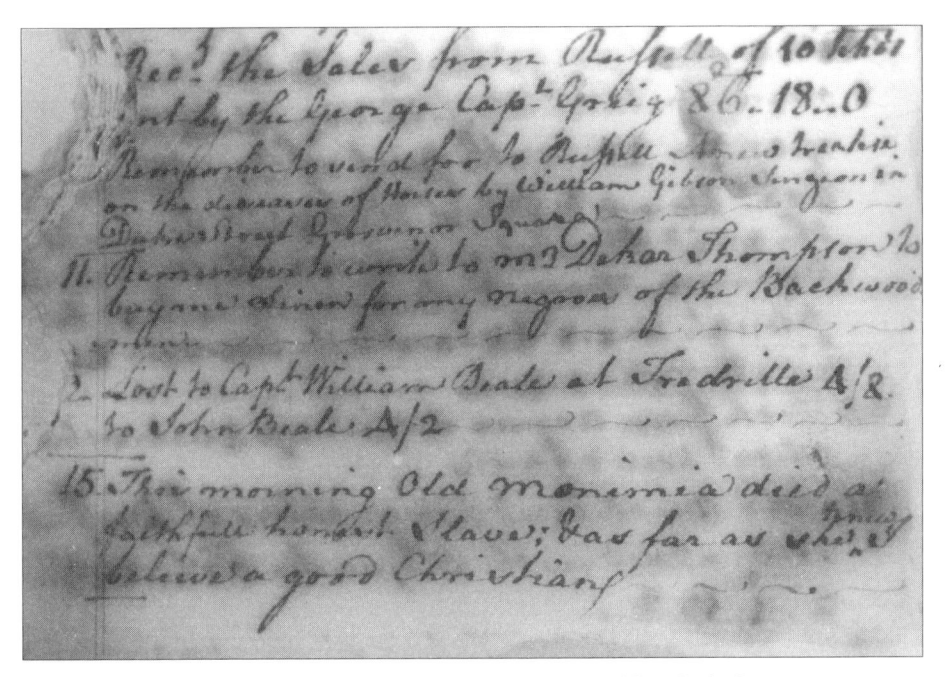

The Diary of Robert Wormeley Carter, March 11, 1766, Manuscripts and Rare Books Department, Swem Library, College of William and Mary, Williamsburg, Virginia

史料4-3-11　黒人奴隷用の靴の製造について［ロバート・ウォームレイ・カーターの日記］
（1769年12月31日から）

The Diary of Robert Wormeley Carter, December 31, 1769, Manuscripts and Rare Books Department, Swem Library, College of William and Mary, Williamsburg, Virginia.

史料4-3-12　1769年にMcKawayによって紡績された糸について［ロバート・ウォームレイ・カーターの日記］（1769年12月から）

The Diary of Robert Wormeley Carter, December 1769. The linen thread spun by McKaway 1769. Manuscripts and Rare Books Department, Swem Library, College of William and Mary, Williamsburg, Virginia.

的として続けるつもりである。私が彼に与えた25ポンドの取り分もさしひかなければならないので、利益はほんの僅かなものとなる。

　ロバート・ウォームレイ・カーターもプランターとしての立場から、黒人奴隷労働力の生産性の向上のために、かれらの衣食住の確保につとめていた。P. ギブズによると彼はG. ワシントンと同様に国内産の布地と輸入品の品質およびコストの比較のための実験を試みたという[49]。結局、結論は輸入品の方が品質がよく、コストも安く、織工の利益にはならない、という結果に至った。

２．ジョージ・ワシントンの場合

(1) ジョージ・ワシントン（George Washington）の経歴[50]

　ジョージ・ワシントン（1732～1799）（図4-3-6）はヴァージニアの富裕な地主の子として生まれた。12歳のとき父を失ったが、父の所有地の大部分は異母兄が継ぎ、彼にはわずかな土地しか与えられなかった。だが、1752年異母兄の死に遭い、広大な所有地マウント・ヴァーノンと、ヴァージニア民兵の第一部隊長の職を受け継いだ。1759年、マーサ・D. カスティス（Martha Dandridge Custis）と結婚し、マウント・ヴァーノンに317人の奴隷を所有するプランターとなる（口絵4-3-7から4-3-9）。彼はプランテーションを５つの農場に分けて管理した。その後1775年、第二回大陸会議によって、

図4-3-6 ジョージ・ワシントン

出典：The Home of George Washington—Mt. Vernon 40 Color Slides and Tape Casette with Narration, Whittier, California, Finley-Holiday Film Corp.

アメリカ大陸軍の総司令官に任命され、さらに、アメリカ合衆国初代大統領に選ばれる。

(2) 奴隷の被服の種類

G.ワシントンは生涯を通じて奴隷の衣服用に大量の布を注文していたが、マウント・ヴァーノンでも、1767年から布の生産が行なわれていた。

第3章で言及したように、ランド・ワシントン（Lund Washington）の会計帳簿（account book）[51]には大半のプランテーションで、1774年には、男の奴隷には1着のジャケット、1本のブリーチズ、2枚のシャツ、1足の靴下および1足の靴がめいめいに支給され、女の奴隷には1着のペティコートと1着のジャケットと2枚のシフトと1足の靴下と1足の靴が与えられた（史料3-1-1）、と記されている。また、この会計帳簿には、家内の奴隷はもっと沢山の衣服が与えられたという多くの証拠がある。例えば、ヘラクレス（Hercules）は1772年に1着のスーツと3着の下着用ズボンを受け取り、ウィル（Will）は繕われた4本のブリーチズを持っていた（史料3-1-2）。年季奉公人で煉瓦職人のジョン・ノールズ（John Knowles）は1774年に1着のウェストコートと1本のブリーチズを受

け取った（史料3-1-3）、と記録されている。

(3) 奴隷用の被服素材の入手方法について
　1757年、G.ワシントンはフレデリックスバーグ（Fredricksburg）の母親に、次のように書いた。

　「私は今まで、グレート・ブリテンから私の黒人の衣服が到着するのを期待して待っていました。だが、季節は移り変わり、危険が彼らに迫っているので（冬が近づいてくるという意味—筆者注）、もうこれ以上待ってはいられません。そこで私はあなたに、約250ヤードのオズナブルグ、200ヤードの木綿、35足の格子柄の靴下と必要なだけの糸……を選んでくれるようお願いしたのです[52]」

　彼は年末に、イギリスから布を受け取っている。ロンドンのT.ノット（Thomas Knot）からの送り状は9月28日の日付であった。G.ワシントンは12月26日、再び送り状を受け取り、品物を近々、受け取れることを期待していると書いている。このとき彼が受け取った布は326エル（ell）（約372メートル）のオズナブルグであった[53]。奴隷のために注文した格子縞の靴下（plaid hose）は、G.ワシントンが注文した数点の品々と一緒には送られなかった。
　1759年の注文[54]には、黒人の召使い用の夏用フロックをつくるための40ヤードの目の粗いジーンズ（Jeans）、またはファスチャン（Fustian）が含まれていた。分量からこの布は家内奴隷用の布と思われる。その他、450エルのオズナブルグ、4ポンドの茶色のロールズ（rolls）、350ヤードのケンダル・コットン（Kendall cotton）、100ヤードのダッチ・ブランケット（Dutch Blankets）、8ダースの格子縞の靴下の注文が含まれていた。これらはおそらく野良の奴隷のための注文であろう。この注文はこの年の代表的な注文であった。
　G.ワシントンの元には、1783年までには黒人用に1,000エルのジャーマン・オズナブルグ（German Oznaberg）、またはティックルンブルグ（Ticklinburg）と200エルのダッチ・ブランケット（Dutch Blanket）が届いたと記されている[55]。このような大量の注文は、おそらく戦争中の布不足によるものであろう。1785年には、彼は召使い用に2級品、あるいは最も粗悪な品質の18枚の南京木綿（Nankeen）を購入した。

(4) 奴隷のお仕着せの生産について
　1764年、ワシントンは彼の仕立て屋のチャールズ・ローランス（Charles Lawrence）に宛てて、お仕着せのスーツについての詳しい説明を付けて、手紙を書いた。

　「同封の色と品質のウーステッドの粗毛で、赤いシャルーン（shalloon）の裏付きのスーツを1着、下記のとおり作ること。コートとブリーチズは、平たい白くメッキしたボタンを付けて同じように仕立て、ボタンホールは同じ色のモヘアでかがること。コートには赤い粗毛の衿を付け、

そのまわりを同封のものと同じような細いモールで縁取ること。コートには、同色のカフスを付け肘まで折り返し、その部分にモールを付けること。赤い粗毛製（ウーステッドの粗毛でもよい）のウェストコートを作り、衿と袖に付けたのと同じモールを付けること。また、もう1着別の寸法のお仕着せを、上記のものとまったく同じように、同じ色の粗毛で作り、モールを付けること。ただし、その代金はマスター・カスティスに請求すること[56]」

口絵3-1-2はピーター・F.コープランド（Peter F. Copeland）によって描かれた、マウント・ヴァーノンの奴隷の従僕のお仕着せのイラストであり、Dewitt Wallace Gallery of Decorative Arts所蔵のお仕着せ（口絵3-1-1①～③）は、このイラストのお仕着せと大変、類似している[57]。

(5) 奴隷の靴の支給と生産について

マウント・ヴァーノンでは何足もの靴が作られていた証拠はある（図4-3-13）が、G.ワシントンは、大量の靴を購入した。例えば、1785年[58]には大きいサイズの丈夫で良くできた黒人用の靴を100足注文した。1786年[59]、M. コックバーン（Martin Cockburn）に手紙を書いて、彼がその年までに黒人の仕立て屋を雇えるかどうか、そして、もし雇えるなら、どのような条件で、何時、雇えるかについて尋ねている。しかし、その結果については不明である。同年、彼はフィラデルフィアで150足の黒人用の靴を作るために、なめし革（leather）を買おうとした。彼は靴をアレグザンドリアで作らせていたが、フィラデルフィアでもっと安いなめし革を買おうと考えたようである。

(6) 奴隷用の衣服素材の生産について

1786年、G.ワシントンは野良の黒人奴隷たちに、着せるのに十分間に合うだけの目の粗いウールを生産したと述べている（口絵4-3-10から4-3-12）が、数量については不明である。G.ワシントンは黒人奴隷用の服地の支給方法について、1792年の手紙で次のように書いている。

「（リネンには）二種類の価格があることをあなたはご存知でしょう。一番、安価なものは少年、少女に支給され、最高の価格の最上のものは、成人した報酬を受けるに値する男女に支給され、余剰品（あなたが要求した布地よりも余分にあるので）は品物を損なわないようにして、保管しておくように[60]」

この手紙は、働く奴隷は働けない奴隷が受け取るよりも、もっと上等の衣服を受け取っていたことを示している。奴隷の衣服費はプランテーション経営においては巨大な額であった。前述のように、マウント・ヴァーノンでは、ある程度の織物生産が行なわれていたが、プランテーションの需要を満たすには決して十分ではなかった。マウント・ヴァーノンで働いていた織工は、雇われるか、あるいは年季奉公人のいずれかであった。雇われた織工も年季奉公人も仕事を手伝ってくれる黒人奴隷を所有していた。

史料4-3-13 マウント・ヴァーノン・プランテーションにおける製織に関するトーマス・デイビスの会計帳簿（1767年，原本の写し）

George Washington Papers, Series Vol. #6, Library of Congress.

　マウント・ヴァーノンにおける製織に関する最も詳しい史料は、1767年から1770年にかけて、トマス・デイヴィス（Thomas Davis）によって作成された会計帳簿（Account Book）（史料4-3-13[61]、4-3-14[62]）である。

　この会計帳簿によると、1767年には188 1/2 ヤードのリンジー・ウールジー（linsey-woolsy）、約25ヤードのコットン（cotton）、および7ヤードのコットンとシルクの交織織物がG.ワシントンのために織られた。同じ年の会計帳簿には各種の布を織る少なくとも11人の織工に対して支払う額が記されている。これらのうち3人は女性であった。T.デイヴィスは奴隷用の布を織っていたようである。他の織工たちはG.ワシントンの家族用のコットンやコットンとシルクの交織織物を織っていた。

　G.ワシントンの1799年の奴隷財産目録（史料4-3-15）[63]には、紡績工および編物工を合わせて9人が記載されている。多くの女性奴隷たちが、衣服生産に従事していたものと思われる。

　史料4-3-16[64]はG.ワシントンが輸入素材と国内産の素材のコストを比較した結果を表している。輸入素材のほうがコストが安いという結果が出ている点は、ロバート・ウォームレー・カーターの場合と同じである。

史料4-3-14　マウント・ヴァーノン・プランテーションにおける製織に関するトマス・ディヴィスの会計帳簿（1767年）（タイプ印刷文書）

To whom belonging	When Brought Months	Days	Weight of the Thread Lbs.	Oz.	When Finished Months	Days	Length Yds.	Qrs.	Weight of the Cloth Lbs.	Oz.	Breadth of Ditto	Hundreds in the Width
John Alton	January	1	6	2	Jany.	2	10				3 Quart.	400
G. Washington	Ditto	1	33	8	Ditto	6	36				Yard	350
Isaac Gates	Ditto	10	13	8	Ditto	10	30				3 Quart.	400
James Wren			30	12	Ditto	17	34	2	31		Yard	550
Geo. Washington	Ditto	17	47		Ditto	26	50		58		Yard	350
Danl. McKay	Ditto		6		February	24	10		6		3 Quarts	500
Gilbt. Simpson	Ditto											
G. Washington	Ditto	27	35		Ditto	26	44		47		Yard	350
Mary Mobbs	February	28	2	8	March	3	6	1	2	8	3 Qurs.	900
G. Washington	Ditto		14	8	Ditto	7	50		27		3 Qrs.	750
Danl. Talbot	March	2	20		Ditto	27	22		20		3 Qrs.	500
Jas. Cleveland	Ditto	3	11									
Isaac Gates	Ditto	9										
G. Washington	Ditto	Do.	34	8	March		56		53	8	Yard	300
H. Y. Peake	Ditto	16	2	14	April	6	12	2	3	12	3 Qurtrs	900
Danl. McKay	Ditto	23	8	6	Ditto	11	19	3	8	6	3 Qrs.	600
Jno. Dulan	April	30	8	10	May	4	23	2	8	12	3 Qrs.	700
Col. Bassett	Ditto		3		Ditto	25	13		3	8	Yard	1200
Jno. Sheridine	Ditto	24	6	12	June	6	17		7	12	3 Qrs.	800
Danl. Talbot	Ditto	27	8	8	May	11	21		9	8	7 eights	800
Jas. Cleveland	May	2	6	2	Ditto	25	17		6	14	3 Qrs.	800
Mr. Washington	Ditto	6	5	4	July	8	8	2	5		3 Qrs.	800
Ditto	Ditto	Do.	5	12	July	12	9	2	4		3 Qrs.	900
Ditto	Ditto	Do.	9	9	Ditto	6	24		11	12	Yard	1000
G. Washington	Ditto	Do.	9	10	May	15	34		21	8	3 Qrs.	650
Ditto	March	16	25		March	21	43		50		Yard	350
brought over												
G. Washington	May	12	15	8	May	21	53	1	31		3 Qrs.	700
G. Washington		15	15		July	8	53		33		3 Qrs.	700
Mr. R. Sanford		18	3	3	June	11	7	2	3	8	7 eights	900
Mrs. Jane Shaw		20	3		Septr.	3	13	2	4	2	Yard	1000
Jos. Moxley		21	3	12	July	18	7	3	4	2	Yard	900
Saml. Johnston		22	3	8	Augt.	21	8	3	4	8	3 Qrs.	1100
G. Washington		29	1	10	June	1	8	2	2	14	Yard	1100

What Kind of Cloth	Price Per Yard s.	d.	Amounts to £	s.	d.	Filling Wanted Lbs.	Oz.	Sickness and other Occurances
striped Woolen		5		4	2			
Woolen plaided		6		18				Jany. 22d. & 23d. Dresed
Cotton striped		5		12	6			pd. thread @ 3/6 pr Day 7/
Linnen		5		14	2			c.
Wool birdeye		6	1	5	0	11		
Linnen		4		3	4			pd.
								Cut out--too bad to Wea'e.
Wool birdeye		6	1	2		12		
Cotton plain	1			6	3			pd. hindd. with sickness fin.
Linnen		6	1	5		13		29th Jany. til 25th Feby.
Cotton filld. Wt. Wool		4		7	4			pd.
								not to be Wove
								Ditto Ditto
Linsay plaided		6	1	8	0	19		
Cotton striped	1			12	6		9	c. March 16th 17th
Thread & Cotton birdeye				19	9			pd. & 18th making
Ms. & Os. Plaided	1	1	1	5	3			pd. Harness for Colo. Bassetts Cloth 0-9-0
Cotton India Dimity	2	6	1	12	6		8	not chargd.
Ms. & Os. Cotton	1			17	1			chargd
Cotton birdeye	1		1	1		1		pd.
Cotton Ms. & Os. Counp. [counterpane]	1			17			10	c. Warpd. to 15 Yds.
Cotton & Wool		8		6	4			
Cotton Jumpstripe	2			19				
Cotton birdeye	2		2	8		2	12	
Linnen		4		11	4	11	6	Warpd. to 33 yds.
Wool birdeye		6	1	1	6	25		
			20	16	11			
			20	16	11			
Linnen filld wt. Tow		4		17	8	15	8	Warpd. to 51 Yds.
Linnen		4		17	8	18		Warpd. to Do.
Cotton birdeye	1	3		9	4		5	c. Warpd. to / Yds.
Cotton stripd. w. silk	2		1	7		1	12	c.
Roman M.	1	6		11	6		4	pd.
Cotton Counterpn.	1			8	9	1		c.
Do. Janes Twilld.	2	6	1	1	3	1	4	

Mr. L. Washington		30	3	4		4	8	2	3	3 Qrs.	1000
Capth. Darnell	June	2	3	2	Augt.	5	8	1	4	2 3 Qrs.	900
Mr. H. Peake		2	1	4	Octr.	17	7		2	7 eights	1200
Thos. Wren Junr.		3	3	14	June	15	7	3	3	15 7 eights	900
Mr. Monroe		12	5	4	Septr.	25	16	3	5	4 3 Qrs.	900
G. Washington		22	10	-	June	26	15	2	18	Ell wide	700
Mr. Abed. Adams			4	8	Do.		14	2	6	6 3 Qrs.	800
Miss Wades	July	1	4	15	Octr.	31	14	2	4	15 3 Qrs.	900
Ditto		1	4		Octr.	24	16	2	5	3 Qrs.	1200
Ditto		1	6	8	Decr.	13	16		6	8 3 Qrs.	900
Robt. Lindsay		3	7	6	Augt.	20	13	3	7	8 3 Qrs.	900
G. Washington		17	11	8	July	22	37	3	20	3 Qrs.	600
Jas. Cleveland		19	10	9	Decr.	18	18	2	10	8 3 Qrs.	400
G. Washington		21	4		July	24	6	2	4	2 Yard	1200
G. Washington		22	10		Ditto	27	3	3		3 Qrs.	600
Wm. Sinclare		24	4		Novr.	21	7	3	4	1 7 eights	900

3 その他の事例

(1) ターナー・サウスホール大佐（Turner Southhall）の事例
　　―Turner Southhall Receipt Book 1776-1784から―

　史料4-3-17①②は、植民地の長官（commissioner）のターナー・サウスホール大佐（Col. Turner Southhall）がヴァージニア邦リッチモンド北のジェームズ川沿いのウェストハム（Westham）に鋳造所の施設と建物を建設した際の領収書である。アメリカ独立革命期にはここで武器や弾薬が製造されていた。史料中にはこの鋳造所の建設者のJ. バレンディン（John Ballendine）によって建設されたウェストハム運河（Westham Canal）のための明細書も混じっている。

　史料4-3-17①②[65]は、上記のうち、黒人奴隷のための被服に関する領収書および明細書が掲載されている部分である。

史料4-3-17①
・鋳造所の黒人奴隷用の衣服を作るために、ターナー・サウスホール（Turner Southhall）から25シ

Do. Do. Do.	1	6	12	9		not chrgd.
Birdeye Cotton	1		8	3	1	c.
Jump stripe	2	6	17	6	12	c.
Cotton birdeye	1	3	9	9		c.
Cotton striped		10	13	9		c.
Woolen		10	12	11	8	
Striped Cotton		8	8	6		c.
Ditto Ditto	1		14	8		c.
Ditto Ditto	1	8	1 7	6		c.
Roman M	1		1 0	0		c.
Birdeye Cottn.	1		13	9		c.
Linnen		4	12	7	19	Wove by Dick
Plain Woolen		4	6	2		c.
Jeans	2	6	16	3		
Linnen		4	10	7		Wove by Dick
Birdeye	1	3	9	9		pd.

Early American History Reprints, Patricia Gibbs, *Cloth Production in Virginia to 1800*, Fiche# 1 of 6, c.1989, Special Collections, John D. Rockefeller, Jr. Library, Colonial Williamsburg Foundation, Williamsburg, Virginia.

リングを1777年12月15日に受領する。

史料4-3-17②

・運河の建設のためにJ. バレンディン（John Ballendine）に雇われた黒人奴隷用の布地にターナー・サウスホールから20ポンドを1777年12月15日に受領する。

　これらの領収書から、ヴァージニア植民地の長官ターナー・サウスホール大佐がアメリカ独立戦争中に、武器、弾薬を製造する鋳造所の建設にあたった黒人奴隷の衣服やストッキングの支給のために、大きな努力をしていたことが明らかである。

(2) カーベル家の事例

　史料4-3-18[66]はカーベル（Cabell）家の黒人奴隷に靴とストッキングおよびブランケットを支給した際の覚書である。75人の黒人奴隷の名前が列記されている。この覚書から、プランターにとっ

史料4-3-15　マウント・ヴァーノンの紡績工、編物工および裁断師の一覧表（1799年）
　　　　　　［ジョージ・ワシントンの奴隷財産目録から］

	Recapitulation															
	Belonging to GW							Dower							Grand Total
Where and how Empld.			Workg.		Childn.					workg		Childn				
	Men	Womn	boys	girls	boys	girls	Total	Men	Wome	boys	girls	boys	girls	Total	
Tradesmen and others, not employed on the Farms....viz															
Smiths	2	--	--	--	--	--	2	--	--	--	--	--	--	--	2
Bricklayers	1	--	--	--	--	--	1	1	--	--	--	--	--	1	2
Carpenters	5	--	--	--	--	--	5	1	--	--	--	--	--	1	6
Coopers	3	--	--	--	--	--	3	--	--	--	--	--	--	--	3
Shoemaker	1	--	--	--	--	--	1	--	--	--	--	--	--	--	1
Cooks	1	--	--	--	--	--	1	--	1	--	--	--	--	1	2
Gardeners	2	--	--	--	--	--	2	--	--	--	--	--	--	--	2
Millers	1	--	--	--	--	--	1	--	--	--	--	--	--	--	1
House-Servants	1	--	--	--	--	--	1	2	4	--	--	--	--	6	7
Ditchers	4	--	--	--	--	--	4	1	--	--	--	--	--	1	5
Distillery	--	--	--	--	--	--	--	4	--	1	--	--	--	5	5
Postilions	--	--	--	--	--	--	--	1	--	1	--	--	--	2	2
Waggoners and Cartrs	1	--	--	--	--	--	1	2	--	--	--	--	--	2	3
Milk Maid	--	--	--	--	--	--	--	--	1	--	--	--	--	1	1
Spinners and Knitr	--	1	--	--	--	--	1	1	7	--	--	--	--	8	9
Mansion Ho								3	9	3	2	8	15	40	40
Muddy hole	3	14	1	--	8	10	36	2	--	--	2	--	--	4	40
River Farm	3	9	2	2	6	4	26	6	9	2	1	5	5	28	54
Dogue Run F	6	7	--	1	7	3	24	5	5	1	--	5	6	17	41
Union Farm	2	1	--	--	--	2	5	4	6	3	--	8	6	27	32
	36	32	4	3	21	19	115	28	42	11	5	26	32	144	259
Passed labr or that do not Work — Muddy hole	--	--	--	--	--	--	--	--	1	--	--	--	--	1	1
River Farm	1	1	--	--	--	--	2	1	1	--	--	--	--	2	4
Dogue Run	--	3	--	--	--	--	3	--	1	--	--	--	--	1	4
Union Farm	--	1	--	--	--	--	1	--	3	--	--	--	--	3	4
Mansion Ho	3	--	--	--	--	--	3	--	2	--	--	--	--	2	5
	40	37	4	3	21	19	124	29	50	11	5	26	32	153	277
Hired frm Mrs. French	9	9	2	4	6	10	40	--	--	--	--	--	--	--	40
Grand Total	49	36	6	7	27	29	164	29	50	11	5	26	32	153	317[a]

[a] From a photostat of the original through the kindness of Judge E. A. Armstrong, of Princeton, N. J.

John C. Fitzpatrick ed., *The writings of George Washington from the Original Manuscript Sources*, vol.37, Washington, United States Government Printing office, 1931(?), Greenwood Press, Publishers, Westport Connecticut, p.268.

史料4-3-16 ジョージ・ワシントンによる輸入素材と国内産素材のコストの比較(1768年)(原文書／タイプ印刷文書)

```
          A Comparison drawn, between Manufacturing & Importing; the Goods on the other side, viz;

  To 509 yds. of best Cotton [sic], to      Wool to make 365 yds. and 144
    supply ye place of 365 yds. wool          yds. of woolen cloth, viz. 499 lbs.
    and 144 yds. Linsey @ 1s.6d.   38.03. 6.  @ 1s.3d.                       32. 5. 0.
  To 773 yds. best Ozbs. as on ye           Hemp to make ye contra cloth
    other side @ 8 d.              25.15. 0.  800 lbs. @ 4d.                 13. 6. 6.
  To 40 yds. Huck @2s.              4. 0. 0. Weaving the above cloth, that is
  To 13 yds. Diapr. @2s.            1.19. 0.   509 yds. woolen, 773 yds. Oznbs.
  To 7 yds. Jeans @5s.              1.15. 0.   Cotton, &c.                   30.15.10.
  To 33 yds. Cotton @2s.            3. 6. 0.                                 76.15. 4.
                                   74.18. 6.
       Charges 12 1/2 p. ct.        9. 7. 4.
                                   84. 5.10.
  25 p. ct. difft. Exch:           21. 1. 5.  Balance                        28.19.11.
       Currency                   105. 7. 3.                                105. 7. 3.

  Note. By this acct, it appears that the above Balance of Lds. 28.19.11 is all that is to defray
  The expence of spinning hire of one white Woman, & 5 Negro Girls—Clothing—Victualling—Wheels &c.
              My own work Lds.         30.15.10.
              For sundries             23. 7. 6
              Total amt. Of Weaving is 54. 3. 4
```

George Washington Papers, M-2075, 116, Special Collections, John D. Rockefeller, Jr. Library, Colonial Williamsburg Foundation, Williamsburg, Virginia.

史料4-3-17 ターナー・サウスホール大佐が黒人奴隷用の衣服に支払った代金の領収書（1777年12月）
① ②

Turner Southhall Receipt Book 1776-1784, 1Vol.[73] pp.MS 31.3,Neg # 99-151, 1s CN, Special Collections, John D. Rockefeller, Jr. Library, Colonial Williamsburg Foundation, Williamsburg, Virginia.

て、労働力としての黒人奴隷への被服の支給が、いかに重要な任務であったかが推察される。

　以上、本章においては奴隷の被服の支給と生産の実態を考察してきたが、最後に得られた結論をまとめておこう。

1. ヴァージニア州ハノーバー・カウンティーのビーバー・ダム・プランテーションで、1800年頃、奴隷によって作られたパッチ・ワーク・キルト（Patchwork Quilt）の実物資料が、ヴァージニア州リッチモンドのValentine Museumに現存しており、この実物資料に見られる多様なストライプと色彩が、ヴァージニア・ガゼット（*Virginia Gazette*）紙掲載の逃亡奴隷広告に見られるヴァージニア・クロスの描写（筆者が第3章で分析）と見事に重なり合っていることが明らかになった。
2. コロニアル・ウィリアムズバーグ振興財団の考古学部門（Department of Archaeological Research）では、カーターズ・グローブ・プランテーション、パレス・プランテーションおよびリッチ・ネック・プランテーションの考古学的発掘調査を進めており、18世紀にプランテーションで使用されていた道具や生活用具が発掘されている。1998年にパレス・プランテーションで発掘された奴隷が用いていた針や指貫は、技術を持った職人の黒人奴隷が衣服の生産に携

史料4-3-18　黒人奴隷の被服に関するカーベル家の覚書（1796年9月27日）

Memo of Cabell Family Papers 1693〜1913,"Memo of shoes, stockings & blankets gave my negroes," 27 Nov., 1796 in Box」, folder 10, Manuscripts and Rare Books Department, Swem Library, College of William and Mary, Williamsburg, Virginia.

わっていたことを裏付ける有用な実物資料である。
3．ヴァージニアの有数なプランターであるカーター家のプランテーションおよびアメリカの初代大統領G.ワシントンが所有していたマウント・ヴァーノンのプランテーションにおいて、奴隷の被服の支給および生産が、どのようにして行なわれていたのか、誰によって行なわれていたのか、という問題について、プランテーションの記録、商人の記録、プランターの日誌や手紙およびその他の公文書に基づいて、その基本的な様相を具体化できた。また、ここで扱った4人のプランターたちが、奴隷の被服の支給および生産に関して実施した政策の特徴と問題点は、次のように整理できる。

(1) 奴隷の被服の支給は、奴隷の健康を管理し、効率よく働かせるために、プランターにとって重要な仕事であった。この点はヴァージニアきっての知識人のプランターであったウィリアム・バード二世が、「病気にかかった奴隷には、1日に1度は必ず、疫病のときには2度も見舞うのが普通であった」という具体的な事実から明らかである。

(2) ランドン・カーターは大陸連盟（Continental Association）が、1774年12月1日をもって大英帝国とアイルランドからのすべての商品を輸入しないことを呼びかけたときの推進者であった。

(3) ヴァージニアにおける布の生産は1770年代の半ばにピークに達した。

(4) ランドン・カーターは年季奉公人は年季があけると独立して、離れていってしまうという問題にもかかわらず、年季奉公人を織工として雇い、彼の黒人奴隷を紡績工や織工として使っていたが、奴隷監督の目を盗んで怠けたり、逃亡したりする奴隷に悩まされていた。

(5) ランドン・カーターは家族と奴隷の衣服や靴の供給のために努力をし、織物生産の設備を整備した。この設備はおそらくヴァージニアのプランテーションにおける布の生産工場の代表的なものであった。

(6) ロバート・カーター・オブ・ノミニ・ホールは、プランテーションにおける最も大きく最も長く続いた布の生産工場を設立した。多くのプランターとは異なり、カーターは大英帝国との貿易が停止に至るまで、工場運営を始めなかった。彼は1776年に布の生産の仕事を拡張し、亜麻、大麻、オズナブルグ、コットン、リネンおよび紡毛織物の生産を推進した。彼の工場は借主によって管理されるようになり、生産量はカーター家の需要を満たす程度のものにとどまった。

(7) ロバート・ウォームレイ・カーターもプランターとしての立場から、黒人奴隷労働力の生産性の向上のために、かれらの衣食住の確保につとめていたが、結局、輸入品の方が品質がよく、コストは国内産より安く、織工の利益にはならなかった。

(8) G.ワシントンは生涯を通じて奴隷の衣服用に大量の布を注文したが、マウント・ヴァーノンにおいても、1767年から布の生産が行なわれていた。G.ワシントンは家内奴隷と野良の奴隷に異なる品質と数の衣服を支給していた。また、労働力として役にたつ奴隷には、働けない奴隷に対してよりも上等の衣服を支給していた。G.ワシントンが輸入素材と国内産の素材のコストを比較した結果、輸入素材の方がコストが安いという結果が出ている点は、ロバート・ウォームレイ・カーターの場合と同じであった。

［注］
(1) Dorothy F. McCombs, *Virginia Cloth: Early Textiles in Virginia, Particularly in the Backcountry Between the Blue Ridge and Allegheny Mountain until 1830*, Unpublished Master's Thesis, Department of History, Virginia Polytechnic Institute, Blacksburg, (Virginia, 1976).
(2) Patricia Gibbs, *Cloth Production in Virginia to 1800*, Research Department, Colonial Williamsburg Foundation, (Colonial Williamsburg, Virginia, March 1978)
(3) 調査日　1999年8月6日。
(4) Linda Baumgartenとのパーソナルコミュニュケーション（1999年8月6日）。
(5) 1999年8月2日聞き取り調査による。
(6) C. カラハンは1996年2月11日から9月7日にかけて、Valentine Museum において開催されたキルト展を担当している。彼女はこのパッチワーク・キルトのラベルに解説を付けている。ここに引用した資料は著者から提供していただいた資料であるが、文献名は不明である。
(7) 調査日　1999年7月27日。
(8) John Hargroveとはどのような人物であったのか。本書のIntroductionには編者によって、次のように著者の紹介が行なわれている。要約紹介する。
　「彼は、1769年、19歳で、母国のアイルランドからメリーランドに移住してきた。この頃、彼は経験豊かな織工であったものと推察される。18世紀の後半に多くのアイルランドの織工が、仕事を求めて新大陸にやってきたのである。それは1750年以降にイングランドからアイルランドに導入された綿業が、徐々にアイルランドのリネン工業と多くの熟練工を追い立てたためである。Hargroveはアメリカでの最初の30年間は、メリーランドの各地に住んでいた。その間、何年間かは熟練した織工であったようである。
　だが、彼は一時、測量技師として働いており、最初の結婚の1776年には　Methodist Episcopal Churchの牧師に任じられた。彼はThe Weaver's Draft Book and Clothiers Assistant の序文において、自らを"Merchant"と記しているが、人生の大半は主に、他の目的に費やしたようである」(Introduction by Rita J. Adrosko, curator of textiles, National Museum of History and Technology, Smithsonian Institutionより要約)。
(9) John Hargrove, *The Weavers Draft Book and Clothiers Assistant* with a new introduction by Rita J. Adrosko, curator of textiles, National Museum of History and Technology, Smithsonian Institution, Worcester American Antiquarian Society, (1979).
(10) John D. Rockefeller, Jr. Library所蔵の本書のコピーを、資料編に添付した。
(11) John Wily, *A Treatise on the Propaganda of Sheep, the Manufacture of Wool, and the Cultivation and Manufacture of Flax, with Directions for making Several Utensils for the Business*, (Williamsburg, printed by F. Royle, MDCCLXV, 1765).
(12) APPENDIX A 1998 Visitor Center Phase Ⅲ Interim Report pp.44-47（kelly Ladd　提供の資料が何という文献、あるいは報告書の中に含まれているものなのかは、筆者の手元では不明である）。
(13) *Virginia Gazette* [Rind], 14 December 1769
　It is with the greatest pleasure we inform our readers that the same patriotic spirit which gave rise to the association of the Gentlemen on a late event, was most agreeably manifested in the dress of the Ladies on this occasion, who, to the number of near one hundred, appeard in homespun gowns; a lively and striking instance of their acquiescence and concurrence in whatever may be the true and essential interest of their country. It were to be wished that all assemblies of American Ladies would exhibit a like example of public service and private oeconomy, so amiably united.
(14) Patricia Gibbs, *Cloth Production in Virginia to 1800*, Research Department Colonial Williamsburg Foundation, Williamsburg Virginia, March 1978, 25-45.
(15) Louis Morton, *Robert Carter of Nomini Hall, A Virginia Tabacco Planter of the Eighteenth Century*, Williamsburg Restoration Historical Studies No.2　(Princeton, 1941), Chapter Ⅰ, 3-30.
(16) Paul P. Hoffman ed., *Guide to the Microfilm Edition of the Carter Family Papers, 1659～1797*, in the Sabine Hall Collection, Microfilm Publication, University of Virginia Library, Number Three, (1967), 7.
(17) Louis Morton, *op.cit.*, 3.

(18) *Ibid.*, 8-13.
(19) *Ibid.*, 26.
(20) The Inventory of the Estate of Landon Carter, Feb. 1779, Manuscripts Print Collection, Special Collections Department, University of Virginia Library.
(21) Jack P. Greene, (ed.), *The Diary of Colonel Landon Carter of Sabine Hall, 1752〜1778*, (Charlottesville, 1965), Vol. I, Vol. II.
(22) *Ibid.*, Vol. I, 383-384.

　　Colonel Harrison's weaver run away and Judy's Cotton is to come down without weaving after being there near 12 months. Thus weavers out of one's own family will never encourage of the least manufactory and I do think it is intirely owing to this that more people do not make a better hand of it.

(23) 池本幸三著『近代奴隷制社会の史的展開―チェサピーク湾ヴァージニア植民地を中心として―』(ミネルヴァ書房、1987年)、286.
(24) Jack P. Greene, (ed.), *ibid.*, 245.
(25) *Ibid.*, 281.

　　Gave Sam, Estate's coachman, 3/9 to pay his ferryages in carrying up the above 70 pairs of shoes for the Estate's negroes.

(26) *Ibid.*, 334.

　　I got his man some years ago to make some negroe shoes.

(27) *Ibid.*, 334.
(28) *Ibid.*, 443.

　　Lucy went away to lay out about 1,500 pounds tobacco in Blare's store for Linnen and cotton for my people.

(29) *Ibid.*, 443.
(30) *Ibid.*, 242.（Typescript掲載）。

　　25　Thursday, November 1763
　　　　Cut out by Betty:
　　　　Boys' suits　　　　10
　　　　Men's suits　　　　⎫
　　　　　　　　　　　　　⎬ 40
　　　　Women's suits　　 ⎭

Landon Carter's Diary, entry dated Nov 17, 1763, Manuscripts Print Collection, Special Collections Department, University of Virginia Library.

(31) Patricia Gibbs, *op. cit.*, 20.
(32) An Inventory of The Estate of Landon Carter esqr. Taken February 1779. Department of the Special Collections, The University of Virginia Library.

　　In the Weaving Manufactory
　　2 looms and gear; 1 quil wheel; 1 cotton gin; 4 flax wheels;
　　5 great wheels; 7 pair cotton cards; 5 pair wool cards;
　　6 slays; 1 coam hackle; 2 pair of low cards; 1 pair clothier cards

　　P.ギブズ (Patricia Gibbs) は、Patricia Gibbs, *op.cit.*, 33-36.で、次のようにタイプ印刷している。筆者としては、P.ギブズのタイプ印刷の方が正しいと思う。
　　coam hackle　→　coarse hackle
　　low cards　　→　tow cards

(33) *Ibid.*, 30.
(34) Louis Morton, *op.cit.*, 26-30, 31-61.

(35) From the Inventory of the Estate of Landon Carter, Feb. 1779 Page 1 " A list of Negroes ……", Item Acc# 1959, Neg# 35-237-A, Manuscripts Print Collection, Special Collections Department, University of Virginia Library.

(36) Patricia Gibbs, *op.cit.*, 33（Cited from Robert Carter Letter Book 2: 189, 116; 13: 128; 3:21. 23, 35, 45, Robert Carter Papers, Duke University Library）

(37) *Ibid.*, 33-34（Cited from Robert Carter Letter Book 2:15, 4:46）

(38) *Ibid.*, 34（Cited from ibid.）

(39) *Ibid.*, 34.

(40) John R. Commons Ulrich B. Phillips, Eugene A. Gilmore, Helen L. Sumner, and John B. Andrews, *A Documentary History of American Industrial Society*, Volume Ⅱ, Cleveland, Ohio, The Arthur H. Clark Company, 1910, 315 （Typescript掲載）。

Nominy Hall, January the 1st, A.D. 1782.

Be it remembered that Mr. Daniel Sullivan, weaver takes the care & management of six negro weavers—namely—George about 19 years old, Ralph, about 18 years old, Jeremiah, about 17 years old, Dennis, about 17 years old, Prince, about 13 years old, William, about 13 years old—four negro winders, namely—Kate, about 65 years old, Sally, about 16 years old, Alice, about 15 years old, Mary, about 14 years old, at the Woolen & Linen Factory at Aires, belonging to Robert Carters, Esq. of Westm'd County.

The said Daniel Sullivan to be allowed twelve pounds, gold or silver money, or the value thereof in country commodities at the former selling prices, also twelve Barrels of Corn, four hundred pounds of Pork & fifteen pounds of picked Cotton, as a full satisfaction for one whole year's work to begin from the first day of January 1782, to the 31st day of December following. As Witness my hand the year and day above written.

Test: Geo. Gordon.　　　　　　　　　　His
　　　　　　　　　　　Daniel　X　Sullivan
　　　　　　　　　　　　　　Mark

(41) Contract of Robert Carter with Daniel Sullivan, overseer, for his negro clothworker, Jan. 1, 1782, MSS1C 2468a 2068, The Virginia Historical Society, Richmond, Virginia.

下線部は写本のとおりにタイプ印刷されているが、現在はyearnはearnと、insuingはensuingと綴られている。

Rates of spinning and weaving, given in by Dan'l Sullivan, 15 Sept. 1787. Dear Sir, Concerning this next year's business in the regard of spinning & weaving, I have to the best of my knowledge & understanding sum'd up what the spinnery would yearn in the run of this next insuing year also I have sum'd up how much the weavers would yearn supposing that spinners and weavers was to have the Blessing laid upon them　that never was to have a Days Sickness throughout the whole year. I am in hopes that you will be at the pains to read it.　I am yr most Humble Servant

　　　　　　　　　　　　　　　　　　　　　　　　　　　　　　　　　　　　　　Daniel Sullivan

To mention the price of spinning
　thread for brown rolls,……………………………………@ 1/4 lb.
　Do. for Oznabrigs………………………………………1/ .
　Do for Bagging…………………………………………6d. per lb
　Do for Coarse Dawlaps …………………………………1/3.
　Do for Cotton warp for Coarse woolen …………………2/ per lb.
　Do for Coarse Woolen Yarn　fill ………………………2　per lb
　Do coarse woolen for Stockings …………………………1/3.
　Do a finer sort for do ……………………………………1/6.
　Do of coarse Tow, ………………………………………4d.
　Do of finer Tow …………………………………………6d.

　Weaving brown Rolls,……………………………………@ 4d.

```
    Do oznabrigs·································································4d.
    Do Bagging ···································································4d.
    Do Coarse Dawlaps··························································6d.
    Do Coarse Woolen & Cotton Warp ······································4d.
    Do finer woolen Cloth is [This stricken out].
    Do Coarse Cotton····························································4d.
    17 spinners ·································································@ £7.16; £132.12.
     4  weavers ································································@ [?]; £110.
```

(42) Louis Morton, *op.cit.*, 177. Louis Mortonは脚注に、次にように記している。
Daniel Sullivan to Carter, Aries, September 11, 1787, Carter MSS, Ⅱ (VHS); December 18, 1790, Letter Book, 1789〜1792, 197.筆者未見。

(43) Deed of Gift, Robert Carter Day Book, Volume XI (Aug. 1, 1791), pages 1-2 MSS. Div., Duke University からのコピー。John D. Rockefeller, Jr. Library所蔵。

(44) John Randolf Barden, " Flushed with Notions' of Freedom": The Growth and emancipation of a Virginia Slave Community, 1732〜1812, Dissertation: Degree Date 1993, Duke University, 465.

(45) Louis Morton, "Robert Wormeley Carter of Sabine Hall: Notes on the Life of a Virginia Planter," *The Journal of Southern History* XII (August 1946), 345-365.

(46) Louis Morton, (ed.,), "The Daybook of Robert Wormeley Carter of Sabine Hall, 1766," *The Virginia Magazine of History and Biography*, Volume 68, 1960, published by The Virginia Historical Society, Richmond, 307 (タイプ印刷掲載)。

March 11th 1766
    Remember to write to Mr. Dekar Thomson to buy me Linen for my Negroes of the Backwoodsmen.

(47) ・The Diary of Robert Wormeley Carter 1764〜1792, 22 (Typescript), Special Collections, John D. Rockefeller, Jr. Library, Colonial Williamburg Foundation, Williamsburg, Virginia.
    ・The Diary of Robert Wormeley Carter, December 31, 1769, Manuscripts and Rare Books Department, Swem Library, College of William and Mary, Williamsburg, Virginia.

December 31, 1769
    Ball told me he had made me 30pr. Of Negroes Shoes at 1/3·········

(48) ・The Diary of Robert Wormeley Carter 1764〜1792, 23 (Typscript), ibid.
    ・The Diary of Robert Wormeley Carter, December 1769, The linen thread spun by McKaway 1769, Manuscripts and Rare Books Department, Swem Library, College of William and Mary, Williamsburg, Virginia.

```
      The linen thread spun by McKaway 1769
                                                        Lbs
    Sold to R. Beverley pd ·····································11. 1/4.
         Thos Wyld ············································16.
    Pd. W. Brockenbrough ·····································10.
    Pd. WmSon Ball ···········································3.9oz.
    Pd. R. W. Carter ··········································1.14.
    Pd. George Garland ········································1.8.
    Pd. Mary Garland ·········································1.8.
    William Buckland··········································1.
    William Beale ············································2.
```

....48.2.oz
48.lbs 2 oz. at 2/6..£6.0. $3^{3/4}$
　　　　　　12.13. $1^{3/4}$
　　　　　£18.13. $5^{1/2}$

By the above it appears that my Weaver earned in 1769.£18..13. $5^{1/2}$..out which must be taken his Clothes; maintenance; Levy & the values of the Hemp which will reduce the sum greatly; I am well convinced there is nothing to be made by weaving at 5d coarse & fine; I shall therefore only carry it on for the conveniency of getting my own work done……also the Interest of the 25£ I gave for him must be deducted; so that the profit will be very small.

(49) Patricia Gibbs, *op. cit.*, 31, 88-89.
(50) Fritz Hirschfeld, *George Washington and Slavery, A Documentary Portrayal*, University of Missouri Press, Columbia and London, 1997, 11-192.
(51) Mount Vernon Ladies' Association of the Union, Lund Washington's Account Books 1772～1787.
(52) John C. Fitzpatrick, (ed.), *op. cit.*, vol.2, 137.
(53) Mount Vernon Ladies' Association, Photocopies of Invoice & Letters 1755～66, 6. Sept.2, 1757.
(54) John C. Fitzpatrick, (ed.), *op. cit.*, vol.2, 332.
(55) *Ibid.*, Vol.27, 6, 175. 428.
(56) *Ibid.*, Vol., 420.
(57) 濱田雅子「18世紀ヴァージニアにおけるお仕着せに関する歴史的考察」(国際服飾学会誌、No.12, 1995年11月)、114-129.
(58) John C. Fitzpatrick, (ed.), *op. cit.*, vol.28, 249.
(59) *Ibid.*, Vol.28.
(60) *Ibid.*, Vol.28, 492.
(61) George Washington Papers, Series Vol. #6, Library of Congress.
(62) Early American History Reprints, Patricia Gibbs, *Cloth Production in Virginia to 1800*, Fiche# 1 of 6, c.1989, Special Collections, John D. Rockefeller, Jr. Library, Colonial Williamsburg Foundation, Williamsburg, Virginia.に基いて、筆者再生。
(63) John C. Fitzpatrick, (ed.), *op. cit.*, vol.37, 256-268.
(64) George Washington Papers, M-2075, 116, Special Collections, John D. Rockefeller, Jr. Library, Colonial Williamsburg Foundation, Williamsburg, Virginia.
(65) Turner Southall Receipt Book 1776～1784, 1Vol..[73] pp.MS 31.3, Special Collections, John D. Rockefeller,Jr. Library, Colonial Williamsburg Foundation, Williamsburg,Virginia.

　Received, Dec.15th, 1777 of Turner Southhall. Twenty five shillings for making Clothes to the Foundery
　　£25　　　　　　　　　　　　Lucy Brazeal

　Received, Dec.15th ,1777 of Turner Southhall. Twenty Two pounds for cloth for the use of the Negroes hired by Ballendine for the Canal.
　　£22.00

(66) Memo of Cabell Family Papers 1693～1913, " Memo of shoes, stockings & blankets gave my negroes," 27 Nov., 1796 in BoxⅡ, folder 10, Manuscripts and Rare Books Department, Swem Library, College of William and Mary, Williamsburg, Virginia.

終　　章

アメリカにおける従来の上流階級の服飾に関する研究では、貴族趣味的な服飾美に着眼して、その実態を博物館に所蔵されている実物資料の調査により明らかにする方法が主流をなしてきた。中産・下層階級の衣服は、貴族スタイルの衣服から装飾を取り去った、粗末な素材を用いたものと見なされ、研究対象としての価値が認められない傾向が強かった。また、中産・下層階級の衣服の実物資料はきわめて僅かしか残存していない。本書で対象としたアメリカ独立革命期ヴァージニアの黒人奴隷の衣服は、現地での調査の結果、1枚も残存していないことが判明した。

　そこで、まずアメリカ独立革命期ヴァージニアの黒人奴隷の被服の考察の前提条件として、第1章において、歴史的背景を、すなわちアメリカ独立革命の背景とアメリカ合衆国の成立、ヴァージニア植民地の成立の背景、ヴァージニアの黒人奴隷制度の成立とその特質、およびアメリカ独立革命期の服飾の特徴をテーマに考察した。なかでもヴァージニアの黒人奴隷制度の成立とその特質は、18世紀の奴隷の被服のあり方を規定する基本的な歴史的条件とみなして、重点的に論述した。つまり、第1章第3節で言及したように、白人年季奉公人制度から黒人奴隷制度への移行についてのデイヴッド・W. ガレンソン（David W. Galenson）の「労働力移行の二段階説」によると、西インドでは砂糖、チェサピーク湾地域ではタバコ、サウス・カロライナでは米やインディゴというように、商品作物こそ異なるが、三地域内のそれぞれのプランテーションでは、第一段階として非熟練分野、つまり野外耕作労働の労働主体が黒人奴隷に移り、熟練労働のみが白人奉公人に委ねられる。ついで黒人奴隷がさまざまな技術を修得するにつれ、熟練労働の分野においても、白人奉公人に取って替るようになる第二段階へ移行した。

　北アメリカ南部のプランテーションでは、上記の第二段階においては、奴隷の身分は労働形態の違いによって、プランターの側仕えの上級の家内奴隷（馬車を引く人、召使い、給仕など）、技術を持った職人奴隷（樽職人、仕立て屋、鍛冶屋、靴屋、大工、ろくろ細工師、車大工、織工、塗装工、木挽き工、医者、御者、樵、屠殺業者、鉄骨組み立て職人など）、および野外耕作奴隷という三つの階層に区分されていた。

　上記の歴史的背景を踏まえて、本書ではアメリカ独立革命期ヴァージニアの奴隷の被服を、その種類、素材、着装実態、および支給と生産の実態に着眼して、社会史的に考察した。

　ピーター・F. コープランド（Peter F. Copeland）および、リンダ・バウムガルテン（Linda Baumgarten）らの先行研究から得られた知見は次のとおりである。

　プランターの側仕えの上級の黒人奴隷、家内の職人奴隷および農園の耕作奴隷といった3階層の奴隷には、それぞれのステイタスを表示する被服が支給されていた。その概略は次の8項目にまとめられる。

(1) 上級の黒人奴隷は、上等ではあるが、奴隷の身分を示す縁取り装飾が施された主人の紋章の色を配したお仕着せをあてがわれていた。
(2) 家内の男の職人奴隷は年季奉公人と同じ種類の被服をあてがわれている場合が多かった。すなわち、コート（coat）、ウェストコート（waistcoat）、シャツ（shirt）およびブリーチズ（breeches）といった上流人や白人の召使いと同じ構成の衣服を支給された。
(3) 職人奴隷は、職種により衣服の特色がみられた。例えば、鍛冶屋は衣服を保護する皮革製のエプロン（apron）をつけ、船頭は水夫の服装をしていた。
(4) 女の召使いの家内奴隷は、白人の召使いのような恰好をしていた。第1章第4節の女子服の項目で言及したように、逃亡奴隷広告にはアグネスやアギーという名の白黒混血の奴隷は、青色のリボンで縁取りされたコルセットを付けて、ノーフォークから逃亡したと記録されている。コルセットを装用した奴隷に関する記録は少ないが、この記事から家内の女奴隷は、コルセットを支給されていたものと推察される。
(5) 家内奴隷は農園の奴隷よりも多くの衣服を支給されていた。
(6) 働く奴隷は、働けない奴隷よりも上等の衣服を支給されていた。
(7) 農園の奴隷はオズナブルグ（osnabrug）のシャツや未晒しのニグロ・クロス（negro cloth）のブリーチズや長ズボン（trousers）という粗末な衣服を支給されていた。
(8) 女の野外耕作奴隷の服装はジャケット（jacket）やショート・ガウン（short gown）にペティコート（petticoat）という貧しい婦人の典型的な服装であった。

　以上の事実から、18世紀北アメリカ南部奴隷の被服は、防寒や自然から身を守るといった実用的な目的だけではなく、奴隷のそれぞれのステイタスを表示するシンボルとしての機能が重視されていた、と結論できる。しかし、以上は奴隷の被服の概観であって、その実態の詳細についてはアメリカの先行研究においても解明されていない。
　そこで、本書では序章で述べた二つの方法を採用し、問題の解明を試みた。以下、二つの方法による考察結果を順次、述べ結論とする。
　第一の方法は、ヴァージニア・ガゼット紙に掲載された逃亡奴隷広告における被服描写の考察である。この考察は第2章第2節、および第3章において行った。「奴隷の被服をいかにイメージ化するか」が、これらの章における課題であった。従来のフィールド・ワークを主とする文化史研究の方法では、実物資料が残存していない場合には、イメージ化は困難である。実物資料が残存していない場合の有用な資料に、絵画や彫刻やイラストがある。P. F. コープランドの描くイラストは中産・下層階級の人々の服装や仕事に従事している姿を実にリアルに表現している。だが、残念なことに、18世紀後半のヴァージニアの奴隷を描いた2枚のイラストは、第3章第1節で紹介したように、プランターの側仕えの奴隷のものであり、職人奴隷や農園でタバコ栽培に従事している奴隷の服装は描かれていない。筆者の周りの人々に聞いても、奴隷といえば「ぼろをまとっているのでは？」というイメージが一般的である。

このような困難な資料状況を打開するカギは何であったのか。それは逃亡奴隷広告に見られる被服情報を丹念に数量化し、得られたデータから実態を明らかにすることであった。この広告の史料価値については、第2章第1節で述べた。
　上記の「奴隷の服装のイメージ化」は三つの方法で進めた。一つは、ヴァージニア・ガゼット紙他掲載の逃亡奴隷広告（1766～1789）に登場する67種の被服素材の解説一覧を作成することである。その結果は表2-3-1から表2-3-2である。これらの表では、67種の素材を繊維別、すなわち、(1) ウール（wool）、(2) ウール（wool）とコットン（cotton）、(3) シルク（silk）とウール（wool）とコットン（cotton）、(4) コットン（cotton）、(5) コットン（cotton）とウール（wool）、(6) コットン（cotton）とリネン（linen）、(7) リネン（linen）、(8) シルク（silk）、(9) その他、および (10) 国産品、に分類し、それらの特徴を概要、組成〈糸と織組織〉、仕上げ、色・柄および逃亡奴隷広告における用途について解説した。素材のイメージをとらえるのに役立つものと確信する。
　二つ目は、第3章第2節で逃亡奴隷の被服の種類、形および着装実態のイメージ化を試みた。本節に示した数量的なデータと逃亡奴隷広告に見られる被服描写に基づいて、1767年から1770年と1776年から1779年の男子の逃亡奴隷の着装スタイルを8タイプに分類し、イラストを描いた。これらのデータ分析の結果、次の結論に至った。

(1) A（帽子から靴までそろっているタイプ）は149人中10人（6.7％）と極めて少ない。

(2) 逃亡奴隷広告の逃亡者の被服の記載に靴の記載があるケースは、149人中40人（26.8％）、つまり4分の1強である。その原因として、a. 靴をもっていない、b. 靴が痛くてはけない、c. 靴が古くなってはけない、という三つのケースが考えられる。
　奴隷の靴の形、はきごこち、素材、耐久性は今後の研究課題である。

(3) B「（上衣と下衣を着て、帽子を被っている）は149人中30人（21.6％）、つまり、5分の1である。

(4) B（上衣と下衣のみを着ている）は149人中74人（49.7％）である。しかも逃亡時に着用していた上衣の枚数が2枚以下の逃亡奴隷は、1767年から1770年、および、1776年から1779年の8年間に逃亡した被験者の80パーセントを占めていることが明らかとなった。プランターが奴隷に年1回、衣服を支給していたが、逃亡奴隷は支給された最低限の衣服を着用して逃亡するか、プランテーションで衣服を盗んで、携行するか、盗んだ衣服に着替えて逃亡するか、のいずれかであった。逃亡広告にはこのような情報が大変多く記載されている。

(5) 下衣については、ブリーチズとトラウザーズの着用の割合が3対1であることが明らかとなった。この時代には家内奴隷も農園の奴隷もきわめて動きにくい、機能性に乏しいブリーチズをあてがわれていることが多かった。ブリーチズは元来、上流階級の男子の衣服であり、プランテーションでの労働には不適切な衣服であった。そのため、なめし皮製の伸縮性のあるブリーチズが用いられる場合もあった。この種のブリーチズは、18世紀を通じて、英国の紳士の乗馬用の日常着として好まれていた。L. バウムガルテンによると、長ズボンは8人のうち、約1人に見られたというが、本研究では4人に1人が長ズボンをはいていたとの結果がでた。さらに、期間を広げて逃亡奴隷広告を調べるべきである。ズボンは後に流行のスタイルとなり、労働者

の衣類となる。さらに種々のスタイルで男性によって、今日にいたるまで、着用され続けている。長ズボンの着用はアメリカ独立革命後、増加していくのであるが、その具体的様相の考察は、今後の研究課題である。

　三つ目には、逃亡奴隷広告に登場する国産の素材に注目し、第3章第3節ではヴァージニア・クロスを取り上げ、布地の定義づけと布地の生産実態の考察を踏まえて、ヴァージニア・クロス製の衣服の特徴を被服の種類、色・柄について分類・分析した。第4節では、ヴァージニア・クロス製の衣服の特徴を示す対照資料として、オズナブルグ製の衣服の特徴を被服の種類、色について分類・分析した。第5節では、逃亡奴隷広告に見られる被服素材の年次変化を輸入素材と自国産の素材の比較という方法で考察した。これらの考察から次の結論に至った。

(1) ヴァージニア・クロスはヴァージニアで製造された織物であり、この用語は一般に輸入織物と区別するために用いられた。ヴァージニアの布地製造は17世紀に遡り、1750年代までにはこの布地は、ヴァージニア・クロスという名前で知られていた。これは当時、ヴァージニアを訪れたアンドリュー・バーナビー牧師（Andrew Burnaby）の旅行日誌から明らかである。

(2) ヴァージニア・クロスに関する多くの記録に記述された繊維のなかでは、コットンが目立つ。だが、コットンにウールが紡ぎ込まれたり、亜麻が紡ぎ込まれたりした織糸を用いた事例もある。コットンにウールが紡ぎ込まれた事例は、第4章で考察したDeWitt Wallace Gallery of Decorative Arts所蔵の男子のコートである。

　以上から、アメリカ植民地時代と独立革命期にヴァージニアで生産されていたヴァージニア・クロスの繊維の種類の代表的なものはコットン、ウールおよび亜麻であったと結論づけられる。

(3) ヴァージニア・クロスの用途は逃亡奴隷広告（1766～1789）に見られる限りでは、奴隷に支給された基本的な衣服（ブリーチズ、コート、ウェストコート、シャツ、ペティコート）である。シャツに多用されたオズナブルグとは対照的である。

　色・柄については、約55パーセントが無地で、約42パーセントがストライプ、3パーセントがチェックであり、ストライプの幅と色の組み合わせは多様であった

(4) 黒人奴隷の被服に用いられた国産品のヴァージニア・クロスは、とくにアメリカ独立戦争中に生産量の高まりが見られた。ヴァージニア・クロスの生産量の伸びを数量的に裏づけるために、1766年から1785年を対象に比率の検定を行った。その結果、1766年および1770年から1779年に至る計11年間ヴァージニア・クロスと輸入品の比率は、これら以外の年との間に有意な差があることが、1％の危険率で立証された。

　このような事実はアメリカの産業史において、どのような社会史的意味を持っていたのか。ヴァージニア・クロスの生産は、確かにプランテーションでの衣服の需要に役立った。この点ではヴァージニア植民地の人々にとっての国内産布地の役割は評価できる。だが、輸入品と比べて、価格および布質の点でどうだったのか。さらに、ヴァージニア・クロス生産の社会史的意味を語るには、これらの問題の解明を待たなければならない。この問題は今後の研究課題と

する。

　本書の第二の方法はヴァージニア・クロス製の衣服と奴隷の被服および被服生産の道具に関する実物調査である。すなわち、DeWitt Wallace Gallery of Decorative Arts（ヴァージニア州コロニアル・ウィリアムズバーグ所在のコロニアル・ウィリアムズバーグ振興財団の一部門）所蔵のヴァージニア・クロス製の男子用スーツの調査、ヴァージニア州リッチモンドに所在するValentine Museum所蔵の奴隷が作ったパッチワーク・キルト（patchwork quilt）の実物資料の調査、コロニアル・ウィリアムズバーグ振興財団の織物部門における織物の調査、当財団の考古学研究部門における出土品の調査を行なった。その結果、次の結論に至った。

(1) 第4章第1節および第2節で紹介した実物資料調査により、奴隷の衣服の実物はもとより、布の断片も残存していないことが判明し、下層階級の人々の衣服のイメージ表現がいかに困難であるかを切実に考えさせられた。だが、第2節で考察したヴァージニア・クロス製の男子用スーツとパッチワーク・キルトから、第3章で逃亡奴隷広告に拠って考察したヴァージニア・クロスの特徴が、具体的に明らかになった。すなわち、前者のスーツのコートの素材は、コットンにウールが紡ぎ込まれた事例であり、後者はストライプや縞柄のヴァージニア・クロスの実物の事例である。

(2) 製織の専門家のマックス・ハムリック（Max Hamrick）提供の布地のサンプルは、18世紀に用いられていたマニュアル本を使って再現された粗悪な布地のサンプルという点で、下層階級の衣服の研究にとっての有用な複製資料である。

(3) ウィリアムズバーグのパレス・プランテーションからの考古学出土品の鋏、針および指貫は、このプランテーションの奴隷の居住地区で、奴隷の手で衣服生産が行なわれていたことを裏付け、また、18世紀には黒人奴隷の中に、技術者がいたことを裏付ける遺品である。

　第4章第3節では、ヴァージニアの有数なプランターであるカーター家（Carter Family）のプランテーションおよびアメリカの初代大統領ジョージ・ワシントンが所有していたマウント・ヴァーノン（Mount Vernon）のプランテーションにおける奴隷の被服生産の実態（18世紀後半）把握のために、プランテーションの記録、商人の記録、プランターの日誌や手紙およびその他の公文書の調査を行なった。「ヴァージニアの有数なプランターであるカーター家のプランテーションおよびアメリカの初代大統領G.ワシントンが所有していたマウント・ヴァーノンのプランテーションにおいて、ランドン・カーター（Landon Cater）、ロバート・カーター・オブ・ノミニ・ホール（Robert Carter of Nomini Hall）、ロバート・ウォームレイ・カーター（Robert Wormeley Cater）およびG.ワシントンという4人のプランターたちは、彼らの黒人奴隷の衣生活をどのようにして管理・維持していたのか」という本書の課題を解明するため、4人のプランターの個々の事業を、彼らが果たした役割も含めて整理した。

(1) ランドン・カーターは年季奉公人は年季があけると独立して、離れていってしまうという問題にもかかわらず、年季奉公人を織工として雇い、彼の黒人奴隷を紡績工や織工として使ってい

た。しかし、奴隷監督の目を盗んで怠けたり、逃亡したりする奴隷に悩まされていた。
(2) ランドン・カーターは家族と奴隷の衣服や靴の供給のために努力をし、織物生産の設備を整備した。この設備はおそらくヴァージニアのプランテーションにおける布の生産工場の代表的なものであった。
(3) ロバート・カーター オブ・ノミニ・ホールは、プランテーションにおける最も大きく最も長く続いた布の生産工場を設立したが、1760年代および1770年代に織工を雇っていた彼の多くの仲間のプランターとは異なり、カーターは大英帝国との貿易が停止に至るまで、工場運営を始めなかった。彼は1776年に布の生産の仕事を拡張し、亜麻（Flax）、大麻（hemp）、オズナブルグ、コットン、リネンおよび紡毛織物（woolen cloth）の生産を推進した。彼の工場は借主によって管理されるようになり、生産量はカーター家の需要を満たす程度のものにとどまった。
(4) ロバート・ウォームレイ・カーターもプランターとしての立場から、黒人奴隷労働力の生産性の向上のために、かれらの衣食住の確保につとめていたが、結局、結論は輸入品の方が品質がよく、コストは国内産より安く、織工の利益にはならない、という結果に至った。
(5) G.ワシントンは生涯を通じて奴隷の衣服用に大量の布を注文したが、マウント・ヴァーノンにおいて、少なくとも1767年から布の生産が行なわれていた。G.ワシントンは家内奴隷と野外耕作奴隷に、異なる品質と数の衣服を支給していた。また、労働力として役にたつ奴隷には、働けない奴隷に対してよりも上等の衣服を支給していた。G.ワシントンが輸入素材と国内産の素材のコストを比較した結果、輸入素材の方がコストが安いという結果が出ている点は、ロバート・ウォームレイ・カーターの場合と同じである。

以上の結果から、白人年季奉公人制度から黒人奴隷制度への移行期に、ヴァージニアの有数なプランターたちが、紡績や織布に携わる熟練職人を白人奉公人から黒人奴隷に切り替えていく過程とそこにおける問題点を、プランター他の手記や手紙や公文書や会計帳簿などの第一次史料から、具体的に解明できた、と考える。

参考文献

【マニュスクリプト】

Diary of Robert Wormeley Carter, December 31, 1769, Manuscripts and Rare Books Department, Swem Library, College of William and Mary, Williamsburg, Virginia.

Diary of Robert Wormeley Carter 1764〜1792, p.22 (Typescript), Special Collections, John D. Rockefeller, Jr. Library, Colonial Williamsburg Foundation, Williamsburg, Virginia.

Diary of Robert Wormeley Carter, December 1769, The linen thread spun by McKaway 1769, Manuscripts and Rare Books Department, Swem Library, College of William and Mary, Williamsburg, Virginia.

Diary of Robert Wormeley Carter 1764〜1792, p.23 (Typscript), Special Collections, John D. Rockefeller, Jr. Library, Colonial Williamsburg Foundation, Williamsburg, Virginia.

Early American History Reprints, Patricia Gibbs, Cloth Production in Virginia to 1800, Fiche# 1 of 6, c.1989, Special Collections, John D. Rockefeller, Jr. Library, Colonial Williamsburg Foundation, Williamsburg, Virginia.

George Washington Papers, M-2075, 116, Special Collections, John D. Rockefeller, Jr. Library, Colonial Williamsburg Foundation, Williamsburg, Virginia.

Hoffman, Paul P., (ed.), Guide to the Microfilm Edition of the Carter Family Papers, 1659-1797, in the Sabine Hall Collection, Microfilm Publication, University of Virginia Library, Number Three, 1967. Colonial Williamsburg Foundation, Williamsburg, Virginia.

Inventory of The Estate of Landon Carter esqr. Taken February 1779. The Albert and Shirley Small Special Collections Library, University of Virginia Library.

Inventory of the Estate of Landon Carter, Feb. 1779 Page 1 "A list of Negroes…", Sabine Hall Papers (♯1959), The Albert and Shirley Small Special Collections Library, University of Virginia Library.

Inventory of the Estate of Landon Carter, Feb. 1779, The Albert and Shirley Small Special Collections Library, University of Virginia Library.

Landon Carter's Diary, Nov. 17, 1763, Sabine Hall Papers（♯1959）, The Albert and Shirley Small Special Collections Library, University of Virginia Library.

Memo of Cabell Family Papers 1693〜1913, "Memo of shoes, stockings & blankets gave my negroes," 27 Nov., 1796 in BoxⅢ, folder 10, Manuscripts and Rare Books Department, Swem Library, College of William and Mary, Williamsburg, Virginia.

Photocopies of Deed of Gift, Robert Carter Day Book, Volume XI(Aug. 1, 1791), pages1-2 MSS. Div., Duke University, John D. Rockefeller, Jr. Library.

Photocopies of George Washington's Account Books, Farm Ledgers, Cash Memoranda, and Weekly Reports, Mount Vernon Ladies' Association of the Union.

Photocopies of Lund Washington's Account Books 1772〜1787, Mount Vernon Ladies' Association of the Union.

Turner Southhall Receipt Book 1776〜1784, 1Vol.,[73] pp.MS 31.3, Special Collections, John D. Rockefeller, Jr. Library, Colonial Williamsburg Foundation, Williamsburg,Virginia.

Typescript of Invoice & Letters 1755〜66, p.6, Sept.2, 1757, Mount Vernon Ladies' Association of the Union.

【新　聞】

Virginia Gazette, Special Collections, John D. Rockefeller,Jr. Library, Colonial Williamsburg Foundation, Williamsburg,Virginia.

【同時代文献】

Burnaby, Andrew, *Travels Through the Middle Settlement in North-America, in the Years 1759 and 1760: with Observations upon the State of the Colonies*, originally published, T. Payne, 1775. Reprint, Great Seal Books, (Ithaca, New York, 1960).

Fitzpatrick, John C. (ed.), *The Last Will and Testimony of George Washington an Schedule of his Property to which is appended the Last Will and Testament of Martha Washington*, The Mount Vernon Ladies Association of the Union, first edition 1939, sixth edition, revised, (U.S.A., 1992).

Hargrove, John, *The Weavers Draft Book and Clothiers Assistant* with a new introduction by Rita J. Adrosko curator of textiles, National Museum of History and Technology, Smithsonian Institution, Worcester American Antiquarian Society,(1979).

Harrower, John, *Journal of John Harrower, an Indentured Servant in the Colony of Virginia, 1773〜1776*, edited, with an Introduction, by Edward Miles Riley, (Williamsburg, Virginia, New York, 1993).

Smith, John, *The General Historie of Virginia, New England and Summer Iles.*, Ann Arbor

［reprinted 1966］(Original ed., 1624).

Wily, John, *A Treatise on the Propaganda of Sheep, the Manufacture of Wool, and the Cultivation and Manufacture of Flax, with Directions for making Several Utensils for the Business*, Williamsburg, printed by F. Royle, MDCCLXV, 1765.

Windley, L.A. (comp)., *Runaway Slave Advertisement: A Documentary History from 1730s to 1790*, Vol.1 of Vol.4, Greenwood, (Westport, Connecticut, 1983).

【法令・議会関係資料】

Bureau of the Census, Historical Statistics of the United States: Colonial Times to 1970, Washington, D.C., U.S. Government Printing Office.

U.S.Bureau of the Census Negro Population in the United States, 1790〜1915.

【研究書】

Andrews, John B., *A Documentary History of American Industrial Society*, Volume Ⅱ, The Arthur H. Clark Company, (Cleveland, Ohio), 1910.

Baumgarten, Linda, *Eighteenth-Century Clothing at Williamsburg*, The Colonial Williamsburg Foundation, (Colonial Williamsburg, Virginia, 1986).

Commons, John R., Phillips, Ulrich B., Gilmore, Eugene A., Sumner, Helen L., and Andrews, John B., *A Documentary History of American Industrial Society* Volume Ⅱ, The Arthur H. Clark Company, (Cleveland, Ohio 1910), 315 (Typescript掲載)。

Copeland, Peter F., *Working Dress in Colonial and Revolutionary America*, Greenwood Press, (Westport, Connecticut, 1977) (濱田雅子訳『アメリカ史にみる職業着－植民地時代〜独立革命期－』(せせらぎ出版、1998年)

Gilgun, Beth, *Tidings from the 18th Century*, Rebel Publishing Co., Inc. Texarkana, (Texas, 1993).

Greene, Jack P.(ed.), *The Diary of Colonel Landon Carter of Sabine Hall, 1752〜1778*, Vol. Ⅰ, Vol. Ⅱ (Charlottesville, 1965).

Harmuth, Louis, *Dictionary of Textiles*, The Third Enlarged Edition, Fairchild Publishing Company, (New York, 1924).

Hirschfeld, Fritz, *George Washington and Slavery*, A Documentary Portrayal, University of Missouri Press, (Columbia and London, 1997).

Köhler, Carl, *A History of Costume*, Dover Publisher, (New York, 1928, reprint 1968).

Montgomery, Florence, *Textiles in America, 1650〜1870: A Dictionary Based on Original Documents, Prints and Paintings, Commercial Records, American Merchant' Papers, Shopkeepers' Advertisements and Pattern Books with Original Swatches of Cloth*, Norton,

New Papers, Shopkeepers' Advertisements and Pattern Books with Original Swatches of Cloth,(Norton, New York, 1984).

Morgan, Philip D., *Slave Counterpoint, Black Culture in the Eighteenth-Century Chesapeake & Lowcountry*, University of North Carolina Press,(Chapel Hill & London, 1998).

Morton, Louis, *Robert Carter of Nomini Hall, A Virginia Tabacco Planter of the Eighteenth Century*, Williamsburg Restoration Historical Studies No.2, (Princeton, 1941).

Morton, Louis, Robert Wormeley Carter of Sabine Hall: Notes on the Life of a Virginia Planter, *The Journal of Southern History XII,* (August 1946).

Mullin, Gerald W., *Flight and Rebellion. Slave Resistance in Eighteenth-Century Virginia*, Oxford University Press, (New York, 1972).

National Museum of American History: "Getting Dressed: Fashionable Appearance, 1750~1800", Smithsonian Institution, (Washington, DC.1985).

Walsh, Lorena S., *From Calabar to Carter's Grove, The History of a Virginia Slave Community*, University Press of Virginia, (Charlottesville and London, 1997).

Warwick, Edward, Pitz, Henry C., and Wyckoff, Alexander, *Early American Dress, The Colonial and Revolutionary Periods*, Bonanza Books, (New York, 1965).

Williams, Gloria M. and Centrallo, Carol, Clothing Acquisition and Use by the Colonial African American(Barbara M. Starke, Lillian O. Holloman, Barbara K. Nordquist, African American Dress and Adornment Cultural Respective, Kendall/Hunt Publishing Company, U.S.A,1990).

【論　文】

Baumgarten, Linda, "Clothes for the People: Slave Clothing in Early Virginia," *Journal of Early Southern Decorative Arts,Vol. 14 No. 2,* (Nov.1988), Museum of Early Southern Decorative Arts, Winston Salem, N.C., 27-70.

Baumgarten, Linda, "Plains, Plaid and Cotton: Woolens for Slave Clothing," *ARS TEXTRINA* 15, (1991), 203-222.

Galenson, David W., White Servitude and the Growth of Black Slavery in Colonial America, *Journal of Economic History* Vol. XLI, No.1,(March 1981), 39-49.

Prude, Jonathan, To Look upon the " Lower Sort ": Runaway Ads and the Appearance of Unfree Laborers in America, *The Journal of American History,* (June 1991), 124-159.

Warner, Patricia Campbell, "Some Kind of Coarse Clothing": Slave Clothes in Eighteenth-Century America, *The Catalog of The 44th Washington Antiques Show,* (January, 1999), 7-10.

【未刊行論文】

Barden, John Randolf, "Flushed with Notions' of Freedom": The Growth and Emancipation of a

Virginia Slave Community, 1732〜1812, Dissertation: Degree Date 1993, Duke University.

Gibbs, Patricia, *Cloth Production in Virginia to 1800,* Research Department, Colonial Williamsburg Foundation, (Colonial Williamsburg, Virginia, March, 1978).

Howard, Bryan Paul, *Had on and took with him: Runaway Indentured Servant Clothing in Virginia, 1774〜1778,* UMI Dissertation Series, Degree Date: 1996. Texas A&M University.

McCombs, Dorothy F., *Virginia Cloth: Early Textiles in Virginia, Particularly in the Backcountry Between the Blue Ridge and Allegheny Mountain until 1830.* Unpublished Master's Thesis, Department of History, Virginia Polytechnic Institute, (Blacksburg, Virginia, 1976).

【邦語・邦訳文献】

アメリカ学会編『原典アメリカ史 第2巻―革命と建国―』(岩波書店、1951年).

有賀貞、大下尚一編『新版 概説アメリカ史』(有斐閣選書、1994年).

有賀貞、大下尚一、志邨晃佑、平野孝編『世界歴史大系 アメリカ史17世紀―1877年』(山川出版社、1994年).

池本幸三・布留川正博・下山晃『近代世界と奴隷制―太平洋システムの中で―』(人文書院、1995年).

池本幸三『近代奴隷制社会の史的展開―チェサピーク湾ヴァージニア植民地を中心として―』(ミネルヴァ書房、1987年初版第1刷、1999年新装版第1刷).

一見輝彦『繊維素材辞典』(ファッション教育社、1995年第1刷、1999年第3刷)

川北 稔『民衆の大英帝国』(岩波書店、1990年).

紀平英作編『世界各国史24 アメリカ史』(山川出版社、1999年).

現代ファブリック事典刊行会編『現代ファブリック事典』(相川書房、1981年).

JIS繊維用語(繊維部門)JISL0206-1976(1984確認)、1976年2月1日改正

清水知久、高橋章、富田虎男『アメリカ史研究入門』(山川出版社、1980年).

『増訂織物染色辞典』(織物染色文化研究所編集発行、1954年).

丹野 郁『西洋服飾発達史―古代・中世編』(光正館、1958年).

丹野 郁『西洋服飾発達史―近世編』(光正館、1960年).

丹野 郁『西洋服飾発達史―現代編』(光正館、1965年).

丹野 郁『近代西欧服飾発達文化史』(光正館、1973年).

丹野 郁、原田二郎『西洋服飾史』(衣生活研究会、1975年).

丹野 郁『服飾の世界史』(白水社、1985年).

丹野郁編『西洋服飾史―増訂版―』(東京堂出版、1999年).

濱田雅子『アメリカ植民地時代の服飾』(せせらぎ出版、1996年).

濱田雅子「アメリカ独立革命と服飾－スミソニアン・インスティテューションの収蔵品に基づいて―」(衣生活研究会「衣生活」第31巻第3号、1988年6月)

濱田雅子「18世紀から19世紀初頭のアメリカ社会と衣服文化の特性について―インフォーマルウェアーを中心に―」(国際服飾学会誌No.8，1991年10月)

濱田雅子「18世紀アメリカの職業着―Peter F. Copelandの業績を中心に―」(衣生活研究会「衣生活」第35巻第5号、1992年10月)

濱田雅子「18世紀ヴァージニアにおけるお仕着せに関する歴史的考察」(国際服飾学会誌、No.12, 1995年11月)

濱田雅子「18、19世紀アメリカにおけるショートガウンの復元作業を通じての一考察」(国際服飾学会誌No.14, 1998年3月)

濱田雅子「ヴァージニア・クロスに関する社会史的考察―逃亡奴隷広告および遺品に基づいて―」(国際服飾学会誌No.17, 2000年5月)

本田創造『アメリカ黒人の歴史 新版』(岩波新書、1991年).

森 呆『アメリカ職人の仕事史』(中公新書、中央公論社刊、1996年).

メアリー・ベス・ノートン他著、本田創造監修、白井洋子、戸田徹子訳『アメリカの歴史①新世界への挑戦 15世紀―18世紀』(三省堂、1996年).

吉川和志『新しい繊維の知識』(鎌倉書房、1974年).

ロナルド・タカキ著、富田虎男訳『多文化社会アメリカの歴史―別の鏡に映して―』(明石書房、1995年).

和田光弘「南部植民地における逃亡奴隷―新聞広告の計量分析―」(社会経済史学、第56巻第5号、1990年12月).

付　　録

資　料　編

資料Ⅰ　逃亡奴隷広告の事例

【資料Ⅰの凡例】
①事例1，2，5，7は引用していない逃亡奴隷広告の事例
②事例3，4，8，9は表3-2-2に掲載している事例。事例9は本文p.96にも掲載
③事例6は本文p.75に，逃亡奴隷広告の実物の写真を掲載。

〔事例1〕

Virginia Gazette（Purdie），March 21, 1766.

GLOUCESTER county, March 18, 1766.

RUN away from the subscriber's plantation, on the 3d instant, two Negro men: One of them named ROBIN*, a very likely fellow, of a yellow complexion, about 6 feet high, 28 years old, by trade a blacksmith, is well acquainted with plantation business, has a large scar on his right arm occasioned by a burn, is very sensible, has been to several parts of the country, and intended when he went off to get on board a man of war, or some other vessel; had on when he went away a gray fearnought waistcoat with metal buttons, osnabrugs shirt, cotton breeches and stockings, Virginia shoes, and felt hat; he carried with him sundry wearing apparel, and it is imagined has a pass and sailors dress, intending to pass for a freeman. Whoever conveys the said slave to me shall have 40 s. reward, if taken out of the county, and if out of the colony 10 1. Also DANIEL, a very likely fellow, near 6 feet high, and about 30 years old; had on a suit of cotton, osnabrugs shirt, Virginia shoes, white yarn stockings, felt hat, and it is thought is gone to Louisa. Whoever brings the said fellow to me shall have 10 s. reward, besides what the law allows.

JOHN FOX.

*L.A.Windley, comp., *Runaway Slave Advertisement : A Documentary History from 1730s to 1790*, Vol.4, Greenwood, Westport, Connecticut, 1983, 38.

〔事例2〕

Virginia Gazette（Purdie & Dixon），August 15, 1766.

RUN away the 26th of June last, a likely Virginia born Negro Man slave named CHARLES, about 30 years of age, about 5 feet 7 inches and a half high, but sparely made, speaks very good English, and pretends he can read; had on when he went away a pair of old leather breeches, a brown kersey jacket without sleeves, and an osnabrug shirt. I have heard he has passed for a free man, by the name of Benjamin Corbin, and has an indenture which he got of another person. Whoever apprehends the said Negro, and delivers him to William Alston, of Halifax county in North Carolina, shall have have [sic] 5 1. reward if taken in North Carolina, or 10 1. if taken in Virginia.

＊Windley, *ibid.,* 46

〔事例3〕

Virginia Gazette (Purdie & Dixon), January 26, 1769.

RUN away from the subscriber in Prince George, a Negro fellow named FRANK* of a yellowish complexion, and has a scar on his right cheek, occasioned I believe by a burn; had on when he went away a double breasted kersey jacket and breeches, of a reddish mixture, and plaid hose, but as he has got several other clothes along with him (viz. an old blue duffil great coat, a long light blue duffil close bodied coat, a pair of buckskin breeches, an old red frieze jacket, several pair of yarn stockings, and two pair of shoes) it is very possible he may change them, and put on some of the others. The person that takes him up, and conveys him to me, shall be entitled to 40 s. besides what the law allows, from

DAVID SCOTT.

＊Windley, *ibid.,* 67

〔事例4〕

Virginia Gazette (Purdie & Dixon), August 16, 1770.

RUN away from the subscriber, some time ago, a very likely Negro boy, named WINDSOR, about 14 years old, of a yellowish complexion, and has a smiling countenance; had on when he went away a blue broadcloth jacket, without sleeves, an Irish linen shirt, and osnabrugs breeches. Whoever brings him to me, in Prince Edward county, shall have 20 s. reward besides what the law allows.

WILLIAM WATTS.

＊Windley, *ibid.,* 87

〔事例5〕

Virginia Gazette (Purdie & Dixon), July 11, 1771.

RUN away from the Subscriber, on the 20th of June, a Mulatto Man named JACK HARRIS, about twenty Years of Age, about five Feet nine Inches high, has a flat Nose, a Scar on one of his Thighs, and grim down Look. He had on a Pair of blue Breeches, a blue Waistcoat without Sleeves, a Plains Waistcoat, Osnabrug Shirt, a Felt Hat bound round the Brim, blue Stockings, and a Pair of Pumps, &c. Whoever will deliver him to me near Shirley, in Charles City County, shall have FORTY SHILLINGS Reward, and reasonable Expense paid.

WILLIAM HARDYMAN.

＊Windley, *ibid.*, 97

〔事例6〕

Virginia Gazette (Dixon & Hunter), January 21, 1775.

THREE POUNDS REWARD.

RAN away from the Subscriber, on the 1st of January, a middling dark Mulatto named STEPHEN, about 21 Years of Age, and thick made; had on, when he went off, a Negro Cotton Waistcoat and Breeches, an Osnabrug Shirt, and Negro made Shoes, with Pegs drove in the Soals; his Hair is cut off the Top of his Head, and but little remains at the Sides. He carried with him a white Mulatto Woman Slave named PHEBE, whose Hair is long, straight, and black; she had on a blue Waistcoat and Petticoat, and took with her two new Osnabrug Shirts, and a Suit of striped Virginia Cloth; she is about 21 Years of Age. They also carried off two Osnabrug Shirts, 6 or 7 Ells of Rolls, a new Dutch Blanket, and one about Half worn. It is imagined they will make for Carolina; and endeavour to pass for free People. All Persons are forewarned from harbouring them, at their Peril. Whoever brings them to me, or secures them in any Gaol, so that I may get them again, shall have the above Reward.

HENRY HARDAWAY

＊Windley, *ibid.*, 160

〔事例7〕

Virginia Gazette (Dixon & Hunter), February 4, 1775.

RAN away from the Subscriber, in New Kent, a little below the Brick House Ferry, in the Night of the 16th inst. (Jan.) a Negro named MOSES, of a very light Complexion, 5 Feet 8 or 9

Inches high, well made, about 23 Years of Age, had on, when he went away, a Kendal Cotton Jacket and Breeches died with Maple Bark, and has flat Metal Buttons on it, Cuffs to his Jacket Sleeves, a Collar of gray Cloth, and a Felt Hat, with a Tinsey worked Button. He went off in a Canoe about 22 Feet long, full timbered, rows with two Oars, and Cleats on each Side to row with a Pair of Sculls; she was sheathed on the outside of her Bottom with thin Pine Plank. Whoever brings him to me, with or without the Canoe, shall have 20 s. Reward, besides what the Law allows; but if they cannot conveniently bring him, and will secure him so that I may get him again, they shall be entitled to the same Reward. I expect he is lurking about Gloucester Town, as he formerly belonged to Mr. Isaac Hobday of that Place.

WILLIAM SLATER.

＊Windley, *ibid.,* 161-162

〔事例8〕

Virginia Gazette (Dixon & Hunter), July 20, 1776.

RUN away from the Subscriber, a Negro Man named BAGLEY, about 20 Years of Age, 5 Feet 5 or 6 Inches high, black Complexion, and well made; had on, when he went away, a white, Russia Drab Coat, brown Linen Breeches, with Waistband, of a lighter Colour, and a Dowlas Shirt much worn. He has several Relations in Gloucester County, and it is probable he may be gone that way. Whoever delivers the said Slave to me in Williamsburg shall have TEN SHILLINGS Reward.

NICHOLAS SCOUVEMONT.

＊Windley, *ibid.,* 177

〔事例9〕

Virginia Gazette (Dixon & Hunter), March 14, 1777.

HANOVER, March 1, 1777.

RUN away from the Subscriber on the 3d of February, at Night, WILL, a Negro Man, by Trade a Carpenter, of a yellow Complexion, middle Statute, well set, flat nosed, and has lost one of his upper fore Teeth; had on when he went away white Virginia Jacket and Breeches, Country made Linen Shirt, striped Wrappers, common Negro Shoes, old Beaver Hat, with a small

Brim, and carried with him a Dutch Blanket almost new, a Pair of old black Lasting Breeches, and a Shirt of the same Linen of the one he had on. I expect he is either lurking about Mr. Braxton Bird's in King and Queen, of whom I purchased him, or Mr. Corbin's in Middlesex, where his Mother lives. He is a cunning sensible Fellow, well acquainted in many Parts of the Country, and is very capable of telling a plausible Story. I will give 5 l. Reward to any Person who will secure the said Slave, so that I get him again, and reasonable Expenses if brought Home.

DANIEL TRUEHEART.

＊Windley, *ibid.*, 181

資料Ⅱ.

John Wily, *A Treatise on the Propagation of Sheep, the Manufacture of Wool, and the Cultivation and Manufacture of Flax*, with Direction for Making Feveral Utensils for the Business, Williamsburg, 1765.

本書はウィリアムスバーグの出版人のジョゼフ・ロイル（Joseph Royle）が1765年に出版したもの。ヴァージニアで織工向けの手引書として用いられていた。

A

TREATISE

ON THE

Propagation of SHEEP,

THE

MANUFACTURE of WOOL,

AND THE

Cultivation and Manufacture of FLAX, with Directions for making feveral Utenfils for the Bufinefs.

By JOHN WILY.

WILLIAMSBURG:
Printed by *J. Royle*, MDCCLXV.

The PREFACE.

AS it is cuftomary for the fmalleft Pamphlets to have a Preface to recommend them to the Publick, I fuppofe it will be expected there fhould be one to this, though I am of Opinion it needs no other Recommendation than the prefent Circumftances of the Generality of the Inhabitants in this Colony, who are more in Debt than they can poffibly raife Money to difcharge, our Paper Currency being almoft exhaufted, little or no Gold or Silver amongft us, Tobacco (our Staple Commodity) of fo little Value that it is fcarce worth making, and Goods at a higher Price than was ever known in this Colony before. I think this a fufficient Recommendation of thefe few Sheets to the Publick, and hope it will plead a fufficient Excufe for my undertaking a Tafk which I muft acknowledge myfelf incapable of in Regard to penning it in a grammatical and methodical Form; but as it is intended chiefly for the Benefit of the common and poorer Sort of People, I hope the Learned will not condemn it, but lend their kind Affiftance to the publifhing a better Piece on the fame Subject, for the Encouragement of Arts and Manufactures amongft us: For as we have got in Debt by our Indolence and Extravagancy, fure there is no better Method to retrieve ourfelves than by our Induftry and Frugality. And I muft believe, and hope, this fmall Treatife will forward thofe Manufactures, as I have given the plaineft Directions

The PREFACE

for the Performance of every Operation in each of them; so that a Person, of a common Capacity, may go through the whole Processes without any other Instructions. Though Fortune hath not placed me in Circumstances to be so great a Benefactor to my Country as she hath those who can afford to lay out two or three Hundred Pounds to improve the Breed of Horses amongst us, yet my Labour in writing this Pamphlet I hope will be serviceable, and as well accepted by the Publick as the Widow's Mite was in the Treasury; and I hope it will prove very beneficial to every Purchaser. This is the sincere Wishes and Prayer of him who begs Leave to subscribe himself the Virginia *Farmer's*

  Most Obedient and
   Very Humble Servant,
    JOHN WILY.

For the Propagation of SHEEP, and increasing the Quantity of WOOL.

THOUGH Sheep are the most beneficial Creatures we can raise, they affording us both Food and Raiment, yet there is no dumb Creature taken so little Notice of in *Virginia* as they; there being but very few People here that take Care to sow any Thing for Winter Pasturage for them, or provide or give them any other Food than a few dry Blades in the Winter. And as Wool is a Commodity greatly wanting in this Colony, I hope it will not be taken amiss if I here give the Readers my Opinion how to manage their Sheep to have more in Number, with finer Wool, and larger Fleeces, than is at present got from the common Flocks.

First. Make choice of a likely large Ram Lamb, that has the finest and longest Wool, and give him always his Fill of good Food, and not suffer him to run with the Ewes until he is two Years old, by which Time he will have a good Growth; and I must likewise be of Opinion it is proper to keep the Ewe Lambs from the Ram until they are a Year old or upwards, for the Ewes having Lambs before they have their Growth is a great Disadvantage to the Breed of our Sheep.

In the Summer remove or change your Sheeps Pasturage as often as you conveniently can, and do not pen them in the Summer Nights, for as they cannot bear the Heat of the Day, it is the only Time they have to feed, unless a little in the Mornings and Evenings; but if you are unwilling to lose the Benefit of their Dung, pen them in the Day Time, and have good Arbours for the Sheep to lie under in the Heat of the Day: The Pens should be frequently removed, or cleaned out, and the Dung carried away; for all Kind of Filth is pernicious to them.

For Winter Pasturage for your Sheep, sow Wheat, Rye, Clover, or Timothy, for them to feed on when the Earth is free from Snow; and sow large Patches of Turnips, to feed them with in snowy Weather, when they have not the Opportunity of getting any green or moist Food. You should take Care to dig your Turnips when your Earth is clear of Snow, and keep them in a Cellar, or Cave made for that Purpose, until you have Occasion for them; then take them out and wash them, and lay them in a clean Trough, and there with a Spade, or some cutting Utensil, cut and chop them to Pieces; then lay them in long Troughs, for your Sheep to feed on. Oats or Pease is exceeding good Food for Sheep in the Winter; and sometimes wet the Oats, and throw a little Salt amongst them, for I look upon Salt to be very serviceable to all Kind of Stock. In the Winter Season, have a good tight Roof for your Sheep to lie under; the Sides to be open, for the Benefit of the Air; have the Shelters often cleaned, and the Dung carried away; and give them fresh litter. You should take Care not to let your Pasture be eaten down about the Time of your Ewes yeaning, but to procure some good Grazing to turn your Ewes on just before their yeaning, which will occasion them to have a Plenty of Milk for the Lambs, and will prevent there being so great a Loss of them as is common where the Ewes have only dry Food to feed on. If any of your Ewes yean whilst the Earth is covered with Snow, that they have not the Opportunity of grazing, you should supply the Defect by giving them a greater Plenty of Turnips. If any of your Ewes refuse to take their Lambs, put the Ewe and Lamb in a close House, and tie a Dog in the same Place, and they will own the Lamb immediately.

The proper Time to shear your Sheep is in the Increase of the Moon, in *May*; and, if you have the Conveniency, make a Pen near some Water Course or Pond, and wash your Sheep before you shear them: As soon as they are washed turn them into a small Enclosure that has a Plenty of Grass, and let them run on it two or three Days, or until you see the fatty or oily Substance shedding amongst the Wool. Then is the proper Time to shear them, for

[8]

that is a great Prefervation to the Wool. If any of the Sheep have fhed Part of their Wool, be fure to clip the young Wool, to prevent its fhedding again. The next Spring, as foon as the Fleece is off, take a Brufh with a little Oil on it, and rub it on the Sheep; and it will occafion the Wool to grow the fafter and caufe the Water to fhed off them the quicker if they are caught in cold Rains, which is very hurtful to them.

I make no Doubt but there may be many more very ufeful Obfervations made on the Propagation of Sheep, but I am in Hopes thofe I have made will be fufficient to ftir up my Countrymen to take more Notice of their Sheep than they formerly have done; and I make no Doubt but the Methods I have prefcribed will be of great Service to the improving our Sheep and Wool, as well as increafing the Quantity of both, if well followed.

As there are different Sorts of Wool on a Sheep, the Neck being the fineft, the Belly next, the Sides next, the Shoulders and Thighs the coarfeft, it will be proper the Perfon employed to fhear the Sheep fhould carefully roll up each Fleece by itfelf, turning it infide out, beginning at the Neck Part, and leaving out the Shanks; that the Perfon employed to fort the Wool may with the greater Eafe feparate the fine from the coarfe, and likewife that which is fuitable to be combed for Worfted from that

[9]

which will anfwer for other Ufes. After your Wool is well culled or forted, the fine from the coarfe, then have it well wafhed; for if you wafh your Wool before it is forted, it afterwards will be very difficult to feparate the fine from the coarfe as it ought to be.

I am perfuaded that many induftrious People have been difcouraged from attempting to have larger Quantities of woollen Cloth prepared and dreft at the FullingMills, onAccount of what they have had done drawing and puckoring up in divers Places, which was altogether owing to the Mifmanagement of the Wool; and this was one Reafon for my undertaking to write this Pamphlet, in Hopes by this Means to put thofe that make any hereafter into a better Method of managing their Wool, and advife them to obferve and be guided by the following Directions.

When your Wool is well forted, the fine from the courfe, and clean wafhed, if you are defirous to have a Piece of fine Cloth, take the fineft of your Wool and fpread it on a Floor, and fprinkle a little Oil, or any foft Greafe, on it; then turn it over, and fprinkle it again; and fo proceed until you think it fufficiently greafed to fpin. Then, with a Pair of coarfe Cards, card it flightly;   fo as to make it into Bats, fuch as is put in Quilts.   Then let three or four Perfons take about an equal Quantity of thofe Bats under their Arm, and, walking round on

[10]

a Circle, with their other Hand pluck off fmall Quantities at a Time, and throw it altogether in a Pile in the Middle of the Circle. Then take it up and card it flightly, and make it into Bats again; and mix them as before. This fhould be repeated two or three Times, or oftener; that the Wool may be well mixed together, which is the only Method to prevent your Cloth being uneven: For if you card or fpin your Wool in the common Way, taking it juft as it comes to Hand, it will certainly be liable to that Misfortune; for the coarfe and fine Wool, nor the Wool of an old Sheep, and Lambs, will not fhrink and mill alike. And if you have a few Quills of fine, and then a few of coarfe Wool, filled or fhot in your Cloth, it is impoffible to prevent its being puckery and uneven, as foon as it gets wet. This I am fully convinced to be the Reafon of Cloths being uneven, for I have always obferved that the Pieces of mixt Cloths which have been brought to the Fulling Mill I am concerned with are not liable to that Misfortune; for by the Owners endeavouring to mix and mingle the different Colours together, they have fo mixed the different Sorts of Wool together that it made the Cloth as even and free from Puckers as that imported here from *England*, or elfewhere. This Method of braking or mixing of Wool I am informed in the old Countries is called fcribbling of Wool, and is Bufinefs many People get a Living by; to perform which they have a Pair of Cards about fourteen Inches long and nine

[11]

Inches wide, the under Card to be nailed to a Plank fixed to a Bench or Form, in the fame Form or Pofition as the Fall of a Defk or Writing Table, and to be about the Height of a Perfon's Breaft, as they fit a-ftraddle on the Bench to work; the Plank that the under Card is fixed to muft be fupported by three other Planks, one to be nailed to the End of the Bench, the other two to the Sides of the Bench, to ftand up endwife, thofe at the Sides to be fawed bevelling at the upper Ends, to nail that on which the Card is fixed to; fo that thefe Planks form a large Pigeon Hole to keep the Wool in ready at Hand : When your Card is thus fixed, put on your Wool; then with the other Card, which hath two Handles, one as common Cards, and the other ftandingupright, fo that the Perfon that works with it hath the Advantage of working it with both Hands, and having a great Purchafe with their Body, makes the Operation much eafier performed than with the common Wool Cards; as a Pair of thefe Cards will make the Bats fo much the larger than the others, a Perfon will brake or fcribble more Wool in one Day with a Pair of thefe Cards than in four or five Days with the other Sort, and will do it much better.   A Pair of thefe Cards will coft about five Shillings Sterling, and I think well worth every Perfon's fending for, that has a large Quantity of Wool to manufacture.

[12]

If you have a Mind for a Piece of mixed (or what is called medley) Cloth, that is, to mix two or more Colours together, put as much of each Colour on the Card as you would have it fhow in the Cloth; then Card it into Bats, and mix it as before mentioned. The oftener you repeat the Operation, the evener and more regular the Colours will appear throughout the whole Piece of Cloth. When your Wool is well broke, or your Colours well mixed together, you muft then with a Pair of common Wool Cards, card and make it into Rolls to fpin.

As to the fpinning your Wool, it will be proper to have your Warp fpun by one Perfon only, as it will likely be nearer of a Size, and twifted nearer alike, than if fpun by different Hands. The Warp fhould be twifted middling hard, and fpun with a ftraight Band in the common Way, as even as poffible. The Filling or Shoot fhould be fpun by one Perfon only, for the Reafons before mentioned; for the Evennefs of the Cloth depends more upon the even fpinning of the Filling thon the Warp. The Filling fhould be fpun with a crofs Band, to twift the Thread the contrary Way to the Warp, which will occafion the Warp and Filling to mill the clofer and tighter together, and not fhow the Threads fo plain as if both twifted the fame Way. The Filling fhould be fpun a Size coarfer than the Warp, and not fo hard

[13]

twifted, but not fo flightly as to want Strength to be fhot in the Cloth.

Woollen Cloth to be milled ought to be wove at leaft five Quarters of a Yard wide, for in milling it fhrinks in Width as well as Length; and if wove but Yard wide will be too narrow for Mens Clothing, if well milled: Therefore, whoever intends to weave Cloth to be milled fhould provide themfelves with a Loom, and proper Slays and Harnefs for that Purpofe; the thicker the Cloth is wove, the thicker it will be when milled.

If you are fcarce of Wool, and have Cotton plenty, you may fpin a Warp of Cotton, to run five or five Yards and a Half to the Pound, fuitable to a Slay Ell wide; for it will fhrink as much in the Width of the Cloth as if it was all Wool, therefore it ought to be wove as wide. Then fpin Wool to fill in two or two Yards and a Half to the Pound, and weave it in the Kerfey or Serge Way, or any double Woof, and have it milled, and it will appear very well until the Wool wears off, and then the Cotton will fhow fomewhat lighter, unlefs you die the Cotton of the Colour you want the Cloth before it is wove, for the Cotton will not take the Die fo eafy as the Wool, and that is the Reafon it will fhow lighter when much worn. This Kind of Cloth will wear exceeding well, and makes very good Clothing for Boys or Houfe Servants. C

[14]

There is another Kind of outfide Clothing for Winter Wear, called German Serge, which is entirely made of Wool, but is a Mixture of Worfted and Yarn. The Method of making it is to pick out a Parcel of Wool fuitable to be combed for Worfted, and have it combed; take the long Wool which is drawn out of the Combs, and fpin it into Worfted for the Warp; fpin it to run about five Yards to the Pound, fuitable to a feven Hundred Slay that is Ell wide; then take what is called the Backing, that is, the fhort Wool that remains in the Combs, and mix it as firft directed; then with a Pair of common Wool Cards card it into Rolls, and fpin it to fill in about three Yards to the Pound, and have it wove in the fame Manner as German Serge; and it will be equally as good as any from the old Countries.

As I have given the Readers fome Information how to manufacture Wool, to make good Cloth for the outfide Clothing for the Winter Seafon, I think it neceffary and my Duty to inform them in the beft Manner I can how to make the Linings, and the Worfted Summer Wear; which I am convinced, by what I have had done myfelf, and what I have feen at Mr. *John Sutton*'s in *Caroline* County (who is my near Neighbour, and Partner in a Fulling Mill) that it may be brought to great Perfection: For I have feen at Mr. *Sutton*'s great Quantities of Wool combed for Worfted (for his own

[15]

Ufe, and fome for the Neighbours) fome of which has been knit for Stockings, which I think far exceeds thofe from Europe on Account of Service, and fome of it applied for the Warp of what we call German Serge, Camelot, Taminies, Duroys, *&c*. Patterns of which may be feen at the aforefaid Mill, where any Perfon may have Cloths dreffed as well as any Where in *America*, and Worfted combed and died of any Colour they choofe.

It requires the longeft and fineft Wool to make good Worfted; and to prepare it for fpinning you fhould have a Pair of Worfted Combs (which will coft about 35 *f*. Sterling) but I look upon the combing of Worfted to be fo great a Difficulty that I believe no Perfon can do it to Perfection unlefs they have ferved an Apprenticefhip to it, or could a Perfon acquainted with it ftand by and direct them, therefore have omitted how the Operation or Procefs is performed. But if you can light on a Perfon acquainted with the Bufinefs, and will comb your Wool fit for fpinning, you may fpin it on a Flax Wheel, as hereafter directed, or on a large Wheel, as Cotton or Wool; only, with this Difference, the Worfted when combed is made into a large Bat, Fleece, or Sliver, and not into Rolls. And to fpin it you are to take for the Bat about as much as would make a Roll, and give it a Turn round the fourth Finger of your left Hand; then join it to a Thread on the Spindle, and, turning the Wheel with your

[16]

right Hand, draw out the Worsted to what Size you think proper. A good Spinner of Worsted will spin Half a Pound a Day, that will warp between 6 and 7 Yards to the Pound, and in 10 Days a good Spinner will spin sufficient to warp 30 Yards suitable for Shalloon, Taminies, Duroys, or any Worsted Stuffs that are but three Quarters of a Yard wide. The German Serge requires more Warp, because of its Width; and Camelot, on Account of its being doubled and twisted.

The Method to make with Wool what is called Camelot (though it often hath Silk or Hair in it) is to have the Wool combed, and take the longest of it and spin it into Worsted, then double and twist two Threads hard together for both Warp and Filling. It is in common wove in the plain Way, but should be flayed as thick as possible, and drove as close together as it can be with the Slay, &c. These plain Camelots after they are wove are put in a hot Press, to give them a glossy Stiffening, and close the Thread. The watered Camelots are those which after weaving receive a certain Preparation with Water, and are after passed under a hot Press, which gives them a Smoothness and Lustre.

Duroys, Taminies, and many other Worsted Stuffs, are wove in the plain Way; and after weaving are passed under a hot Press, to give them a Gloss and Lustre.

[17]

Shalloon, Sagathy, Calimanco, Plaids, and many other Worsted Stuffs, are made of raw Worsted, but are double wove; and the Difference in them is performed by the different Methods the Weavers have of putting the Warp in the Harness, and by working it with a larger Number of Treadles than they make Use of in the weaving plain Cloth.

To oblige some of the worthy Gentlemen who are pleased to favour me with their Names to my Subscription Paper, for the Encouragement of the publishing this Pamphlet, I shall here give some Account of the Methods for milling, dying, shearing, and pressing Cloths, though I thought to have concluded the Woollen Manufacture of the Worsted Stuffs; for I am of Opinion these Processes concerning the Woollen Cloth will be but of little Use to the Publick in general, as it will be only serviceable to those who erect a Fulling Mill for that Purpose. And whoever undertakes to carry on the Business must provide themselves with People that are acquainted with every Branch of the Business, or they cannot carry it on to Perfection; and it is a very great Difficulty to find one Man acquainted with the whole Processes, for I am credibly informed that in the Mother Countries the Milling of Cloth is a Branch of the Woollen Manufacture by itself, the Dying another, the Shearing another, and the Pressing another, and that each of these a Man is to serve a regular

[18]

Apprenticeship to before he is permitted to set up any of those Branches of the Business.

When the Cloth is wove, the next Thing to be performed in common is the Milling (though sometimes it is died first) which I think is the best, as the Cloth then being thin and open the Dies will strike it the better. But the best Method of dying is in the Grain, for the Cloth to retain the Die. What is meant by dying it in the Grain, is dying the Wool of the Colour you want the Cloth, which stands to Reason it will hold the Colour better; for as the Wool is all loose and open, the Dies have the freer Access to the Wool.

For the milling of Cloth, you should have what is called a Fulling Mill. There are several Methods of building them, though they are all worked by a Water Wheel, which is in common 10 or 12 Feet diameter, and is either over or under shot; or what is called a Breast Mill. This last the Water is delivered near the Centre of the Wheel, and is turned the same Way as the under shot. They have all a large Stock of Timber, about 30 Inches square, and about 8 Feet long, which is called the Bed, to which there is an upright Post or Stock of Timber of the same Dimensions fixed, by letting them into each other, and fastening them by dovetailed Keys; and in the front Side of the Post that is next the Shaft of the Water Wheel, there is to be a large Hole or Cavity made, at the Bottom

[19]

of which there is another Piece fixed, and a Piece on each Side the Post to enlarge the Cavity, or what is more properly called the Cup of the Mill. In this the Cloth is put when it is to be milled, and there to be beaten with two large Mallets, which are raised or lifted by two Arms which go through the Shaft of the Water Wheel. In the Top of the upright or main Post there should be two Mortices or Places cut for what is called the Leavers; these are Pieces which are morticed through the Mallets, and extended so far through as for the Arms before mentioned to take Hold enough of them to raise the Mallets to a proper Height to fall with a good Force on the Cloth; the other Ends of the Leavers are fixed to Rollers, which work or turn in a Hollow, made suitable to the Size of the Rollers, in the back Side of the Post at the upper End. The Mallets are about 4 Feet long, and almost in the Shape of the upper Beak or Bill of a Hawk; they are about 6 Inches thick, 24 Inches wide at Top, and 6 at Bottom, so that the Foot which strikes on the Cloth is 6 Inches square; the Back of the Mallets should be cut with a Sweep suitable to the Cup in which the Cloth is laid to be milled. There are three other Pieces, called Fenders, which are cut in the Inside by the same Sweep as the back Part of the Mallets; one End of each of them is fixed to the Piece at the Bottom of the Cup; they have a Piece morticed on the Top of them, and from that Top Piece there are three other Pieces fixed to the main Post and the said Top Piece,

[20]

to keep the Fenders steady. The Use of the Fenders are to keep and guide the Mallets from striking against the Sides of the Cup. The Fenders are planed straight on both Sides; one of them stands between the two Leavers, and one on each Side.

I have here given an Account of the principal Parts of a Fulling Mill, and shall now proceed to give some Account of the Method of milling of Cloth. First wet it with warm Soap Suds or Chamber Lie, then lay the Cloth in the Cup of the Mill, and set the Mill to work. The Cloth should be kept moistened with warm Soap Suds, Chamber Lie, Rye Meal, or Fullers Earth, mixed with warm Water, to make and keep the Cloth slippery, that it may turn a little at every Stroke the Mallets give it; for if you see the Cloth remain in the same Position for several Strokes together, you may depend the Mill, or Cloth, is not in proper Order. The Cloth should always have a moderate Warmth in it, first raised by the warm Liquid it is moistened with, which Heat is afterwards to be kept up by the hard and quick Strokes of the Mallets, which are ordered or regulated by the Quantity of Water delivered on the Wheel once in 5 or 6 Hours. The Cloth should be taken out of the Mill, and overhauled, beginning at one End and examining it through, to see if it is not united or milled together in Places that ought not to be, which will sometimes happen if the Mill continues working too

[21]

long at a Time without examining. When the Cloth is thickened or milled enough, it should be scoured, to cleanse it of the Grease, Soap, or other Ingredients made Use of in milling the Cloth. To scour it, lay it in the Cup of the Mill, and have a small Trough to convey a small Quantity of Water into the Cup amongst the Cloth, and set the Mill to work, and as she keeps going the Water will dash out as fast as it runs in; this Method will cleanse the Cloth of all Filth, and make it in Order to receive the Die.

To die Cloth you should have a large Copper fixed in Brick, in the same Manner as a Still is set up, having a wooden Frame on the Top with two upright Posts about 18 Inches high; on the Top of these Posts the Axletree of a Reel should turn to receive or take up the Cloth out of the Liquid it is dying in, and to let it into the Copper of Liquid again, that by shifting, changing, and running it through the Die, it may be all of one Colour, which it would not if thrown into the Copper, and let lie without being moved.

As to my pretending to give a full Account of the Die Stuffs made Use of in every particular Colour, I must ingenuously confess I am not so well acquainted with the Business as to give a proper Account of dying, as I was not brought up to it, but will endeavour to satisfy

D

[22]

the Reader's Curiosity, as far as lies In my Power, what Dies are in common made Use of, and the Colors they die.

There are several Ingredients made Use of in dying, some of them only to prepare Stuffs for better taking the Die and to heighten the Lustre of the Colours, some to colour it, and others to fix or set the Colours.

The Ingredients commonly made Use of in dying Scarlet are a Decoction of Alum, Aquafortis, and Cochineal; a Pewter Vat is the best to die this Colour in.

For dying common Reds, Purples, &c. Alum, Redwood, Brazil, Madder, &c.

For dying Yellow, Alum, Woad, Fustick, &c.

For dying light Colours, Alum, Copperas, Galls, and several Kinds of Barks.

For dying dark Browns, Snuff Colours, &c. Alum, Copperas, Logwood, Madder, Walnut Hulls, Sumach, Alder, Galls, &c.

For dying Black, Copperas, Galls, Sumach, Alder, &c.

For dying Blue, Indigo, and Woad, with which a Decoction is made, should be fermented

[23]

in a Lead Vat fixed in a Brick Furnace; the Vat should be in Resemblance of a Sugar Loaf, or Mill Hopper, the small End set a little Way in the Earth, the Bricks not to close to the Side until they rise near the Top, that the Fire may have free Access to the Side of the Vat to keep it with a moderate Heat. Lime Water or Pot-Ash are sometimes used in working of blue Vats; the over-heating a blue Vat will spoil its Process.

All the other Colours I have mentioned, except the Scarlet, may be died in a Copper in boiling Liquid which the Drugs are boiled in; any of the Colours are to be heightened or lowered according to the Proportion of the Ingredients put into the Liquid, which must be left to the Knowledge and Skill of the Dier.

To die Green, first die it a good Yellow, then put it into a blue Vat, and if the Blue is good it will be a good Green; but if either the Yellow or Blue be of a bad Colour, it will not make a good Green.

As soon as Cloth is taken out of the Die it should be rinsed in clean Water, to wash off the loose Dregs of die; and whilst it is wet it should be carded with a Pair of what is called Clothiers Cards, to make a Grain on the Cloth, and to lay the Wool all one Way. The Method of carding the Cloth is to hang one End of the Cloth over a small Bar fixed to the Joists

[24]

of a House, or supported by two Posts; then take a Card in each Hand, and as the Cloth hangs over the Bar reach up as high as you can with the Cards; bear them hard against each other, and pull them down the Cloth the Side you purpose for the Outside. When you have the End carded as high as you can reach, then pull it down to your right Hand, and so proceed until you have laid the Wool all one Way; which is necessary, that the Garments which are made of it may shed the Water off better when taken in Rain. This you may observe by stroking your Hand on any of the fine Cloth imported here, for it will feel much smoother and finer one Way than the other. As soon as the Cloth is finished carding, before it gets dry it should be streched on the Tenter Bars to dry, to make it smooth, and free from Wrinkles, that it may be in the better Order for shearing.

To erect a Set of Tenter Bars, you should get as many Posts as are necessary for the Distance you purpose to set up the Bars; the Posts should be set about 10 Feet apart, to have a Tenant at the Top for the Top Rail or Bar to have a long Mortice for the Bottom Bar to work up and down in, to stretch the Cloth according to its Width; the lower Bars to have a double Tenant, one to be in the Mortice, the other to be in the front Side of the Post; the Tenter Hooks are square, and have two Points, one to be drove into the Bars, the other to hang the Cloth on; those drove in the upper Bars should

[25]

have their Points standing upright, and the Points of those in the Bottom Bars should be downwards. To stretch out the Cloth, begin at one End, and hang one Selvage on the Hooks in the upper Bars, and the other Selvage to the lower Bars; then squeeze them down, and confine them so until the Cloth is dried.

When the Cloth is thorough dry it is in Order for shearing; and to perform this Branch of the Manufacture, you should provide a Pair of Clothiers Shears, and have a Shear Board made suitable to the Shears. To make a Shear Board, or Bench, get a Piece of Timber about 5 Feet long, 2 Feet wide, and 4 or 5 Inches thick; fix 4 good strong Legs to it, to keep it steady; the Top of the Bench to be about the Height of a Man's Waistband that is to work at it; the Top of the Bench should be made rounding, exactly to fit the Hollow of the Blade of the Shears; then fold up a Piece of Cloth, and lay it on the Bench; then lay a Piece of brown Linen, or good Rolls, over the Cloth, and draw it over the Cloth, and as tight as possible to the under Side of the Bench, to make a good firm Cushion to shear the Cloth on; then you should have 6 small Iron Hooks about 4 Inches long, Half an Inch wide in the Middle, and small at each End, with a Hook to each End, one to hook in the Selvage of the Cloth, the other in the cover of the Cushion, to stretch the Cloth to be sheared so tight on the Cushion as to make it free from any Puckers or Wrinkles.

[26]

A Pair of Shears will weigh about 40 lbs. notwithstanding there is very often 15 or 20 lbs. of Lead fixed on the under Blade of the Shears, to make them clip the Wool the closer to the Threads; they are made chiefly of Steel, and have a large Bow of well tempered Steel, near as large as a small Man's Wrist, which is so stiff, as they are obliged to be worked by a Purchase with a Handle, and a Cord to draw the Edges together when working with them.

When you have your Shears and Shear Bench fixed as before mentioned, fold up your Cloth, and lay it at the Backside of your Shear Bench; then take the End of the Cloth which the Wool is laid towards, that you are going to shear, and with the Tenter Hooks stretch the Cloth tight on the Cushion, and with a Pair of Tweezers made for that Purpose pick off all the Knots, and with a Clothier's Card, or a Set of Teasels, card the Cloth towards you, and then lay on the Shears, and begin to work close at one Selvage, and so work across the Cloth to the other; then make your Tenter Hooks loose, and take over some more of the Cloth, and so proceed until you have sheared the whole Piece of Cloth.

The next after shearing is the pressing. To perform it there must be a Press erected, a Press Hearth, Press Boards, and Press Papers. A Press is made with two large Posts 12 Feet

[27]

long, 16 Inches wide, and 12 thick; two other Pieces, of the same Width and Thickness of the Posts, to be 8 Feet long; one is for a Bottom, and the other a Top Piece. These Pieces are to be tenanted through the Posts, with a double Tenant to each End. The Posts should be 4 Feet apart in the clear. The Inside of them, and the Edges, should be smooth and straight, that the Foot Board, or Follower, may slide up and down between them without Interruption. The Bottom and Top Piece to be 5 Feet apart in the clear, and then there will be sufficient Timber at each End of the Posts to prevent the Tenants tearing out. There should be Keys in the Tenants at the Backside of the Posts, to keep them in Place. There must be a Hole cut through the Top Piece in the Centre, between the Posts, just sufficient for the Screw to work through the Piece. Then fix the Box or Nut of the Screw to the under Side of the Top Piece, so that the Screw may work exactly perpendicular through the Hole in the Top Piece. When the Posts are set upright, the lower ends of the Posts may be set in the Earth even with the Bottom of the Bottom Piece; then a Floor of Bricks to be raised on each Side the said Piece, even with the Top of it; then have some Pieces of Plank 3 Inches thick and 5 Feet long, and lay them across the Bottom Piece, from one Post to the other; the Ends of the Plank to lie on the Brick Floor which is raised on each Side the said Piece; then make a Brick Hearth on the said Planks, and

[28]

run up a Pillar of Brick, close to the Inside of each Post, a Foot high, and one Pillar in the Middle; on these Pillars the Press Plate, or Hearth, is laid; it is a Plate of cast Iron, about 3 Feet 10 Inches long, 2 Feet 8 Inches wide, and 2 Inches thick; then get a Piece of Timber for the Foot Board, or Follower, 5 Inches thick, 4 Feet 8 Inches long, and 2 Feet 8 Inches wide; then from within 3 Inches of the Centre adze it away bevelling to each End, to be about 2 Inches and a Half thick at the Ends; then cut again, or guide in each End of it, exactly to fit in between the Posts, and leaving an equal Part at each Corner to guide it to slip up and down the Posts; then fix the Foot or Step exactly in the Centre of the Follower. What is called the Step or Foot is a Piece of Iron, which with large Nails is fixed on the Top of the Follower, by which the Follower is raised or forced down to press the Cloth, the Step having a Hollow in the Centre of it for the Point of the Screw to work in; and by turning the Screw one Way it takes up the Follower, and turning it the other forces it down on the Cloth. Then have some Press Boards made of white Oak Plank, Inch thick; they should be about 3 Feet long and 2 Feet and a Half wide, with Ledges to the Ends of them, to keep them together; they should be planed smooth on both Sides; 6 or 7 of them will be sufficient for a common Press. Then have a sufficient Number of Blocks, 2 Feet and a Half long, tied up 6 Inches square, to lay between the

[29]

Follower and the Pressing Board that is over the Cloth to be pressed.

When you have a Press fixed as here mentioned to press Woollen Cloths or Stuffs, make a small Fire in the Stoves underneath the Iron Plate, or have a large Quantity of good hot Coals to put in the Stoves, to make the Press Plate as hot as you can endure your Hands on it for a small Space of Time; and it should be supplied with fresh Coals, to keep with a moderate Heat as long as there are any Cloths in the Press. To fold up the Cloth to put in the Press, there should be a large Table to lay the Cloth and Pressing Papers on; then begin at one End of a Piece of Cloth, and lay on a Paper; then turn the Cloth over that Paper; then lay another Paper on the Cloth, aud bring the Cloth back again over the second Paper; and so proceed until the whole Piece of Cloth is folded up, with a Paper between every Fold; then lay two or three of the sorry Papers on the Hearth or Press Plate, and the Cloth that is papered on them; then lay a Press Board upon the Cloth, and give it a Squeeze with the Screw, and let it lie until it is warmed; then take it off the Plate, and lay another Piece, papered in the same Manner, on the Plate, and a Pressing Board on it; then lay the first Piece on the Board, and another Board on that, and so proceed until the Press is full of Cloth; or until you have all in that you have ready for the

E

[30]

Press; observing always to put the fresh Pieces next the Papers on the Plate, and to have a Press Board between every Piece of Cloth, if large, but if small two or three Pieces may be between two Boards. Every large Piece of Cloth you put in Press, or two or three small Ones, you should take a good hard Set on it, with an Iron Crow Bar, which is to have one End made suitable to the Holes in the Screw to turn it by. In the Press, Shalloons, Taminies, Duroys, and many other Worsted Stuffs, have a Paper put in only every other Fold, to make a Gloss only on one Side of the Stuffs; but the Worsted requires a harder Set with the Screw than Cloth. There are some Kinds of Stuffs which are watered when put in the Press, which will show a long Time after being worn.

On the Cultivation and Manufacture of FLAX.

FLAX thrives the best, and grows to the greatest Perfection, in moist Lands, that have a fine rich mellow Soil; but it will sometimes grow to great Perfection on high Land, that has a fine Soil, if well manured, especially if the Season of its growing should prove moist, in which Case it will probably be as good as any on the low Lands. I am of Opinion the Ground that will bring good Tobacco will bring good Flax; for I this Year sowed about two Acres of Ground in Flax, which had been tended

[31]

fifteen Years successively, without any Kind of Manure the whole Time of its being cleared and tended: Therefore I think no Person need doubt of making it, as Ground so long tended would bring it to Perfection.

To prepare your Land for Flax, tend it the Year before in Tobacco (if you choose to make any) or in any Thing else that will clean the Ground of Weeds and Grass Seeds; for if a great Quantity of either comes up with the Flax it will be very hurtful to it, unless picked out, which is very troublesome, as it is to be done by Hand, in the same Manner as you weed Tobacco Plants. You should plow the Ground in the Month of *March*, two or three Times over, until you have well broken the Clods; then go over it with a Tooth Harrow, until you have laid it as level, and made it as fine, as possible.

The proper Time to sow Flax Seed is between the Middle of *March* and Middle of *April*, though it will sometimes come to good Perfection if sowed at any Time before the Middle of *July*; but if sowed after the Time first mentioned it is liable to be hurt by the Weeds or Grass, if the Ground throw out a large Quantity of either, or the Summer Drowth will be apt to hurt it, if on high Land.

Flax should be sowed promiscuously (as Wheat or Oats, &c.) but somewhat thicker.

[32]

Though the Seed is much smaller than Wheat, it will take a Bushel and a Half to sow one Acre of Land to make it fit for Linen or Thread. The thicker it is sowed in Reason the better, for the smaller the Stalk is the thinner the Bark will be (which the Thread and Linen is made of) and it stands to Reason the Fibres of the Bark are the smaller, and therefore can be separated the finer, and made fit for the finest Linen or Thread; but if you want to get a larger Quantity of Seed, according to the Seed sowed, sow a Bushel to the Acre, and it will bring very good Flax for common Use; but as the Stalk is larger than that which is thick sowed, the Bark will be thicker, the Fibres larger, and therefore cannot be separated and made so fine as thin barked. As soon as the Seed is sowed, go over the Ground with a Tooth Harrow, or a larger Quantity of scragged Brush dragged after a Horse or Ox, to cover or mix the Seed with the Earth.

Flax sowed at the Time first mentioned will be fit to gather about the first or Middle of *July*, and I have known two Crops in one Year off the same Piece of Ground, by cleaning of the Grass and Weeds as soon as the first Crop is off, and sowing it over again. The second Crop will sometimes be as good Flax as the first, but not common; and it seldom brings so good Seed, or so much as the first Crop, therefore shall not advise any One to attempt it until they are well stocked with Seed.

[33]

To know when your Flax is fit to gather, you must observe the Leaves turning yellow, and the lower Ones dropping off the Stalks, hardening and beginning to dry, and the Seed ripening, which may be known by its Colour.

The Method to gather your Flax is to pull it up by the Roots with one Hand, and deliver it into the other until you have as much as you can grasp, holding it near the Middle, and observing to put all the Roots one Way and the Tops the other; then lay that Handful behind you, and so proceed through the whole Patch. If the Seed is not full ripe, as it seldom all ripens together, you may let it lie in the Field two or three Days, to dry and ripen the Seed that is not full ripe. As soon as the Seed is dried gather up the Handfuls, and carry them to some clean hard Yard or Floor, to get off the Seed.

The best Method to get off the Seed is with what is called a Rippling Comb, which is made as followeth: Get a Piece of Plank about eighteen Inches long, three broad, and one thick; then have fourteen or fifteen Teeth made of Iron or Steel, about six Inches long, in the Shape of a flooring Brad; then bore as many Holes lengthwise in the Plank as you have Teeth to put in it, letting the Teeth stand about a Quarter of an Inch apart; then nail the Comb to some heavy Timber or other, to keep it

[34]

steady whilst working with it; then take a Handful and strike it on the Teeth, and draw it through; repeat it until you have the Seed clean of the Handful, and so proceed until you have cleaned all the Flax. Some People whip out the Seed on a small Cask, or thresh it off with a Flail; but I like the Comb best, for this Reason; that it lays the Boughs all straight, by drawing them through the Comb, and prevents it being entangled when it is spreading out to dry after being watered; and the other Methods break and entangle the Flax, and make it troublesome to spread to dry, or to be dew-rotted. As chief or many of the Pods or Bolls will come off whole, and not shed the Seed out of them, it will be proper to spread them out in the Sun on a Cloth, which will cause many of them to burst open as they dry; and when they are thorough dry, put them in a Mortar, Cask, or Trough, and beat them slightly with a wooden Pestle, then wind the Seed, and run it through a suitable Sieve for the Purpose, by which Means you will get the Remainder of the Pods or Bolls together; then beat them again, and so proceed until you have got the Seed clean, and fit to sow or sell to the Oil Manufactures.

Flax is in some Respects of the Quality of Hemp, having a gummy glutinous Substance, or Sap, which occasions the Bark to cling and stick to the Stalk, and must be soaked out of it by lying in Water, or being exposed to the Rains and Dews, spread thin on the Grass:

[35]

Therefore, as you ripple off the Seed tie it up in Sheaves, about the Size of a Sheaf of Wheat, ready to be watered, or carried to a convenient Place to be dew-rotted. If you thresh off the Seed it should be tied in Sheaves before you thresh it, or it will be greatly entangled, and occasion great Loss in the Flax. That which is to be water-rotted should be tied with some good strong Bark, or Withe, for fear of its breaking loose in the Water.

On the Manufacture of FLAX.

THE watering or rotting Flax is looked upon to be the most mysterious and difficult Part of the whole Manufacture, but I am of Opinion if those that go upon making Flax will observe and be guided by the following Directions they will find it not so great a Difficulty as they may imagine; though it is out of the Power of any Man to tell the exact Number of Days it will take to water or dew-rot Flax, yet it may be performed with great Safety by the following Observations: To water your Flax, take the Sheaves before mentioned and put them in Water, and confine them down so that no Part of them appear above the Water; and go to it once or twice a Day, and draw out a few Stalks from about the Middle of a Sheaf, and break them; and if the Stalk and Bark both break very short, and appear very rotten and tender, it is likely to be rotted enough. But

[36]

for further Trial, take a few Stalks and dry them; then take four or five, or more of them, and snap them, holding your Hands about an Inch apart; repeat snapping them, and giving them little Rubs together, until you have broke them for six or eight Inches; then give them small Twitches with your Hands, and if the Flax is properly watered you will see the woody Part called the hard separate and fall from the Bark, which will remain strong and good if not over-watered, but if over-watered the Bark when dry will break short and tender; and if this Misfortune should happen there is no Remedy to restore it to its proper Strength, and the chiefest Part of it will make nothing but Tow; and if the Flax is not watered enough the woody Part of the Stalk will stick to the Bark, and occasion the Linen Thread to be harsh and full of Hards.

Some People choose standing Water to soak or rot their Flax in, and others to dew-rot it; but I should choose a Stream of fresh running Water, for these Reasons: The Motion and running of the Water through the Flax will the better cleanse it of the gummy Substance which causes the Bark to stick to the Stalk, and the running Water being cooler than Pond Water it will not rot it so soon, and therefore it is not so liable to be over-watered; and to prevent this Misfortune I would advise you to take it out of the Water before it gets hurt, for you may then have it sufficiently rotted by the same

[37]

Method as those who never water it at all, but do it entirely by exposing it to the Rains and Dews, spread on a grassy Place. When you find or believe your Flax to be watered enough, take it out and carry it to a grassy Place (where no Stock can walk amongst it to tangle it) and there untie the Sheaves and spread it in straight Rows, as thin as possible; for if it is sufficiently watered, the sooner it gets thorough dry the better; and as soon as you find it so take it off the Grass and tie it up in Sheaves again, and put it in a House where it may be kept dry, in Order for breaking.

The Method to dew-rot your Flax is after the Seed is cleaned off: Whenever it suits you carry it to a grassy Place, where the Grass is rank (for the rank Grass is best for dew-rotting, as it will the longer retain the Moisture of the Rains and Dews among the Flax) and there spread it in straight Rows, so that you may pass between them to turn it over once in four or five Days, that it may all rot alike; this need not be spread so thin as that which had been watered, and required drying soon. To know when it is rotted enough, and fit to take off the Grass and put in a House, make Use of the same Methods as before mentioned in the water-rotting, by breaking and trying a few Stalks when dry.

As I before mentioned it is out of the Power of any Man to inform the Publick what Number

F

[38]

of Days, or Length of Time, it will take to water or dew-rot Flax, or Hemp, to a proper Medium (for in the water-rotting the Length of Time depends chiefly on the Water it is soaked in, and the Heat of the Weather, if it is in a Pond of Water, and the Weather hot, two or three Days will be sufficient, but in a Stream of running Water it will take about a Day or two longer) I must advise those who are not in immediate Want of their Flax to water it about the first of *October*, as the Weather then being moderate there will not be so great Danger of its being over-watered. Salt Water will not answer for watering Flax, for the Salt will occasion it to give in moist Weather, and may cause it to mildew, funk, and spoil in the House.

And in dew-rotting Flax the Length of Time depends chiefly on the Heat and Wetness of the Weather, and the Month of *August* is accounted a very proper Time for dew-rotting. You must always observe to have your Flax entirely dry when you take it out of the Field, and bind it up in Sheaves, and put it up in a House, or it will heat and spoil.

I hope what I have said, in Regard to rotting Flax, will be sufficient for any Person to manage it without spoiling; and if the Readers are doubtful of my Directions not answering, they are under no Obligation of watering their whole Crop at once, as it takes so little Time to do it,

[39]

but may do it at different Times, to try the Experiment, and for their better Information.

The next Operation is the breaking your Flax, to perform which there are two Methods, one with a wooden Machine called a Brake, the other is with a Hand-Mall called Beatles. A Brake is made as follows, with a good stiff four-legged Bench about five Feet long, with an upright Post near each End of it, the Posts to be about five Inches one Way and three the other, the Tops of the Posts to be near the Height of the Person's Waistband as he stands by it to work; in the Tops of these Posts let in four or five Pieces of white Oak, three Quarters of an Inch thick and three Inches broad, to stand up edgewise in the said Posts; then get three or four more Pieces, according to the Number of the under Ones, and of the same Dimensions as the others; then get a Piece about a Foot long, and of the same Size of the Post in the Bench, and bore a large Hole through the Middle of it, and put a Pin in it about a Foot long, for a Handle to lift the Fall or upper Jaw of the Brake by; then make a Mortice or Place in one End of it, to fasten the other three or four Pieces of white Oak in, in the same Manner as those in the upright Posts, and pin them fast; the upper Pieces must be about a Foot shorter than the under Ones; then you must put the Ends of the upper Pieces between the others, and bore a Hole through them all, and put in a slack Pin with a Head

[40]

at one End, and a Nail through the other, to prevent its working out; the upper Pieces should work or slip easily between the others which are fixed in the upright Posts, and the Edges of all these Pieces should be made Half round, or they will be apt to chop or break the Bark of the Flax too short; if they have sharp or square Edges, these Pieces should lock about one Inch near the Head of the Brake; when there is no Flax between the Jaws, the Head should strike on the Top of the foremost Post.

When you have a Brake thus fixed, untie one of your Sheaves and take out as much as you can grasp in your left Hand; then raise the upper Jaw of the Brake with your right Hand, and lay one End of the Handful of Flax you have in your Hand on the lower Slats or under Jaw of the Brake, and strike on it with the upper Ones, or Fall; these Strokes should be repeated very quick, and at every Stroke turn or move the Flax a little; and when you have well broke one End of the Handful about two Thirds of the Length of the Flax, turn the other Ends, and use them in the like Manner, by which Means great Part of the woody Part of the Stalk will separate and fall from the Bark through the lower Jaws or Slats of the Brake. When you think it is sufficiently broke, make it up into Twists, about the size of a large Twist of Tobacco, to be scuchened, or swingled.

To break your Flax with what the *Irish* call Beatles you must have Hand Malls made, the

[41]

Mall Part to be about six or seven Inches long and three or four Inches through, according to the Strength of the Person that works with them; then untie a Sheaf, and let a Person take as much as he can confine down with his left Hand and lay it on some smooth solid Timber or Stone, and then take the Mall or Beatle in the right Hand, and begin at one End of the Handful and beat and turn it over until it is well mashed or broken better than Half Way; then turn the other Ends, and use them in like Manner, until it is all well mashed or broken; then lay by that Handful to be scuchened, as the *English* and *Dutch* call it, or swingled, as the *Irish* call it.

A Brake is the most expeditious Method for breaking Flax, and it is the easier swingled, as great Part of the hard is beaten out in breaking; but it is apter to make a larger Quantity of Tow, for the Beatles only mash and split the Stalk and Bark: Therefore the Bark is likely to be longer than that which is done in a Brake, unless it is a very good One; but that which is done with Beatles requires to have the Hards snapped and rubbed out by Hand, and will take a longer Time in the swingling than that which is done with a Brake.

The next Operation is the swingling your Flax, to perform which there are two Methods; one is performed by a Wheel, the other with a wooden Knife, which is the common Method,

[42]

and to be performed as followeth: Get a Piece of Plank about 5 or 6 Inches wide, 1 Inch thick, and 3 Feet long; plane one Side of it a little ovalling, tenant one End of it in a Block about 14 Inches long and 10 wide, so that the said Plank may stand upright; then within 3 Inches of the Top saw it within one Inch of being through, then split off the sawed Part for the Flax to lodge on, and leave the other Part as a Guard to keep you from striking your Hand with the Knife, which should be made of the hardest and heaviest Wood you can get; the Knife should be made almost in the Shape of a Dagger, the Blade to be about 16 or 17 Inches long, 2 and a Half broad, and 3 Quarters of an Inch thick on the Back. When you are thus fixed with a Swingling Board and Knife, take one of the Twists before mentioned, or a Handful of beaten Flax, in your left Hand, and give it a Stroke or two, to open and loosen it; then lodge it on the Top of the Swingling Board, and let about two Thirds of the Length of the Flax hang down the planed Side of it; then take the Knife in your right Hand, and strike the Flax just where it hangs over the Board with the Edge of the Knife, letting the Side of the Knife slide down the Flax with a quick Motion, and the Edge a little inclining towards the Flax; you should grasp it hard, to prevent its beating out amongst the Hards. As soon as you have one End cleansed of the Hards, turn the other, and use it in the like Manner. You will still find some Hards remaining in the

[43]

Middle of the Twist or Handful; then hold it up by one Hand, and draw out that which seems the longest with the other Hand, and put it together again; repeat this, and the swingling it, until you have well cleansed it of the Hards and made it soft and pliable, which is the Intent of the swingling; then make it up into Twists again, about the Size of a large Twist of Tobacco, and lay it by for heckling.

As a Swingling Wheel will be somewhat expensive, and I suppose but small Quantities of Flax made for some Years, I have omitted a Description of one; though one would greatly expedite the Operation, and would be very serviceable where there is a large Quantity of Flax or Hemp to be manufactured.

When your Flax is scuchened, the next Thing to be done is the heckling, to perform which you should have a Set of Heckles, to make the finest of Linen or Thread; but many People have only one, of a middle Size, which will cost about 20*s*. Sterling, though I think they be made as cheap here, therefore shall give the following Directions how to make one of a middle Size: First, it will take 176 Teeth, to be made of Steel about 4 Inches long, and at the But End to be square about one Inch, and to be about the Size of an Eightpeny Nail, and from thence to be made round, and to be brought with a gradual Taper to as fine a Point as possible, and neatly polished; then get a Piece of

[44]

Plank of some Wood that will be hard to split, and plane it to one Inch thick; let the Plank be 12 Inches long, and 7 Inches wide; then with a Moving Gage make a Schribe lengthwise, the Piece one Inch from the Edge; then move your Gage, and make another Schribe Half an Inch and Half a Quarter from the first; and so proceed making Schribes at the same Distances until you have made seven; then one Inch and a Half from one End, with a Square, make a Schribe crossways; then with your Compasses make a Prick Half an Inch and Half a Quarter from the Schribe; and so proceed, and make them at the same Distances until you have made 14. Then make Schribes across at every Prick; and where these and the other Schribes intercept or cross each other, bore Holes of a proper Size to hold the Teeth fast when drove into them; then with your Moving Gage make other Schribes lengthwise, exactly between all them you made first, and likewise make other Schribes exactly between them you first made crossways; and where these last Schribes intercept or cross each other, bore other Holes of the same Size as the first; then drive in your Teeth, and bore a Hole in each Corner, to nail it to a heavy Block or Bench to keep it steady whilst working with it.

You must observe that a coarser Heckle will require longer and larger Teeth, and to be set at a little further Distance from each other; and a finer Heckle should have smaller Teeth, and be set closer together.

[45]

When you have your Heckle thus fixed to a Block, or Bench, take one of the Twists which has been scutchened and untwist it; then hold it up by one End, and give it a Shake or two, to loosen or open it; then wrap one End of it round the fourth and middle Finger of your right Hand, and fling the other Ends of the Flax on the Points of the Heckle Teeth, and bear your Hand a little downwards and draw the Flax through the Teeth; these Strokes should be repeated very quick, and observe to hold the Back of your left Hand against the Side of the Heckle Teeth, as a Guide to prevent your striking your Hand that holds the Flax against the Points of the Heckle Teeth; and when you have one End of the Twist cleansed of the Hards and short tangled Flax, which is called Tow, turn the other End, and use it in like Manner. You will still find both Hards and Tow remaining in the Middle of the Twist; you should then endeavor to turn it inside out, and rub it a little between your Hands, to loosen the Hards; you must continue heckling, until you have it clean of Hards; you should draw out the longest of the Flax that hangs on the Side of the Heckle next to you, and heckle it again, and may add it to the long Flax which remained in your Hand, as it will make very good Thread, or may lay it by itself, to be twisted up and spun by itself; then take that which remains in the Teeth of the Heckle, which is called Tow, and

G

[46]

throw it altogether, to make coarse Linen, which I shall say more of hereafter.

The Intent of the Heckles is to cleanse the Flax of the Hards and Tow, and to split and separate the Bark, and make it as fine as possible; and as soon as you have it in that Order, lay by that Handful and heckle another in the same Manner, until you have sufficient to make a Twist, as before mentioned; then twist it up, and lay it by for spinning, or Sale.

To spin your Flax you should provide yourself with a Wheel for that Purpose, which is worked with the Foot; the Band must go twice round the Wheel Ream, and cross at the under Part; one is to be in the Whirl, which is one Part of the Spool or Quill, which receives the Thread from the Fliers; and the other Part of the Band is to run in the Whirl, which is fixed on the Spindle with a Screw.

When you have a Wheel thus fixed, take one or Part of the Twists before mentioned and untwist it, and open and spread it on a Table about two Feet long and one wide; then take the Distaff from the Head of the Wheel, and lay it on one End of the Flax you have spread on the Table, and roll it up in the Middle of the Flax; then tie a Fillet to the Top of the Distaff, and wind it slightly round the Flax on the Distaff, until you get it near the Bottom, and there tuck it in so as to keep the Flax from drawing out too fast whilst you are spinning it; then fix

[47]

your Distaff to the Head of your Wheel again, and take a Piece of Thread of any Kind, tie one End round the Spool or Quill, and put the other End through the Eye of the Spindle, and carry it up to the Flax on the Distaff, and lodge the Thread on one of the Wires in the Fliers; then hold the Thread in your left Hand up to the loose Flax which hangs at the Bottom of the Distaff, ready to join it; then turn the Whirl with your right Hand, and keep it in a Motion with your Foot on the Treadle or Foot of the Wheel; as soon as your Thread twists and joins to the Flax, draw it out to what Size you choose, and so proceed until you have spun all on the Distaff. You should often turn round the Distaff, to bring the Flax suitable to your Hand; and should often move the Thread to different Teeth of the Flier, to fill the Quill or Spool equally alike.

The Tow which I before mentioned is what they make coarse Linen of, and it answers, and will wear exceeding well, if spun and filled in with a Warp of Cotton, for common Sheets or Table Linen, or any other Use that coarse Linen is applied to.

And to prepare it for spinning you must provide a Pair of Tow Cards, and card it in them a few Strokes; then lay one Card on the other, with the Handles both one Way, and hold them fast in your Lap with one Hand and draw out the longest of it from between the Cards with your other Hand; this Kind of Tow will

[48]

make good coarfe Linen, and that which ftill remains in the Cards may be carded to fill in coarfe brown Linen or Rolls; when you have got a fufficient Quantity carded and fpread on a Table, as before mentioned, you muft roll it round your Diftaff, and fet your Wheel to work in the fame Manner as with the long Flax.

Shoe Thread is fpun in a different Manner from fewing Thread, or that for Linen : For to fpin your Shoe Thread take the longeft Flax you have, and open one of the Twifts and give it a fhake or two, to feparate the Fibres from each other; than tie it to the Top of your Diftaff, and let the Flax hang ftraight down it; then fet your Wheel to Work, and join the Thread to the Fibres which hang down the Diftaff, fo that you may draw it out lengthwife, that the Shoemaker may have fine long Fibres to faften on his Briftles with ; and it fhould be twifted as much as it will bear without kinking.

The Thread you fpin for Linen fhould be hanked, for which Purpofe you ought to provide yourfelf with a Jack to hold your Spool, and what is called a Clock Reel that will ftrike at being twined 120 Times, fo that you may know when you have 120 Threads on your Reel, which is called a Cut. Thefe Cuts, or Skeines, fhould be tied feparate from each other, fo that you may know, by counting the Cuts, exactly what Number of Threads is in each Hank, and if your Reel is exactly two Yards round, which

[49]

is a proper Size. You will then have 240 Yards of Thread in each Cut; 15 of thefe Cuts is a Day's Work for a good Spinner, fo that in 12 Days fhe will fpin as much Thread as will warp 30 Yards fuitable to a 720 Slay, and in 12 Days more fhe will fpin the Filling, fo that you may have Thread fpun for 30 Yards of Cloth in 24 Days. To calculate it, for Example:

1 Cut contains	120 Threads
1 Thread	2 Yards long
1	240 Yards
1 Day's work	15 Cuts
	1200
	240
Contains	3600 Yards.
	12
Contains	43,200 Yards,

which, divided by 1440, the Number of Threads in a 720 Slay is 30, the Number of Yards it will warp.

Threads in the Slay 1440)43200(30 Yards of Warp.
4320
————
0000

By thefe Methods, when you have a Quantity of Thread fpun and hanked, and know what Slay will fuit it, you may know what Quantity of Yards to warp it to, fo as not to have any Lofs. You fhould hank your Filling as well as the Warp, for it fhould all be boiled in Water and Afhes, to make it foft and pliable, that it may weave the clofer and tighter together. You fhould boil it until you fee it begin to lint, that is, when you fee a Lint or Fuzz rife on the Thread.

[50]

Thread for fewing muft be wound together on a Ball, then twifted and hanked; and if it is only for coarfe Work, it will anfwer by boiling in Afhes and Water two or three Times, and being well rubbed with your Hands when cooled a little, or being beaten on a fmooth folid Timber or Stone with a fmooth heavy Stick made in the Shape of a Butter Stick (it is properly called a Bat Staff) which is to make the Thread foft and pliable ; but if it is fine Thread, and you want it whitened or bleached, obferve the Proceffes hereafter given for bleaching of Linen.

The weaving Linen I fuppofe I need fay little about, as it is wove in the plain Way, but muft inform thofe who are not acquainted with weaving it that it requires good ftrong Stays, made of Steel or Cane; for as the Thread is fo hard and wiry, it requires harder ftriking and driving together with the Slay than Cotton or Woollen Cloth, and therefore our common Reed Slays will anfwer the Purpofe.

After your Linen is wove, the next thing to be performed is the bleaching. This Procefs I muft confefs I never faw performed, but have taken great Pains to collect the eafieft and beft Methods how to manage it in every Particular, from Perfons who have been employed in the Manufactures at home; and according to the Information I have had, I fhall here give as plain and fhort an Account of the Proceffes as poffible, which I expect will be fufficient for

[51]

any private Family; though at home they have calendering Mills, which I fuppofe we fhall be many Years without, unlefs fome Gentlemen would fet up a Factory for that Purpofe.

To bleach your Linen firft put it in warm Water, and foak it thirty fix or forty eight Hours; then rinfe it, and dry it; then make a ftrong Lie, and mix it with foft Cow Dung, and ftir them well together; then put in Linen, and let it lie about 48 Hours; then carry it to your Bleach-Yard, where you fhould have a fine green Grafs Plat to ftretch it out, and you fhould have feveral Loops at the Ends made with the Thrums, and Loops put along the Sides, within two or three Yards of each other, to ftretch it tight, with fmall Sticks drove in the Earth, fo that the Linen may fcarcly touch the Grafs in any Part. You fhould keep it ftrecthed out in this Manner 4 Days, and to be kept always wet. As foon as you perceive it begin to dry fprinkle it again with clean Water, fo as to keep it always moift; and at the End of 4 Days and Nights take it off the Grafs and wafh it clean of the Cow Dung; and whilft it is wet lay it in a Heap on a fmooth Stone or Timber that lies folid, and there beat it with large BatStaffs for two or three Hours, and frequently turn it over, and keep it wet with warm Lie; then take it out, wafh it and ftretch it out again 24 Hours, and keep it watered as before mentioned; then beat it again with the Bat Staffs, and wet it with Lie as before directed. Con-

[52]

tinue this Method of steeping it 24 Hours in Lie, then washing it out and stretching it 24 Hours; and when you take it up wet it every Time with warm Lie, and beat it with the Bat Staffs. This Method is to be followed for 8 or 10 Days; then lay it in sour Milk, or Butter Milk, one or two Nights; then take it out, wash it, and beat it again; then stretch it out, and water it a Day or two; then steep it in the Souring again; and so proceed for about a Week, or until you have bleached or whitened it to your Satisfaction.

A Bat Staff should be about 3 Feet and a Half long, 2 Inches thick, and the Blade about 5 Inches wide and 18 long, the Sides a little ovalling; the Edges to be rounded off, to prevent their cutting the Linen; the Handle to be of a proper Size, for a Person to hold it to work with.

To make a proper Lie for bleaching they make Use of Potash at home, but the common Lie will do.

And if you have not a sufficient Quantity of Butter-Milk, or sour Milk, mix some Wheat Bran and warm Water together, and let it stand a few Days, until it begins to sour; then throw in what Butter-Milk or sour Milk you have, and it will make a very good Souring for that Purpose.

F I N I S.

This Edition of *A Treatise on the Propagation of Sheep* has been composed using the types of William Caslon, printed on an English Letterpress, and bound in the prevailing Styles of the Eighteenth Century at the Printing Office, Williamsburg in Virginia.

A Treatise on the Propagation of Sheep was written by John Wily of Caroline County. Published at the time of the Stamp Act, the Pamphlet did much to promote Manufactures in Virginia. John Wily wrote to the Virginia Gazette of John Dixon and Alexander Purdie the week of September 28, 1769:

To the P R I N T E R.
S I R,
When you have nothing better to offer to the publick, I shall be obliged to you to give the following piece a place in your useful and entertaining paper. JOHN WILY.

THE late resolves and commendable association of our late representatives, and some pieces which I have observed in your papers, have convinced me that it is the indispensable duty of every member of society to do all he can for the good of his country. I must therefore beg leave to inform the publick that I was some years concerned in a woollen manufactory, which thoroughly convinced me a large sum of money might be saved in this colony annually by manufacturing the wool that is raised differently from the usual method (spinning it up into coarse cloth for the Negroes) which I look upon to be next to throwing it away, as may appear by the following calculations, viz. I value a pound of good clean wool at 1 s. 3 d. the spinning a pound for Negro Cloth at 10 d. and the weaving a yard (which will take near a pound) at 4 d. in all 2 s. 5 d. by which it appears one yard of good cloth for the Negroes will cost about 2 s. 5 d. and for that sum a yard of cotton may be purchased, that would answer the purpose fully as well.

But, for the good of the colony, suppose the wool was all to be manufactured into good cloth (or worsted stuffs) for the wear of the white people, the expense may be calculated as follows, viz. I value a pound of good clean wool at 1 s. 3d. the spinning a pound for good fine cloth at 1 s. 3 d. the weaving, milling, dying, shearing, and pressing one yard (which will take about a pound of wool, to make it the width of narrow broads) at 2 s. in all 4 s. 6 d. by which it appears there may be 5 s. 6 d. saved to the colony on every pound of good wool that is raised in it, by manufacturing good cloth; and I believed the worsted manufacture would be a greater advantage.

I cannot pretend to say the exact quantity of wool that is raised in this colony annually, but suppose there is at least 150,000 weight, and that at 5 s. 6 d. a pound amounts to 41,250l. which may be saved to the colony annually, a sum I think well worth our notice.

I am in hopes the calculations I have here offered to my countrymen are sufficient to convince them there may be a large sum of money saved to the colony by this economy, and that they need nothing more to put them on this saving scheme, and to encourage so beneficial a manufacture amongst us.

To conclude, I must beg leave to inform the readers I am but a poor Buckskin, with a slender education; therefore hope no one will be offended at this poor unpolished piece, but kindly accept of it as my honest endeavours herein to serve my country. And let that make atonement for all errours herein committed.

The Printing Office of the Colonial Williamsburg Foundation would like to express its appreciation to the Virginia State Library for the kind assistance that allowed this Pamphlet to be reprinted.

資料Ⅲ.

John Hargrove, *Weavers The Draft Book and Clothiers Assistant*, Worcester, American Antiquary Society, 1979

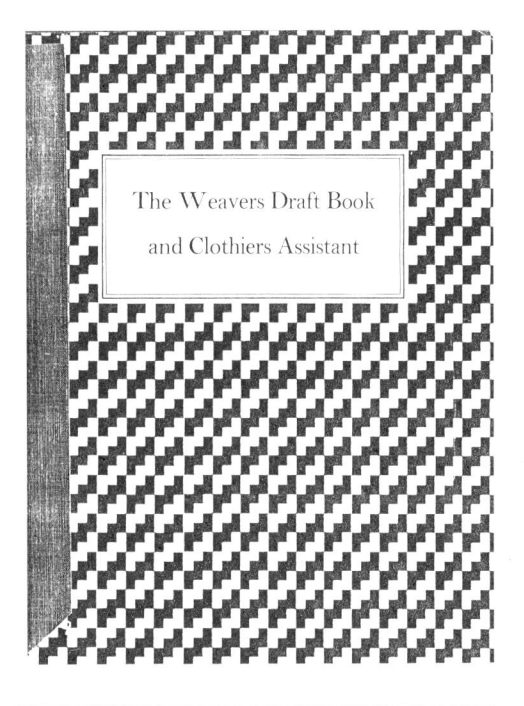

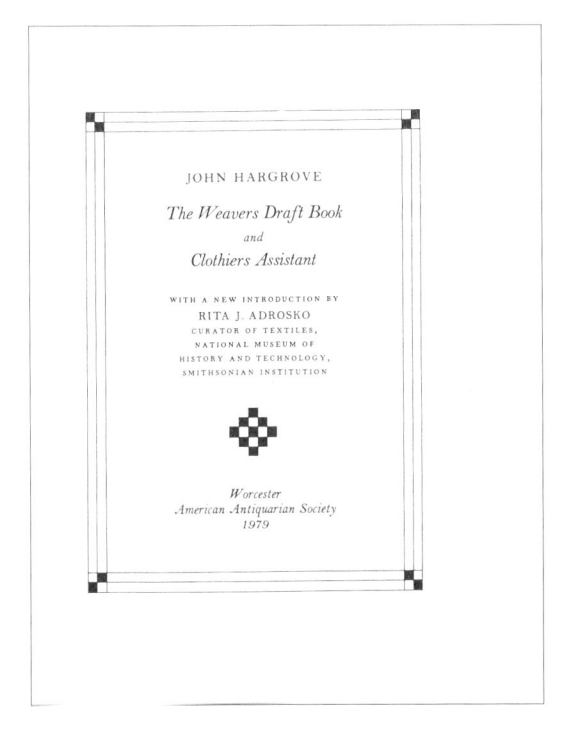

Introduction

THE excellent condition, beautiful design, and rarity of the copy of *The Weavers Draft Book and Clothiers Assistant* (Baltimore: Hagerty, 1792) reproduced here makes it an ornament, as well as an interesting historical document. Acquired by the American Antiquarian Society in 1977, it is only the second known copy of this work to surface. Seven years ago the first copy had been found and sold to the library of the Merrimack Valley Textile Museum in North Andover, Massachusetts. Previous to 1970, the volume was known only through advertisements in newspapers of 1792 and through an entry (number 24996) in Charles Evans's *American Bibliography*.

This beautiful volume, according to John Hargrove, its author, is the first weavers' draft book printed in the United States. While authors of other early (nineteenth-century) draft books have made the same claim, no earlier book of its kind has been found to refute Hargrove's claim. Today, besides being a significant historical document, this little book can serve contemporary weavers who wish to expand their vocabulary of weaves.

The Author

Although John Hargrove described himself as a 'mechanic' in the preface to *The Weavers Draft Book and Clothiers Assistant*, most of his life seems to have been spent mainly in other pursuits. The only evidence that Hargrove had been a weaver is in a note that appears in the entry in Evans's *American Bibliography*.[1] It states that his book was 'compiled by an experienced weaver, of Harford County, in this State.' Unfortunately Evans did not record the source of the quotation.

It is quite possible that Hargrove was an experienced weaver when the nineteen-year-old youth emigrated from his native Ireland in 1769. Many Irish weavers came to this country seeking work during the latter

[1] Charles Evans, *American Bibliography* 8 (Chicago: privately printed, 1914): 881.

half of the eighteenth century. Although overpopulation was the root cause of emigration from Ireland during this period, the cotton industry, introduced into that country from England after 1750, had gradually displaced the Irish linen industry and many of its operatives. Henry Wansey, an English traveler who recorded in his journal that in June 1794 a ship arrived in New York from Ireland with over 435 passengers, noted that almost 200 of these were weavers of diaper and dimity who had left because 'times were hard and things so dear' that 'with all their industry, they could not live.'[2]

During Hargrove's first thirty years in this country he lived in various parts of Maryland; for some of those years he might have been a practicing weaver. It is recorded, however, that he once served as a land surveyor, and that in 1776, at about the time of his first marriage, he was ordained a minister of the Methodist Episcopal Church. About 1788, the year after Cokesbury College opened in Abingdon, Harford County, Maryland, the Reverend John Hargrove was chosen to join this Methodist institution's four-man faculty. His settling in Baltimore a few years later must have coincided with his mission to combat the Swedenborgian sect in that city. In researching the latter faith, presumably to become better armed to discourage its spread, he himself was won over to it, and in 1799 became the first Swedenborgian minister ordained in the United States. As a rule, neither the Methodist nor the Swedenborgian Ministry was yet a full time calling, so Hargrove may well have continued to pursue the weaver's trade even after ordination.

Although Hargrove did not have a 'collegiate or classical education,' his son-in-law and biographer states that he 'valued principles in science as well as in religion for the sake of use,' and that his 'checkered life' afforded him many opportunities for acquiring knowledge of a wide range of subjects. He stated further that Hargrove had 'felt an interest in the political events of his time, and in whatever concerned the wel-

[2] Henry Wansey, *Henry Wansey and His American Journal*, ed. David John Jeremy, Memoirs of the American Philosophical Society, vol. 82 (Philadelphia: American Philosophical Society, 1970), p. 129.

fare of his fellow citizens, and the honor and prosperity of his adopted country.'[3]

These assessments of Hargrove's character and beliefs partly suggest why, as an active minister who probably had been a weaver, he might take time out from his other affairs to compile the material for this book.

Textile Manufacturing in Maryland

Scattered references to textile manufacturing in late eighteenth-century Maryland suggest that such efforts were confined mainly to relatively small-scale production of utilitarian goods for local consumption. It is clear that domestic producers could not compete with the great quantity and variety of materials imported from England and India during and immediately after the Revolutionary War. In the 1780s, awareness of this fact prodded a number of patriotic Maryland citizens to take positive steps toward developing domestic manufactures, which could provide a cheap American supply of cotton and other materials, and thus reduce their dependence on foreign manufactures.

In February 1789 a number of Baltimore tradesmen and manufacturers met, produced, and sent to Congress a petition that urged the imposition of tariffs on imports and expressed the hope that Congress would give top priority to the encouragement of American manufactures. Although earlier efforts to manufacture textiles in Baltimore had been limited, on May 1, 1789, an advertisement in the *Maryland Journal* announced a meeting of 'citizens desirous of promoting American manufacture,' who, it was hoped, would then set up a cotton manufactory in Baltimore. The result was the Baltimore Manufacturing Company, recorded as the first establishment of its kind in the city. While this venture ended in failure two years later,[4] the patriotic sentiments of its patrons were clear.

[3] Edward Hinkley, 'John Hargrove,' *New-Jerusalem Magazine* (Jan. 1853), pp. 3, 5, 7. On Hargrove, see also Marguerite Beck Block, *The New Church in the New World: A Study of Swedenborgianism in America* (1932; repr. New York: Octagon Books, 1968), pp. 90–95.
[4] William R. Bagnall, *The Textile Industries of the United States*, vol. 1, pt. 1 (Cambridge: The Riverside Press, 1893), pp. 151–53.

Interestingly enough, John Hargrove specified that cotton warp yarns be used for most of his drafts at a time when very little cotton yarn spun in America was strong enough to be used for warp. In the mid-1780s Arkwright's machinery for carding and spinning by waterpower was arousing a great deal of interest among those wishing to promote the development of the American cotton industry. It was reported that around 1785 Thomas Somers had 'visited England at his own risk and expense to prepare machines for carding and spinning cotton.' Because of British legislation that forbade the export of textile machinery, he could only 'bring away descriptions and models of such engines with which he returned to Baltimore. Finding little to be done there, he set out for Boston,' where he had built a 'model of an early and imperfect form of the Arkwright machine.'[5] Among other early efforts to introduce cotton spinning machinery into the United States was one reported in the June 6, 1789, issue of the New York *Gazette of the United States*: 'There is now in the possession of William Pollard, Esq. of Philadelphia, a valuable spinning machine on a new construction and far superior to anything of the kind which has appeared in Pennsylvania.'[6] Pollard's machine, which was based on the Arkwright system, worked, but because of business difficulties, his efforts to establish a manufactory for producing cotton yarn and stockings failed.

It was not until Samuel Slater set up water-powered spinning frames, also based on the Arkwright system, in Pawtucket, Rhode Island, in 1790 that the mechanical spinning of cotton warp yarns began in earnest in the United States. Although carding and spinning machinery was operating successfully by 1792 when Hargrove's book was published, the volume of cotton yarn produced could not have been great. Whitney's cotton gin had not yet appeared, to solve the problem of separating the seeds from raw cotton, so the supply of raw cotton, whose seeds had to be picked out by hand, must have been rather limited. Hargrove may simply have been trying to provide new outlets for this

[5] J. Leander Bishop, *A History of American Manufactures from 1608 to 1860* 1 (Philadelphia: Edward Young and Co., 1861): 398–99.
[6] Anthony F. C. Wallace and David J. Jeremy, 'William Pollard and the Arkwright Patents,' *William and Mary Quarterly*, 3d ser. 34 (1977): 408.

infant industry's product in recommending cotton warp yarns for most of the cloths made from his drafts.

Hargrove's Draft Book

Hargrove's contribution to the development of Baltimore's textile industry was the collection and compilation of weavers' drafts[7] into a book that could be disseminated among weavers of the area. Because of the port city's accessibility to both northern and southern cities (it was only a day and a half's stagecoach ride from Philadelphia), and because it was served by six newspapers whose advertisements reached distant cities, Hargrove must have been aware that his publication had many potential customers beyond Baltimore's city limits.

It was natural that, as a Methodist minister, John Hargrove would have chosen John Hagerty and his nephew, George, to print the book. Both were circuit-riding Methodist preachers. Also, Hagerty apparently was superintendent of the Methodists' Baltimore book business.[8]

Almost all records of the activities of Alexander Ely, the book's engraver, place him in Massachusetts and Connecticut; however, his Methodist connections must have brought him to Maryland and in contact with Hagerty and Hargrove. An unsigned drawing of the Cokesbury College building 'prepared as for engraving' was found at Drew University with other manuscripts by Dr. W. W. Sweet, author of *Methodism in American History* (New York, 1933). It was inscribed with Ely's 'characteristic script,'[9] and is the only link, besides the Hargrove book, that connects the three men. Hargrove's volume is unusual, partly because of its elegant style, but also because it includes so many pages

---

[7] Hargrove's comment in the book's preface that 'the secret has . . . lately fallen into the hands of one, who is willing . . . [to] . . . share in the benefit' suggests that the drafts were collected, rather than used by Hargrove himself. This is emphasized by Hargrove's statement that 'there are many more drafts of figured Cottons, Diapers and Coverlids, which I have not yet been able to procure.'
[8] Louise Hall, 'Artificer to Architect in Anglo-America' (Ph.D. diss., Radcliffe College, 1954), pp. 23–27, number 15.
[9] Ibid.

of engraved text. Such engraving, in the music book tradition, relates the draft book to *The Baltimore Collection of Church Music*, compiled and engraved by Ely, and published by Hagerty three days before the draft book appeared. The music book's plain, modest appearance vividly contrasts with the grace and flourish of the weavers' manual.

Harry Dorsey Gough, to whom the weavers' draft book is 'humbly dedicated,' was also a Methodist. This merchant and gentleman was a sheep-fancier who encouraged home manufactures and who became the first president of the Maryland Agricultural Society. Such interests could have quite naturally drawn Gough and Hargrove together, and inspired Hargrove's dedication.

Other American Weavers' Draft Books

Every trained weaver undoubtedly had his own repertoire of patterns. However, each could benefit by new ones and by the variations of standard weaves that might be found in a book devoted to weavers' drafts. The value of such a volume can scarcely be assessed today but if conditions in 1792 were similar to those in 1818 it was, indeed, an important contribution. Philo Blakeman wrote that in 1818, when he was writing his own weavers' manual, single drafts were selling for from three to five dollars, and some sold for as high as ten dollars.[10]

Most available evidence of pre-1800 American weavers' patterns is in fabrics, rather than written records, since very few manuscript weavers' patterns remain. The earliest handwritten draft book that might be American is one found in Rhode Island, inscribed by 'Nathaneil S[?]earell,' and bearing the date September 3, 1685. Comments on the warping of worsteds appear on the second of its fourteen pages. Its location is unknown, and because its contents were not recorded, no information about the drafts is available at the present time.

John Landes's book of coverlet drafts is assigned an eighteenth-century date. Several eighteenth-century-dated German weavers' handwritten

---

[10] Philo Blakeman, *The Weaver's Assistant* (Bridgeport, Conn.: N. L. Skinner, 1818), p. 3.

books of coverlet patterns in American collections were quite likely made up in Germany, then later used here by their owners, who emigrated to this country.[11] It is known that American weavers of German background also used printed books such as Johann Michael Frickinger's *Weber-Bild-Buch* (Schwabach and Leipzig: Johann Jacob Enderes, 1740) and Johann Michael Kirschbaum's *Neues Weberbild-und Musterbuch* (Heilbronn and Rothenburg ob der Tauber, Echebrechtischen Buchhandlung, 1771). None of these includes the simple four- to ten-shaft patterns found in Hargrove.

In spite of the progress made by this country's textile industry during the thirty years that followed Hargrove's publication, only four more weavers' manuals are known to have been printed here during that time. All of them may be found in the collections of the American Antiquarian Society. Three of these, Joseph France, *The Weaver's Complete Guide* ([Providence?, 1814]); J. and R. Bronson, *The Domestic Manufacturer's Assistant* (Utica, N.Y.: William Williams, 1817); and Philo Blakeman, *The Weaver's Assistant* (Bridgeport, Conn.: N. L. Skinner, 1818), cover steps preparatory to weaving, but are mainly devoted to drafts for three- to sixteen-shaft patterns. The fourth, Philip W. Miller, *The Young Weaver's Assistant* (Boston: Munroe and Francis, 1815), contains no drafts; its text is limited to explaining how to prepare the yarn and the loom for weaving. Such explanations, found in the introductory chapters of the other three works, must have been badly needed, for Joseph France commented that 'out of a thousand tradesmen who manufacture goods of various kinds, there is scarce one . . . who knows the internal structure . . . or . . . the real texture or make of those goods' and that 'there is scarce one in a hundred of the weavers themselves' that knows how to make a draft by analyzing fabric or a 'remnant' of cloth.[12]

---

[11] Johann D——'s book of 59 patterns, Darmstadt, 1766; Johann Conrad Schleelein's book of 280 geometric patterns, Windsheim, Middle Franconia, late 18th or early 19th century; and Johann Ludwig Speck's book of 54 patterns, 1723. All three manuscripts and John Landes's pattern book are in the library of the Philadelphia Art Museum.
[12] Joseph France, *The Weaver's Complete Guide, or the Webb Analyzed* ([Providence?, 1814]), p. iii.

The Drafts

A brief comparison of Hargrove's drafts to those in the other three pre-1820 books serves to point up how different his book is from those that followed. Eighty-five percent of Hargrove's fifty-two drafts were for four-, five-, and six-shaft patterns, while the other three books devoted only about sixty-two percent of their drafts to such patterns. Hargrove concentrated on basic goods and simple little patterns; the others included some of these, but Blakeman and the Bronsons also offered drafts for coverlets, carpeting, and fancy linens; and France included several ribs, spots, and cords requiring eight to sixteen shafts. Oddly enough, comparatively few of Hargrove's patterns are repeated in the three later volumes.

Summarizing the drafts included in Hargrove, we find eighteen designed for four shafts; three for five shafts; twenty-three for six shafts; three for eight shafts; and five for ten shafts. It contains patterns for two different stockinets, three birds-eyes, denims, and fustians, four thicksets and velverets, five satinets, and seven cords and dimities (six of the latter simply labelled 'A Dimity'). The remaining drafts are for a variety of fabrics, several of which have colorful names such as 'Deception Diaper' and 'Worm and Cord.'

It should be made clear that Hargrove's drafts supply only the skeletal structure of fifty-two fabrics. Individuals wishing to make faithful reproductions of eighteenth-century cloths will need more information than Hargrove has provided. In fact, actual fabric samples showing color and texture are essential to making a good reproduction.

Hargrove's instructions to sley most cloths 'as high as linen' but to sley eight of the drafts 'full ⅛ higher than sheeting linen' are not useful without knowing the exact sett of sheeting linen of that period and place. The density of the filling is merely alluded to by Hargrove, who suggests that the warp be sleyed less densely if the desired effect is to show up the filling pattern by 'admit[ting] more filling to be drove in.'

Hargrove's comment that 'altho' most of the figures . . . appear, and wear best with Cotton Warps . . . almost all of them wear very well with Linen Warps, and several of them look very beautiful in Worsted' is helpful. Unfortunately it does not give details of the warp yarns' size, color, twist, ply, or texture, and we are given no information at all about the weft. Finishing processes, at least in the case of the thirty-two drafts that Hargrove says 'require no other finishing from the Loom but dying or bleaching,' offer no problems. Correctly finishing the other ten—goods that must be 'cut, singed, and calendered, by proper Machines'—would be more difficult, especially because the degree of finishing and the specific finishes required for each of the cloths are not known.

Hargrove intended his tie-ups for sinking sheds, applicable to the counterbalance and countermarch looms that were most common in the late eighteenth century. His terminology is quite clear; only his references to a 'leaf of the harness' (shaft)[13] and 'cording' (tie-up) might be confusing today.

The drafts are clearly and beautifully illustrated, and threadings and treadlings are all numbered from right to left. Because shafts and treadles are numbered, they can be interpreted easily and transposed from side to side and top to bottom, to conform to a modern system of notation. The tie-up, marked by 'Xs' (and labelled 'Cording' in Draft No. I), can be shifted from the left to the right side of the threading notation. The threading order (labelled 'Draft' in No. I) is arranged so that the shaft closest to the weaver is numbered '1,' and threaded with the first thread of the repeat, and the shaft furthest from the weaver is numbered '4.' The numbers indicating the treadling order, which appear on the left below the tie-up, can be rewritten to the right of the threading order and above the tie-up. Thus, with the threading, treadling, and tie-up notations transposed, and the pattern sketched in, Draft No. II for 'English Huckabag' (*sic*) would read as in the accompanying sketch. The dark squares indicate wefts that float and other wefts on the surface that tie down warp ends; the light squares indicate warp ends that float and other ends on the surface that tie down wefts.

[13] The word 'shaft' is preferred to 'harness,' the term most contemporary handweavers apply to the frame that lifts the heddles and the warp ends threaded through them.

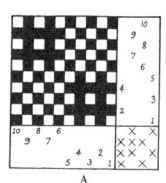

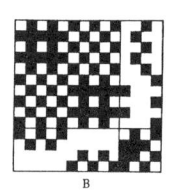

As is true of most other early weavers' drafts, errors can be found in some of these; Nos. XVII, XXIV, and LII have the most obvious errors. Some drafts may have longer floats than today's weavers would consider practical. Both of these facts point up the necessity for weaving trial samples of all patterns chosen for reproduction, then making adjustments or corrections that satisfy the individual weaver's needs.

In addition, it is worth noting that two different six-shaft drafts for 'Plain Thickset' (Nos. XXXIX and XLIII) are identical, and that the draft for a four-shaft 'Plain Thickset' (No. XVI) produces a weave similar to that of the six-shaft thickset. A number of drafts (such as No. IX) group two or three warp ends in a single shed. While this may appear to be an error, it was apparently an accepted practice at the time. Blakeman, writing in 1818, even tells us the name for these sheds: '*That* which raises two threads together, two up and two down, makes, what is called *doublers*, or *flats*; and may also be performed on any number of shades [sheds], *above* one.'[14]

For some unknown reason, three of the fifty-two drafts are threaded from front to back; forty-eight are threaded from back to front, and in the ten-shaft pattern (No. XLVI), the threading starts on the sixth shaft and proceeds toward the shaft furthest from the weaver. All of these irregularities add credence to the idea that Hargrove assembled these drafts from several sources.

[14] Blakeman, *Weaver's Assistant*, p. 7.

The Recipes for Sizing and Dyeing

The seven dye recipes included and the two for sizing cotton warp are variations on many found in other early sources. The high cost of indigo should discourage experimentation with those recipes in which lavish amounts of indigo are used. It is recommended that dyers try updated recipes for using indigo and other dyestuffs included in Hargrove's recipes. Trying out old dye recipes is, indeed, a fascinating activity which calls for as careful a plan as does any other chemical experiment. Such exploration is most profitably undertaken by experienced dyers who have worked with a range of modern dye recipes and who are familiar enough with early dyers' materials and techniques that they can adapt them to current conditions.[15]

Conclusion

It is curious that while John Hargrove's draft book appeared to be the first of its kind, it also represented one of the late remnants of the prefactory period of the American textile industry. The latter fact did not diminish the book's value to handweavers of the time, who continued to work in the old ways well into the nineteenth century, nor does it make the book less useful for modern handweavers, who wish to recapture a flavor of the past in their own weaving.

Rita J. Adrosko

[15] Two reprints that may be useful to contemporary dyers are J. and R. Bronson, *Early American Weaving and Dyeing* (New York: Dover Publications, Inc., 1977), a reprint of *The Domestic Manufacturer's Assistant and Family Directory in the Arts of Weaving and Dyeing*, published in 1817; and Elijah Bemiss, *The Dyer's Companion* (New York: Dover Publications, Inc., 1973), a reprint of the book's second edition, originally published in 1815.

The Weavers Draft Book

THE WEAVERS DRAFT BOOK AND Clothiers Assistant;

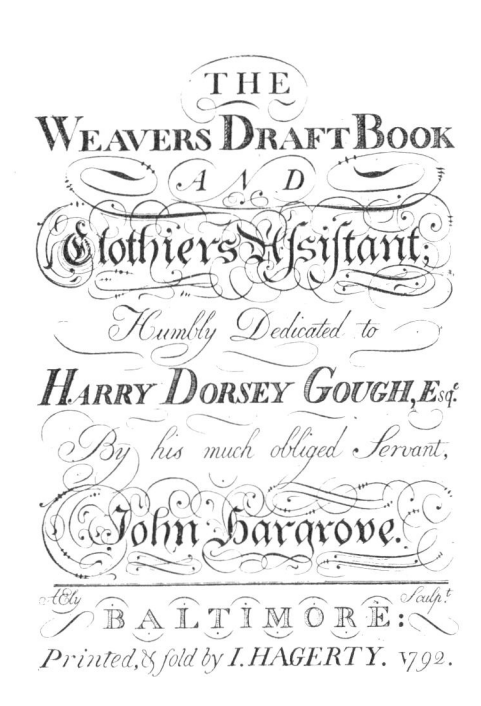

Humbly Dedicated to
HARRY DORSEY GOUGH, Esq.

By his much obliged Servant,

John Hargrove.

Ely Sculp.t

BALTIMORE:

Printed, & sold by I. HAGERTY. 1792.

2 Preface

IT is with singular pleasure I reflect, that I am the first Mechanic, who has ever favored the American Weaver and Manufacturer, with a public Assistant of this kind. Long! too long! has the Weaving trade remained a mystery (at least in the figured line) to hundreds, and thousands, who have served a regular Apprenticeship to that business, & followed it afterwards for many years: Selfish motives have prevented those, who *were* capable of giving Instructions, from revealing the art, least it might operate against their own personal interest (having no desire to promote the Prosperity of their Country at the risk of their own) but the secret has (in a good measure) lately fallen into the hands of one, who is willing, that all concern'd should share in the benefit.

I am not ignorant, however, that the following collection of drafts and receipts (although very valuable) is not altogether perfect as to number; there are many more drafts of figured Cottons, Diapers, and Coverlids, which I have not yet been able to procure: but if any Person, into whose hands this book may come, is possessed of any such Materials, and feels a generous inclination to enrich this little treasury, will please to forward their collection of drafts or receipts, unto Mr. John Hagerty, Stationer in Water-street, Baltimore, their Patriotic Zeal, and Public Spirit shall be gratefully acknoledged, & justly rewarded; besides the pleasing

ing consciousness they will feel, in contributing their mite towards enriching their Country, in the Manufacturing Arts, & rendering the second edition of this work more valuable.

In the following collection of Drafts are included, as well those kind of Goods which require to be cut, singed, & calendered, by proper Machines, as those which require no other finishing than Bleaching alone; and altho' most of the figures herein laid down & Drafted appear, and wear best with Cotton Warps; yet almost all of them wear very well with Linen or Thread Wapps, & several of them look very beautiful in Worsted, particularly the numbers 7, 10 & 48.

Most of them may be fleyed as high as Linen, except you want them to show very rich with the filling, in which case you must fley them a little lower, and thereby admit more filling to be drove in.

There are however a few of them, that must be fleyed full 1/8 higher than Sheeting Linen requires, or they will take too much filling (and not be square) however, the grist of the filling must help to determine; for the coarser the filling is, the lower you may fley.— The few drafts, that more particularly require to be fleyed higher than Linen, by about 1/8, are the numbers 1, 7, 10, 19, 21, 22, 48 & 52.

The Drafts, which require no other finishing from the Loom but dying or bleaching, are the numbers 1, 2, 4, 5, 6, 7, 8, 9, 10, 11, 12, 13, 14, 18, 19, 20, 21, 22, 23, 26, 27, 30, 31, 32, 33, 34, 35, 36, 38, 40, 48, & 52, in all 32 patterns.

After an attentive view of the following Drafts, it will appear evident, that I consider the different spaces between any two of the lines, which run across the book, as representing the different leaves of harness, and the spaces between the upright lines at the left hand side of each page, and just below the cross lines, as the different treddles.

4

The Figures to the right hand side of every page represent the manner of your drawing in the Web through the harness (for one single course in each Draft) and the little crosses, marked thus (×) between the spaces of the cross lines, at the left hand side of the page, denote the different leaves of harness, that are taken or trod down by every treddle; and lastly, the Figures, contained between the spaces of the different upright lines at the left hand of each page, and below the cross lines, represent the manner of your treading with your feet, in order to raise the figure.

But, to make it still more obvious, suppose you wish to set to work, and weave a piece of English Huckabag, N.º 2, you will perceive from the Draft, that it is to be wove in four leave of harness, and with 4 treddles. 1.ˡʸ You must begin to draw in your warp on the leaf of harness next to you, which I call the First leaf; the Second thread on the second leaf; Thirdly on the first leaf; Fourthly on the second leaf; Fifthly on the first leaf; Sixthly on the leaf farthest from you, or the fourth leaf; Seventhly on the third; Eightly on the fourth; Ninthly on the third, & Tenthly on the fourth, which ends your course. 2.º You must next tie it up, so that the outside right foot treddle will take down the 4.ᵗʰ and 2.ᵈ leaves of harness; the outside left foot treddle the 3.º, 2.º, & 1.ˢᵗ leaves; the inside right foot, treddle the 3.º and 1.ˢᵗ and the inside left foot treddle the 4.ᵗʰ, 3.º, & 2.º leaves. 3.º & Lastly, you must tred on your 4 treddles, as directed by the lower figures from 1 to 10, which ends your course, and compleats the figure; more plain instructions I judge superfluous.

John Hargrove

Hartford County Maryland,
24.ᵗʰ June, 1792

Nº I.
Garret's Birdeye.

Nº II.
English Huckabag.

Nº III.
A Plain Corp.

Nº IV.
A Denim.

Nº V.
A Pillow Fustian.

Nº VI.
Large Mˢ and Oˢ.

Nº VII.
Mᶜ Cluin's Birdeye.

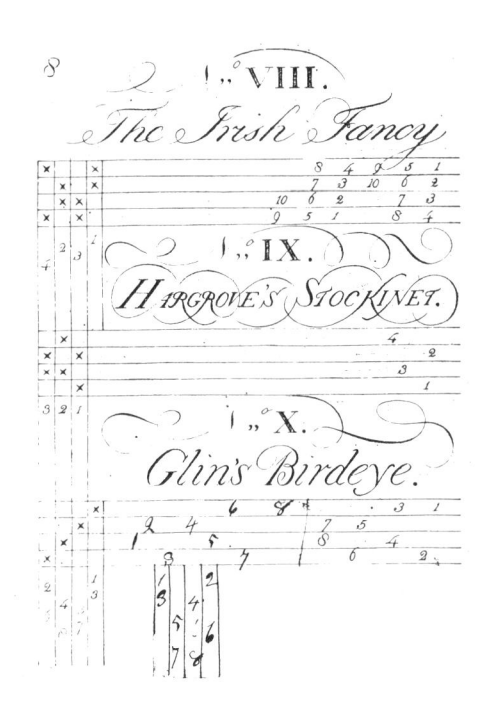

N.º VIII.
The Irish Fancy

N.º IX.
HARGROVE'S STOCKINET.

N.º X.
Glin's Birdeye.

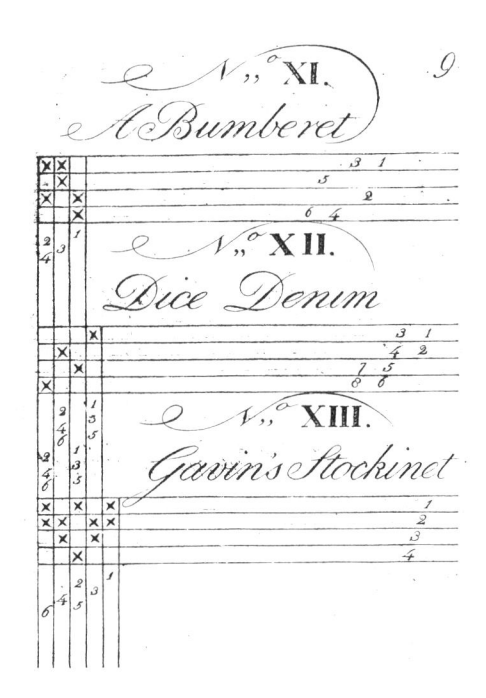

N.º XI.
A Bumberet

N.º XII.
Dice Denim

N.º XIII.
Gavin's Stockinet

N.º XIV.
Ducape.

N.º XV.
Eaton Cord.

N.º XVI.
A Plain Thickset

N.º XVII.
A Velveret & Cord.

N.º XVIII.
A Plain Velveret

N.º XIX.
A Satinet

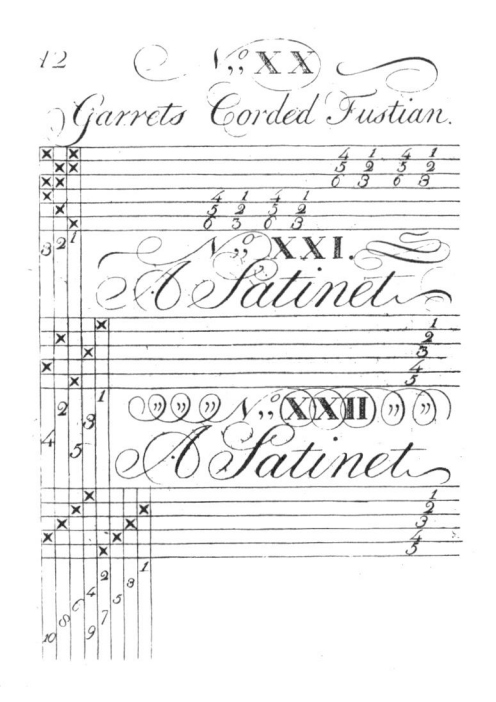

N.º XX
Garrets Corded Fustian.

N.º XXI.
A Satinet

N.º XXII
A Satinet

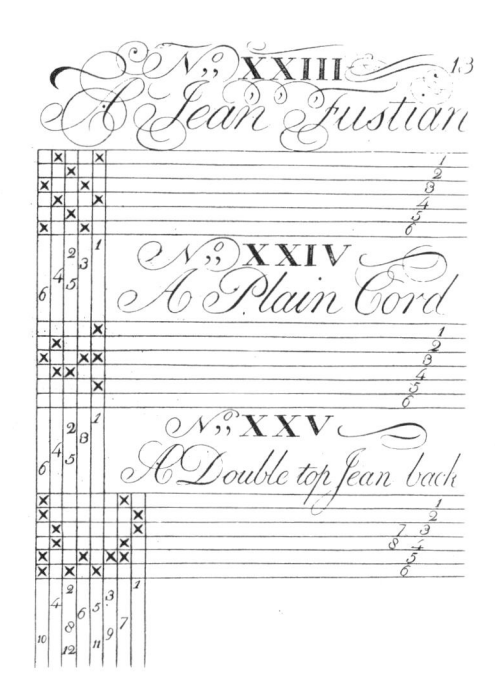

N.º XXIII
A Jean Fustian

N.º XXIV
A Plain Cord

N.º XXV
A Double top Jean back

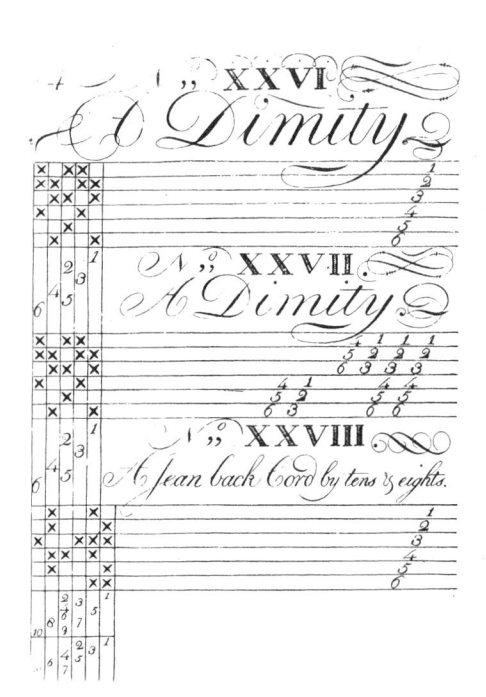

N.º XXVI
A Dimity

N.º XXVII
A Dimity

N.º XXVIII
A Jean back Cord by tens & eights.

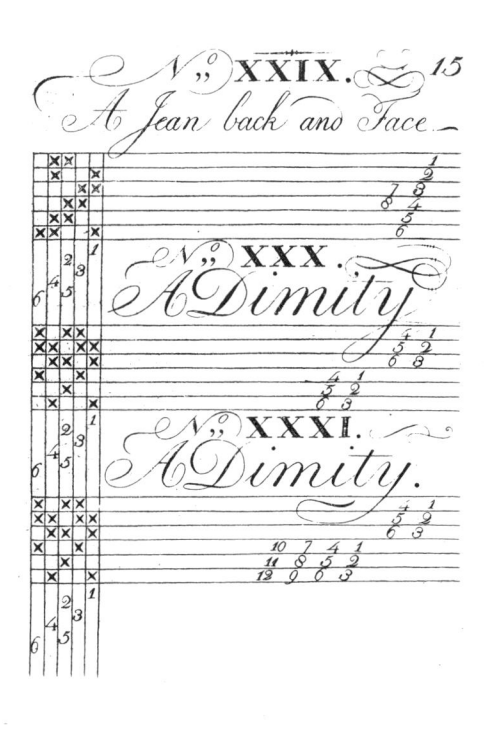

N.º XXIX.
A Jean back and Face

N.º XXX.
A Dimity

N.º XXXI.
A Dimity.

資料Ⅲ 207

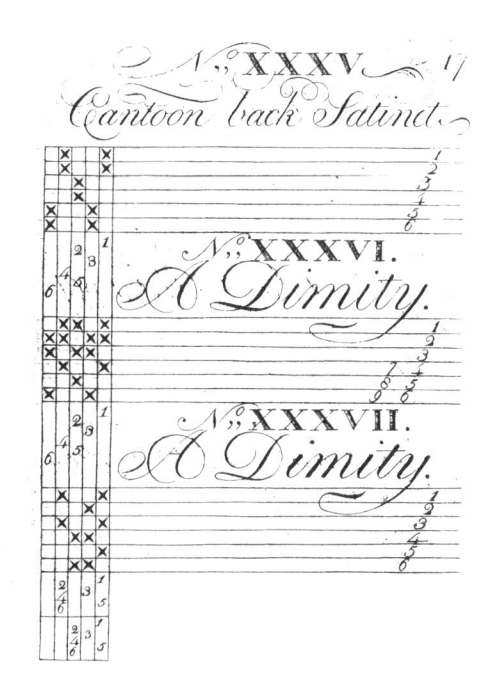

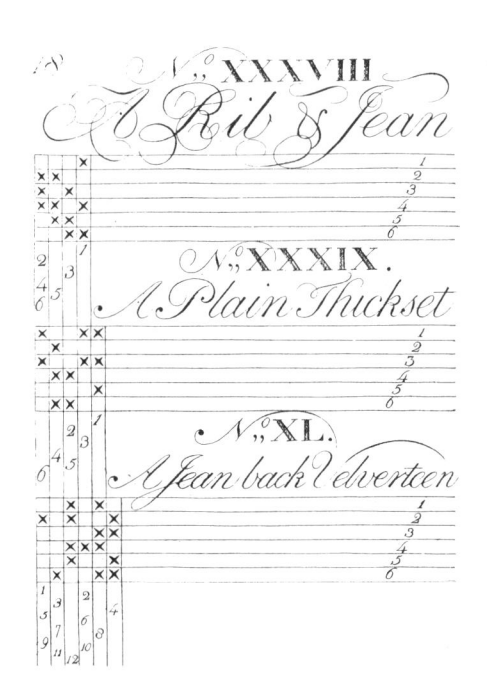

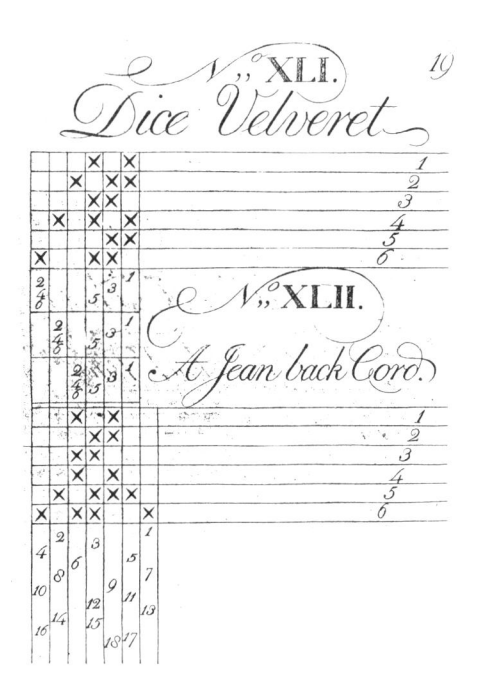

N.º XLIII. *A Plain Thickset.*

N.º XLIV. *A Jean back Thickset.*

N.º XLV. *A Balloon Cord.*

N.º XLVI. *Dice Dimity.*

N.º XLVII. *Dice King's Cord.*

N.º XLVIII. *Liliputian Stuff.*

N.º XLIX. *Worm & Cord.*

N.º L. *Mild Worm & two Cords.*

Nᵒ LI.
Rodney's Cable and Cord.

Nᵒ LII.
The Deception Diaper.

An approved Receipt for Sizing Cotton Warps.

TO every lb. of twist or cotton thread, that you intend for warp, take 2 ounces of superfine wheat flour, two pennyworth of gum arabic, and half an ounce of glue; you may also add one ounce of starch: dissolve the glue by itself, making a thin liquor of the flour, by mixing the above quantity in 2 quarts of water; and when it comes to a boiling state (over a slow fire) put in the dissolved glue & gum arabic; the starch may be mixed with the flour & water, a few minutes boiling will be sufficient; after it comes off the fire, you may add a small quantity of stone lime.

N.B. The following receipt will do very well where the above gum and glue are not to be had. Viz.

FOR every lb. of twist, take 3 ozs. of fine flour, and 2 ozs. of starch, mixed in about 2 quarts of water, & after it boils (over a slow fire) and is taken down, add a little stone lime; you must not wring it hard when you put it to dry, but slip it softly through your hands, and hang the hanks on a pole, running the pole through, so that the hanks may hang straight down; put the pole out of doors in the open air and sun, or, if it is wet weather, hang the pole about 2 or 3 yards from a good fire, in a close room, & attend to it constantly, until it be dry, turning the hanks round on the pole every 4 or 5 minutes, that the sizing may be prevented from running in the hanks towards the bottom.

Receipt for Dying Cotton or Linen Yarn of a Beautiful Blue.

DISSOLVE 3 lbs. of powder'd spanish indigo, in a strong solution of potash, for 24 hours, over a slow fire; then take 3 lbs. of slack'd stone lime; put it into a vessel, with 6 quarts of soft water, and boil it about an hour; when this is settled, pour off the clear by inclination; then 3 lbs. of green copperas is to be dissolved in this lime water, & the whole to rest and settle until the next day; then you make a mixture with water of about 300 quarts, and so in proportion for a greater or less quantity.

A 2ᵈ Receipt to Dye Cotton or Thread Blue.

GET one barrel of rain water; fill it within 4 inches of the top; then take two buckets full out of the barrel, and put it in a brass or copper kettle; then put one lb. of indigo into an earthen vessel, putting as much strong lye over it as will cover it, and let it stand by the fire side all night; then make the indigo as fine as you can, and put it in the kettle, with the two buckets of water; then take 2 lbs of good copperas and two of lime, and make them as fine as you can, and put them in the kettle also, and hang it over the fire, and stir it until it boils; after which pour it in the tub or barrel, and stir it well; when so done you may die in 12 hours; but you must not stir it when you are going to die but stir it 3 times a day, whither you die or not; for by so doing, the die remains good many years; only you must strengthen it now and then, with a little of the above ingredients; a day before the cotton is to be dyed, it must be boiled in water, with a peck of bran, and lie in it all night.

A 3ᵈ Receipt to Die Cotton or Thread Blue.

TAKE one lb. of logwood chip'd or beat fine; boil it 4 hours, in as much water as will cover 2 lbs. of cotton; then take the wood out, and put in one oz. of blue vitriol, and let it boil 2 minutes, stirring it all the time; then put in the cotton, and let it boil 2 minutes; then boil it in soap suds, and rinse it out well.

A Receipt to Die with Aranetta.

TAKE one ounce of aranetta, and tie it up in a little fine linen bag, and steep it in as much strong soap suds, as will cover 3 lbs. of cotton or thread (or that weight of cotton or linen cloth) for 6 or 8 hours, until it be soft enough to rub through the bag, in the same manner as women rub their blue bag; when you rub it all out of the bag, put in the cotton or thread, and let it remain in for 24 hours, keeping it hot all the time by the fire, it will come out a beautiful deep aranetta, and the same liquor will die as much more a pale colour.

To Die Cotton or Woollen Yarn a fine Green.

FIRST die your cotton yarn a blue, according to the directions in the preceeding receipts; or, if woollen yarn, die it blue by indigo and chamberlie; if you wish to have a deep green, you must first die it a deep blue, and if a light green, it must be only a light blue; then procure a sufficient and equal quantity of black oak bark & hiccory bark (the inside bark) as will make a strong decoction when boiled in water; you may then take out the barks from the brass or copper kettle in which they must be well boiled, and, having steeped your yarn a little while in strong alum water, put it in the bark liquor, and let it remain in 6 hours, kept warm, giving it air now and then, and you will have a beautiful green.

N.B. You must rinse the woollen yarn well from the chamberlie, before you put it in the alum water, and, after it is soaked there, wring it out dry, before you put it in the bark liquor.

28. To Die Woollen Yarn a Madder Red Colour.

TAKE about ½ bushel of wheat bran, and soak it in a tub of water (enough to cover 8 lbs. of yarn) for 3 or 4 days, until it becomes quite sour; after which you will squeeze out the bran, & after the liquor settles, pour of the clear by inclination; then take one lb. of madder, & soak it in this strained liquor, for about 12 hours; after which put it over the fire, in a brass or copper kettle, and boil it 2 or 3 hours; then soak your yarn in strong alum water a few minutes, and wring it out dry, and put it in the kettle over a flow fire, and keep it to a scalding heat, for 2 or 3 hours more, and you will have a good madder red; but, if you were to add one lb. of brasil or red wood, chip'd or bruised fine, to your madder, & boil'd with it, the colour would be more beautiful.

To Die Woollen Yarn a good Black.

FOR every pound of yarn you intend to die, procure 3 or 4 pounds of indian walnut tree bark, & boil it well 5 or 6 hours, in a large iron pot, keeping it fill'd up with water as it boils down, then take out the bark, and add 2 ounces of green copperas, for each pound of yarn you intend to die, and, having liquor enough to cover your yarn, put it in, and let it hang over a flow fire for 6 or 8 hours, keeping it to a scalding heat all the time, it will come out a good black.

N.B. 1st Shumack berries will answer in the room of walnut tree bark, but, if both are united in a sufficient quantity, the colour will be better.

2d. The root bark of any tree is the strongest & best for dying, if a sufficient quantity can be procured.

3d. If the yarn is previously boil'd in a strong decoction of common sorrel water, it will take the die the better.

The Weavers Draft Book

あとがき

　本書執筆の動機は、アメリカ黒人作家アレックス・ヘイリー作、安岡章太郎、松田銑共訳の『ルーツ』（社会思想社、1977年）にある。ヘイリー氏がアフリカのジュフレの村をたずね、みずからの先祖を探しあて、7代200年を描いた小説『ルーツ』は、世界的なベストセラーとなり、ピューリッツァー特別賞を受賞した。この作品はテレビドラマ化され、話題作として脚光を浴びた。作品中の「主人公のクンタ・キンテが着ていたものを考証できるのは、歴史学と服飾史学の研究に従事しながら、アパレル産業の現場で実際の服作りに携わって来たあなたしかいないですよ。」とアメリカ黒人史のご専門家で、神戸大学文学部の恩師である故本田創造先生から「奴隷の着るもの」研究をお勧めいただいた。これは1985年ころのことである。「奴隷の衣服」とおっしゃらなかったのが印象的で、今も鮮明に記憶している。師のご助言こそ、私が「奴隷の着るもの」の解明に取り組みだした直接的な動機である。私自身は、このようにお勧めいただく前に、『ルーツ』の翻訳書を読んだり、テレビドラマをビデオで観たりしていたのだが、小説中やテレビドラマのなかの奴隷の被服描写に疑問をいだいていた。

　本田先生からこのようなご助言をいただいた頃、私は武庫川女子大学大学院家政学研究科に在籍しており、西洋服飾史の草分けでいらっしゃる丹野郁博士のご指導のもとに、アメリカ服飾史研究に従事していた。修士論文のテーマは「アメリカ植民地時代の服飾の歴史的考察—ヴァージニア、ニューイングランド、ニューネザーランドの場合—」であった。このテーマに取り組む一方で、アメリカの中産階級や下層階級の人々の衣服についても、P. F. Copelandの "Working Dress in Colonial and Revolutionary America" Greenwood Press, London, 1977. の翻訳を並行して進めていた。

　修士論文は『アメリカ植民地時代の服飾』（せせらぎ出版、1996年）と題して刊行され、後者の翻訳書は『アメリカ史にみる職業着—植民地時代〜独立革命期—』（せせらぎ出版、1998年）というタイトルで出版の運びとなった。

　前者の研究の基礎資料をなす、アメリカ服飾史の古典的な名著、Edward Warwick, Henry C. Pitz and Alexander Wyckoff, "Early American Dress, The Colonial and Revolutionary Periods" Bonanza Books, New York, 1965. には、黒人奴隷の被服について詳しい記述はみられない。著者は

このシリーズの近刊書では、黒人奴隷の衣服が明らかにされるでしょう、と予告はしているのだが、結局、実現されてはいない。その他のアメリカ服飾史の研究書においても、奴隷の被服は扱われていない。そのため、私には1993年まで奴隷の被服をテーマとする研究は具体化できなかった。具体化のきっかけは、Linda Baumgartenの論文、"Clothes for the People: Slave Clothing in Early Virginia", *Journal of Early Southern Decorative Arts*, Vol.14, No.2, Nov.1988.である。これ以降の研究の進展については、本書の序論の先行研究をお読みいただきたい。

私の「奴隷の着るもの」研究は、丹野郁博士をはじめ、武庫川女子大学生活環境学部の風間健博士、天野敏彦博士、森谷尅彦教授の厳格で心温まるご指導のもとに、紆余曲折を経て、ようやく、2000年11月8日、『アメリカ独立革命期ヴァージニアの奴隷の被服に関する社会史的考察』と題し、博士学位論文として武庫川女子大学大学院家政学研究科に提出するに至った。その結果、2001年3月17日、家政学博士を取得した。

学位取得の半年後に、丹野郁博士からご紹介いただいた東京堂出版の編集部の堀川隆氏から、当該学位論文を、研究者は勿論のこと、一般読者をも対象とする専門書として刊行することが決まりました、とのお知らせがあった。電話でお知らせをうかがった瞬間は、夢ではないかと呆然としてしまった。

ここで、本書が成るに至るまでの経過を振り返ってみる。本研究に当って、武庫川女子大学から在外研修の機会を与えていただき、アメリカ合衆国ヴァージニア州の Williamsuburg 所在の John D. Lockefeller, Jr. Libraryを拠点として、調査を進めるという幸運にめぐまれた（1999年7月12日から9月21日）。以下に述べることからも明らかなように、本図書館は、私の研究テーマに最適の願ってもない機関であった。

本図書館は米国ヴァージニア州ウィリアムズバーグに、1997年4月、Colonial Williamsburg Foundation によって開設された。Rockefeller の孫娘のAbby M. O'Neilと夫 George O'Neilが、Lockefeller の遺産から200万ドルを本図書館の建設資金に提供したとのことである。

当該図書館には18世紀関連の建築、考古学、芸術、歴史、経済、政治、社会生活および貿易などの分野の希覯本やマニュスクリプトやマイクロフィルムや地図などを含めた貴重な第一次史料およ

び第二次史料が所蔵されている。本書の基礎史料である*Virginia Gazette* 紙の実物やマイクロフィルムも所蔵されている。

　国内・外の研究者や学生や Colonial Williamsburg Foundation のスタッフは平日9時から5時まで利用できる。土、日は休みである。私自身はワシントンD.C.に所在するSmithsonian Institution のアメリカ歴史博物館の学芸員、Claudia Kidwell 女史とヴァージニア州ウィリアムズバーグのDeWitt Wallace Gallery of Decorative Arts の学芸員、Linda Baumgarten 女史からの紹介で、18世紀を研究している在外研修員（Visiting Scholar）として、招聘していただいた。お二人ともアメリカ服飾学会（Costume Society of America）を通じての知人であり、アメリカではテキスタイル、パターンおよび中産階級や下層階級の衣服研究で著名な研究者である。当該図書館の3階に研究スペースがあり、そこにデスクを用意して下さり、インターネットも接続していただけた。明るく、静かで、なかなか快適な環境で、お陰様で研究に専念でき、感謝に堪えない。基本的に週5日、ここへ通って午前9時から午後5時まで、資料検索と資料整理をして過ごし、必要に応じて、下記の場所に史料や実物資料の調査に出かけた。

1) DeWitt Wallace Gallery of Decorative Arts, Colonial Williamsburg Foundation, Willimasburg, Virginia
2) RichmondのValentine Museum
3) Colonial Williamsburg Foundation の Weaving Room
4) Colonial Williamsburg Foundation の Department of Archaeological Research
5) Mount Vernon Plantation
6) College of William and Mary の Swem Library
7) The Virginia Historical Society
8) The Library of Virginia, Library of Mount Vernon Ladies Association
9) The Alderman Library of The University of Virginia
10) Library of Congress

さて、ヴァージニアにおける奴隷の被服研究はスムーズに進んだのであろうか。上記の諸機関のスタッフの方々は大変、親切で、私のために、誠心誠意、資料検索にご協力下さった。さまざまなエピソードがあるが、そのなかから一つのエピソードをご紹介しよう。
　ハーバード大学と並んで古い、17世紀に設立された公立大学、College of William and MaryのSwem Library 司書のMargaret Cook 女史は、司書歴40年のベテランの方である。奴隷の被服関連のマニュスクリプトが見つかるとすぐに、Lockfeller Jr. Library のマネージャーの Inge Flester 宛てにお電話をかけてきて下さるのである。「まさに見せたい史料が見つかったので、いつ見に来るか、連絡するように伝えて下さい」と。そして、私は連絡を受けるが早いか、胸をワクワクさせて調査に出かけた。大学構内の広い芝生の中庭を通り過ぎ、風格ある大学図書館を訪ねると、Margaret Cook女史は、いつも得意げに、18世紀の奴隷の名簿やプランターの日記など、黄色く色褪せてはいるが、価値の高い史料を見せて下さった。入館して、書類に必要事項を記入して、ロッカーに手荷物をしまうと、鉛筆を1本渡され、貴重本専用机に案内された。そして、びっしり英文で書かれた注意事項を読んでから、緊張の面持ちで調査に向かったものだ。この緊張感は今も思い出される。このようにして入手した第一次史料は、本書本文中にも掲載させていただいている。Margaret Cook女史のような熱意とご好意を示して下さったのは、彼女ひとりではない。ヴァージニアで知己を得た20人余りもの人々が、こちらの調査の意気込みに心動かされてか、調査の右腕となって力を貸して下さったのだ。
　さて次に、本書の概要を一般読者の方々に分かりやすくまとめよう。
　本書の中心的課題のひとつは「奴隷の被服をいかにイメージ化するか」にある。この点について、筆者の周りの人々に聞いても、奴隷といえば「ぼろをまとっているのでは？」というイメージが一般的である。
　では、本書では奴隷の被服についてどのような方法で、どのようなイメージを打ち出すに至ったのであろうか。
　まず、先行研究からアメリカ独立革命期のヴァージニア黒人奴隷は労働形態により、プランターの側仕えの上級の黒人奴隷、家内の職人奴隷および農園の耕作奴隷といった3階層に区分されてお

り、それぞれのステータスを表す被服が支給されていたことを確認した。しかし、先行研究では、奴隷被服の概観しか明らかにされていない。

　そこでさらに、本書では当時の新聞に掲載された逃亡奴隷広告を調査し、奴隷の被服の実態を明らかにした。①逃亡奴隷広告から抽出した67種類の被服素材の一覧を作成し、②奴隷の被服のデザイン、色柄の分析から着装実態を筆者の下絵を基に、橋本裕佳子さんに描いてもらったイラストにより視覚化し、③ヴァージニア・クロス製の衣服の特徴を示し、さらに数量的データに基づいて、逃亡奴隷広告に見られる被服素材の年次変化を輸入素材と自国産の素材の比較という方法で考察した。

　いっぽう奴隷被服の実物調査の点では、困難が立ちはだかっていた。本研究は、現地調査で奴隷の被服の実物を見つけることができなかったため、資料面で大変困難な研究であった。ヴァージニアに行く前に、筆者は逃亡奴隷広告に着眼し、まったくの試行錯誤で研究を進めた。すなわち、L.A.Windley 編集の1983年に出版された*Runaway Slave Advertisement: A Documentary History from 1730s to 1790*, Vol.4, Greenwood, Westport, Connecticut, 1983.を用いて、コンピュータにより統計処理を行なった。「逃亡奴隷広告」、これはすでに書いたように、プランテーションから逃亡した奴隷を捕獲した人には、何がしかの報償金をあげますよ、という趣旨で出された新聞広告である。広告主はプランターである。この広告には、逃亡奴隷の逃亡時の服装が被服管理簿に基づいて描写されている。今日流に表現するならば、いわゆる犯罪人の指名手配文書である。従来、このようなまとまった史料はアメリカにおいても決して十分に活用されてきたとは言えない。そこでまず、1,000以上もの逃亡広告をコンピュータ・ソフト（Omnipage Professional）で取り込んだ。この作業に20時間以上の時間を費やした。次に、逃亡広告の被服情報から、67種類の素材をMicrosoft wordを用いて検索し、Microsoft excelを用いて一覧表にする作業は何時間かかったか記憶していない。ヴァージニアでも日中、Lockefeller Libraryで資料検索をし、住まいに帰ってからパソコンに向かった。確かに大変便利であるが、パソコンに使われることがどれほど大変だったか。

　本書のもうひとつの中心的課題は「プランターたちはプランテーションにおいて、奴隷たちの被服をどのようにして調達・支給していたのか」という問題である。

そこで、奴隷の被服とその生産手段の実物調査を行い、多くの史料から当時のプランターの家族とかれらの奴隷の被服の生産状況を裏づけた。また、収集した記録（プランターの日記、公文書等）からプランテーションにおける奴隷使用と被服調達の実態を示した。

　従来の上流階級の服飾に関する研究では、貴族趣味的な服飾美に着眼して、その実態を博物館に所蔵されている実物資料の調査により明らかにする方法が主流をなしてきた。中産・下層階級以下の衣服は、貴族スタイルの衣服から装飾を取り去った、粗末な素材を用いたものと見なされ、研究対象としての価値が認められない傾向が強かった。また、中産・下層階級の衣服はきわめて僅かしか残存していない。実物が残存していない場合は特に、コンピュータ・ソフトを用いた新しいタイプの文化史研究の方法は、従来のフィールド・ワークを主とする研究に、さらに新たな価値を生み出すことを可能にしてくれた。すなわち、数量化により過去の服飾や被服の実態を明らかにすることを可能にしてくれたと確信する。

　このようなわけで、本書には多数の表やグラフが収まることとなった。拙著がアメリカ史や他の関連領域の諸研究に役立てば幸いである。

　次に、今後の研究方針について述べる。
1. 本書の形の良い発展として「トマス・ジェファソンのプランテーションにおける奴隷被服の国産化の推移」をテーマとして研究を進める方針である。1811年にジェニー紡績機を導入したジェファソンは、プランテーションにおいて、奴隷被服の国産化の事業を促進し、一定の成果を挙げた。今後の研究により、その実態を明らかにし、下層階級の被服の生産と流通の実態に迫る方針である。
2. 19世紀アメリカ服飾史を中産・下層階級による衣服生産に焦点をあてて、考察する。アパレル産業で衣服生産に従事してきた者の立場から、パターンシステムにも着目し、アメリカにおける衣服産業の発達をヨーロッパとの比較において考察する方針である。

　本書刊行に至るまで、国内外の大変、多くの方々のご指導やご支援・ご助力をいただいた。お世

話になった皆様に対して、筆舌に尽くしがたい感謝の気持ちでいっぱいである。本紙面を借りて、御礼を申し上げたい。アメリカの皆様への謝辞は、英文要旨の末尾に記させていただいた。

　とりわけ、本研究を進めるにあたって終始温かくご指導・ご鞭撻下さった丹野郁博士ならびに風間健博士には、拙著のために本書の目的を読者の皆さんに大変、的確に伝えて下さる序文をお寄せいただき、衷心から厚く御礼申し上げたい。また、在外研修に際して、その実現にご尽力下さり、帰国後、論文の内容、研究方法、さらに文章の書き方に至るまで綿密にご指導下さった天野敏彦博士に深謝申し上げる。また、本研究の進展を温かく見守って下さった森谷尅久教授に厚く御礼申し上げる。さらにまた、著者の意図に沿って、逃亡奴隷のイラストを描いてくれた長女、橋本裕佳子にありがとうを言いたい。

　最後に、東京堂出版編集部の堀川隆氏には、本書刊行にあたって、終始、大変、細やかに、また、著者の意向を十分お汲み取りの上、このように格式ある書物を誕生させて下さり、心から厚く御礼申し上げる。

2002年8月

濱　田　雅　子

Summary
(英文要旨)

1. The Purpose of This Study

　　Recently, with the progress of the study in the new fields such as the methodology of quantitative study, social history and the history of public movements, it is becoming a pressing need to deepen and integrate the conventional fields of academic study on American history for further development. The theme of this study is the slave clothing during the period of the American Revolution, and this study is positioned in the field of the so-called "material culture." The term "material culture" here means culture as it relates to materials such as food, clothing and shelter indispensable for human daily life. The mainstream of the study on the history of European and American costume has so far been related to the clothing of the upper classes. As to the clothing of the middle and the lower classes, only a small number of reports have been presented, with very few reports on that of the lower classes. In this study, therefore, various items of slave clothing are investigated, focusing on their types, textile materials, and the actual conditions of their supply.

　　The scope of this study is the 24-year (1766~1789) period of the American Revolution and the geographical area of Virginia (**Fig.1-3-3**), the first colony in the United States of America. The "clothing" taken up in this study includes not only garments but also accessories such as headgears (hats, caps, etc.), shoes and stockings.

　　In 1661, the colonial assembly of Virginia legalized black slavery. In 1790, when the first census was carried out in the United States, most of about 700,000 black slaves lived in the Southern States. Particularly in the State of Virginia, the population of black slaves reached 292,627, the largest in the United States. Among the 13 colonies, Virginia was a typical area where the slavery system and the republic system made a coincidental and very paradoxical development. Though colonial Virginia, along with colonial Massachusetts, lead the van in the American Revolution and produced a large number of "Founding Fathers of America," the black slavery continued to remain there. There are only a few papers that delved squarely into the issue of continuation of the black slavery during the period of the American Revolution. The purpose of this study is to clarify the real aspect of the clothing of black slaves as their status symbol, by investigating the issue of the slavery in Virginia in the period of the American Revolution.

"How should we image to ourselves the slave clothing?" It is the main subject of this study.

This study covers the period from 1766 to 1789. In this study, the types of the items of slave clothing and the textile materials used for them during the said periods are analyzed quantitatively.

The actual clothing of the upper classes are preserved in museums, but as to slave clothing, there hardly remains anything. If the scope of study was limited only to the clothing of the upper classes, it would be impossible to grasp the nature of their clothing habits. Therefore, recognizing the historical value of runaway slave advertisements as a source of useful pieces of information about the clothing of runaway slaves, the descriptions of the types of various items of slave clothing and their textile materials are extracted from such advertisements, and the obtained data are analyzed. The combination and the number of the items of male runaway slaves are also investigated. The study method is explained later in Section 3.

2. Earlier Studies

A comparative study is made on the purposes and the methods of the earlier studies on the history of European and American costumes, as well as those of the earlier studies which were made based on "runaway slave advertisements." The studies on the slave clothing in Virginia during the period of the American Revolution are very scarce. The work of Peter F. Copeland and that of Linda Baumbarten are outstanding. However, the scopes of their works were limited to a general survey of slave clothing, without mentioning the details of the actual conditions of the clothing.

3. Study Method

First, in this study, the descriptions of various items of slave clothing are extracted from the runaway slave advertisements that appeared in the newspapers such as *Virginia Gazette* (1766 ~1789), and the types of the extracted items and their textile materials, as well as the combination of the items of clothing worn by male slaves when they ran away, are investigated. The characteristic features of the clothing made of Virginia cloth and osnabrug, which frequently appeared in the runaway slave advertisements, are also clarified. Moreover, 67 textile materials are extracted from the advertisements, and the changes in the use of home made textiles, which were generally called "Virginia cloth," are analyzed quantitatively, referring to their social background.

Next, some actual materials, including the clothing made of Virginia cloth and the tools used for making clothing, are investigated. The investigated materials are a man's suit made of Virginia cloth, which is in the collection of the DeWitt Wallace Gallery of Decorative Arts, (a department of the Colonial Williamsburg Foundation, Virginia); a patchwork quilt made by slaves, which is in the collection of the Valentine Museum (Richmond, Virginia); the textiles which were reproduced by the Weaving Department of the Colonial Williamsburg Foundation; and other archaeological finds excavated by the Archaeological Department of the same Foundation. To grasp the actual conditions of the production of slave clothing at the plantations of the Carter Family, the most prominent planters in Virginia, and at the Mount Vernon Plantation owned by the first president George Washington, the records at plantations, the letters written by traders, the diaries and letters of planters, and other official records are investigated. "How did the planters manage and maintain the production and supply of the clothing of their family of black slaves?" is one of the main subjects of this study.

Summary 221

4. The Composition of This Study

This study is composed of a total of six chapters, including "Introduction," and "Conclusion." "Introduction" describes the purpose and the method of this study, briefly reviews the earlier studies, and explains the significance and the composition of this study. Chapter 1 reviews the historical background. Section 1 deals with the background of the American Revolution and the birth of the Unites States of America. Section 2 deals with the history of colonial Virginia (Fig. 1-2-1). Section 3 deals with the establishment of black slavery in Virginia and its specific features (Fig. 1-3-1, 1-3-2, Table 1-3-1~1-3-4). Section 4 investigates the characteristic features of the costumes on the eve of the American Revolution (Fig. 1-4-1~1-4-4, 1-4-6, 1-4-7, Fig. 1-4-5, Table 1-4-1). Above all, a special emphasis is placed on the establishment of black slavery in Virginia and its specific features, because they can be considered to be the fundamental historical factors that determined the nature of the slave clothing in the 18th century. The significance of the shift from the white indentured servant system to the black slavery system is pointed out here, referring to its historical background. The social status of slaves at plantations in the southern part of North America varied depending on their labor categories, that is, slaves were classified into three groups — high-ranking house servants who served close to planters, skilled slave artisans, and slaves as field hands.

Chapter 2 describes the significance and the method of the study based on runaway slave advertisements.

Section 1 explains the historical value of the descriptions of the slave clothing that appeared in the advertisements, and Section 2 gives the method of analyzing these descriptions (Fig. 2-2-1). In Section 3, the textile materials of the clothing (67 types) that appeared in the advertisements are classified into nine groups — (1)wool, (2)wool & cotton, (3)silk, wool & cotton, (4)cotton, (5)cotton & silk, (6)cotton & linen, (7)linen, (8)silk, and (9)others - and their respective characteristic features are explained according to their out lines, compositions (threads and textile weaves), finishes, colors and patterns, and the uses described in the advertisements (Table 2-3-1, 2-3-2, Fig.2-3-1〜2-3-24, 4-2-4-1, 4-2-4-2, 4-2-5-1〜4-2-5-6). The data presented in this section will be helpful in grasping the concrete images of slave clothing.

In Chapter 3, the descriptions of the clothing that appeared in the advertisements are analyzed quantitatively. Section 1 makes an investigation into the types of slave clothing, clarifies the changes in the status of slaves and their labor categories, and then presents the patterns of the clothing that would represent the status of the slaves in different strata (Doc.3-1-1〜3-1-3, Fig.3-1-3〜3-1-6, Fig.3-1-1-1〜3-1-1-3, 3-1-2)

Section 2 investigates the actual conditions of the clothing of male slaves when they ran way (Doc.3-2-1, 3-2-2). The results of the analysis of a total of 149 instances reveal the following facts (Table 3-2-1〜3-2-5). (1) The number of those who had all the items, from head coverings to shoes, was very small (only about 7%). (2) "Shoes" were found in about 27% of the descriptions of the clothing of male runaway slaves in the advertisements. (3) About 50% of male runaway slaves had only upper and lower clothes, and as many as 80% of all the male runaway slaves were not wearing more than two upper clothes when they ran away (Table 3-2-6, 3-2-7). (4) As to lower clothes, the ratio between those who were wearing breeches and those who were wearing trousers was 3:1 (Table 3-2-8).

Based on the data obtained through the quantitative analysis of the descriptions of slave clothing in the advertisements, the wearing styles of male runaway slaves are classified into eight patterns, and their illustrations drawn by Yukako Hashimoto, based on the author's drawings, are also presented here.

Section 3 discusses the characteristic features of Virginia cloth that appeared in the advertisements (Table 3-3-1〜3-3-4, Fig. 3-3-1〜3-3-3), and Section 4 deals with Osnabrug (Table 3-4-1, 3-4-2, Fig. 3-4-1, 3-4-2). Then, in Section 5, the year-to-year changes in the use of textile materials for slave clothing are investigated, comparing the cases of imported textile

Summary 223

materials and home made ones. The obtained data indicate that the percentage of the use of home-made textiles, which were called Virginia cloth, began to increase after the Revolutionary War in 1776 (Table 3-5-1, Fig. 3-5-1). The background of this change is also discussed here.

Chapter 4 discusses the actual conditions of the production of slave clothing in Virginia, based on the results of the investigation of the actual materials preserved in Virginia and various primary sources. Section 1 reviews the trend of the study on this subject, arranges the materials for this study, and explains the study method adopted here.

Section 2 presents and discusses the results of the investigation of the actual materials preserved in Virginia. A man's suit made of Virginia cloth (Table 4-2-1, Fig. 4-2-1-1〜4-2-1-6) and a patchwork quilt made by slaves (Fig. 4-2-3-1〜4-2-3-4) clarify the concrete characteristic features of Virginia cloth that frequently appeared in the runaway slave advertisements. The archaeological finds such as scissors (Fig. 4-2-6-1), pins (Fig. 4-2-6-3) and thimbles (Fig. 4-2-6-2), which were discovered at the Palace Plantation in Williamsburg, prove that the production of clothing had been performed by slave artisans at slave quarters.

Then, to grasp the actual conditions of the production and the supply of slave clothing, Section 3 examines various primary sources such as the records at plantations, the letters written by traders, the diaries and letters of planters, and other official records at the Carter family's plantation (Doc.4-3-2〜4-3-12, Fig.4-3-1〜4-3-4) and the Mount Vernon plantation of George Washington (Fig.4-3-6, Doc.4-3-13〜4-3-16). This section also clarifies the process in which the prominent planters in Virginia, during the period of the transition from the white indentured servant system to the black slavery, switched their skilled artisans, who were engaged in the spinning and weaving work, from white servants to black slaves.

"Conclusion" summarizes the essential points of the findings of this study on slave clothing during the period of the American Revolution.

Acknowledgement

I would like to express my appreciation to all of the curators, librarians, archivists and another staffs in Virginia, United States of America, who helped me with the research and writing of this book. Many of them have been extremely generous with their time and information.

Foremost among them are Claudia Brush Kidwell of Smithsonian Institution, Linda Baumgarten of Colonial Williamsburg Foundation and Susan Berg of John D. Lockefeller, Jr. Library, Colonial Willinamsburg, Williamsburg, Virginia. They were so kind to arrange for my study at the John D. Lockefeller, Jr. Library.

I am deeply indebted to all the staffs of above Library. They are Mary Haskell, Juleigh Muirhead Clark, Inge Flester, Gail Garfinkle Greve, George Yetter, Marianne Martin, Doug Mayo and Joanne Proper. Above all I should like to thank Inge Flester who was a manager of this Library and was always helpful and patient to take care of my study life in Virginia.

Much gratitude goes to Patricia Gibbs and Lorena Walsh for their counsel, direction and advice. I wish to thank Toshihiko Amano who had just graduated from College of William and Mary. He drove me to several plantations for my fieldwork. Without his great help, I could not have gotten so many kinds of useful information.

I would like to thank following staffs of Colonial Williamsburg Foundation: Carl L. Lounsburg, William E. Pittman, Kelly Ladd, Max Hamrick, Janea Whitacre, Wendy Sumerlin and John Markham Ferguson(Jr.).

I also would like to express my appreciation to Rhonda Russell who rent me her comfortable room. She was a very kind and nice advisor and friend during my stay in Virginia. And Margaret Cook of Swem Library of the College of William and Mary, Colleen R. Callahan of the Valentine Museum, Bryan Clark Green of the Virginia Historical Society, Pauline Page and

Kirsten Thorsen of the Alderman Library of the University of Virginia, Barbara McMillan and Mary V. Thompson of Mount Vernon Ladies Association. They were most helpful to me and without their kind help, my work would be most difficult.

For the permission to reproduce the photographs, illustration, materials from manuscripts and microfilms, I would like to thank John D. Lockefeller, Jr. Library; Smithsonian Institution; DeWitt Wallace Gallery of Decorative Arts, Colonial Williamsburg Foundation; Valentine Museum, Richmond; Weaving Department of Colonial Williamsburg Foundation; Department of Archaeological Research of Colonial Williamsburg Foundation; Library of Mount Vernon Ladies' Association; Swem Library, College of William and Mary; The Virginia Historical Society; The Library of Virginia; The Alderman Library, The University of Virginia; Library of Congress; Duke University; Greenwood Publishing Group; W.W. Norton & Company; Dover Publications, INC.; The University of North Carolina Press, Chapel Hill & London; and Rebel Publishing Co., Inc., Texarkana, Texas.

Masako Hamada

索 引

【凡　例】
①本文および口絵に掲げた主な語句を「人名索引」「地名索引」「事項索引」に分類し、それぞれ《アルファベット表記》《日本語表記》等に分けて掲出した。
②事項索引の《アルファベット表記》は、原則として、本文中に（　）でアルファベット表記を併記したもののみを項目化した。
③事項索引のゴチック体で表記した事項には、当該事項に該当する事項を、五十音順に配列した。
④＊は本書に記載のない原語に付した。
⑤（　）の付いた頁は口絵を示す。

人名索引

≪アルファベット表記≫

【A】
Andrews, John B. ·······························*161*
【B】
Bacon, Nathaniel ······························*24*
Barden, John Randolf ·······················*162*
Baumgarten, Linda
　　　　·········*7,9,10,13,14,36,64,100,115,159,166,168*
Botetourt, Norborne Berkeley ···········*122,123*
Burnaby, Andrew ·····························*104,115,169*
Byrd Ⅱ, William ·······························*129,158*
【C】
Cabell ··*153,157*
Callahan, Colleen ·····························*119-120,159*
Carter Family ···*3,11,12,39,40,68,69,118,123,124,158,170*
Carter Jr., John ·································*125*
Carter of Nomini Hall, Robert
　　　　·········*3,113,124,126,134,136,158,170,171*
Carter, King ·····································*125,126*
Carter, John ····································*124,125*
Carter, Landon ·······························*3,124,126-134,142,158,170*
Carter, Robert ································*43,67,126,134-138,140-142*
Carter, Robert King ··························*43,125,126,142*
Carter, Robert Wormeley
　　　　·········*3,124,126,142-145,149,158,170,171*
Centrallo, Carol ·······························*7,13*
Charles Ⅰ ···*125*
Commons, John R. ····························*161*
Copeland, Peter F. ···························*5,33,36,68,115,148,166,167*
Custis, Martha Dandridge ···············*145*
【D】
Davis, Thomas ·································*149*
Diderot, Denis ·································*118*
Dunmore, John Murray ····················*122*
【F】
Fauquier, Francis ····························*122*
Fitzpatrick, John C. ·························*13*
【G】
Galenson, David W. ··························*25,166*
Gibbs, Patricia ································*10,113,116,118,134,159-161,163*

Gilmore, Eugene A. ···························*161*
Greene, Jack P. ································*160*
【H】
Hamilton, Alexander ························*113,118*
Hamrick, Max ···································*(14),121,123,170*
Hargrove, John ································*12,121,159*
Harmuth, Louis ································*10,43*
Harrower, John ································*104,115*
Henry, Edward Warwick ···················*35*
Hirschfeld, Fritz ·······························*163*
Hoffman, Paul P. ······························*160*
Howard, Bryan Paul ·························*8-10,43,110,111*
【J】
Jefferson, Thomas ···························*18,74,118*
【K】
Kidwell, Claudia ·······························*5,6*
Köhler, Carl ····································*36*
【L】
Ladd, Kelly ······································*122*
Lawrence, Charles ····························*147*
【M】
McCombs, Dorothy F. ························*43,104,115,118*
Montgomery, Florence ·····················*10,42,43*
Morgan, Philip D. ······························*25-27,35,115*
Morton, Louis ··································*124,159,161,162*
Mullin, Gerald W. ······························*6,7*
【N】
Norton, Mary Beth ···························*35,115*
【P】
Phillips, Ulrich B. ·····························*161*
Prude, Jonathan ·······························*7,8,13*
【R】
Raleigh, Sir Walter ···························*20*
Rolf, John ·······································*20*
【S】
Smith, John ····································*20,35*
Southhall, Turner ·····························*11,152,153,156*
Sullivan, Daniel ································*136-139*
Summer, Helen L. ·····························*161*
【W】
Walsh, Lorena S. ·······························*39,40,43,68,115*
Warner, Patricia Campbell ···············*14*
Washington, George ··························*3,11,
　　　　12,18,19,67-69,124,126,145-149,155,158,170,171*
Washington, Lund ·····························*68-70,146*

Williams, Gloria M. ·················· 7,13
Wily, John ························ 12,159
Windley, Lathan A. ········ 6,7,10,36,40,42,43,74,115

≪日本語・かな漢字表記≫

【あ】
有賀　貞 ························· 35,115
池本幸三 ······················ 7,8,13,35,160
一見輝彦 ····························· 43
大下尚一 ························· 35,115
【か】
川北　稔 ···························· 35
紀平英作 ························· 35,116
【さ】
清水知久 ·························· 16,35
志邨晃佑 ························· 35,115
下山　晃 ···························· 35
白井洋子 ························· 35,115
【た】
高橋　章 ·························· 16,35
丹野　郁 ······················· 4,13,35,36
戸田徹子 ························· 35,115
富田虎男 ························· 13,16,35
【は】
平野　孝 ···························· 115
布留川正博 ··························· 35
本田創造 ························· 35,115
【ま】
森　杲 ··························· 25,35
【や・わ】
吉田和志 ····························· 43
和田光弘 ···························· 8,14

≪日本語・カタカナ表記≫

【ア】
ウィリアムズ, グロリア・M.（Groia M. Williams）··· 7
ウィンドレイ, ラーサン・A.（Lathan A. Windley）
　　　　　　　　　 ········ 6,7,10,35,40,42,43,74,115
ウォルシュ, ロレーナ・S.（Lorena S. Walsh）
　　　　　　　　　 ··················· 39,40,43,68,115
エリザベス女王 ·························· 20
エンリケ航海王子 ························ 21

【カ】
カーター家（Carter Family）
　　　　·········· 3,11,12,39,40,68,69,118,123,124,158,170
◇カーター・オブ・ノミニ・ホール, ロバート・
　　（Robert Carter of Nominy Hall）
　　　　················· 3,113,124,126,134,136,158,170,171
◇カーター, ジョン・（John Carter）·········· 124,125
◇カーター Jr., ジョン・（John Carter Jr.）········ 125
◇カーター（ロバート・カーター）婦人 ············ 33
◇カーター, ランドン・（Landon Carter）-大佐
　　　　················· 3,124,126-134,142,158,170,171
◇カーター, ロバート・（Robert Carter）
　　　　················· 43,67,125,126,134-138,140-142
◇カーター, ロバート・ウォームレイ・（Robert
　　Wormeley Carter）
　　　　················· 3,124,126,142-145,149,158,170,171
◇カーター, ロバート・キング・（Robert King
　　Carter）···················· 43,125,126,142

カーベル（Cabell）·················· 153,157
カスティス, マーサ・D.（Martha Dandridge
　　Custis）······························ 145
カラハン, コリーン・（Colleen Callahan）··· 119-120,159
ガレンソン, ディヴィド・（David W. Galenson） 25,166
キドウェル, クローディア・（Claudia Kidwell）··· 5,6
ギブス, パトリシア・（Patricia Gibbs）
　　　　················· 10,113,116,118,134,159-161,163
「キング」カーター→カーター, ロバート・キング
ケントラッロ, キャロル・（Carol Centrallo）······ 7,13
コープランド, ピーター・F.（Copeland, Peter F.）
　　　　················· 5,33,36,68,115,148,166,167
ゴンサルヴェス, アンタン・ ·················· 21
【サ】
サウスホール, ターナー・-大佐（Turner Southhall）
　　　　·························· 11,152,153,156
サリバン, ダニエル・（Daniel Sullivan）······ 136-139
ジェファーソン, トマス・（Thomas Jefferson）
　　　　································ 18,74,118
スミス, ジョン・（John Smith）················ 20
【タ】
ダンモア総督（John Murray Dunmore）·········· 122
チャールズ1世（Charles I）·················· 125
デイヴィス, トマス・（Thomas Davis）·········· 149
ディドロー, デニス・（Denis Diderot）·········· 118

【ノ】
ノートン, メアリー・ベス・ ·················35,115
【ハ】
ハーグローブ, ジョン・(John Hargrove) ···12,121,159
バード二世, ウィリアム (William Byrd Ⅱ) ·····129,158
バーナビー, アンドリュー・(Andrew Burnaby) 牧師
 ·······································104,115,169
ハーミュス, ルイス・(Louis Harmuth) ·········10,43
バウムガルテン, リンダ・(Linda Baumgarten)
 ········7,9,10,13,14,36,64,100,115,159,166,168
ハミルトン, アレグザンダー・(Alexander Hamilton)
 ·······································113,118
ハムリック, マックス・(Max Hamrick)
 ·······································(4),121,123,170
ハロワー, ジョン・(John Harrower) ·········104,115
ハワード, ブライヤン・P.(Bryan Paul Howard)
 ·······································8-10,43,110,111
フォクイエル総督 (Francis Fauquier) ············122
プルード, ジョナサン・(Jonathan Prude) ······7,8,13
ペイン, トマス・(Thomas Paine) ·················18,74
ベーコン, ナザニエル・(Nathaniel Bacon) ········24
ボティチュール総督 (Norborne Berkeley Botetourt)
 ·······································122,123
ホフマン, ポール・(Paul Hoffman) ············160
【マ】
マッコム, ドロシー・F.(Dorothy F. McCombs)
 ·······································43,104,115,118
マリン, ジェラルド・W.(Gerald W. Mullin) ······6,7
モーガン, P. D.(Philip D. Morgan) ······25-27,35,115
モートン, ルイ・(Louis Morton) ·········124,159,161
モンゴメリー, フローレンス・M.(Florence M. Montgomery) ···············10,42,43
【ラ】
ラッド, ケリー・(Kelly Ladd) ·····················122
ローランス, チャールズ・(Charles Lawrence) ···147
ローリー, ウォルター・(廷臣ローリー) ············20
ロルフ, ジョン・(John Rolf) ·····················20
【ワ】
ワシントン, ジョージ・(George Washington) ···3,11, 12,18,19,67-69,124,126,145-149,155,158,170,171
ワシントン, ランド・(Lund Washington) ···68-70,146

地名索引

≪アルファベット表記≫

【A】
Alexandria, Virginia ·······························148
【B】
Boston, Massachusetts ···························123
【C】
Chesapeake Bay ··················20,23,25,27,166
Concord, Massachusetts ·······················18,113
Connecticut ·······································2
【D】
Delaware ···2
【G】
Georgia ···································2,6,18,24
【J】
James City County, Virginia ······················43
Jamestown, Virginia ·····························20
【L】
Lexington, Massachusetts ·····················18,113
【M】
Maryland ·································6,23,24
Massachusetts ·································2,9,18
Mount Vernon, Virginia
 ······················3,12,39,145,146,148,154,158,171
【N】
New England ·······································4
New Hampshire ···································2
New Jersey ·······································18
New Netherland ···································4
New York ·································2,17,18
North Carolina ·································2,6,7,23
【O】
Old Orchard, Virginia ·····························142
【P】
Pennsylvania ·······································18
Philadelphia, Pennsylvania ··············18,19,31,148
【R】
Rhode Island ·······································2
Richmond, Virginia ·······························3
【V】
Virginia ·································2-4,6,7,9-14,17,

18,20-25,27,29,31,33,38,42,67,68,104,105,111,113,
114,118,119,121-126,129-131,134,140,145,156,158,
166,167,169-171

≪日本語・カタカナ表記≫

【ア】
アレグザンドリア（Alexandria, Virginia）………148
ヴァージニア（Virginia）…2-4,6,7,9-14,17,18,20-25,27,29,
 31,33,38,42,67,68,104,150,111,113,114,118,119,121-
 126,129,131,134,140,145,156,158,166,167,169-171
オールド・オーチャード（Old Orchard, Virrginia）…142
【カ】
コネティカット（Connecticut）……………………2
コンコード（Concord, Massachusetts）………18,113
【サ】
ジェイムズ・シティ・カウンティ（James City County,
 Virginia）……………………………………43
ジェームズタウン（Jamestown, Virginia）…………20
ジョージア（Georgia）……………………2,6,18,24
【タ】
チェサピーク湾（Chesapeake Bay）…20,23,25,27,166
デラウェア（Delaware）………………………………2
【ニ】
ニュー・イングランド（New England）……………4
ニュー・ジャージー（New Jersey）………………18
ニュー・ネザーランド（New Netherland）…………4
ニュー・ハンプシャー（New Hampshire）…………2
ニュー・ヨーク（New York）……………………2,17,18
ノース・カロライナ（North Carolina）………2,6,7,23
【ハ】
フィラデルフィア（Philadelphia, Pennsylvania）
 …………………………………………18,19,31,148
ペンシルヴェニア（Pennsylvania）…………………18
ボストン（Boston, Massachusetts）………………123
【マ】
マウント・ヴァーノン（Mount Vernon, Virginia）
 ……………………………3,12,39,145,146,148,154,158,171
マサチューセッツ（Massachusetts）…………2,9,18
メリーランド（Maryland）……………………6,23,24
【リ】
リッチモンド（Richmond, Virginia）…………………3
レキシントン（Lexington, Massachusetts）……18,113
ロードアイランド（Rhode Island）…………………2

事項索引

≪アルファベット表記≫

*は本書に記載のない言語。

【A】
African American*……………………………………7-9
apron………………………………………………30,67,79
archaeological field school………………………121
Aries………………………………………………136,142
【B】
Bacon's Rebellion*……………………………………24
baize…………………………………………………67
banyan………………………………………………34
barvell*………………………………………………34
bath coating………………………………………44,54
Battles of Lexington and Concord*………17,18,113
bearskin………………………………………44,54,71-73
beaver coating………………………………38,42,44,54
beaver hat……………………………………………96
belted jacket*………………………………………34
blacksmith………………………………………78,84,86
blanket………………………………………34,76,153
blanket coat*…………………………………………34
block print*…………………………………………120
blouse…………………………………………………34
bob wig*………………………………………………34
body shirt*……………………………………………34
bonnet………………………………………………67,108-110
boots*………………………………………79,81,83,85,87,89-93
boss………………………………………………27,40,134,158
breasted………………………………………………42
breeches……………………(11),30,34,39,42,45,47,49,51,
 53,66,68-71,73,76,78,80,82,84,86,88,90-93,95-98,100,
 103,105110,114,119,120,146,147,167-169
bricklayer*………………………………………69,146
broadcloth……………………………………(4),44,54,67,71-73
brocade*………………………………………………31
buckskin………………………………………………44,54,71-73
bullycock*……………………………………………34
butcher………………………………………………27,78,166
buttom*………………………………………………121

【C】
calico······(7),48,59
calimanco······(4),44,54
camlet (camblet)······44,54,73,98
canvas (duck)······(15),50,61,67
cap······34,40,49,51,67-68,79,81,83,85,87,89-93
cape and cuffs······98
carpenter······27,80,82,84,86,167
carter······78
casimer······(4),44,55
castor······44,55
check······(8),50,61,73,74,106,114,120,169
chemise······34,66
cloth······44,55,72,112
clothing of corn field Negroes······79
clothing of field Negroes······81
clothing of labouring Negroes······79
common dress of field slaves······83
coat······(10),30,31,45,47,49,51,53,66-68,72-74,78,80,82,84,
 86,88,90-93,97,98,100,102,103,105-107,109,110,
 114,119,120,122,147,167,169,170
coating······(14),44,55
coif*······34
Continental Association······2,111,131
cooper······27,80,82,86,88,166
corduroy······48,50,59
corset bodice*······34
corset*······33,34,67,68,70,167
cotton (7),(8),(15),7,10,42,48,50,59,68,70-74,97,98,104,109,
 112-114,119,120,122,129,130,136,142,149,158,168
 -171
cotton & flax······73
cotton & yarn······73
cotton cloth······105
cotton stuff······50
country cloth······52,63,74
country linen······97
country made linen shirt······96
crocus······50,61
crop Negro······68
crop Negroes usually wear······81
【D】
Dewitt Wallace Gallery of Decorative Arts
······3,6,11,67,114,119,148,169,170
dimity······(8),48,59

doctor······5,27,34,43,166
double-breasted······42
dowlas······52,53,61,72,73
drab, Russia drab······44,55,72
dreadnaught······44
dress······49,66
driver······5,27,34,166
duffel (duffil, duffle)······(5),38,41,42,44,55,56,72,73,76
duroy······(5),44,56
Dutch······76
Dutch Blanket······96,147
【E】
elk skin······44,56
everlasting······(5),44,56
【F】
Factory Production······123
farmer······84
farnothing (dreadnaught, fearnaught, fearnought)
······44,56,71-73,96
felt······52,62,112
felt hat······34,96
flannel(nel)······(5),46,48,56
flax······4,46,50,52,66,67,104,114,134,136,158,169,171
foot wear······79,81,83,85,87,89
freedom dues······23
frieze······(5),38,43,46,56,71,72,97
frock······30,40,66,109,110
frock coat*······30,34,49
fustian······39,50,60,68,147
【G】
gauze······50,59
German oznaberg······147
German serge······71,72
gown······66,106,107,109
great cloak*······38,41,45
great coat······34,43,76
【H】
half-thicks······46,56
handkerchief*······34
hat······45,67,79,81,83,85,87,89-93,129
head covering······77,79,81,83,85,87,89,90,94-96,98
helmet*······34
hemp······4,134,136,158,171
Holland······52,61
Home Production······123

Homespun ·················46,57,119,120
hose ·················79,81,83,85,87,89-93
hunting shirt* ·················34
【I】
Indentured Servant ·················6,14,22-25,68,166,171
indigo* ·················6,24,25,120,166
Irish Holland, Holland ·················52,61
iron worker ·················27,166
【J】
jackboots* ·················34
jackcoat ·················66,106,107
jacket ······34,39,45,47,49,51,53,66,68-73,76,78,80,82,84,86,
88,90-93,97,100,102,103,105-107-110,146,167
jacket, jackcoat ·················66
jeans, janes ·················50,60,147
Jocky Cap ·················98
joiner ·················80
【K】
Kendall cotton ·················48,59,147
kerchief* ·················34
kerzey·················(4),46,57,70-73
knit ·················52,62
【L】
lace* ·················148
lasting ·················96
leather ·················31,52,62,70,72,73,148,168
leather Jockey Cap ·················98
leggings* ·················34,49
linen ···(8),(15),39,42,43,50,52,62,67,68,70,71,104,110,112,
113,130,134,136,140,143,144,148,158,168,171
linsey-woolsy ·················(15),149
livery suits ·················129
lower clothes ·················78,80,82,84,86,88,90-93,96-99
Lund Washington's account book ·················68,69
【M】
market coat* ·················45
Merchant's Hundred Plantation ·················39,40,68
mob cap* ·················34
moccasin* ·················34
Mount Vernon Plantation ·················3,68,124,158,170
【N】
nankeen ·················50,60,147
National Museum of American History ·················5
neckerchief* ·················34
negro cloth ·················34,50,60,70,167

negro cotton ·················34,38,42,50,61,71-73,76,97
negro shoes ·················96
Nomini Hall ·················134,142
【O】
one-piece* ·················66,68
osnabrig, osnabrug, oznabrig, oznabrug
3,11,12,52,62,68,70-74,76,96,98,108-110,112,113,
134,138,140,147,158,167,169,171
over coat* ·················66
overall ·················66,109,110
【P】
painter·················27,166
Palace Plantation ·················121-123,156,170
Patchwork Quilt ·················(12),(13),3,11,119-121,156,170
pattens* ·················34
petticoat
34,40,45,47,49,53,66,68,69,105-110,114,146,167,169
petticoat trousers* ·················34
Phrigian cap* ·················34
pilot ·················80
plaid hose ·················40,68,98,147
plaid, plaiding ·················(7),7,48,58,71,72
plains ·················(6),7,46,57,72,73
plantation ···3,6,8,12,25,27,31,67,69,70,123,166,168,169,171
Plantation Production ·················123
planter ······3,12,24,25,27,28,33,38,39,67,126,129,134,158,
168,170,171
ploughman ·················78
plush ·················(6),46,57,73,74
polonaise gown* ·················31
preacher ·················78
print* ·················119,120
pumps ·················79,81,83,85,87,89-93,97
【R】
rackoon ·················46,57
red frieze ·················42
reproduction ·················5,6
Rich Neck Plantation ·················121,156
robe* ·················34
rolls ·················52,62,71,72,73,147
Roquelaure* ·················34
Russia drab (Russia drill) ·················44,55,73
【S】
Sabine Hall ·················126,130,131
sabot* ·················34

sack*	49,66,106
sacking cloth*	134
sagathy	(6),46,57
sailor	78,88
Salutary Neglect	10,17
sash*	34
sawyer	27,78,82,166
sea boots*	34
serge	(6),46,57,70,72,73
servant	25,31,67,82,129,147,166
shag	(6),46,58
shalloon	(6),38,41,46,58,147
sheets	105
shift*	39,49,66,69,108-110,146
ship carpenter	78,80
shirt	34,38,39,42,47,49,51,53,66,68,70-74,76,78,80,82, 84,86,88,90-93,96-100,102,103,105-110,114,146, 167,169
shoemaker	27,38,67,68,78,80,82,86,166
shoes, pumpus	2,34,40,40,41,67,69,76,77,79,81,83, 85,87,89-97,108,129,130,143,146,148,153,168
short coat	38,42,45
short gown	5,49,66,68,106,167
silk	4,42,48,52,62,168
silk stuff	50
silvers	34
skilts	34
slops	34
smith, black smith*	67,166,167
Smithsonian Institution	5
smock	34,66
Stamp Act	16,17,111,123,142
status symbol*	3,9,14,33,70
stays	67
stocking, hose	2,19,34,40,41,53,67-69, 77,79,81,83,85,87,89-99,106,107,146,147,153
straw hat*	34
stripe*	49,106,108,114,120-122,156,169,170
stuff	50,60,71,72
suit	5,11,34,39,45,66,69,78,82,84,86,88,105-107,109, 110,119,120,122,131,146,147,170
surtout coat*, surtout*	34,47,49
swanskin	48,58,71,72

【T】

tammy	48,58
tanner*	27
taylor	27,67,166
thick*	73,74
thickset	(8),50,60,73
thread	52,63
three-piece-suits*	30,31
ticking*	120
ticklinburg*	147
tow	97,134,140
trousers	31,34,66,68,72,78,80,82,84,86, 88,90-93,97,100,103,106,107,109,110,167,168
turner	27,82,166

【U】

under jacket	49,51,66
under shirts*	66
under vest*	45
uniform*	34,68,119,120
upper and under coats	105
upper clothes	78,80,82,84,86,88,90-93,96-99,102,103
usual cloathing for labouring Negroes	81
usual clothing of crop Negro	83

【V】

Valentine Museum	3,11,119,156,170
veil*	34
velveret	50,60
velvet	48,59
vest	45,47,66
Virginia	2-4,6-9,11,12,14, 17,18,20-25,27,31,38,42,67,73,104,113,114,118, 119,122-126,129-131,145,156,158,166,167,169-171
Virginia cloth	3,10-12,52, 63,71,72,74,76,96,104-114,118-122,156,169,170
Virginia cotton	108
Virginia Gazette	3,6-8,11,35,38,40, 35,75,76,9699,108,113,118,121,123,156,159,168
Virginia Jacket	96
Virginia knit stocking	105
Virginia linen shirts	105
Virginia yarn stocking	105

【W】

waggoner	86
waistcoat	30,34,38,42,45,47,49,51,53,66, 68-70,71,72,73,74,76,78,80,82,84,86,88,90-93,96-98,100,102,103,105-107,109,114,147,148,167,169
waistcoat lapelled	42

索　引　235

waiting man ································· 80,84
waterman ································· 78,167
weaver
　　27,84,129,131,134,138,143,148,149,158,166,170,171
wheelwright ································ 27,166
wig, periwig ···································· 34
wilton ·· 48,58
woodworker ································· 27,166
wool ········(15),4,10,42,44,46,50,67,68,72,104,105,111,113,
　　114,119,120,122,134,148,168,169
wool & cotton ······························· 73,168
woolen ····································· 48,58,71
woolen cloth ············ 44,46-48,52,74,136,138,140,158,171
worsted ·································· 67,147-148
wrapper ································· 96,105-107
wrap-rascal* ···································· 34
【Y】
yarn ································ 52,63,68,73,74
yarn jacket ······································ 99
yarn serge ······································· 71
yarn stocking ···································· 96

≪日本語表記≫

【あ】
藍（インディゴ）（indigo）* ············· 6,24,25,119,166
茜 ··· 119
麻織物 ··· 50
　◇亜麻（flax）
　　　　 ··· 4,46,50,52,66,67,104,114,134,136,158,169,171
　◇大麻（hemp） ············· 4,134,136,158,171

アフリカ人奴隷貿易 ······························ 21
アフリカン・アメリカン（African American）* ···7-9
編物工 ······································· 149,154
アメリカ合衆国憲法（合衆国憲法） ·········· 16,17,19
『アメリカ史にみる職業着』 ························ 5
アメリカ植民地時代 ················ 4,6,33,114,169
　―の服飾 ······································· 4
アメリカ製品愛用運動→（国内産の素材） ······ 18,111
アメリカ独立革命（独立戦争） ········ 2-6,9-11,16-18,30,
　　31,50,74,100,113,120,134,136,152-153,166,169
アメリカ服飾史 ································· 4,6
綾織毛布 ······································· 42
アリーズ（Aries）の工場 ···················· 136,142

【い】
イギリス商品ボイコット運動 ················ 16,123
イギリス製品不輸入協定 ···················· 18,111
衣服生産 ·································· 4,122,131
印紙法（Stamp Act） ········· 10,16,17,111,123,142
インディアンの奴隷化 ························ 22,24
【う】
『ヴァージニア、ニューイングランドおよびサマ
　ー諸島の一般史、1584～1624』 ············· 20
「ヴァージニア・ガゼット（Virginia Gazette）紙」
　　　3,6-8,11,36,38,40,43,75,76,96-99,108,113,118,121,
　　　123,156,159,168
ヴァージニア・クロス（Virginia cloth）
　　　3,10-12,52,72,74,104-114,118-122,156,169,170
ヴァージニア・コットン（Virginia cotton） ········ 108
ヴァージニア植民地議会（―議会）··· 2,9,111,118,123,140
ヴァージニアの黒人奴隷数 ······················ 25
【お】
欧米の中産・下層階級の職業着 ················ 33,34
　◇医　者 ··································· 33,34
　◇煙突掃除夫 ···································· 34
　◇追いはぎ ······································ 34
　◇開拓者（フロンティア開拓者） ············ 5,33,34
　◇下級の召使 ···································· 34
　◇下級判事 ······································ 34
　◇騎馬郵便配達人 ································ 34
　◇行商人 ·· 34
　◇御　者 ·· 34
　◇公　僕 ·· 34
　◇護　衛 ·· 34
　◇裁判官 ·· 34
　◇左馬御者 ······································ 34
　◇商　人 ··································· 5,33,34
　◇使用人 ··································· 5,33,34
　◇少年馬丁 ······································ 34
　◇消防士 ·· 34
　◇職　人 ·· 34
　◇正規軍（正規兵） ························· 5,33,34
　◇聖職者 ··································· 5,33,34
　◇大世帯の従僕 ·································· 34
　◇知的職業人 ···································· 34
　◇地方労働者 ···································· 34
　◇肉　屋 ·· 34
　◇農　民 ··································· 5,33,34
　◇墓掘り女 ······································ 34

◇馬　丁 ……………………………………… 34
◇馬丁助手 …………………………………… 34
◇犯罪人（犯罪者） ………………………… 5,9,33,34
◇船乗り ……………………………………… 5,33,34
◇辺境地の住民 ……………………………… 34
◇法律家 ……………………………………… 5,33,34
◇民族諸集団 ………………………………… 5,33,34
◇民族服 ……………………………………… 34
◇民　兵 ……………………………………… 5,33,34
◇夜　警 ……………………………………… 34
◇宿屋の主人 ………………………………… 34
◇輸送労働者 ………………………………… 34
◇呼び売り …………………………………… 5,33,34
◇漁　師 ……………………………………… 5,33,34
◇路上の商売人 ……………………………… 34
◇罠猟師 ……………………………………… 34

お仕着せ …………………………… 6,67,68,70,147,148,167
織　機 ……………………………………………… 121,136
織物生産 ………………………………………… 148,158,170
織物生産の設備 ………………………………… 158,170
女の召使い ………………………………………… 34,68,70,167
女の召使いの家内奴隷 …………………………… 70,167
【か】
カーターズ・グローブ・プランテーション
　　（Carter's Grove Plantation）………… (1),121,156

下　衣
◇下着用ズボン ……………………………… 69,146
◇スカート（petticoat）…………………… 34,66
◇スキルト（skilts）………………………… 34
◇トラウザーズ（長ズボン）(trousres)
　　31,34,66,68,71,72,78,80,82,84,86,88,90-93,95,97,
　　100,103,106,107,109,110,167,168
◇幅広のズボン（petticoat trousers）*………… 34
◇ブリーチズ（半ズボン）(breeches)
　　(11),30-32,34,38,39,42,45,47,49,51,53,66,68-71,73,
　　76,78,80,82,84,86,88,90-93,95-100,103,105-107,
　　110,114,119,120,146,147,167-169
◇ペティコート（petticoat）
　　34,40,45,47,49,53,66,68,69,105-110,114,146,167,169
◇レギンス（leggings）* ………………………… 34,49

解放給付（freedom dues）……………………… 23
家事サーヴァント ………………………………… 22

下層階級 ………………………… 2,7,108,113,122,123,170
合衆国憲法→アメリカ-
家内生産（Home Production）………………… 123
家内奴隷 ………………………… 67-70,100,147,158,167,171
家内の職人奴隷の職種
◇医　者（doctor）………………………… 5,27,166
◇鍛冶屋（smith, black smith）* ……… 27,67,166,167
◇革なめし（tanner）* ……………………………… 27
◇樵（woodworker）………………………… 27,166
◇給　仕 …………………………………… 25,67,166
◇御　者（driver）………………………… 5,27,166
◇靴職人・靴屋（shoemaker）
　　　　………………… 27,38,67,68,78,80,82,86,166
◇車大工（wheelwright）………………… 27,166
◇木挽き工（sawyer）…………………… 27,78,82,166
◇仕立て屋（taylor）……………………… 27,67,166
◇織　工（weaver）
　　27,84,129,131,134,138,143,148,149,158,166,170,171
◇製樽工，樽職人（cooper）……… 27,80,82,86,88,166
◇船　頭（water man）* ………………… 29,78,167
◇大　工（carpenter）…………… 27,80,82,84,86,166
◇鉄骨組み立て職人（iron worker）………… 27,166
◇屠殺業者（butcher）…………………… 27,78,166
◇塗装工（painter）……………………… 27,166
◇馬車を引く人 …………………………… 25,67,166
◇召使い（servant）……… 25,29,67,82,129,147,166
◇煉瓦職人（bricklayer）* ………………… 69,146
◇ろくろ細工師（turner）……………… 27,82,166

柄
◇幾何学的紋様 ……………………………………… 45
◇格　子 ……………………………… 49,53,119,120,147
◇縞（stripe）*
　　…… 47,49,106,108,114,119,120,122,156,169,170
◇透かし模様 ………………………………………… 45
◇花の模様 …………………………………………… 45
◇プリント（print）* …………………… 51,119,120
◇ブロック・プリント織物（block print）* ……… 120
◇無　地 ……………………………………… 45,47,49,120

カラヴェル船 ……………………………………… 21
【き】
絹織物（silk）………………………………………… 4,52
強制された召使い ………………………………… 22
強制労働制度 ……………………………………… 23

キルト ……………………………………………119-121
【く・け】
「クロップ・ニグロ（crop negro）」……………………68
毛織物 ……………………………4,44,46,72,111,134
憲法制定会議 ……………………………………19
【こ】
航海法 …………………………………18,104,111
工場生産（Factory Production）……………………123
工場制手工業 ………………………………18,111
公文書…………………………………………11,12,170
国産の織物 …………………………………………52
黒人奴隷 ………………2,3,6,9,22-25,27,30,31,67,68,95,171
　　　　－数 ………………………………25,126
　　　　－貿易 ………………………………25
黒人奴隷制度 …………………2,10,14,21,23-25,67,166
　　　　－存続の問題 ………………………………3,9
　　　　－の廃止 ………………………………3
　　　　－の法制化 ………………………………2,9
国内産の素材 ……………3,10-12,72,134,149,158,159,169
国立アメリカ史博物館（National Museum of
　　American History）………………………………5
米 …………………………………………6,24,25,166
「コモン・センス」………………………………18
コロニアル・ウィリアムズバーグ振興財団（Dewitt
　　Wallace Gallery of Decorative Arts）
　　　　………………3,6,11,67,114,119,121,148,156,169,170
　　　　－織物部門（織物工房）………………11,121,170
　　　　－考古学研究部門（Department of
　　　　　　Archaeological Research）……………121,156
混　紡 …………………………………………………72
◇ウールン（woolen）とコットンの－ ……………72
◇コットンと亜麻（flax）の－ ………………………72
◇コットンとシルクの交織織物 …………………149
◇木綿と紡毛の－ …………………………………48
◇木綿とリネンの－ ………………………………50
◇リンジー・ウールジー（linsey-woolsy）……(15),149
【さ】
サーヴァント ………………………………………22
裁断師……………………………………131,149,154
裁　縫 …………………………………………27
砂　糖 ………………………………………6,25,166
砂糖法 …………………………………………16,123
サビーン・ホール（Sabine Hall）…………126,130,131

【し】
仕上げ
◇両面起毛 ……………………………………47
◇起　毛 ……………………………………47,52
◇毛　羽 …………………………………45,47,49
◇毛羽のない ……………………………………47
◇縮　絨 …………………………………………45,47
◇縮絨しない ……………………………………47
◇添毛織物 ………………………………………48

自由の娘たち ……………………………………123
熟練労働（熟練工、熟練職人）…………25,27,166,171
主人のお下がり ……………………………………67
主要商品作物 ……………………………………6,25
上　衣
◇アンダー・シャツ（under shirts）* ……………66
◇アンダー・ベスト（under vest）* ……………45
◇ウェストコート（waistcoat）
　　(10),30,34,38,42,45,47,49,51,53,66,68-74,76,78,80,
　　82,84,86,88,90-93,96-98,100,102,103,105-107,109,
　　114,147,148,167,169
◇ガウン（gown）……………………………66,106,107,109
◆コート（coat）
　　30,31,45,47,49,51,53,66-68,72,74,78,80,82,84,86,
　　88,90-93,97,98,100,102,103,105-107,109,110,114,
　　119,120,122,147,148,167,169,170
　□大型外套（great cloak）* ……………38,41,45
　□大型コート（great coat）* ……………34,43,76
　□オーバー・コート（over coat）* ……………66
　□シュルトゥー・コート（surtout coat, surtout）*
　　　　……………………………………34,47,49
　□ショート・コート（short coat）………38,42,45
　□ブランケット・コート（blanket coat）* ………34
　□フロック・コート（frock coat）*………30,34,49
　□マーケット・コート（market coat）* ………45
　□ヨーロッパ製のコート …………………………30
　□ラップ・ラスカル（wrap-rascal）* ……………34
　□ロクロール（Roquelaure）*……………………34
◇コルセット（corset）* ……………33,34,67,68,70,167
◇コルセット・ボディス（corset bodice）*…………34
◇サック（sac）* ……………………………49,66,106
◇シフト（shift）* ……………39,49,66,69,108-110,146
◆ジャケット（jacket）
　　34,39,45,47,49,51,53,66,68-73,76,78,80,82,84,86,
　　88,90-93,97,100,102,103,105-110,146,167

□アンダー・ジャケット（under jacket）…49,51,66
□外着用ジャケット………………………………66
□下着用ジャケット………………………………66
□ベルト付きジャケット（belted jacket）*………34
● シャツ（shirt）
　　　34,38,39,42,47,49,51,53,66,66,68,70-74,76,78,80,
　　　82,84,86,88,90-93,96-100,102,103,105-110,114,
　　　146,167,169
　□狩猟用のシャツ（hunting shirt）*……………34
　□ボディー・シャツ（body shirt）*………………34
◇ジャケット［ジャックコート］（jacket, jackcoat）
　　　………………………………………66,106,107
◇シュミーズ（chemise）……………………34,66
◇ショート・ガウン（short gown）5,49,66,68,106,167
◇ステイズ（stays）……………………………67
◇スモック（smock）………………………34,66
◇ドレス（dress）……………………………49,66
◇バンヤン（banyan）……………………………34
◇ブラウス（blouse）……………………………34
◇フロック（frock）………………30,40,66,109,110
◇ベスト（vest）……………………………45,47,66
◇部屋着………………………………………108
◇ポロネーズ型のガウン（polonaise gown）*………31
◇ローブ（robe）*…………………………………34
◇ワンピース（one-piece）*……………………66,68

上衣の着用枚数……………………………102,103
上級-家内-奴隷……………………25,34,67,69,70,166-167
上級の白人の召使い………………………………67
小世帯………………………………………………34
商人の記録………………………………11,12,170
上流階級……………2,5-7,10,14,30,33,34,113,166-168
　－人の立ち居振る舞い…………………………5
女子服（上流階級）………………………………31
職業着………………………………………………5
織　布………………………………………………171
植民地議会…………………………………17,122
植民地時代……………………………………7,9,66
人口センサス………………………………………2,9
【す】
スーツ（suit）
　　　5,11,34,39,45,66,69,78,82,84,86,88,105-107,109,
　　　110,119,120,122,131,146,147,170
◇少年用スーツ……………………………120,131
◇女性用スーツ……………………………………131

◇スリー・ピース・スーツ（three-piece-suits）*……30,31
◇男性用スーツ……………………………120,131

スミソニアン協会（Smithsonian Institution）………5
ステイタス・シンボル（status symbol）*…3,9,14,33,70
【せ】
製靴業…………………………………………18,111
製　織…………………………………………149
製織工場……………………………………131,134
　－の設備…………………………………………134
製織工………………………………………………138
制服（ユニホーム）（uniform）*………34,68,119,120
製　粉………………………………………………27
西洋服飾史…………………………………………4
繊維工業…………………………………………18,111
組成（糸と織組織）
◇綾　織……………………………44,46,48,50,67
◇一重織……………………………………………44
◇畝　織……………………………………48,50,51
◇カシミア梳毛糸…………………………………44
◇サテン織…………………………………………44
◇斜文織……………………………………………52
◇粗　毛……………………………………………148
◇梳　毛……………………………………………48
◇梳毛糸…………………………………………44,46
◇梳毛織物…………………………………………44
◇粗毛製（ウーステッド）………………………148
◇梳毛撚糸…………………………………………44
◇二重織……………………………………………44
◇平　織…………………………………44,46,48,50
◇紡毛糸………………………………44,46,48,140
◇紡毛織物（woolen cloth）
　　　………………44,46-48,52,74,136,138,140,158,171
◇細綾木綿…………………………………………50
◇紋　織……………………………………………52
◇四綜統織…………………………………………46

【た】
第一回大陸会議…………………………………18
体　形………………………………………………5
大西洋奴隷貿易…………………………………21
第二回大陸会議………………………………18,145
「代表なければ課税なし」……………………17,111
大プランテーション……………………………27,67
大陸連盟（Continental Association）………2,111,131

タウンゼンド諸法 …………………*16-18,111,123*
ダッチ・ブランケット（Dutch Blankets）……*96,147*
タバコ・プランテーション ……………*22,24,25*
タバコ栽培………………………*6,20,22-25,166*
タバコの需要 …………………………………*30*
タバコの生産過程 ……………………………*27*
ダブルの打ち合わせ …………………………*38*
樽つくり ………………………………………*27*
男子逃亡奴隷の逃亡時の着装実態 ……*11,74,166,168*
男子服（上流階級）………………………*30,34*

【ち・て】

茶　法 ………………………………………*18,111*
中産階級 ……………………………………*2,113*
中産・下層階級…………………*5,31,123,166,167*
　　－の衣服 ………………………………*33*
　　－の職業着 ……………………………*5*
鋳造所 ……………………………………*152,153*
手織り布地 ……………………………………*123*

【と】

逃亡奴隷………………*6,39-41,68,70,74,77,94,95,100*
逃亡奴隷広告 …………*3-4,6-8,10-12,33,38-42,48,66,68,69,*
　　　71-74,95,100,102-103,105-112,114,122,168,169
　　－数 ……………………………………*40,41*
　　－にみる男子奴隷の被服の組み合わせ
　　　　　　　　　　　　　　　　74,77,90,94-95

逃亡奴隷広告にみる67種の被服素材 ……*10,11,42,168*
　①ウール（wool）
　　　　　(15),10,42,44,50,67,68,72,104,105,113,114,119,120,
　　　　　122,148,168,169
　◇ウィルトン（wilton）………………………*48,58*
　◇ウーレン（woolen）………………*48,58,71,136*
　◇エヴァー・ラスティング（everlasting）…*(5),44,56*
　◇エルクスキン（elkskin）……………………*44,56*
　◇カシミア（casimer）……………………*(4),44,55*
　◇カスター（castor）…………………………*44,55*
　◇カムレット（camlet, camblet）……*44,54,73,78*
　◇カルゼ，カーセー（kerzey）…………*(4),46,70-73*
　◇キャリマンコ（calimanco）……………*(4),44,54*
　◇クロス（cloth）…………………*44,55,72,112*
　◇コーティング（coating）………………*(4),44,55*
　◇サージ（serge）………………*(6),46,57,70,72,73*
　◇サガスィー（sagathy）……………………*(6),46,57*
　◇シャグ（shag）……………………………*(6),45,46*
　◇シャルーン（shalloon）………*(6),38,41,46,58,147*
　◇スワンスキン（swanskin）…………*48,58,71,72*

　◇ダッフィル（duffil），ダッフェル（duffel）
　　　　　………………*(5),38,41,42,44,55,56,72,73,76*
　◇タミー（tammy）…………………………*48,58*
　◇デュロイ（duroy）………………………*(5),44,56*
　◇ドラブ（drab），ラシア・ドラブ（Russia drab）
　　　　　……………………………………*44,55,72*
　◇ドレッドノート（dreadnaught）……………*44*
　◇バース・コーティング（bath coating）……*44,54*
　◇ハーフスィックス（halfthicks）………*46,56*
　◇バックスキン（buckskin）…………*44,54,71-73*
　◇ビーバー・コーティング（Beaver Coating）
　　　　　………………………………*38,42,44,54*
　◇ファーナッシング（farnothing）……*44,56,71-73,96*
　◇フィアノート（fearnought）………………*44,72*
　◇プラッシュ（plush）………………*(6),46,57,73,74*
　◇フランネル（flannel），ネル（nel）……*(5),46,48,56*
　◇フリーズ（frieze）………*(5),38,43,46,56,71,72,97*
　◇プレインズ（plains）……………*(6),7,46,57,72,73*
　◇ブロード・クロス（broadcloth）…*(4),44,54,67,71-73*
　◇ベア・スキン（bearskin）…………*44,54,71-73*
　◇ホームスパン（homespun）…………*46,57,119,120*
　◇ラックーン（rackoon）……………………*46,57*
　②ウール（wool）とコットン（cotton）……*73,168*
　◇プレード（plaid），プレーディング（plaiding）
　　　　　………………………………*(7),7,48,58,71,72*
　③シルク（silk）とウール（wool）とコットン（cotton）
　　　　　………………………………………*48*
　◇キャリコ（calico）…………………………*(7),48,59*
　◇ベルベット（velvet）………………………*48,59*
　④コットン（cotton）
　　　　　(7),(8),7,10,42,48,50,52,59,68,70-74,97,98,104,109,
　　　　　112-114,119,120,122,129,130,136,149,158,168-171
　◇ガーゼ（gauze）……………………………*50,59*
　◇ケンダル・コットン（kendall cotton）……*48,59,147*
　◇コーデュロイ（corduroy）……………*48,50,59*
　◇スィックセット（thickset）………………*50,60,73*
　◇ディミティー（dimity）……………………*(8),48,59*
　◇ナンキーン（nankeen），南京木綿 ………*50,60,147*
　◇ベルブレット（velveret）………………*(8),50,60*
　⑤コットン（cotton）とウール（wool）……………*50*
　◇スタッフ（stuff）…………………………*50,60,71,72*
　⑥コットン（cotton）とリネン（Linen）……………*50*
　◇ジーンズ（jeans）……………………*50,60,147*
　◇ジェーンズ（janes）………………………*50*
　◇ニグロ・クロス（negro cloth）………*34,50,60,70,167*

索　引　239

◇ニグロ・コットン（negro cotton）
　　　　　　　　　　　　……34,38,42,50,61,71-73,76,97
◇ファスチャン（fustian）………39,50,60,68,147
⑦リネン（linen）
　　　39,42,43,50,52,62,67,68,70,71,104,110,112,113,
　　　130,134,136,138,140,143,144,148,158,168,171
　◇アイリッシュ・オランダ（Irish Holland），オラ
　　　ンダ（Holland）………………………52,61
　◇オズナブリグ（osnabrig），オズナブリュグ
　　　（osnabrug），オズナブリグ（oznabrig），
　　　オズナブルグ（oznabrug）
　　　　3,11,12,52,62,68,70-74,76,96,98,108-110,112,113,
　　　　134,138,140,147,158,167,169,171
　◇キャンバス（canvas），ダック（duck）…(15),50,61,67
　◇クロッカス（crocus）………………………50,61
　◇ダウラス（dowlas）………………52,53,61,72,73
　◇チェック（check）……(8),50,61,73,74,106,114,120,169
　◇リネン（linen），亜麻糸　…………(8),52,130,140
　◇ロールズ（rolls）………………52,62,71-73,147
⑧シルク（silk）………………4,42,48,52,62,168
⑨その他　………………………………………52
　◇スレッド（thread）………………………52,63
　◇なめし皮（leather）………31,52,62,70,72,73,148,168
　◇ニット（knit）………………………………52,62
　◇フェルト（felt）…………………………52,62,112
　◇ヤーン（yarn）………………………52,63,68,73,74
　◇レザー（leather）……………………………52
⑩国産品　………………………………………52
　◇カントリー・クロス（country cloth）……52,63,74
　◇ヴァージニア・クロス（Virginia cloth）
　　　(10),(11),3,10-12,52,63,71,72,74,76,96,104-114,118-
　　　122,156,169,170

逃亡奴隷広告に登場しない被服素材
　◇ウーステッド（worsted）……………67,147-148
　◇サッキング・クロス（sacking cloth）…………134
　◇ジャーマン・オズナブルグ（German Oznaberg）
　　　　　　　　　　　　　　　　　　　　　　…147
　◇ジャーマン・サージ（German serge）………71,72
　◇スィック（thick）……………………………73,74
　◇ティッキング………………………………………120
　◇ティックルンブルグ（ticklinburg）……………147
　◇トゥ（tow）……………………………97,134,140
　◇南京木綿………………………………………147
　◇皮革……………………………………………72

◇ブロケード（brocade）………………………31
◇ベーズ（baize）………………………………67

逃亡奴隷数　………………………………10,77
独立宣言　…………………………………………19
都市労働者　………………………………………34
徒弟サーヴァント　………………………………22
奴　隷　……………………………………………5,34
奴隷解放　…………………………………………3,140
奴隷監督（boss）………………27,40,134,158
奴隷小屋　………………………………………121,122
奴隷制度　…………………………………………2,39
奴隷制問題　………………………………………7,9
奴隷の職種　………………………………………27
奴隷の職人の年齢構成比　…………………………27
奴隷の被服生産の実態　…………………………170
「奴隷の被服のイメージ化」………………3,11,67,168
奴隷の被服の種類→被服の種類　…………9-11,66-67,69
奴隷の被服描写　…………………………………3,10
奴隷貿易　…………………………………………21
奴隷労働力　………………………………………39

【な・に・ぬ】
7年戦争（フレンチ・アンド・インディアン戦争）
　　　　　　　　　　　　　　　　　　　　…16,17
任意の召使い　……………………………………22
布の生産………………11,104,113,118,123,131,158,169
布の生産工場　………………………134,158,170,171

【ね】
年季奴隷　…………………………………………23
年季の限られた奉公人　…………………………23
年季契約奉公人
　　　…5,9,20-24,33,69,70,125,131,146,148,158,167,170

【の】
農園の奴隷（野外耕作奴隷）
　　　　　　…25,27,30,67-69,70,100,158,166-167,171
農業サーヴァント　……………………………22,23
農具や家具の製作　………………………………27
ノミニ・ホール（Nomini Hall）………134,142

【は】
白人年季奉公人（Indentured Servant）・白人奉公
　人，白人年季奉公人制度………6,14,22-25,68,166,171
白人年季奉公人制度から黒人奴隷制度への移行
　　　　　　　　　　　　　　　　…24,25,166,171
白人の召使い　……………………………33,68,70,167
鋏　…………………………………………(12),121,170

パッチワーク・キルト（Patchwork Quilt）
　　　　　　……………(12),(13),3,11,119-121,156,170
パトン（木製）(pattens)*……………………………34
針……………………………(13),121,123,156,170
パレス・プランテーション（Palace Plantation）
　　　　　　………………(12),(13),121-123,156,170
【ひ】
東インド会社……………………………………18,111
非熟練分野……………………………………………166
被服管理………………………………………………123
被服情報……………………………39,40-42,74,76,77
被服生産の道具………………………………………12
被服素材の年次変化………………………11,111,169
被服の携行情報………………………………………76
被服の種類→上衣,下衣,スーツ,付属品他……11,30,31
被服の着用情報………………………………………74
被服描写……………………………………10,38-41,95
比率検定………………………………………………3
【ふ】
複製（reproduction）……………………………5,6
付属品他
◇エプロン（apron）………………………30,67,79
● 鬘（wig）………………………………………34
　　ボブ・ウィック（鬘）(bob wig)…………34
◇被り物（head covering）*
　　　　　　……………77,79,81,83,85,87,89,90,94-96,98
◇靴（shoes, pumpus）
　　2,34,40,41,67,69,76,77,79,81,83,85,87,89-97,108,
　　129,130,143,144,146,148 153,168
　　□モカシン（moccasin）*………………………34
● 靴下（stocking, hose）
　　2,19,34,40,41,53,67-69,77,79,81,83,85,87,89-99,
　　106,107,146,147,153
　　　格子縞の靴下（plaid hose）…………40,68,98,147
◇小物入れ……………………………………………34
◇棍棒…………………………………………………34
◇サボ（木製）(sabot)*……………………………34
◇スカーフ（kerchief）*……………………………34
◇ずきん（coif）*……………………………………34
◇ストッキング（stocking）…………19,53,67,153
◇提灯…………………………………………………34
◇杖 34
◇手袋…………………………………………………34
◇刀剣…………………………………………………34
◇ナイフ………………………………………………34

◇ネッカチーフ（neckerchief）*…………………34
◇ハンカチ（handkerchief）*……………………34
● ブーツ（boots）*………………79,81,83,85,87,89-93
　　□騎手用のブーツ……………………………34
　　□シー・ブーツ（sea boots）*…………………34
　　□ジャックブーツ（jackboots）*………………34
◇ブランケット（blanket）……………………34,76,153
◇ベルト………………………………………………34
● 帽子 2,34,45,53,67,79,81,83,85,87,89-93,95,100,129,168
　　□バリーコック（bullycock）*…………………34
　　□フェルト帽（felt hat）…………………34,96
　　□縁付き帽（縁付きの帽子），ハット（hat）
　　　　　　…………………………………45,67,129
　　□縁なし帽,キャップ（cap）
　　　　　　…………34,40,49,51,67-68,79,81,83,85,87,89-93
　　□フリジア帽（Phrigian cap）*………………34
　　□ヘルメット（helmet）*………………………34
　　□ボンネット（bonnet）………………67,108-110
　　□麦わら帽子（straw hat）*……………………34
　　□モブ・キャップ（mob cap）*………………34
◇サッシュ（緋色）(sash)*…………………………34
◇バーベル（barvell）*………………………………34
◇ベール（veil）*……………………………………34
◇ボタン（buttom）*………………………………121
◇モール（lace）……………………………………148

プランター（planter）……………………3,12,24,
　　25,27,28,30,33,38,39,67,126,129,134,158,168,170,171
プランターの手紙…………………………………12,170
プランターの日誌…………………………………12,170
プランテーション（plantation）
　　………3,6,8,12,25,27,31,67,69,70,123,166,168,169,171
プランテーション生産（Plantation Production）…123
プランテーションにおける被服管理………………11
プランテーションの記録…………………………11,12,170
古着……………………………………………………30
【へ・ほ】
ベーコンの反乱（Bacon's Rebellion）*…………24
帆………………………………………………………51
縫製……………………………………………………27
紡績および製織費用………………………………139
紡績工………………………129,131,134,138,142,149,154,158
紡績工場……………………………………………134,138
紡績・製織事業……………………………………138,171
法律家………………………………………………5,33,34

ホームスパン運動 …………………………16
ボストン茶会事件 ………………………16-18,111
ポルトガル人 ………………………………21
【ま】
マウント・ヴァーノン・プランテーション
　　（Mount Vernon Plantation）…(16),3,68,124,158,170
マーチャント・ハンドレッド・プランテーション
　　（Merchant's Hundred Plantation）……39,40,68
マテリアル・カルチャー（物質文化）……………2,39
【め・も】
綿織物 ………………………………48,50,52,104
紋　章 ………………………………67,68,70,166
【ゆ】
「有益な怠慢」政策（Salutary Neglect）…………10,17
輸入素材 ………………10-12,114,149,158,159,169,171
輸入品……………………………10,111-113,158,169
指　貫 ………………………………(13),121-123,156
【ら〜わ】
ライフスタイル・サーヴァント ……………………22
酪　農 ………………………………………27
ランド・ワシントンの会計帳簿（Lund Washington's
　　account book）………………………………69
リッチ・ネック・プランテーション（Rich Neck
　　Plantation）……………………………121,156
リネン織物 ……………………………………138
レキシントン・コンコードの戦い（Battles of
　　Lexington and Concord）……………17,18,113
労働力移行の二段階説 ……………………………25
ワシントンの奴隷財産目録 ……………………154

・著者紹介・

濱田　雅子 (はまだ・まさこ)

1965年　神戸大学文学部史学科西洋史学専攻卒業。
1988年　武庫川女子大学大学院家政学研究科被服学専攻修士課程修了（家政学修士）。
現　在　武庫川女子大学生活環境学部教授。家政学博士。

【主要研究業績】
［著　書］
『アメリカ植民地時代の服飾』せせらぎ出版、1996年
丹野郁編著『西洋服飾史―増訂版―』東京堂出版、1999年（現代の服飾・担当）
［翻　訳］
Peter F. Copeland著『アメリカ史にみる職業着―植民地時代～独立革命期―』（単訳）
　　せせらぎ出版、1998年
アルベール・ラシネ著、アイリーン・リベイロ英訳・再編（日本語版監修・丹野郁、翻
　　訳編集・国際服飾学会）『世界服飾文化史図鑑』（共訳）原書房、1992年
ジョン・ギロウ、ブライアン・センテンス著（日本語版監修・丹野郁、翻訳編集・国際
　　服飾学会）『世界織物文化図鑑』（共訳）東洋書林、2001年
［論　文］
「17世紀ニューイングランドのピューリタン衣裳の史的考察」（国際服飾学会『国際服
　　飾学会誌』No.2所収、1985年7月）
「ウィリアム・ブラッドフォードの洗礼用衣服の歴史的考察」（国際服飾学会『国際服
　　飾学会誌』No.11所収、1994年12月）
「ヴァージニア・クロスに関する社会史的考察―逃亡奴隷広告および遺品に基づいて」（国
　　際服飾学会『国際服飾学会誌』No.17所収、2000年5月）
［所属学会］
国際服飾学会（理事）、ユネスコ・イコム・コスチューム部門、アメリカ服飾学会（The
Costume Society of America）、アメリカ学会、初期アメリカ学会、日本風俗史学会、
日本家政学会他

黒人奴隷の着装の研究
―アメリカ独立革命期ヴァージニアにおける奴隷の被服の社会的研究―

2002年9月10日　初版印刷
2002年9月24日　初版発行

著　者――濱田雅子
発行者――大橋信夫
印刷所――東京リスマチック株式会社
製本所――渡辺製本株式会社

発行所――**株式会社　東京堂出版**
　　　　〒101-0054　東京都千代田区神田錦町3－7
　　　　電話 03－3233－3741　振替 00130－7－270

ISBN4-490-20460-4 C3022　　　　　Masako Hamada©2002
Printed in Japan

西洋服飾史 〈増訂版〉
丹野　郁編著　　B５判　　本体2700円＋税

アパレル業界・日中韓英
対訳ワードブック
村尾康子編　　B６変形判　　本体2300円＋税

世界帝王系図集 〈増訂版〉
下津清太郎編　　B５判　　本体15000円＋税